SHELTER, SIGN & SYMBOL

SHELTER, SIGN & SYMBOL

edited by Paul Oliver

The Overlook Press
Woodstock, New York

First published in the United States in 1977 by
The Overlook Press
Lewis Hollow Road
Woodstock, New York 12498
Copyright © by Barrie & Jenkins Ltd.
First published in Great Britain in 1975 by
Barrie & Jenkins Ltd.

Library of Congress Catalog Card Number: 77-77809
ISBN: 0-87951-068-4

The illustrations listed below (by page numbers) are reproduced by kind permission of the owners, copyright holders and photographers. Copyright obtains on the whole contents of the book; no illustration may be reproduced without the authority of owner, copyright holder or photographer.

Julian BEINART 160, 161, (161), 163, 164, 166, 167, 168, 169, 170, 171, 172, 173, (174), 175, 176, 177, 178, 179, 180, 181, 182
Corrie BEVINGTON 6, 35b, 209, 212
BOCKNER (Photo in Rapoport) 40tl
Professor BOURAS (139), 144l
R. E. Cole BROWN 125, 126
Timothy BRUCE-DICK 11t, 18, 85
David BUXTON 198, 204
Keith CRITCHLOW 221, 223, 225
Ulker COPUR 104b
Bobbie COX (11b)
Tore HAKANSSON 89b, (89), 87, 88, 89, 90, 91, 93
Hasan-Uddin KHAN 183, 185, 186, 187, 188, 189, 190, 191, 192, 194, 195
Romi KHOSLA 70, 72, 73, 74, 75, 76, 77, 78, 79, 80, 81, 82, 83
Wilfred KRÖGER 52.
Zeynep KURAL 97, 98
Prof. A.-Ph. LAGOPOULOS (1) 211, 213, 214
Ronald LEWCOCK 107, 108, 109, 110, 111, 112, 113, 114, 115, (116)
Fritz MORGENTHALER 4, 150, 151, 152, 153, 154, 155, 156
Selhattin ONUR 98b
Paul OLIVER 10, 14, 17, 19, 20, 21, 12, 22l, 25, 26, 27, 28, 29, 30, 33, 199, 201, 202, 210
Suha OZKAN 94, (96), 99, 100, (101), (102t), 102, 103, 104, 105
Jan PIEPER 53, 54, (56–58), 59, 61, 62, 63, 64, 65, 66, 67 (also air photos 54, 61, 65)
Eugenia POLITIS 22r, (135) (19, 11, 136), 137, 138, 139, 140, 141, (142), 143, 144, 145, 146, 147
Amos RAPOPORT 38, 39, 42, 45, 46, 47, 48, 49
(Transvaal Chamber of Mines) (in Walton)
James WALTON 117, 118, 119, 120, 121, 122, 123, 127, 128, 130, 131, 132, 133, 134
Elizabeth WILKINSON 35t

CONTENTS

INTRODUCTION

Paul Oliver

A TONGA KRAAL RESETTLES

There is an extended passage in Henri A. Junod's *The Life of a South African Tribe* in which he describes the processes that take place when a Tonga village moves its location.[1] Predominantly an agricultural people, who also keep cattle, fowl and other live-stock, the Tonga live in dispersed settlements which are scattered across the country in Southern Rhodesia and Moçambique. Their *kraals* are centred on cattle pens and surrounded by fields of maize and Kaffir corn as well as rice, manioc and other crops. There are times when it is decided that a *kraal* must be moved – when a head-man dies, and his successor has to seek a new site; when a village is struck by lightning; or when the land becomes exhausted. Settled though their villages are, a headman, his wives and children, together with his married sons and their wives and off-spring, constitute a usual kraal unit so that the responsibility for deter-mining the place where a new location will be rests with the head-man, who leaves the kraal and selects a number of possible locations for the new site.

When the possible sites have been selected the headman breaks off small twigs from selected trees in the area of each prospective site, and returning to the village tests them by astragalomancy, or the use of divining 'bones'. According to the interpretation of the information he receives from the falling of the *kanye* (actually an abnormal *stone*) and its proximity to the twig, he ascertains which site will prove to be the most appropriate and propitious. This done, he gathers building materials for the new hut – grasses for the thatch of the roof, saplings and mud for the wattle-and-daub walls. He leaves the older site for good and consummates the choice of the new by sexual intercourse with his principal wife, on the new dwelling site. The following morning they tie a knot in the grass where they have slept and on this every member of the village is obliged to step, 'to tie the village'.

So the site is determined and the village confirms its allegiance to its head. But the process is by no means over; a month of rigorous taboo, *bahlapfa,* follows during which time abstinence from sexual relations is demanded of the villagers. Breaking the taboo will bring illness upon the headman to whom they have re-pledged their relationship and the guilty woman will be unable to bear children. During this month the circular mud walls of the huts are built and the roofs of the houses are then transported from the old site to the new, the frames being carried by the men to the taunts and insults of their women, who sing obscene songs at them as they dismantle the old village and assemble the new one. In turn, the women are subjected to the obscene songs of the men when they are smearing the ground with mud, which will harden to make the floors.

When the new village is completed it is protected from evil spirits and witches by a fence, treated with magical substances. The entrance has poles smeared with drugs and medicine is poured into the post holes; 'those who come to try their chance against us will be attacked by disease and go and die in their houses'. With this protection afforded, the married couples within the village com-munity celebrate their union and the founding of the new village with sexual relationships, performed strictly in order of their kinship to the headman.

Eventually the headman's authority in his new village is established by a ritual in which his principal wife takes his *assagai* and his shield, and closing the gate of the new village to the outside world makes an offering to the spirits of the ancestors. She makes a declaration to the villagers to 'bring forth children; live and be happy and get everything', and addresses the ancestral spirits, calling on them to witness: 'I have no bitterness in my heart. It is

Frontispiece
From their rock shelters, effigies of the departed watch over the living at Toradja, Celebes, Indonesia. The carved and clothed figures of the cliff cemetery symbolise the eternal presence of the ancestral spirits, and of the living members of the society.

Facing page
A Dogon ancestral shrine. Projections in phallic form bear evidence of libations and offerings of food. The building in its entirety is strongly zoomorphic.

pure.' Declaring her part-jealousy and anger over his taking other wives she makes an end to it. 'We shall have friendly relations together' she announces, and the headman pushes the thorn branch aside and opens up the village. Finally the village sits down to a ceremonial feast and invites neighbouring villages to share it.[2]

This account of the establishment of a new village is the description of a process. But the process contains within it many levels of sign and symbol, belief, superstition, ritual and religion, which indicate the range of symbolisation whereby a community focuses on the huts of its own village its interpretation of its own social structure; its indications of conflict within the community and its desire to mend them, its struggle for social adhesion, its concept of allegiance and hierarchy, its restrictions and controls upon behaviour and the imposition or flouting of taboos for the cohesion of the society, its dependence upon divination and its belief on the spiritiual presence of the ancestors of the tribe.

Much of the process described has a symbolism which is acknowledged by the members of the village. One Tongan described the obscene songs sung at the time of the dismantling and transportation of the village huts: 'the village is broken to pieces, so are the ordinary laws. The insults which are taboo are now allowed.' He may have described the custom alone, but the relationship between the disassembly of the village and the breakdown of tabooed behaviour during this period was close enough in his mind for him to make a direct comparison.

Other aspects of the symbolic ritual in rebuilding the village may have been less overtly acknowledged, but the conflicts brought about by jealousies among the women, the stresses that the break from the village structure of the young men with their new wives could create, and the phoenix-like opportunity for rebirth of the community with the rebirth of the village, were acknowledged in the prayer of the principal wife to the headman. There were however, elements of sign and symbol which were less immediately apparent or less expressly stated; the signs by which the headman selected the possible location for the situation of his new village; the signs which the divining bones gave to him in their accidental fall, and which indicated the special advantages of the site finally selected; the knot of grass which was recognised as a symbol of the marital knot and a symbol of the knot tied between the villagers and their headman. Perhaps the fact that the grass was growing from the earth further symbolised their ties with the earth, the source of their livelihoods and their lives, and with the bodies and spirits of their departed ancestors. Whether these were consciously acknowledged or not, every member of the village was obliged to step across it, and in so doing to make not only a symbolic gesture of linkage and union but a clear sign of his own participation in the ceremony. There was much in common with the rites of passage, the initiation of the boys, or mourning over the dead, which revealed that the creation of the new village was itself a passage to a new life.

The eventual village, with its cluster of huts walled protectively by a fence of magical substances, was itself a symbol of the unit of the newly-born community. Its protective role was magical only—the fence was not substantial enough to be a physical barrier. In its

traditional forms and instantly identifiable building details it was a sign to neighbouring villages of their larger unification within the Tonga lands. A sign too, of the existence of the village itself, signifying the presence of its occupants and the nature of their way of life.

To the independent observer the village may present an unprepossessing appearance. Its stockade of thicket, smeared with mud and other substances, presents a casual, and even dirty surface. The huts, with their wattle-and-daub walls and their thatched roofs, show a level of competence in house building average among the peoples of Africa; they do not compare for technical skill and beauty of form with the *indlu* of the Zulu.[3] It is easy to dismiss them as 'cylinder-and-cone' structures, or to classify them in terms of their functions, their arrangement, their materials; not difficult to assess their performance in terms of durability, the use of materials, the protection they afford from wind or rain or sun.

In their construction, structure, performance, accommodation, serviceability, these are analysable buildings, relatively simple and satisfying the material needs of the community that uses them. In some examples of vernacular architecture they may meet demands in a precise and even sophisticated manner; in other instances they may make demands of adaptation upon the dwellers who are obliged to accommodate themselves to discomforts or the limitations that technology, resources and economy may impose.

But beyond the material demands made upon the house, the village or settlement there are other aspects that are not immediately apparent. These are the equivalents of the symbols, rituals and beliefs associated with the structures which are to be found in the Tonga example. They constitute the central theme of the present book, and may be summarised as those aspects which identify, seek or invest meaning in the structures of vernacular architecture. Their purposes are varied and the forms in which they gain expression, multitudinous. Together they present a spectrum of rites, customs, superstitions, religious practices, signs, two and three-dimensional symbols, hierarchies of space, patterns of behaviour, expressions of built form and other aspects of symbolic usage which centre upon the building, the village or settlement.

SIGN, SYMBOL AND THE PROBLEM OF DEFINITION

To the sophisticated mind of the anthropologist, sociologist, administrator, architect or educationalist who may encounter the phenomena of indigenous attributions of meaning and significance to built structures, there is a powerful motivation to fit such experiences into classifications which accord within the philosophical constructs of his own tradition. Classifications of signs, comparative studies of rites and ritual, analysis of the formal elements in common among cultures in the choice of symbol or identification of symbolic attributes, would contribute some of the conceptual frameworks in which the combination of shelter, sign and symbol are comprehended.

And this is possibly inevitable. For we read through the windows of our own heritage of culture and learning and in a Cartesian tradition understand them best as we observe and classify. That the processes of signification by which we identify the phenomena are themselves determined by the philosophical constructs of our own tradition, would seem inescapable.

Our inclination to interpret other societies through the filters of our classifications is no more special than their perception of the alien from the west through the filters of their own language categorisations. However, in this one-way traffic where the curiosity of the west is focused on the cultures of others, our communication is heavily conditioned by our categorisation which threatens to draw distinctions in the structure of the cultures where, within the cultures themselves, none exists. Those aspects of the culture which are particularly suited to structural analysis and comparison consequently tend to receive more attention than their importance to the people may warrant. In this connection Professor George Murdock wrote with reference to the Shona (a Bantu people related to the Tonga people whose hut-raising was discussed earlier): 'as an example of overemphasis in anthropology the author should perhaps record his experience in attempting to ascertain the nature of the Shona economy. After reading the fourteen sources on this nation which appeared most promising from the available 376 African bibliographies, he found that he had obtained nine independent lists of kinship terms but not a single mention of the crops grown by this basically agricultural people.'[4]

While the kinship of the Shona lends itself to structural analysis and itemisation, though not, apparently, without disagreement as to what that analysis might be, it is unlikely that to the Shona themselves the abstract concept of the kinship structure is likely to be important, while their exact kinship relationships undoubtedly are.

Though this is no more than stating the obvious, it is the obvious that may suffer in any analysis of tribal or non-literate societies and their cultures, and this may apply to shelter as much as to any other aspect. In fact, as any random sampling of anthropological works of almost any school shows, even including that of material culture, shelter seldom rates for much attention, as previously noted in this series.[5] In contrast, the vast documentation of the myths of societies throughout the world, the extensive classification of them as motifs, as in the work of Aarne Antii and Stith Thompson,[6] or in comparative studies of myth and totemism seen as structural systems as in the work of Lévi-Strauss and his followers, lays emphasis on the oral tradition and the non-material determinants of the culture.[7] These studies seek to uncover the internal systems of thought, motivation, social structure, morals and codes of behaviour in terms of moral tale, allegory, or the narrative of preternatural beings and their behaviour, which the myths serve to define as the values of the society to its members.

The systems of mythology, of superstition, magic, belief and religion which are properly the concern of anthropologists, are ones through which man comes to terms with the phenomena of the world of his experience. They determine his world view and place him in relation to his environment, to the natural and inanimate beings and objects with which he shares the physical world. They provide explanations for the mysteries of life and death; the unaccountable fact of his presence on earth and the mystery of the departed souls of his ancestors; and for his own unknown future. To make them comprehensible he has created constructs of ritual which placate the gods of his own devising. He has evolved patterns of behaviour which place him in accord with the phenomena he has perceived, he has invented terms and names to identify the world of his experience and invested some of them with qualities which parallel those that he has perceived in himself and his fellow creatures. To make the unknown known, to make the incomprehensible at least recognisable, to make the unknowable identifiable, to make the unseen visible he has read, identified and named the signs of his experience.

It can be argued that all phenomena experienced by man exist in the form of messages and that the signs of their existence are there to be read by those who wish to see them. The Whorf hypothesis[8] that language not only reflects the basic assumptions and orientations of a given culture but also contributes to the definition or the quality of experience, has its corollary, as Professor Roger Brown has shown, in the fact that language perpetuates the assumptions and orientations of the culture, not only defining, but also to a large extent determining, the way in which a culture views itself and the world.[9]

The processes of identifying, naming, investing with value and meaning are those of signification and symbolisation. The nature of these processes and the different qualities of sign and symbol have been the concern of philosophers and anthropologists in countless studies since the late nineteenth century. As stated simply by Ogden and Richards in *The Meaning of Meaning* 'If we stand in the neighbourhood of a cross-road and observe a pedestrian confronted by a notice *To Granchester* displayed on a post, we commonly distinguish three important factors in the situation. There is, we are sure (1) a Sign which (2) refers to a Place and (3) is being interpreted by a person.'[10]

All situations in which signs are considered are similar to this. 'When we consider the various kinds of Sign-situations (instanced above) we find that those signs which men use to communicate one with another and as instruments of thought, occupy a peculiar place. It is convenient to group these under a distinctive name; and for words, arrangements of words, images, gestures, and such representations as drawings or mimetic sounds, we use the term *symbols*.'[11] The eminent reasonableness of Ogden and Richards' definition opened up a complex but logically developed argument on the nature of sign situations, the canons of symbolism, the theory of definition and the nature of symbol situations. Though the three-part character of the sign situation that Ogden and Richards defined has been widely, if not by any means universally, accepted, many semiologists have offered different definitions for the use of the terms 'sign' and 'symbol'.

The nineteenth century American philosopher Charles Pierce identified sign, symbol, index, icon and information as the basis of a possible science of semiosis. In his view, a sign 'is something which stands to somebody for something in some respect or capacity' which should 'stimulate its recipient into making some

Sign and Symbol. *As sign, the plaster surface of a Hausa mud building denotes 'brickwork'; as symbol it has the connotations of Western technology, and hence sophistication and prestige.*

In contrast, as sign, the surface of press-moulded aluminium veneer by 'Golden West' on a Californian mobile home denoted 'rubble stonework'; as symbol it has the connotations of pioneer vernacular, and hence the frontier spirit and rugged, unsophisticated individualism.

response which itself may be capable of acting as a sign for the same object signified.'[12] The symbol was for Pierce a 'conventional sign depending upon habit', while a signal was an 'artificial index, a fact that provides an indication and has been produced expressly for this purpose.' Pierce argued that 'signs are only used in relation to one another, in a working system of signs, but never in isolation. Every sign requires another to interpret it.' But these definitions, though made at the close of the nineteenth century, have been subject to a wide measure of disagreement and confusion. With the development of the study of semiotics, or semiology (to their respective adherents not precisely the same thing), there has been a plethora of new definitions. So, to Roland Barthes, everything that has signification is a sign,[13] whereas for Doede Nauta 'every conventional form functioning as human communication is a symbol.'[14] To George Mounin, a symbol is a sign produced by its interpreter,[15] while for S. I. Hayakawa symbolic process is the

House decoration for the celebration of the Festival of Laxshmi Puja, Orissa.

means whereby men can make one thing stand for another. To him the symbol differs from the sign in being 'plurisituational', meaning the same thing in many differing contexts.[16] These few examples among many may indicate that the subject of signification and symbolisation is complex; there is considerable disagreement among scholars on the terms they use and the meanings that they ascribe to the terms they use, even when they agree upon them.[17] There is a real risk that the abstractions of the discussion become so seductive that they draw attention from the nature of the subject. Whatever the definitions of the nature of the process, we ascribe meaning and value to the signs we perceive, and, as far as religious architecture is concerned, specifically build or construct forms in order to invest them with that value.

In view of the confusion over the definitions of sign and symbol, no precise instruction has been given to contributors to this book as to the use of terms, but they have been invited where necessary, to supply the definition for the context of their own argument and examples. In general, the definition used by Carl Jung in *Man and His Symbols* has been found most useful, identifying *signs* 'which do no more than denote the objects to which they are attached' and the *symbol* which 'possesses specific connotations in addition to its conventional and obvious meaning'.[18] He instanced badges and insignia as signs; the wheel and the cross as symbols. 'Thus a word or image is symbolic when it implies something more than its obvious and immediate meaning. It has a wider 'unconscious' aspect that is never precisely defined or fully explained.' Because there are limits to human understanding, he argued, mankind uses 'symbolic terms to represent concepts that we cannot define or fully comprehend.' This is the reason why religions use symbolic language and images. Man uses both conscious and unconscious symbols. 'The sign is always less than the concept it represents, while a symbol always stands for something more.'[19]

But what are the symbolic connotations of shelter? To Christian Norberg-Schultz it is evident that 'human life cannot take place anywhere; it presupposes a space which is really a cosmos, a system of meaningful spaces.' He emphasised the 'importance of supplementing the physical milieu with a symbol-milieu, that is, an environment of meaningful forms'.[20] Norberg-Schultz was writing in a book devoted to the problems of the identification of meaning in architecture and the task of the architect as form-giver, and hence as symbol-giver. 'The task of the architect,' he continued, 'is not to do as little as possible,' but 'to create forms with an adequate capacity. The capacity of the forms defines their range of meaning.'[21]

The contributors to *Meaning in Architecture,* from which Norberg-Schultz's observations are quoted, take predominantly a structuralist-semiological position of analysis that is cross-referential rather than specific to one physical milieu. But it is illuminating that the only consistent symbol-milieu to stand up to scrutiny in the volume, indeed the only one to be identified as a whole, was one of vernacular shelter – the 'Basket-House-Village-Universe' as Aldo Van Eyck described it. of the Dogon of the Bandiagara escarpment in Mali; the Dogon who, in his description 'rely on an all-pervading framework which embraces every facet of

their existence, material, emotional, and transcendental' yet who include 'within the intricate, closely-knit fabric of their system a gratifying kind of scope (flexibility) which permits circumstantial and incidental modification' by the individual.[22]

There is a fundamental difference between the product of the architect as form-giver and symbol-giver and the symbolic elements that exist within the shelter of a vernacular society. The architect determines the forms that seem appropriate to the needs of a particular building or building complex within a society, while in the case of an indigenous society, the form of its dwellings is symbolic of its self-image. Vernacular shelter takes the form that is seen as appropriate to a society's nature, organisation, family structure, aesthetic. The individual within a tribal or folk culture does not become the form-giver for that society; instead he employs the forms that are essential to it, building and rebuilding within determinants that are as much symbolic as physical or climatic.

Though the constraints may be ones of availability of materials, or of the suitability of the structure to withstand solar radiation or heavy precipitation of rain or snow, the symbolic connotations of the building to the society generally take precedence over such considerations of resource or comfort. So a people that has moved from one region to another may take with it a building form that is inappropriate to the climatic context and cling to it because, in terms of its symbol value, it is necessary to the community. Only over the passing of generations may the adaptations of form and structure necessitated by a better fit to the environment take place. As for individual expression, it is evident within the symbolic norms that the society recognises.

Generally speaking, individual expression is of small importance in vernacular shelter, for the similarity of the buildings within a cluster is symbolic of identification with the group that resides within them. Circumstances of terrain or family size may condition the form to some extent but this is usually within constraints that are determined by the culture. Individual interpretations are far more likely to occur in the decoration of buildings. In some contexts any variations from a prescribed canon of symbolism would be unacceptable, but in other societies variants may be permissible within the limitations admitted by the cultural milieu; the materials employed or the devices used in conveying the symbolic content of the theme depicted. The Festival of Laxshmi Puja in the province of Orissa, India, is a case in point. Laxshmi, the Hindu Goddess of Wealth is said to have incurred the wrath of her husband, the god Jaganath, because she visited the house of an Untouchable. By a trick she deprived him of all his possessions and all food; each attempt to obtain sustenance met with failure and Jaganath was obliged to eat at the home of an Untouchable. Whereupon Laxshmi forgave him his anger on condition that she could visit any home she wished. The women of Orissa wash down their houses during the Festival of Laxshmi Puja, and then decorate them with linear patterns drawn in rice (or chalk) mixed with water. Elephants, doves, fowl, mythical animals and other symbolic devices are used, the women competing to attract the goddess to their homes. Brahmin and Untouchable alike paint their houses, often speaking of the process as "feeding" the buildings, the concept of nourishment adding a further layer of symbolism. A wide range of expression is permissible within the constraints of tradition, religious purpose and a culture-determined pattern range. Their participation in Laxshmi Puja declares the women's faith in the goddess, and though they vie with each other in originality the patterns do not challenge the custom but reinforce tradition. Their individuality has expression but is subordinated to the collective purpose of the Festival.

For this reason, the structures built by strongly motivated folk members of the urban society fall outside the scope of the present volume. There is no doubt that the Watts Towers in Los Angeles, built by the Italian-born tile-setter and ex-construction worker Simon Rodia,[23] or the 'Palais idéal' of the postman Ferdinand Cheval, in the French village of Hauterives,[24] are charged with personal symbols. Cheval's *palais imaginaire*, which was claimed by André Breton as the work of 'the undisputed master of mediumistic sculpture and architecture' is loaded with erotic and sexual forms and symbols. But these examples are of singular, purposeful, simple men within urban and suburban contexts whose place within society has been threatened with eclipse, and whose own personalities break through the bonds of formal, meaningless constraint, to build in a declaration of independence against a bureaucratic, mechanical, stereotyped environment. Their gestures are noble, but their work is in a spirit of individualism and defiance, proud claims that symbols matter. Their work may be read as peaks of achievement that express the creative spirit of man, but they can also be read as challenges to a society which has no common language of symbol and significance to which all its members may relate.

PRIMARY SYMBOLISM IN LOCATION AND FORM

There is no one reason why mankind should find it necessary to worship his deities in a specific structure, or why he should place his revered images in a particular volume. But the temple, the mosque, the synagogue, the monastery, the shrine, cult house, ceremonial lodge or sanctuary are at all levels of religion and belief, man-made structures which house worshippers, officiates, novices, initiates, priests, and provide protection for their votive offerings, their graven images, sculptures, religious paintings, gods, idols, relics or other articles of veneration. Some structures symbolise the condition of a tribal origin or creation myth, providing a simulation of the mysterious other world from which man appeared. Others provide a cavity, which symbolises the womb from which he is re-born after initiation; still others screen religious or magical objects from the eyes of unbelievers, the unitiated, or from women. The reasons why men build such special structures are many, but there is no denying that a large proportion of man's building activity is devoted to the provision of shelter for the use of specialist castes of priesthoods, or for worshippers within a particular belief or religion. Frequently the material from which such structures are built is more permanent than that from which the domestic dwellings are constructed; a people may live in houses

of branches, leaves and thatch, but will build great and monumental structures to its gods of stone, which may last for generations. Domestic dwellings of Egyptian or Aztec may be lost to us, or perpetuated only in buildings or similar construction of recent date, but the evidence of ziggurat, pyramid, or temple at Ur, Chíchén Itzá or Angkor Wat remain as enduring testimony to man's fear of, and devotion for, his gods.

Frequently the siting of places of worship is on land with ritual or religious implications as the spiritual homes of ancestors or mythological figures, or on the ground and among the groves inhabited by spirits. It seems likely that early British mark stones were placed on sites associated with legendary heroes, leaders and 'persons of skill and power' as Alfred Watkins termed them. Watkins' research, supported by a wealth of data, led him to the conclusion that almost 'all the wayside and churchyard crosses evolved from mark stones'.[25] The purpose of the mark stones was to identify trade routes and movements through trackless prehistoric forests, but some assumed considerable importance, to become sites for open-air courts, and, as at Kingston-on-Thames, for the crowning of Saxon Kings. Some were selected as sites for Roman altars, and these in turn were incorporated into early churches. Other churches were sited directly on the mark stones, and as Walter Johnson noted 'it is on record that Patrick, Bishop of the Hebrides, desired Orlygus to build a church wherever he found the upright stones or menhirs.'[26] The places where heroes and kings and seers were laid to rest were similarly regarded.

The example of the mark stones and the situation of churches and places of worship on the ley-lines between them indicates a sequence from a functional location which, through its importance in use, became a centre for religious or chieftainly activities and which subsequently became revered for these associations before becoming the traditional core of a historic association which led to the siting of places of worship upon them. This is a progression from the functional to the symbolic, and it seems possible that some sites had secular and practical beginnings as signs whose symbolic attributes eventually led to their being venerated.

Among the most important of the elements that determine siting in shelter are those related to subsistence, and this in turn provides a reason for venerating the location itself. The recurrence of a certain natural phenomenon, or source of food in a particular place, may appear to endow it with particular properties, or give it the attributes of a place preferred by the gods or spirits. In his study of the Netsilik Eskimo, Asen Bilikci noted that places where the caribou were hunted or where salmon trout were trapped by stone weirs were holy: 'the *saputit*, like most other hunting and fishing sites of importance, was considered a holy place, and numerous work taboos had to be observed' though the Eskimos were free to pitch camp there.[27] Balikci concluded that many hunting taboos had as their objective the intent to appease the anger of the hunted animals and ensure future success in the hunt. Female 'impurity' was a particular source of concern, but the taboos protected society from the danger of pollution. Pregnant and menstruating women were confined to their tents at the carbou hunting and fishing places so that the sacredness of the places could be preserved.

13

The tendaana, *or land-priest of a Fra-Fra compound, Northern Ghana. His totem, a Christian cross, and empty Schnapps bottles constitute a mixture of religious symbols.*

Countless other examples could be cited to show the relationship between subsistence and the sacred; for innumerable cultures there is no clear distinction between the religious and the secular. The miracle of life, the cycle of the seasons and the years, are mysteries whose recurrence is matched by a cycle of ritual and ceremony to the spirits and gods who ensure them. Men recognise their animal form, perceive their dependence on, and their shared characteristics with nature and relate their dwellings and their habitat to their observations of the natural world and their perceptions of the spiritual world. Their understanding of these phenomena is frequently expressed in symbols – by name, by the attributes ascribed to them, by pictographs, by their formal similarities with other phenomena which imply spiritual associations. No people exist without some form of shelter, but among some cultures a windbreak, a cave, a 'shallow depression like a scooped nest of shore birds on a beach'[28] may suffice. But even in these instances the symbolic connotations of site and structure can be essential. Few cultures have simpler dwellings than did the Australian aborigines, but as Amos Rapoport shows in the first contribution in this book, the definition of place and location through its symbolic value determined their movements and the location of their camps.

In many societies the decision to place a building or village on a particular site is the special reserve of a priest. Endowed with particular qualities, or the right to speak with the spirits, he may seek auspicious signs for guidance in the choice. Among the Fra-Fra of Northern Ghana, as among many other related peoples along the border region with Upper Volta, this responsibility rests with the *tendaana,* or land priest. A totem of a crocodile, symbolis-ing the origin myth of the tribe, is sculpted on the mud wall of the entrance room to his compound. Above the entrance itself a cross is painted, for though the Fra-Fra are not Christians they have a respect for the power of 'the white man's god'. European influence is indicated in another way, for the path to his compound is lined with Schnapps bottles, each one a sign of a ritual related to the location of a compound. On behalf of a young villager who has taken a wife and wishes to build a compound of his own, the tendaana speaks with the land spirits, offering them libations of Schnapps, which, long ago, the Dutch traders managed to have instated in place of the locally brewed *akpateshie.* Eventually the tendaana designates the site which has been approved by the land spirits and the ancestors and the new compound is begun.

The transition from camp to permanent settlement must be accountable in many ways, but the form that a group of dwelling units may take, and their plan upon the landscape, is often trace-able to a desire to relate directly to natural phenomena. In many tribal societies, man is very aware of his relationship with the rest of nature; he is frequently concerned with maintaining the stability of his environment and attempts to act in harmony with it. Some of his symbols, including those of his dwelling place, can stem from his observations of the rising and setting of the sun, the move-ment through the heavens of moon and stars, and his classification of the world of his experience. A widely observed shape or form may thus acquire symbolic significance. The Oglala Sioux consider the circle as sacred 'because the Great Spirit caused everything in nature to be round except stone', – a Sioux version of the familiar adage that 'nature abhors a straight line'. To the Oglala 'stone was the implement of destruction. The sun and the sky, the earth and the moon are round like a shield, although the sky is deep like a bow. Everything that grows from the ground is round like the stem of a plant.'[29] The circle marked the edge of the world and the winds that travelled around it; it was the symbol of time, for in their observation the day, night and the moon go in a circle above the sky; it became symbolic of the divisions of time and con-sequently the symbol of time itself. 'For these reasons the Oglala made their tipis circular, their camp circle circular, and sat in a circle in all their ceremonies. The circle is also the symbol of the tipi and of shelter.'[30] As in the structures of so many other peoples, the cosmos as they perceived it was symbolised in their dwelling type and their settlement pattern.

Of course, for many vernacular societies the concept of place and the symbolism of location is of relatively little importance compared with the determinants of availability of water or grazing land, of prevailing winds, or access to communication routes – though a number of these may be ascribed spiritual significance. But if among those that ascribe special importance to the meaning of a specific location for the siting of its settlement the Australian aborigines represent one end of a scale, the prescribed siting, dimensioning and orientation of village and town in traditional China must represent the other.

Two centuries before the birth of Christ, at the commencement of the Han dynasty, Chinese town planning was already deter-mined by precise geometry and strict conventions that related the courtyard house, centre of the family, to the *fang,* or a small square grouping of houses. Status in the town was determined by the position of a house within the *fang,* an orderly arrangement of *fangs* comprising the town. *The Book of Rites,* or *Li Chi,* compiled in the Han dynasty, carefully delineated the elaborate rules of etiquette considered appropriate to behaviour in the house, symbolic gestures which had already become ritualised. The orientation of buildings was invested with profound meaning through rites and ceremonies of dedication, and the *K'ao-kung Chi* or 'code book of works' in the *Li Chi* defined an ideal plan. 'The capital city is a rectangle of nine square li. On each side of the wall there are three gates.'[31] A Chinese mandala of nine squares with man at its centre was formed. The south is drawn at the top on Chinese plans so 'The Altar of the Ancestors was to the left, east, and the Altar of the Earth was to the right, west. The court was held in front, and marketing in the rear. The Chinese mandala embraces the concept of *tien-yuan, ti-fang,* or 'heaven round, earth square', and 'as it radiates from the centre in a series of alternating and concentric circles and squares, beginning and end-ing with the square (order and knowledge of man) or the circle (chaos and truth of nature)'[32] is as implicit in the Chinese courtyard house as it is in the city. This formalism, deeply and profoundly embedded in Chinese planning, carries a weight of symbolism in ancestor worship and philosophy, and was sustained at all social levels from the Emperor's palace to the house of the simple town dweller. The rules of the *Book of Rites* have their parallels in the Hindu system and the town plans of their equivalents in the plan-ning principles of the *Manasara.* This collection of design canons, or the 'Vastu Sastras' laid down the principles of town design which was intended to be an image of the cosmos in the form of a great *mandala.* The complexity of this symbolic system and the applica-tion of the *Manasara* to three Hindu towns in Nepal, with the many problems of reconciling ideal principle to site and topography, is examined by Jan Pieper.

In spite of the fundamental differences between the great eastern religions, there are elements in common in the importance of contemplation and inner spiritual harmony. The *mandala,* as a graphic symbol of the universe, may be contemplated at many scales in both the Hindu and the Buddhist religions. The mandala is also the planning principle of Buddhist monasteries in Tibet, as Romi Khosla shows, and his analysis of the symbolism of the monastery also delineates the significance of the Tantric mandala painted as a mural on the walls of the temple. Other symbolic representations include the Wheel of Life and the three animals that reside within it – the red cock of desire, the green snake of hatred and the black hog of ignorance. It is interesting to note how widespread are the associations with these animals and these colours, the former being metaphoric associations, the latter more abstract.

In graphic symbolism literal images may have profound associa-tions, the attributes of the device being deeply associated with its visual form. By this means, complex philosophical ideas, or the limitless qualities of a deity, may be interpreted in visual form,

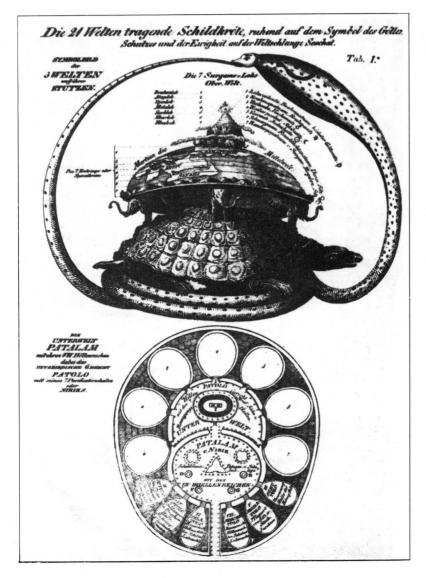

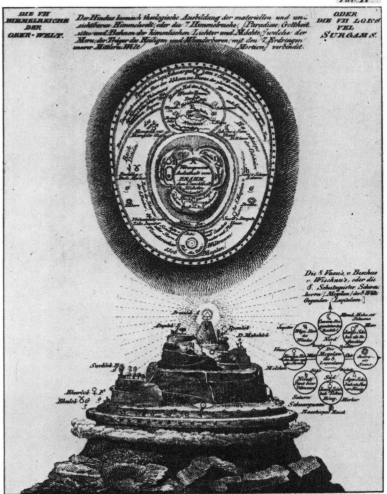

A nineteenth century depiction of Hindu cosmology by N. Müller from Glaube, Wissen und Kunst der Alten Hindus, *Mainz, 1822 (two etchings).*

layers of meaning being unfolded as the enlightened teach. So in Hindu symbolism the essential nature of Mahesha, or Shiva, is represented by a number of basic symbols, including the *damaru* (the Drum), the Crescent Moon, the Tiger's Skin, the Bull, the Trident and the Snake. In simple terms the Moon symbolises Time, the Bull symbolises Spiritual Strength, the Tiger Skin Spiritual Energy. As the consciousness of Mahesha embraces the whole of the manifested Universe 'evil must be present, for there can be nothing outside His consciousness',[33] so the Snake represents Evil, which plays harmlessly round the neck of Mahesha, and the Trident represents the punishment that brings those who stray from the path of *dharma* back to righteousness. Yet this level of interpretation does little justice to the depth of Hindu symbolism: *damaru*, the two-note drum, represents more than Perfect Balance. A ball

strikes both membranes alternately at a speed that produces the effect of a third, combined sound. 'It is eminently suited, therefore, to represent the important function of Mahesha to bring into some kind of relationship the unmanifest state of *Shiva-Shatki-tattva*, and the manifestation of *Ishwara-tattva* represented by Brahma, Vishnu and Rudra',[34] the opposite states of Real and Unreal, the Unmanifest and the Manifest. *Maheshvara-tattva,* which the *damaru* represents, is a critical state between the *Nirgu a-Brahman* or 'attributeless Brahma', and the *Saguna Brahman,* or 'Brahma with attributes', a concept of balance and unity between irreconcilable states.

All aspects of Hindu symbolism have their deeper significance, but this does not mean that they are all appreciated at every level by the populace. The advantage of the literal, figurative symbol, is

Ancestral figures outside a Grunshi compound. The remains of the ancestors are kept in a gourd vessel inside the earth pinnacle. It is 'fed' daily with libations which are also seminal in acknowledgement of its phallic form and the principle of life increase and regeneration.

that it may be comprehended at a very elementary level, but can be unfolded as having layers of meaning, as the Christian church likewise realised with the didactic purpose of the Mediaeval bestiaries, the misericords and carved bosses of the churches.

The woman who bathes the cylindrical stone *Siva-lingam* and places her offerings beside the phallic emblem in Siva's village temple may take the symbol very literally, and the few women who go to the temple do so early in the morning to avoid the laughter of the schoolboys.[35] Their comprehension of the *lingam* as 'a symbol of that Dual, Transcendent, Unmanifest Reality'[36] is probably not intellectualised at these levels. Certainly, in much of South Asia the use of sexual motifs is explicit and purposeful, with the generation of species, the sexual education of the young and the propagation of the crops by symbolic association being their prime purpose. This Tore Hakansson has indicated in his chapter on forms of house decoration among the Muria, the Konds and contiguous peoples. He considers the phenomenon of the youth house or dormitory and its distribution among South East Asian peoples, showing how Hinduism has permeated the tribal, indigenous religions. The form and symbolism of the decorations for the *ghotuls* and of the Saora pictographs, or *ittals,* for fertility rites and for the curing of disease, show how certain basic symbols of a figurative kind are widely distributed and perform similar roles.

In a number of the *ghotuls* and other buildings described by Tore Hakansson, pillars are important as foci for symbols, drawn, painted or carved upon them. These devices are overtly sexual and frequently female. The relationship of the post to phallic worship

may have been forgotten by the celebrants, as the phallic maypole has lost its significance to those who still dance round it on the First of May; the symbolic values of the celebration itself may persist after the precise meaning of the post has been forgotten – or unacknowledged to the anthropologist. The transition from tree worship to post worship, to centre post of a shrine, is a progressive one. George Riley Scott, in giving innumerable examples of the phallus as pillar, either within shrines or before them, notes that 'there are signs of the phallicism inherent in the religion of the Maoris in the manner of decorating the rafters of their sacred houses with representations of the male and female genitalia. The reason for this practice, according to Mrs Rout (in *Maori Symbolism*) is that 'the reproductive organs are considered by the Maoris to be the ribs of the Human House – in other words that the human race is carried and supported on the reproductive organs, just as the house is carried and supported by the rafters.'[37]

Such a conception brings a level of abstract connotation which relates to that of Christian symbolism. To the builders of country churches and cathedrals alike, the stones of the walls were symbolic of the simple faithful, while the pillars, piers and buttresses symbolised the great mystics and teachers 'or the kings and the powerful ones of the earth, whose duty it is to support and uphold the Church by their intellectual and moral power'.[38] If, to the Maori, the support of the roof by the rafters had a symbolic association with the support of the human race by the generative organs, for the Church the vaulting of the nave symbolised 'the firmament, surrounding in its radiant beauty the visible creation'.[39] The form and structure of the church was to be read as a book of symbols which could elevate the spirit with their revelation of Christian meaning.

It is this power to influence and generate responses, as well as to make concepts visible, that gives the symbol its longevity.

17

DIFFUSION AND ABSTRACTION

In his 'theory of needs' Bronislaw Malinowski maintained that the 'symbol is the conditioned stimulus which is linked up with a response in behaviour only by the process of conditioning', and symbolism 'the development of conventional acts for the co-ordination of concerted human behaviour' Its effect is as a 'catalyzer of human activities, as a stimulus which releases responses in a chained reflex, in a type of emotion, or in a process of cerebration'.[40]

Malinowski's definition of symbolism was essentially pragmatic; he considered that most definitions were 'metaphysically tainted' and stated that 'in reality', as he termed it, 'symbolism is founded not in a mysterious relation between the sign and the contents of the human mind, but between an object and a gesture, and an action and its influence upon the receptive organism'.[41]

Fear of the capacity of symbols to stimulate responses caused missionaries to destroy tribal symbols and substitute them with their own. During the nineteenth century in particular, the missionaries of Christianity demolished the phallic and ancestral figures, the gods and idols of the shrines and temples – to establish the Cross as the universal symbol of religion, without acknowledging its own potent, pagan origins. In an earlier century there was less ambivalence in the use of the Christian symbol, and Payne Knight in 1786 could write of the male sexual organs as the 'symbol of symbols. One of the most remarkable of these is a

A recently excavated temple at Aihole, Mysore State, India. Though constructed of stone it reveals a timber technology, symbolic of the persistence of a conservative religion.

A new church at Agios Nicholaos, Crete, is being constructed in reinforced concrete in the form of the traditional stone churches.

cross, in the form of a letter T, which thus served as the emblem of creation and generation, before the Church adopted it as the sign of salvation; a lucky coincidence of ideas.'[42] Numerous examples may be cited in support of this, but the Cross, once forbidden as a Christian symbol because of its pagan associations, is today so powerful a symbol, that few could break a cross on the altar of a Christian church without consciously attempting to destroy that which it symbolised.

The effect of so strong a symbol can be startling. In his study of *Chan Kom, a Mayan Village,* Robert Redfield has noted how pervasive is the recognition of the cross as a symbol within the construction of the Mayan house. 'The shape of the cross as a symbol of power and protection, pervades the thinking and imagery of the people so that they see crosses everywhere . . . each house (of the old Maya type) has its protecting crosses, formed by the intersections of vertical poles with horizontals, to which

offerings are made. Indeed a home is a lacework of crosses.'[43] The most important are four pairs of large wooden crosses that stand at the four entrances of the village and keep evil from entering it. Street intersections are seen as crosses and so they are considered as appropriate places for the performance of magical rites.

The persistence of religious beliefs and symbols associated with building may have extraordinary duration. During the excavations at Ur, miniature bricks were found in the foundations of a building of about 1000 B.C. which were in imitation of the bricks that had been in use nearly two thousand years before.[44] In our own day, the forms of new churches and cathedrals still bear the elements that relate them to those of the Gothic centuries although there has been a conscious determination to introduce new structures and forms that are inspiring but are no longer dependent on tradition. In the vernacular, however, no such self-conscious rejection of the symbolic charge within traditional forms has been made; a new

A corrugated iron Methodist church in Sussex, England. The essential symbolic elements of the Gothic porch and cusped roundel remain.

church, cast in concrete in a small village in Crete will retain the forms of its stone predecessors; a corrugated iron Methodist church in Sussex, England, has the plan, door and window details that relate back to the Early English period. When the monks of Cappadocia hollowed out their monasteries and churches from the tufa rock of Southern Anatolia their traditional symbolism was incorporated in the new churches. The meanings they attached to the pillars, arches, altars and floors were deeply ingrained in their architecture. As Suha Ozkan and Selahattin Onur have shown in their chapter, the Cappadocian way of carving out spaces lent itself to very free internal forms, for the house-sculptor was able to carve out spaces that were not defined by normal structural considerations. To a very large extent, however, the monks kept to the forms that were related to the symbols of their religion. They did not respond to the new material in a totally plastic way, but kept to the forms that were symbolically relevant to them, modifications only taking place over centuries, until eventually

stone-built churches imitated the forms of the rock-hewn ones. Conceptually, the churches were turned inside-out, the carver striking back to the surfaces he required until he achieved the appropriate forms, a symbolic process in itself.

Continually developed from the fourth to the thirteenth centuries, the painted symbols in the churches became progressively more abstract. At first, the walls were decorated with painted symbols of the rooster, the stag or the lion, pagan devices to which new and complex meanings were attached. Later, in a period of iconoclasm the cross was to become the only symbol that could be painted on the walls, roofs and arches of the churches.

Many factors may account too for the tendency to abstraction of symbols, not least of which being that the sign becomes symbolic. In no longer having to be described according to its attributes, it assumes those attributes itself, or in other words, gains in value. Sometimes this may be a matter of protection spurred on by retreat from alien pressures or by religious persecution. It seems likely that this defensive purpose adds further to the value of the symbol.

'In a number of cases it has been shown that a series can be arranged in which we may place at one end a realistic representation of an object. By degrees we may pass to more and more conventional forms that show a distinct similarity to the preceding one, but end in a purely conventional geometric design in which the initial stage can hardly, if at all, be recognised',[45] wrote Franz Boas in a pioneering study of symbolism in primitive art. According to him, the first to discover the phenomenon of a chain of this kind was Frederic Ward Putnam, who traced a progression from fish forms to pure abstraction in the slit feet of Chiriqui pottery dishes. A more dramatic series was illustrated by Charles H. Read in 1892, when he traced a chain of decorations on Polynesian maces, from a pair of figures back to back, through degrees of conventionalism to a final, fused, single abstract blade form.[46] Boas hypothesised on the possible evolution in reverse from geometric form to increasingly realistic development, but could summon little evidence to support such a progression. The importance of the boat as a ceremonial vessel among maritime societies of the coastal regions of South East Asia extends not only to the use of the boat in particular rites and customs, but also to its conservation within land-based villages. Representing in physical form the values of the society's ceremonial life, it has been incorporated as a symbol in the structure of buildings in many coastal cultures. In their study of the boat as an architectural symbol, Ronald Lewcock and Gerard Brans have shown how the features of the ceremonial boat have been incorporated into the structure and symbolism of house types in the island regions, and bring much linguistic evidence to show the persistence of boat symbolism in nomenclature and use. The dissemination of the custom of boat/house building is related by the authors to the diffusion of the maritime Dongson culture. Named after the Vietnamese village of Dong-Son where evidence of the transmission of bronze manufacture and working was first identified in South East Asia as having its roots in China, the Dongson peoples were Mongoloid Deutero-Malay immigrants from Yunan whose culture spread through the Malay archipelago.

They show how in the process of diffusion the roof details have become abstracted as they move further to the conventional from the representational in a typical symbolic series.

It is in the nature of the abstract symbol that any connotations attached to it are projected by man and not intrinsic to the figurative character of the symbol itself. As a result, many symbols may take on different meanings in different societies, though the motif may remain essentially the same. Nevertheless, the distribution of certain symbols through many cultures while retaining the same essential meaning is remarkable, and generally a mark of diffusion. The most notable instance is the swastika, the symbol of Vishnu in Hindu religion. Vishnu was the protector of life and it is notable that the swastika is almost universally, apart from its use by the Nazis, a symbol of good fortune, and a protection against the evil eye. Many examples of the use of the swastika were found by Schliemann in the successive layers of the cities of Troy while the curved swastika occurs in a Middle Minoan clay vessel nearly four thousand years old, and an earlier origin in Anatolia is suspected. The swastika has been found in every Asiatic country including Japan, to the east,[47] and was extensively used among the mound-building prehistorical Amer-Indian cultures in Alabama and Tennessee regions. But whereas the swastika is generally recognised as a sun symbol, Swanton has suggested that the swastika pendants found in mounds in Alabama 'were symbols of the wind clan, which was one of the most important of the Muskhogean people',[48] Both the connotation of the sun and of the wind seem to derive from the perceptual phenomenon of implicit movement or gyration conveyed by the characteristic swastika form – especially interesting among a people which did not discover the principle of the wheel. Is the Amer-Indian use of the swastika related to the known Asian origin of the American aborigine and an example of diffusion, or was it developed separately in the Americas?

Another symbol which implies movement is the spiral or double volute, which was used by the Hopi Indians as a symbol of their migrations, and found from Mesa Verde and Chaco Canyon to Chíchén Itzá, which latter source attests to Hopi belief that the Mayas were simply aberrant Hopi clans who did not complete the migrations. The distribution of the spiral motif has been studied by Dr. Andreas Lommel, who has suggested an origin in the X-ray style painting of Central Asia, where the spiral commenced as a convention for the intestines. Later, he suggests, the spiral was incorporated in body painting. 'In Oceania as a whole, the spiral seems to have accompanied the spread of the south-east Asian Dongson culture around 300 B.C.' he goes on, suggesting that 'the spirals of New Zealand, and especially the spiral derivatives of the Merquesas Islands, point to association with the spirals of the late Chou period of China'.[49] His chart of the distribution of the spiral shows it to be strongly identified with early cultures in Europe and South East Asia, but thinly distributed in Africa. In the transmission the significance of the spiral motif changed, being associated with the snake in some cultures, and with the leaping of kangaroos among some Australian aborigines.

Comparing the facial paintings of the Caduveo Indians, Brazilian remnants of the Guaicuru nation, with the tattooing of the Maoris,

Claude Lévi-Strauss emphasised the split representation of both, though the Maori was systematically symmetrical, and that of the Caduveo Indians asymmetrical. The elements of the latter comprised 'simple and double spirals, hatching, volutes, frets, tendrils, or crosses and whorls' and the four hundred examples that he collected in 1935 of which no two were alike, were improvised within the limits of a complex, traditionally defined range of themes. Their use was to express 'rank differences, nobility, privileges, and degrees of prestige', but, Lévi-Strauss noted, 'we know nothing about their archaic character. It is possible that the themes of these paintings, whose import has become lost today, formerly had a realistic, or at any rate symbolic meaning.' He did not dismiss entirely the possibility of some relationship between the Brazilian and Maori examples, though he made an aside concerning the 'ambitious reconstructions of the diffusionist school'.[50] Certainly in this example there would seem to be little evidence as yet to support a theory of historic contact.

Yet the principle of diffusion can be seen to operate. There are many examples of specific motifs which have been diffused over many centuries and over thousands of miles, have assumed different meanings among different societies, and have sometimes lost their meaning or acquired new ones. In his study of Bantu mural art on the house walls of the Ndebele, Sotho and other peoples, James Walton has summarised the evidence to show the distribution and movement of these motifs and designs through the migrations of peoples, often from remote regions. In the processes of migration and cultural transmission, much of the symbolic meaning has been

The spiral motif of the Hopi migration symbol as recorded in Oraibi, Chíchén Itzá, Chaco Canyon and Mesa Verde; after Frank Waters.

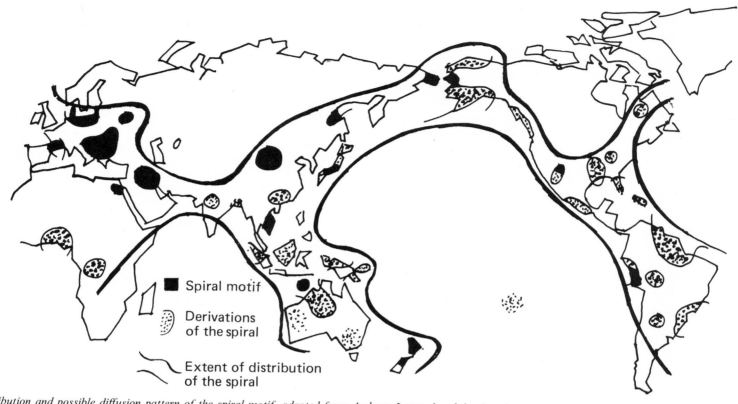

Distribution and possible diffusion pattern of the spiral motif, adapted from Andreas Lommel and developed.

Handpainted hex signs from Pennsylvania Dutch barns, painted by Johnny Claypool of Lenhartsville, Pa.

Motifs of similar form to the Pennsylvania Dutch signs on the wall of a House in San Moritz, Switzerland.

Within the map legend:

- ■ Spiral motif
- Derivations of the spiral
- Extent of distribution of the spiral

lost. but the decorative elements persist, to be used in new contexts.

Many symbols are essentially geometric and therefore have a greater propensity for interpretation by differing societies. Sometimes the degree of symbolisation may change within a single society – S. A. Barrett, in a study of Pomo Indian basketry, gave examples of a simple triangle repeat counterchange pattern which was interpreted by the northern and eastern Pomo as butterflies, but by the central Pomo as arrow-heads. Still more open to interpretation was a counterchange of rhomboids, which were identified as 'broad back', deer back, or darts by the northern Pomo, symbolised crow-foot or crow-tracks to the central Pomo, and to the eastern Pomo were marks indicating orientation. Other geometric designs listed were open to similar diversity of interpretation.[51]

Confusion as to the continuity of the meaning of the symbol becomes greater as it approaches the abstract where, as noted above, other interpretations may develop. Eventually meaning may have gone, to leave a residual compulsion to continue to decorate in the traditional forms. A detailed example in vernacular architecture has been traced by August C. Mahr in the decoration of Pennsylvanian barns by the descendants of German and Swiss peasantry, the Pennsylvanian 'Dutch' (Deutsch). A large number of these signs are swastikas, and stars with five, six, eight or even more points. Comparing these with the motifs of harness ornaments from Austrian pack saddle ornament from the Tyrol, and weaving, washing and other implements from Poland or decorations on the frames of barn doors in Westphalia, Mahr gives ample evidence in tracing them to earlier custom in Europe where the signs have an ancient history as devices to ward off the evil eye, and, even earlier, as symbols of the Sun cult. To many Pennsylvanian Dutch today, these symbols no longer have significance as magic, and are not used to deter evil elements. Nevertheless, barn symbols are still restored and the group still feels the need for their presence. 'The unquestionable credence these magic symbols have been receiving, both in Europe and in Pennsylvania, can only be explained on the basis of peasant psychology, which is group psychology. The *individual* peasant may be entirely honest in telling the stranger that he does not believe in "such things". Just the same, as a *member of his peasant community,* he cannot extricate himself from the *group belief,* which is super-individual. He applies symbols to his barn or household utensils, not because he, as a person, feels that he must have them, but because "one has to have them". The group spirit commands so.'[52]

A similar situation apparently exists in Pyrghi, Chios, which is discussed by Eugene Politis, herself a Chiote. Her study of the decorated houses of the mastic town traces the technique of *xisto* back to its possible origins. But the decorations, though they may relate to archaic symbols that could in some instances be traced to Mycenae, have no significance now for the artists.

Ernst Cassirer in his *Essay on Man* stated that symbols 'cannot be reduced to mere signs. Signals and symbols belong to two different universes of discourse: a signal is a part of the physical world of being; a symbol is a part of the human world of meaning. Signals are operators; symbols are designators.'[53] In a functional sense this is true, but when the symbol has lost its function, it can, as in the example of the Chios, still persist as a sign. Like the face paintings of the Caduveo Indians, they are improvised within a tightly defined group of shapes, whose significance has been lost. Until the pressures of the West threatened to change attitudes by establishing links between the isolated town and the rest of the world through tourism, the painting of xisto flourished, because, like the Pennsylvania Dutch barn symbols, the group need for their presence demanded that they were there.

SIGNS AND SYMBOLS IN CULTURAL CHANGE

In a large number of examples given in this volume, there is a quality of design, building technique and refinement of detail, a quality of workmanship and attention to form, texture or decoration which have a strong appeal in aesthetic terms. Admittedly this statement takes into account none of the special characteristics of the aesthetic of one culture or another – the '*horror vacuui*' of Melanesian decoration or the economy of means and purity of form discernible in the houses of many African peoples whose only decoration may arise from the nature of the materials which have been employed in their construction. If standards consciously sought and attained are very different among various vernacular cultures, the evidence is clearly of a seeking after quality in the vehicles of symbolism. But, as Jaeger and Selsnick observed 'the cultural symbol is not necessarily an aesthetic symbol, nor is the aesthetic symbol necessarily part of a high culture. A village square, a pile of ruins, or an historic personage may become a cultural symbol without having much in the way of aesthetic quality.' They argued that there is a 'strain' toward the aesthetic among cultural symbols, but not that all cultural symbols were works of art. In their view 'when a village square has symbolic meaning, it will have, or there will be some effort to lend it, aesthetic elaboration. But we recognise that there are other sources of symbolic "imprinting" e.g. the recurrent use of the square as a locale for ritual gatherings.'[54]

So it can be argued that the strain to the aesthetic is the outcome of the value placed upon the symbolic attributes of the village square. But the implication is that care, craftsmanship, and aesthetic quality are lavished upon the object *because* it is symbolic; Freud on the other hand suggested that it was through its value as art that the symbol could serve its purpose of stimulating the emotional response in the beholder. 'Art is a conventionally accepted reality in which, thanks to artistic illusion, symbols and substitutes are able to provoke real emotions. Thus art constitutes a region half-way between a reality which frustrates wishes and the wish-fulfilling world of the imagination, a region in which, as it were, primitive man's strivings for omnipotence are still in force.'[55]

Sigmund Freud's researches were to inspire the field of psychological anthropology, especially in the work of Géza Róheim in Hungary, and a number of American anthropologists, among them Clyde Kluckhorn with the Navaho, George Deveraux who worked with the Mohave, David Aberle and the Hopi, and Irving Hallowell, whose studies were especially important in his long contact with the Ojibway and Salteaux. As might be expected, their applications of psychoanalysis to anthropological research concentrated particularly on the interpretation of dreams, the study of myth and the examination of the relationship between personality and culture. Little research has been devoted to the symbology of shelter as revealed through psychoanalysis, although sidelights have been thrown on the subject in the pursuit of other studies. Irving Hallowell, in studying the importance of cultural factors in spatial organisation among the Salteaux, showed that the attention to directional orientation in the ceremonial of the Salteaux represents a spatial universe 'that penetrates religious as well as secular life. And it is obvious that it has psychological implications qualitatively different from directional orientation in Western culture. The build-up of associations of north, south, east and west with symbolic and mythological meanings makes the directions meaningful places. It further integrates other aspects of the culture and behaviour so that a "living in" the world is experienced which has its own peculiar character.'[56]

That the spatial experience is culturally different among the Salteaux suggests that the imposition of alien spatial concepts through Western urban patterning could create a cultural disorientation. The impact of Western concepts upon those of African and Oceanic peoples has been the concern of Dr. Fritz Morgenthaler, a psychiatrist and anthropologist who has done field studies and psychoanalytical studies among West African and New Guinea peoples. Using Darcy Ribiero's terminology as an index, he summarises the symbolism of house and village form among the peoples he has studied and the effects of reflex-modernisation which in the course of civilisational processes has created the breakdown of traditional symbolic values.

Though the influence of European art and values has been evident in the art and architecture of tribal cultures for more than a century, and in some instances for much longer, a significant impact upon the cultural expression through the symbols and forms that have been used has been generally of comparatively recent date. A case in point is the Mbari house of the Ibo of Eastern Nigeria. As the life of the mud sculptures within these clay houses is only about three years, detailed documentation of their past history is almost impossible, but today the typical Mbari house contains both traditional and modern elements. They are to be found mainly south of Owerri and are built wherever Ala, the Ibo fertility goddess, sends a 'sign' to a priest. Open-sided, their zinc roofs supported by four cubic columns, the Mbari houses present four stages with their backs to a hollow sealed chamber. One stepped stage of the Mbari house contains a mud statue of Ala, while the opposite side has a figure of Amadi Oha, representing thunder and the sky deity. The water goddess, Ekunochie, is often represented but the other figures crammed into a Mbari house may represent district officers, teachers, tailors, animals, with steamships and other objects in surrealistic juxtaposition. The figure of Christ may appear, crucified in schoolboy uniform with short pants, for the villages are largely Christian. Cultures overlap and

so do symbols; 'motor cars and policemen are found side by side with the most sacred symbols. This is a contrast only in the eyes of the Western spectator' wrote Ulli Beier. 'To the Ibo whose life is still dominated by traditional concepts and beliefs, there is no essential difference between the sacred and the profane, and no sharp line of division between the world of the spirits and human life.'[57]

A somewhat similar adaptation has taken place among the Fanti of the Ghanaian coast, but in the case of the secular 'Asafo Regiments' only with continuing changes in their role. Originally the Fanti Asafo companies were warrior societies who formed what was tantamount to a 'home guard' during the Ashanti wars, centred on the village of Anomabu near St. George Castle. With the subjugation of the Gold Coast tribes by the British the Asafo societies lost their warrior status, but the companies persisted with quasi-military names after a British model. They found a new role in acting as paddling crews for unloading the trading vessels from the deep water offshore and carrying goods and passengers over the breakers in their long canoes. The establishment of ports and the decline in the work of the paddling crews left them using their canoes primarily for fishing. Today the Asafo companies operate as men's clubs in an African form of Freemasonry, their identity now symbolised in the regalia and magical objects, which are kept in the massive concrete 'Asafo monuments'. Symbols of their own image and their view of European power are to be found in the concrete lions, whales, tin clocks and palm trees of the No. 2 Dontsin Company's monument, or the concrete gunboat complete with sidegate thoughtfully provided for access, of the No. 3 Company.

Within the structure of tribal life, even when assailed by the onset of industrialisation, technology and rapid communications through mass media, there is a system, complete and sufficient within itself, which gives the individual member of a society a sense of relationship to the community as a whole, reinforced by the belief system and values of its culture. In turn the beliefs are expressed in symbols which are not seen as dissociated from those aspects of the phenomena of life and death of the real and the spiritual world which they symbolise. Meyer Fortes and E. E. Evans-Pritchard observed that in an African society its members 'feel their unity and perceive their common interest in symbols, and it is their attachment to these symbols which more than anything else gives their society cohesion and persistence. In the form of myths, functions, dogmas, ritual, sacred places, and persons, these symbols represent the unity and exclusiveness of the groups which respect them. They are regarded however not as mere symbols, but as final values in themselves.' They pointed out that Africans do not understand or attempt to comprehend the objective meaning of the symbols, and that these symbols would lose their power if if they did, dependent as it is essentially on their symbolic content. Africans, they argued, do not analyse their social system but live it, thinking and feeling about it 'in terms of values which reflect, in doctrine and symbol, but do not explain the forces that really control their social behaviour.'[58] The stability of African community structure lies in this and the norms that are woven into the

Above and overleaf. The 'monuments' of the Asafo Companies, Dontsin Regiment, Anombu, Ghana.

duties, rights and patterns of behaviour that they express. Were these to be questioned or flouted, the fabric of the society would loosen and traditional society would ultimately disintegrate.

Nevertheless the pressures of a changing economy and the pulling factor of urban development cause thousands of rural village dwellers to move to the city. Whereas the Ibo Mburi houses embrace the modern elements within a traditional framework of belief, the city often offers only the abandonment of the traditional customs and the acceptance of new and bewildering scales of values, or sometimes a transitional system which reconciles the urban environment with the need for stability of traditional structures of belief. This has been studied by Dr. D. K. Fiawoo and Dr. Kenneth Little, who have reported on the rise of syncretist cults in urban west Africa. The cult of Blakete has a supernatural power vested in two principal male and female gods, and a minor female goddess. Cult meetings take place in a shrine. Some of these are privately owned and others owned by the

community and established with the permission of the chief as a protective agency for the town against the growing incidence of witchcraft, minor crimes, marital infidelity and social problems. The shrine bears the symbols of the deities and the ritual, and rules of membership are a heterogeneous assimilation of Christian, Moslem and animist beliefs.[59]

Instances such as the Blakete cult show that the need for the structure of tribal life within an urban context has generated a synthesis of disparate religious elements, and a pantheon of new gods represented by old and new symbols.

Communications have brought about this confusion; contacts between the settled tribal community and the new urban environments that are of a new kind, more rapidly made, more supported by technological institutions than ever before. From transistor radio to masthead television or mobile film show the media have contributed to the fragmentation of tribal life, demonstrating the dubious attractions of the city and showing even in their own

press-button magic the vast disparity between indigenous, rural life and the impact of westernisation. Melanesian cargo cults, which are based on the belief that the present world will end in a cataclysm to be followed by an age of peace and plenty when the spirits of the ancestors would bring goods from the Land of the Dead, summoned by mysterious writing, as the Europeans summoned their ships, are one extreme symptom of the stress experienced by some societies by this cultural collision.

But the circumstances of cultural contact are not always so disastrous though confusion in the conflict of one symbol-system with another can still be real. When the impact is less dramatic the absorption of the symbols of one religion into another may produce strange results. When speaking of the transmission of motifs, signs and symbols, whether from society to society through the contiguity of cultures, or through the movements of peoples and the conquest of others, we tend to assume that with each new settlement the design elements of a past tradition are re-established. For a migrant or nomadic people, or for the missionary spreading the beliefs of an expanding religion, adherence to the symbols and ritual associated with its origin is a necessary component of the process. Nevertheless, as the study of any evangelical movement for the transmission of any religion tends to reveal, adaptation to new cultures, adjustment to the dogma and practices of established religion newly encountered, may cause substantial changes in the form and content of the symbols employed, and the meaning attached to them. And, as already noted, the process of transmission may lead to an abstraction of elements which may ultimately be without meaningful significance in any literal form though the motivation to decorate with abstract symbols may remain.

Whatever the circumstances, the passing on of motifs and symbolic configurations is dependent upon contact with, or the resettlement and location of, the priesthood, the converted, or the artist-craftsmen who interpret the symbols in their work. To these however, may be added the smaller, but not wholly insignificant transmission of motifs through the form of mobile shelter itself. This is possibly most evident in the use of boats which bear the blazons of their occupants, and which are in themselves highly charged symbolic forms whose existence, as has been shown, may influence architectural form.

Pakistan truckers, who travel long distances between *addas,* or truckers' hostels, to maintain communication and supply routes in a national network, use the truck, its cab and its whole structure as a mobile shelter richly embellished with symbols from various sources. Many of these motifs are frankly derivative, adapted from the high art of Islam, but they are reinterpreted in a genuinely original folk expression. Though the horse-drawn carts of Palermo, Sicily and its environs are employed within a narrower compass, and do not provide shelter to the same degree, much of the spirit which motivates their decoration and even the pictorial adaptation from high art forms, is comparable.

Sicilian cart decoration poses many problems – why was it so light a structure when used for heavy loads? Why was the axle box made of bronze and not iron? Why were some parts entirely painted and others with little care? Why was the dominant colour a golden yellow? Dorothy Leadbeater showed that the elaborate carts were a folk artist's adaptation of the lavishly decorated and gilded coaches used throughout Europe by royalty and nobility in the late seventeenth and first two-thirds of the eighteenth centuries. The sources of the decorations of the carts are frequently prints of high art paintings and engravings, and sometimes postcards. The prints present a conventionalised form of the painting which the folk artist can adapt to his cart panels. But the painter is one of a hierarchy of craftsmen, from the apprentice who stripes the wheels, the *indoratore* who paints the cart yellow and does the lesser decoration, to the *pittore* who paints the panels. The artists show an eclecticism in their choice of sources, but a freedom in their approach to their work which is 'with critical discrimination but without prejudice, diverse channels which ultimately merge to reveal themselves as a tradition.'[60] But though the choice is his, and he draws on his sources with a lively imagination, the range is limited by what is considered appropriate in the culture. Any relationship to the carriages of seventeenth-century Europe has been long forgotten; the tradition has its own independence, the scenes of battles from the Crusades or the Franco-Prussian war are welded together in a time-free pictorial space. They are now their own symbols of values as a reality.

But there is a transitional period today, where some of the motorised carts bear traditional decorations, while others have something of the symbols, some adhesive and plastic, some painted, that the motorised carts of Iran or Turkey sport. Young drivers in these countries spend much time decorating their vehicles with eye-lashes round the headlamps, stick-on heroes of popular films and fiction, labels and pendants of places unseen and unvisited – signs of a modern age of plasticised media still used with the freedom and lack of cultural restraint of the folk artist. Many of these embellishments, though sportive and personalised with tinted photographs, pelmets, fringes and tassels, are ready-made

for the purpose by accessory shops; ultimately they will stultify invention.

The trucks of Pakistan are different both in scale and importance. But they are decorated by a team, including an apprentice to an *unstad* or master painter and the calligrapher, corresponding to the teams of Sicilian cart artists. The symbols employed by the truckers are a combination of religious ones which reflect traditional beliefs, popular folk tales and personal emblems. Hassan Khan shows how these have moved from rural to urban and technological content, symbolic both of the trucker's trade and their aspirations in the modern world, befitting a form of expression which has

A traditionally painted cart, Palermo, Sicily.

Motorised 'taxibar' vehicle in Iran.

developed since the Second World War. The trucker, most of whose adult life is centred upon the vehicle, which constitutes his 'home', focuses upon its decoration an anthology of signs and symbols that represent both the impact and conflict of cultures in which he finds himself, and to which he contributes.

So the traditional mode has followed the migrant to the city, overtaken him and accommodated to the urban environment; as such it is new and an expression of the city, or rather the dilemma in which the tribal migrant finds himself. Those that settle and become urban dwellers must either adhere to such a quasi-tribal structure or forge out a new way of life for themselves. Today the cities of Africa and the East are alive with new signs, new and dramatic paintings, motifs, emblems, symbols, painted sometimes with a vivacity of colour and breadth of treatment that eclipses the naivety of the technique, or sculpted with bravura in concrete. In a study of the Western Native Township on the edge of Johannesburg, Julian Beinart recorded the designs of the dwellers in the two thousand 'identical boxes, each two-roomed, 400 square feet' arranged on 'the most straightforward grid-iron that irregular

land allows' and rented as housing. The formula seemed grim, but the people liked the buildings, formed their own community and began to develop 'a communication system on the front façades of their houses. Only the front 22 ft. by 7 ft. rectangle; there was no point in decorating the other walls, which no one could see'—a principle not dissimilar from the decoration of the Pakistan trucks, emblazoned for the world to admire. Beinart asked many of the occupants why they decorated the houses: 'I told the builder a tree design would have great significance with the people that used to come for prayer at my house' said one. Another: 'I wanted something that would look modern instead of the decorations we do on the farms', and another, enigmatically: 'We need the extra space on the *stoep*'. Asked what the designs made them think of, they suggested 'dignity', 'a butterfly', 'the Queen's crown', 'the money I spent on it'. 'I think of the wealth in the form of a diamond', said one, and another: 'I think of a razor which together with the black colour signifies "danger" '.[61] These and other replies revealed an essentially African response to the motivation to decorate, the challenge presented by the hundreds of identical blockhouses, and a

'Chop Bar' near Tarkwa, Ashanti. The contrast between traditional tribal life and sophisticated modern living is symbolised through the paintings of the [st]able diet 'fufu' being prepared, and a couple eating at a table with a knife and fork.

[si]gnificance in the designs they painted and moulded that was at [o]nce symbolic in group terms and meaningful as an individual [e]xpression. Where the inhabitants came from, which tribes they [r]epresented and how much their decorations represented those

origins, their response to new conditions and the community of the Western Native Township itself is the subject of Julian Beinart's chapter.

[S]HELTER, SYMBOL AND SCIENTIFIC METHOD

[O]nly a few examples of the kind quoted in Julian Beinart's inter-[v]iews are necessary to demonstrate the fact that the meanings [as]cribed to symbols in different societies, even in a modern urban [c]ontext, are considerable. When the difference of meaning of a [si]milar device is dramatically demonstrated by quite sharp distinc-[ti]ons between one culture and another, the differentiation is [c]omprehensible; it is less so the closer they are, for the nuances and [sh]ades of interpretation may not be apparent. Words are them-[s]elves integral elements in the symbolic system of a language, and [th]e translation of words from one language to another creates

many difficulties arising from the nature of classification and cultural symbol systems. Meanings, explained the linguist Edward Sapir, 'are not so much discovered in experience as imposed upon it, because of the tyrannical hold that linguistic form has upon our orientation in the world. Inasmuch as languages differ very widely in their systematization of fundamental concepts, they tend to be only loosely equivalent to each other as symbolic devices and are, as a matter of fact, incommensurable in the sense in which two systems of points on a plane are, on the whole incommensurable to each other if they are plotted out with reference to two differing

Moenkopi, Northern Arizona, the most recent of the Hopi towns. Its architectural forms are clearly defined though unspecified by name.

systems of coordinates.'[62] This problem of correlation applies in the very naming and identification of parts of a building; still more so in the identification of its symbolic attributes.

In a classic and highly influential study, Benjamin Lee Whorf discussed a large number of linguistic factors in the terms used by the Hopi Indians when making reference to their architecture. He showed that whereas the Hopi have a large number of very specific terms for architectural details, such as *te. wi,* 'ledge, shelf or setback'; *e'ci,* 'partition', or 'closure' of any kind; *'pa'wi,* 'plastering clay', and so on, there was an 'absence of terms for interior three-dimensional spaces, such as our words room, chamber, hall, passage, interior passage, cell, crypt, cellar, attic, loft, vault, storeroom etc., in spite of the fact that Hopi buildings often have many rooms, and frequently for specialised use. In Hopi it is not possible to say the equivalent of 'my room'. Hopi and other Uto-Aztecan languages consider building spaces as purely relational concepts, 'thus hollow spaces like room, chamber, hall, are not *named* as objects are, but are rather *located*; i.e. positions of other things are specified so as to show their location in such hollow spaces'.[63] This, Whorf points out, has nothing to do with paucity of space types, for the architectural forms of the Hopi are quite rich. Again, the Hopi have buildings which are designated for different uses as schools, churches, stores and so on, as well as traditional uses which do not reflect white influence. But for all of these, whether jail, barn, garage or whatever, there is only one Hopi word, *ki.hi,* meaning 'house' or 'building'.

The Hopi, Whorf indicated, do not associate occupancy with the building as in English where 'school', 'garage', 'theatre', 'hospital', etc., are words where the use and the structure fuse. For the Hopi, it is the occupancy and the spot of ground or floor where the occupancy occurs which is called *ki.hi.* Perhaps the most startling observation is that 'there should be no name for the *kiva,* that structure so highly typical of pueblo culture and so intimately connected with their religion. Many people know that our word kiva is taken from the Hopi, but they think that it is the Hopi word for a kiva, which it is not'.[64]

Edward Sapir subscribed strongly to the view that signification in turn structures thought and perception. 'The fact of the matter is that the "real world" is to a large extent unconsciously built upon language habits of the group', he wrote 'We see and hear and otherwise experience very largely as we do because the language habits of our community predispose certain choices of interpretation'.[65] It follows that the study of vernacular architecture of non-Western societies in particular should take into consideration the values attached to the terminology used to describe the building and its use. If the symbolic value of a built structure is recognised as something special to the society which builds it, there seems ample linguistic evidence to show that it may still be conceptualised in a linguistic framework which is itself of a different order of emphasis and signification. The values attached to the building or settlement may be such as to perceive relationships between built form and environment, or meanings in the built structure which fall outside the conceptual framework within which we ourselves structure the world in the West. This is the subject of David Dalby's study of the noun *gàrii* as used among the Hausa. His study shows that the term, which may loosely be defined as meaning 'town' or 'settlement' has also the meaning of 'sky'. Dalby's article reveals that these two apparently unrelated terms are in fact, within the construct of Hausa thought and language, closely related in one concept. The signification of the town in Hausa thought is of quite a different order from that in the West, and its physical limits and abstract connotations are also of a different, and varying, kind. This example emphasises that when the building, settlement or town, or any of their parts from internal spaces to streets or settlement limits, are perceived and noted from a western viewpoint, they may still be conceptually far removed from the way in which they are recognised and symbolised within the culture itself.

When we consider the orientation of buildings, or siting of them in relation to physical phenomena or a code of rules; when we examine the values ascribed to the parts of a structure and to the paintings or carvings which it bears; when we consider the meanings of the words which are used to describe the nature of a settlement as culturally determined, we are talking not about one kind of symbol system, or sign system, but of many. Brief mention has been made earlier of the difficulties that have arisen in the precise definition of the meaning of sign and symbol. Ferdinand de Saussure's classification in his *Course in General Linguistics* of the 'sign', the 'signified' and the 'signifier' has been widely accepted as establishing the three-part relationship of any sign system, and this has been applied with refinements to semiology, the science of signs, which he postulated as one which would embrace all sign systems, with linguistics being only one branch of the science.[66] Now well established and embraced within the theory of structuralism, the aim of semiological research is, in Roland Barthes' words to reconstitute the functioning of the systems of significations other than language in accordance with the process typical of any structuralist activity, which is to build a *simulacrum* of the objects under observation'.[67]

Essential to semiology is the application of a precise method, unambiguous terminology and the rigorous use of its own discipline. This Professor A-Ph. Lagopoulos has done in an analysis of the settlements of the western Sudan, taking the ideological values of these societies related to their settlements, and expressed in the settlement forms. Many aspects already encountered in this volume, including the expression of cosmic order in the organisation of a compound or village, the relation of the village to the earth and sky, the anthropomorphic projection onto the plan of a community, the incorporation of clan, phallic, religious and other symbols within the organisation of the community are examined on a comparative basis among the Dogon, Fali, Bamako, Yoruba, Kotoko and other peoples. The structural principles underlying the symbolic significance of the plan organisations of these West African settlements enable him to make deductions concerning the importance of these integrated sign-systems compared with the freedom of choice of sign in the architecture and planning of the West, a freedom which may ultimately contribute to urban disintegration.

In his summary of the Dogon conception of the large house, Professor Lagopoulos observes that it is considered as a 'cosmic egg' in which the 'plan of the house is converted into a sort of summary of its three-dimensional spatial reality', and shows that the signs 'ground floor', 'ground floor ceiling' and 'floor ceiling' of the two-storey house lead to the signified 'earth', 'space between this earth and the sky' and 'sky' respectively. This might lead one to deduce that the use of *gàrii* among the Hausa for both 'house' and 'sky' is similarly derived, and indeed it might be, although David Dalby's extensive linguistic studies suggest that it is not a matter of extension through symbolisation, but that the 'house' and 'sky' meanings of *gàrii* are conceptually the same, being related to a notion comparable with 'environment' with its domestic, village, regional and still more extensive applications. That a semiological analysis which provides a systematic structure through which to examine the systems of symbolism within tribal societies is itself subject to the same problems of precise definition and meaning is of course inevitable, bearing in mind the difficulties of translation and interpretation.

Looking down upon a Dogon village it is hard to discern any similarity between its physical plan and the idealised form which the symbolism of the homestead and settlement implies. The precise symbolic meaning of the altars and shrines, grinding stones and storerooms remain, but their disposition is subject to the difficult topography of the falaise and the rock debris of the escarpment on which Dogon dwellings are built. This demonstrates the semiological principle of the *langue* and the *parole,* as de Saussure termed it, the difference between language and speech. The rules of the symbolic principles of layout are the langue; the individual expression of these rules which is indicated in the physical organisation of the homestead on its site, the parole.

Even among the Chinese, the geomancer exercises in the practice of his craft discretion as to the situation of buildings, as J. E. Spencer has shown in *Houses of the Chinese.* Geomancy, or cosmic orientation through the applications of the principles of *feng shui* is, in Wheatley's terms, 'the art of adjusting the features of the cultural landscape so as to minimise the adverse influence and derive maximum advantage from favourable conjunction of forms.'[70] In other words it is not a precise geometry but rather the perception of propitious orientation, the balancing of favourable elements according to symbolic, perhaps scientific principles. So the location of the building that it may face South while getting the benefit of the spirit of wind and water, which gives *feng shui* its name (*feng,* wind and *shui*, water) also contains within it the *yin/yang,* female/male principle, the *yin* in Mandarin corresponding to the shaded side of a hill, the *yang* to the sunny side.

A Japanese symbol-system related to the cardinal points in a building may also have a purely practical base. With the south to the top and the north at the bottom it represents an eight-sided figure which commences on the north side and progresses through twenty four positions, three to a face, in a clockwise direction. At the first position it is 'good for building a storehouse or barn and receding ground has the promise of good luck', while 'a lavatory does no harm'. Due northeast, 'A Shinto shrine built here brings misfortune; a miniature hill in the garden, good luck, a gate, misfortune.' While to the south 'a pond here causes deaths from drowning or the intemperance of the master of the house; a lavatory, perpetual diseases, a garden or wood does no harm.'[71] The system gives advice and rules on the siting of storehouses, cooking-stoves, wells, fireplaces, gates and so on. Some may be seen to have very practical implications when the propitious and disadvantageous sites for a lavatory and cooking places are considered. But the system makes no hard and fast rules; the choice is still that of the builder though the principles are associated symbolically with concerns of luck, religion, ancestral respect or family peace which may give him pause.

Niike is a Japanese farm community comprising a score of homesteads. Keith Critchlow has examined the evidence of the information on the siting of the buildings and has related it to the *hogaku* system of zodiacal orientation. Linking the pattern of orientation to the cycle of the festivals in the year, the passage of time, the health of an individual at various times of the day related to zodiacal characteristics and the patterns of Essences or 'elements', he suggests that a comparison may be made with the principles underlying acupuncture. Acupuncture has been proved to work, but the reasons are still unknown; the rules governing the geomacy of feng shui or the siting of the Japanese house may belong to similar orders of esoteric knowledge. The principles have been handed down from the observations of sages to become absorbed within the vernacular. He does not propose a scientific explanation for the use of hogaku, but makes an analogy which is now being seen to have a scientific basis, revealed by cross-referential studies of magnetotropism in plants. Here, he suggests, the placing of buildings in relation to the earth's geomagnetic field may have a direct relationship with the findings of A. V. Krylov on the effects of magnetic fields on the growth of plants.

Can symbolism have a scientific base, then? Concluding his article on the architectural symbolism of Tibetan monasteries, Romi Khosla expresses the hope that eventually 'we may be able to study their culture . . . and interpret their beliefs in a scientific language'. There is clearly an argument against the possibility. Professor Lagopoulos, in his semiological study of the Western Sudan settlements has applied a precise discipline to the study of the subject and has expressed the symbolism of those societies in a language of a social science; in this he has 'interpreted their beliefs in a scientific language'. But there are some that would argue that the folk or tribal mind is fundamentally unscientific and that the structure of symbolism is likewise. To this Claude Lévi-Strauss argued in *The Structural Study of Myth* that 'the logic in mythical thought is as rigorous as that of modern science, and that the difference lies, not in the quality of the intellectual process, but in the nature of things to which it is applied'.[72] Is the nature of symbolism such that scientific logic cannot be applied to it? Presumably not, if the internal logic is as consistent and rigorous.

But if this is the case, the question remains whether, outside the logical consistency of symbolism itself, there can be any scientific basis to the symbols. The fact, demonstrated earlier, that symbols may stand for different concepts and associations suggests that there can be no one-to-one relationship, no means whereby symbols may be rationalised into a scientific system. Yet apart from the shifting connotations of the symbols there is the persistence of the symbol forms themselves to reckon with, and these, as has been shown in a number of examples, are sometimes widely, even universally employed. That a rational basis for the ritual structures and usages of tribal or 'primitive' man was identifiable when based on magic and sympathetic association would have seemed highly unlikely only a short while ago.

Recent research on age-old problems has produced, sometimes with the aid of computers, some remarkable discoveries. Stonehenge has been the subject of countless claims and refutations as to its origin, the methods of construction, the rites that may have taken place there and the purpose of the great dolmens. Professor Gerald Hawkins, however, in his studies of Stonehenge employing computer checking, identified that Stonehenge I had eleven 'key positions, every one of which paired with another, often more than one other, to point 16 times to ten of the twelve extremes of the sun or moon; Stonehenge III with its five trilithons and heel axis pointed eight times to eight of those same extremes. Such correlation could not have been coincidental.'[73] He speculated on the possible use of such accuracy and skill in these alignments and why they should have been employed to conclude as a possibility that 'They made a calendar, particularly useful to tell the time for planting crops; they helped to maintain priestly power . . . by enabling the priest to call out the multitude to see the spectacular risings and settings of the sun and moon, most especially the midsummer sunrise over the heel stone and midwinter sunset through the great trilithon'.[74] He also gave convincing evidence to show that the fifty-six Aubrey holes which had never been satisfactorily explained 'served as a computer. By using them to count the years the Stonehenge priests could have kept accurate track of

the moon, and so have predicted danger periods for the mo[st] spectacular eclipses of the moon and the sun' as well as oth[er] celestial events.

Meanwhile Dr. Alexander Thom made detailed studies of ancie[nt] stone circles throughout Britain to conclude that instead of bei[ng] circles, they were rings of flattened proportion whose circum[-]ference-diameter ratio was almost exactly three; in other word[s] that they were attempting, for my[s]tical reasons, to make *Pi* 1[:] He could not suggest the precise purpose for doing so, but co[n-]cluded that prehistoric Britons could measure the length of [a] curved line 'with an accuracy better than 0.2 per cent'.[75]

The implications here are clearly that in their mystic rites a[nd] structures prehistoric men incorporated a remarkable knowled[ge] of geometry and astronomical observation which gave scienti[fic] basis to their constructed symbols.

Other discoveries that suggest a knowledge by prehistoric m[en] of the workings of our own and other planets of unsuspect[ed] depth include the tracing of geodetic lines by divining, unravell[ed] by Guy Underwood. He identified the water line, the aquastat a[nd] the track line and showed that 'they appear to be generated with[in] the Earth; to involve wave motion; to have great penetrati[ng] power; to form a network on the face of the Earth; to affect t[he] germination and growth of trees and plants', which is perceiv[ed] and used by both animals and men. 'These geodetic lines for[m] spiral patterns which involve the number seven in their constructi[on] and follow mathematical laws which involve the number three.' This discovery suggests the scientific basis in symbolic importan[ce] of the numerals 3 and 7 in many religions and rites, and likewi[se] the form of the spiral. In the course of his work, Underwo[od] became interested in the prevalence of the serpent symbol [in] religions and the 'subsequent emergence of the serpent as a g[od] believed to control fertility, and always associated with water a[nd] usually with the moon. As the serpent is the one land-livi[ng] vertebrate which naturally and frequently reproduces all t[he] geodetic spiral patterns it seems reasonable to assume that bo[th] the serpent and the spiral symbols are representations of t[he] geodetic spiral.[72] Such studies and hypotheses may not come with[in] the compass of what is acceptable in the most rigorous definiti[on] of scientific discovery. But this is perhaps, as Keith Critchlow h[as] suggested, the fault of the viewpoint.

THE RELEVANCE OF SYMBOL AND SHELTER

Throughout the United States today, and increasingly in Gr[eat] Britain and other countries, new settlements are being create[d.] Most of them are being formed for purely economic reasons; th[ey] comprise groupings of trailer houses or 'mobile homes', mova[ble] structures which leave the assembly line of the factory to take [a] single trip before being 'hooked up' to a servicing unit at a mob[ile] home park. Close on 20 per cent of new American housing is n[ow] of the mobile home type, and just as these well-serviced, relativ[ely] nexpensive homes for the young and the retired illustrate the fundamental demand for shelter, they also illustrate the need for a symbol-milieu. These trailer homes, semi-permanent dwellings of a rootless society in search of a base, bravely bear the symbols of another age and another culture, which seems to have the cohesion and the quality that they seek. So mobile homes sport windows with echoes of Early English lancets, or carry panels of aluminium press-moulded stonework in imitation of a pioneer vernacular, or support their sun porches with extruded aluminium 'wrought iron' scrollwork; the elements are banal, the designs trite, but the search for symbols in vestigial links with recognisable motifs of the past is real enough. A Los Angeles mobile home is painted in the colours of a Japanese vernacular, the house is approached by way of a tiny *tori* arch, yet the nameplate carries the name of Massey. But it is situated on Sir Gawaine Drive. The owner of Prince Arthur Mobile Homes had hoped to wring what little romance and spirit remains in the debased symbols and associations of an age of chivalry that never was.

What they are seeking is the unifying language of a symbolism that denotes the values of their microcosmic social group. To some extent, the mobile home parks are succeeding, in the smallness of their scale and the social integration that some have achieved, to gain the cohesion that man needs in relation to his fellows in a community of a size that ensures interaction and communication. They have yet to create a symbolism of their own, and the pre-packaged, frame and panel assembly lines of the manufacturers do not create a vernacular. Theirs is not a shelter that stems from the expression of the society that is appropriate to their own social order; not yet, anyway.

Or so it would seem, although we are probably ill-equipped to make such an assumption. To date we have had remarkably little material on which to base any conclusions concerning man's search for symbols appropriate to his shelter in an urban society, and we know too little about the fundamental relationship between

Entry through a tori *gate to a Los Angeles 'Vagabond' mobile home, decorated in 'Japanese' fashion.*

shelter, sign and symbol to be confident of any such evaluation. Much needs to be done in the study of the symbolism of shelter and signs and symbols that decorate it, or are incorporated within its forms and structures. Though this has not been a major concern of anthropologists in general, there are valuable descriptions and observations in countless works whose principal purpose was other than the study of either symbolism or shelter, and some of these have been unashamedly quoted in this introduction in order to draw attention to the fact. Nevertheless such references can be seen as a valuable spin-off, a bonus from a work which was quite differently directed; as the anthropology of shelter is in its infancy at the present time, so too the relationship of sign and symbolism to it is no less immature.

There is little guidance in this direction, unfortunately. The Royal Anthropological Institute's volume of *Notes and Queries on Anthropology* which is intended as a guide to field workers scarcely mentions the subject. Page counts can be invidious, but indicative in this case: in a volume of four hundred pages, twenty five are devoted to political organisation and only three to habitations. A few lines are devoted to 'Ceremonies in construction', but the paragraph on 'Arrangement of Camps, Villages and Towns' makes no mention of the symbolic connotations of settlement. As for the section on 'Objects of Art' it is merely recommended that 'it should be noted' . . . whether a work of art 'is part of a building, canoe, or other artifact' while the section of two pages on 'symbolic art' makes no mention of shelter at all.[78]

In spite of this limited concern for the anthropology of shelter, there is good reason for pursuing the study. We know too little about the value of buildings as sign vehicles in vernacular cultures, but a semiological, scientific or aesthetic approach to the study of the subject will only be possible in limited circumstances until we are far better informed.

In this volume, some of the important aspects of sign and symbol in vernacular shelter are discussed, from the symbolism of man's location in space to natural phenomena, to the formalisation of symbols into codes which determine his settlement patterns. It illustrates aspects of the relationship of such a code to both spatial concepts and physical image-making, and the elaborate complex of meanings associated with figurative symbols, and it shows how these may, by acceptance, use and custom pass through successive stages of abstraction in built form, as well as in decoration. Contributors indicate how the symbols of one culture or generation may be passed on and spread through other cultures, changing their meaning in the process, or even losing it altogether, reducing the symbols to a system of signs, which nevertheless retains vestiges of symbolic connotations. How certain abstractions of symbol gain in strength and meaning under duress, and how some symbolic forms persist, even when material and other factors could enable them to change, through the persistence of their values, is shown—and so too are the pressures upon a culture whose symbol-system is assailed by the values of other societies. Processes of transmission by physical means through mobile shelter or by the carrying of motifs, the hybridisation of the symbols of different belief systems, and the establishment of new symbol patterning

within an urban culture by an integrated social group are contrasted with the disintegration of others through culture contact from alien societies with incompatible symbol-systems.

That shelter and symbol can be seen as related in semiological terms within contiguous societies with related value systems is shown in semiological analysis but the difference of meaning through linguistic diversity acts as a caution against over-simplified conclusions; we are warned in another paper that alien symbol systems may be based on esoteric knowledge not available or lost to the west, while the possibility of a universal code of signs serving protective purposes that has a bearing on geomagnetic fields could be hypothesised.

There are many aspects of sign and symbol in vernacular shelter which are not discussed in this collection, or have been referred to very inadequately. One might instance the progressive importance of symbolic spaces, the relationship of totems to the structure of vernacular buildings, the determination of settlement or compound form by ritual or ritualistic dance. But this volume makes no claims to encompass all forms of shelter in which symbolism is important, because, it is not unreasonable to argue this might apply to all vernacular shelter; nor does it assume to cover the range of possible ways in which signs and symbols operate in settlements and buildings, or how symbolism is incorporated within their form and structures.

One aspect of the study of signs and images on buildings that has not been discussed at length in this volume is that of aesthetics. The aesthetics of tribal societies constitutes an area which has been dealt with rather sketchily by anthropologists, who are happier to describe than to interpret, and equally lightly by art historians and critics who are more ready to comment upon tribal art in western terms and values. Many cultures do not identify an 'artist' within their midst; all members of the group may be potential artists, or may be involved in activities of embellishment, configuration, carving or painting, which in European contexts would constitute 'art', but which are essentially a part of belief or ritual in the cultures observed. Tracing the development of a style, or placing objects in a series as they move from the naturalistic to abstraction can be justifiably a part of the documentation of art but they do not reveal to us the nature of an aesthetic sensibility in tribal cultures, or the aesthetic values of folk societies. External interpretation has been avoided here as much as possible, and where reference has been made to the purposes of art as vehicles of symbolic content, their functional role and a description of the forms has been emphasised rather than their purpose to the artist or the meaning that they have for him. Interestingly, some of the most revealing comments on signs as art come from the painter of the decorated houses of Pyrghi whose designs are now almost divested of identifiable symbolic meaning – although, at a deeper level, they clearly contain one.

Unless we can relate the aesthetics of vernacular shelter to the values of the culture, such studies place us at stages removed from the societies concerned, separating us by intellectual abstraction rather than leading us to a better understanding of the needs of the communities. But this is only possible when the requisite anthropo-

…rey Wethers, stone circles on Dartmoor, indicate the site of Bronze Age ritual and ceremonial.

…unding crops for food in a Dogon compound. On the wall of the granary is the symbol of 'the life of the world' depicting in abstract form the heavenly …acenta and the earthly placenta.

35

logical data is available and applies to any other kind of scientific or semiological approach to the study of signs and symbols of shelter.

In recent years, archaeological and anthropological data – such as the distribution of artefact-types, the subsistence strategies of nomadic peoples or the location and territory of village units – have been subjected to intensive computer analysis. From the massive accumulation of data in such areas and the application of different methods of analysis which are 'mathematical rather than scientific', Dr. David L. Clarke has come to the tentative conclusion 'that cultural systems are primarily information systems', and he acknowledges that 'the concept of material and non-material culture as information in an information system has been deliberately emphasised because it appears to be more than a simple analogy'.[79] He argues that artefacts and their attributes are the physical outcome of actions or sequences of actions which produce a specific type which, through usage behaviour, leads to further actions. Embedded, so to speak, in the artefact, whether arrowhead or shelter, is the symbolic value that has been attached to it and generated through evolution and adaptation. 'The symbolic information content of such artefacts and assemblages becomes more than an academic conceptualisation' Clarke continues. In his view 'socio-cultural systems are the transmission systems of acquired knowledge, supplementing instinctive behaviour in man. Culture is an information system of signs and symbols of great advantage in the face of natural selection and possibly the coded forerunner of true speech. The artefacts and rituals may well have provided the intermediate stage of abstraction in the transformation from instinctive behavioural information to adaptive cultural information, from animal behaviour to forethought and symbolic perceptivity.'[80]

Man shares with a vast majority of animals and insects and birds the need for shelter of a kind. Burrowing, cocoon-making, nesting, spinning, weaving, fabricating shelter from mud and earth, twigs and straw, man must have witnessed in animals the reflection of his own need for protection from the elements and other creatures. In the transitional stages from animal behaviour to hominid behaviour, from instinctive action to forethought and problem solution, shelter must have been a major subject of man's symbolising perceptivity and processes in their earliest formative times. In turn, he has projected upon his shelter symbolic designations which relate the hut and the compound to the states of the observable universe of natural phenomena and his projection, through myth and religion, of his conceptions of the non-observable, non-material world of his belief.

So the significance of shelter, sign and symbol is very probably deeply rooted in man's being. The fact of the shrine and the temple is less mysterious when viewed as an element in man's emergence as a symbolising animal. A better understanding of the interrelationship of the processes of signification and shelter-making would lead us to a more profound appreciation of the state of man in the dwelling, compound, village or settlement on which he can project his symbols, and his dilemma in urban conurbations of indefinable scale which defy his symbolic configurations.

One could hope for a situation where our knowledge of the importance of sign and symbol in the provision of shelter is no longer so minimal; where we are in a position to regard with respect and understanding the importance of the building in representing the values of the culture through the embodiment of its symbolism. Perhaps then we shall be more cautious of the housing projects that we in the West, or those designers, architects and planners in non-Western countries who have assimilated Western modes of design and planning, provide for indigenous peoples. We may even be able to turn to the needs of our own society in symbol as well as in shelter. Better still, the people themselves will be able to determine the shelter which embodies their own symbol-systems without suffering the decisions made by designers for them. The lead perhaps, is already coming from the mobile home parks, the squatter settlements or the instant cities of pop festivals and dropout communities. Whether or not such a situation becomes universal is unknown but unlikely. With a better understanding of the relationship of sign and symbol to shelter we may be able to recognise it if and where it does happen. We may eventually encourage the expression of group identity through symbols in vernacular architecture, rather than repressing it on grounds of taste, bye-laws or planning regulations. Then perhaps there may be less dissatisfaction on the part of the community as a whole with the decisions of architects, and the gap between the professional designer and the community, whose environment he largely determines, may be narrowed.

NOTES

[1] JUNOD, HENRI A., *The Life of a South African Tribe,* Vol. 1, 'Social Life', Macmillan & Co., London 1927, pp. 320–323.

[2] Ibid p. 323.

[3] See BIERMANN, BARRIE, 'Indlu: The Domed Dwelling of the Zulu' in Paul Oliver (ed.), *Shelter in Africa,* Barrie & Jenkins, London 1971, pp. 96–105.

[4] MURDOCK, GEORGE P., *Africa: Its Peoples and their Culture History,* McGraw-Hill, NY 1959, p. 376.

[5] OLIVER, PAUL, *Shelter in Africa* (Ibid), pp. 11–13.

[6] Published as THOMPSON, STITH, *Motif-Index of Folk Literature,* Indiana University Press, Bloomington, 1955, 6 Vols.

[7] Discussed in LEACH, EDMUND (ed.), *The Structural Study of Myth and Totemism,* Tavistock Publications, London, 1967.

[8] Developed in WHORF, BENJAMIN LEE, (John B. Carroll ed.), *Language of Thought and Reality,* M.I.T. Press, 1956.

[9] Developed in BROWN, ROGER, *Words and Things,* The Free Press, NY, 1958.

[10] OGDEN, C. K. and RICHARDS, I. A., *The Meaning of Meaning,* Harcourt, Brace and World, 1923, p. 21.

[11] Ibid, p. 23.

[12] PIERCE, CHARLES, S. *Selected Writings* (ed. J. Buchlev) Harcourt, Brace, N.Y. 1940.

[13] BARTHES, ROLAND, *Elements of Semiology,* Jonathan Cape, London, 1969.

[14] NAUTA, DOEDE, *The Meaning of Information,* Mouton, Paris, 1972.

[15] MOUNIN, GEORGE, *Introduction à la Semiologie,* Les Editions de Minuit, Paris, 1970.

[16] HAYAKAWA, S. I., *Language in Thought and Action,* Harcourt, Braced World, N.Y. 1964, p. 25 et seq.

[17] I am indebted to Rafael Ros for his work in tracing the confusion in the terminology of sign and symbol in ROS, RAFAEL, *Notes on Semiotics,* Architectural Association Graduate School, Unpublished thesis, London 1973.

[18] JUNG, CARL G. and others, *Man and his Symbols,* Aldus Books, London, 1964, p. 20.

[19] Ibid, p. 55.

[20] NORBERG-SCHULTZ, CHRISTIAN, in George Baird and Charles Jencks (eds), *Meaning in Architecture*, Barrie & Jenkins, London, 1969, p. 226.

[21] Ibid, p. 229.

[22] VAN EYCK, ALDO, 'Basket-House-Village-Universe', *Ibid*, p. 188.

[23] See LANGSNER, JULES, 'Sam of Watts' in *Arts and Architecture*, July 1951; also CARDINAL, ROGER, *Outsider Art*, Studio Vista, London, 1972, pp. 170–72.

[24] BRUNIUS, JACQUES, 'Le Palais Ideal' in *Architectural Review*, October 1936; also CARDINAL, op. cit., pp. 146–153.

[25] WATKINS, ALFRED, *The Old Straight Track*, Methuen & Co., London, 1925, p. 32.

[26] Ibid, p. 117.

[27] BALIKCI, ASEN, *The Netsilik Eskimo*, Natural History Press, NY, 1970, p. 36.

[28] Adapted from the description of the Bushman *werf* in THOMAS ELIZABETH MARSHALL, *The Harmless People*, Penguin Books, London, 1969, p. 49.

[29] 'The Sun Dance of the Oglala Division of the Dakota', *Anthropological Papers of the American Museum of Natural History*, XVI, Part II, p. 160.

[30] Ibid.

[31] 'Chon Li, K'ao-chi' in *Li Chi*, Shih-san-ching edition, Shanghai Commercial Press, n.d. p. 129.

[32] WU, NELSON I, *Chinese and Indian Architecture*, Prentice-Hall, London, 1963, p. 46.

[33] TAIMNI, I. K., *An Introduction to Hindu Symbolism*, Theosophical Publishing House, Madras, 1969, p. 51.

[34] Ibid, p. 42.

[35] LEWIS, OSCAR, *Village Life in Northern India*, Vintage Books, (1958), 1965, pp. 228–229.

[36] TAIMNI, op. cit., p. 31.

[37] SCOTT, GEORGE RILEY, *Phallic Worship*, Luxor Press, London, 1966, p. 101.

[38] NIEUBARN, Father M. C., *Church Symbolism*, (Trans. Rev. John Waterreus), Sands & Co., London, 1910, p. 45.

[39] Ibid, p. 55.

[40] MALINOWSKI, BRONISLAW, *A Scientific Theory of Culture*, Oxford University Press (1944), 1960, p. 153.

[41] Ibid, p. 139.

[42] KNIGHT, RICHARD PAYNE, *A Discourse on the Worship of Priapus*, Privately printed, 1786.

[43] REDFIELD, ROBERT, and VILLA ROJAS, ALFONSO, *Chan Kom, A Maya Village*, Phoenix Books, NY (1934) 1962, p. 111.

[44] Reported in *The Times*, London, July 15, 1932.

[45] BOAS, FRANZ, *Primitive Art*, Dover Books, NY (1927) 1955, p. 113.

[46] Ibid, pp. 114–115, Illustrations of both series.

[47] ELWORTHY, FREDERICK, *The Evil Eye*, John Murray, London, 1895, pp. 289–292.

[48] SWANTON, JOHN R., *Social Organisation and Social Uses of the Indians of the Creek Confederacy*, Bureau of American Ethnology Annual Report (1924–1925) 1928, pp. 110–112.

[49] LOMMEL, Dr. ANDREAS, *Prehistoric and Primitive Man*, Paul Hamlyn, London, 1966, p. 78

[50] LÉVI-STRAUSS, CLAUDE, *Structural Anthropology*, Allen Lane, The Penguin Press, London, 1968, pp. 252–258.

[51] BARRETT, S. A., *Pomo Indian Basketry*, Publications in American Archaeology and Ethnology, Vol. VII, No. 3, University of California, (n.d.) pp. 180–190.

[52] MAHR, August C., 'Origin and Significance of Pennsylvanian Dutch Barn Symbols', *The Ohio Archaeological and Historical Quarterly*, Vol. 54, Ohio Historical Society, 1945, pp. 1–32.

[53] CASSIRER, ERNST, *An Essay on Man*, New Haven, 1944.

[54] JAEGER, GERTRUDE and SELZNICK, PHILIP, 'A Normative Theory of Culture' in *American Sociological Review*, 29, American Sociological Association, 1964, pp. 653–669.

[55] FREUD, SIGMUND, 'The Claims of Psychoanalysis to Scientific Interest', *Standard Edition*, Hogarth Press, London 1955, Vol. 13, p. 187.

[56] HALLOWELL, A. IRVING, *Culture and Experience*, Schocken, New York (1955), 1967, p. 201.

[57] BEIER, ULLI, *African Mud Sculpture*, University Press, Cambridge, 1963, p. 38.

[58] FORTES, M., and EVANS-PRITCHARD, E. E., (Eds), *African Political Systems*, Oxford University Press, 1940, p. 17.

[59] LITTLE, KENNETH, *West African Urbanisation*, University Press, Cambridge, 1966, pp. 38–42.

[60] LEADBETTER, DOROTHY, 'The Sicilian Cart: Origins of a Western European Folk Art' in SMITH, MARIAN W., *The Artist in Tribal Society*, Routledge & Kegan Paul, London, 1961, p. 46.

[61] BEINART, JULIAN, 'WNT: The Same and the Change' in DONAT, JOHN (ed.), *World Architecture 2*, Studio Vista, London, 1965, pp. 186–193.

[62] SAPIR, EDWARD, 'Conceptual Categories in Primitive Language', *Science*, LXXIV, 1931, p. 578.

[63] WHORF, BENJAMIN LEE, 'Linguistic Factors in the Terminology of Hopi Architecture' in *Language, Thought and Reality* (John B. Carroll, ed.) MIT Press (1956), Cambridge, Mass., 1964, pp. 199–206.

[64] Ibid, p. 205.

[65] SAPIR, EDWARD, quoted in WHORF, 'The Relation of Habitual Thought and Behaviour to Language', Ibid, p. 134.

[66] DE SAUSSURE, FERDINAND, *Course in General Linguistics*. McGraw-Hill, N.Y. 1966 (1915), p. 65 et seq.

[67] BARTHES, ROLAND, *Elements of Semiology*, Jonathan Cape, London, 1967, p. 95.

[68] GRIAULE, MARCEL, *Dieu d'Eau: Entretiens avec Ogotemmeli*, Editions du Chêne, Paris, 1948, p. 36.

[69] GRIAULE, MARCEL and DIETERLIEN, GERMAINE, 'The Dogon' in FORDE, C. DARYLL (ed.), *African Worlds*, Oxford University Press, London, 1954, p. 97.

[70] WHEATLEY, P., *The Pivot of the Four Quarters*, Quoted in DULYACHINDA SUMED, *Fragrant Harbour*, Architectural Association Graduate School, Unpublished thesis, 1973.

[71] From TAUT, BRUNO and HIRAL, SHIRO (trans.) *Fundamentals of Japanese Architecture*, Kokusai Bunka Shinkokai, Tokyo 1936. Illustrated in DULYACHINDA, (Ibid).

[72] LÉVI-STRAUSS, CLAUDE, op. cit., p. 230.

[73] HAWKINS, GERALD S., *Stonehenge Decoded*, Fontana Books (1966), 1970, p. 150.

[74] Ibid, p. 177–178.

[75] THOM, Prof. ALEXANDER, 'Megalithic Geometry in Standing Stones', *New Scientist*, March 12, 1964.

[76] UNDERWOOD, GUY, *The Pattern of the Past*, Abacus (1969), 1972, p. 34.

[77] Ibid, p. 185

[78] Committee of the Royal Anthropological Institute, *Notes and Queries on Anthropology*, Cortledge and Kegan Paul, (London) 1960. pp. 310–314.

[79] CLARKE, DAVID L., *Analytical Archaeology*, Methuen, London, 1968, p. 659.

[80] Ibid, p. 658.

AUSTRALIAN ABORIGINES AND THE DEFINITION OF PLACE

Amos Rapoport

INTRODUCTION

The essence of place lies in the quality of being somewhere specific, knowing that you are 'here' rather than 'there'. Those architects who have been interested in the concept of place – for example Aldo Van Eyck and Charles Moore – stress the separation of *inside* from outside. Enclosure becomes a very important aspect of place-making which also seems, in some way, to be related to the concept of territory. For these architects, as for many cultures and civilisations throughout history, the establishment of place and the taking possession of it is accomplished by means of building structures and boundaries and personalizing the resulting places in some way.

There is one culture at least – that of the Australian aborigines – in which the building of structures and boundaries is so unimportant that it becomes interesting to discover whether they have any concept of place at all – and if they do, how they define it. This would throw light on the essence of place and the range of means available for defining it. While other peoples – Tierra del Fuego Indians and Bushmen for example – build no major dwellings they do build cult buildings; aborigines do not. Therefore a survey of the ethnographic literature on aborigines with this particular question in mind should be enlightening.

I have previously suggested[1] that socio-cultural and symbolic factors dominate the organisation of dwelling space, and have also suggested that this is the case for cities.[2] A case study of the Pueblo and Navajo Indians[3] illustrated this point in more detail. The present case study of the Australian aborigines extends the generality of the hypothesis that shelter is only one function of architecture and that other, and more important, functions are the symbolic, place-defining and socio-cultural—to *any* environment in which people live, whether built or not built.

HUNTERS AND GATHERERS

Aborigines are hunters and gatherers. As such they share certain general characteristics with that larger group.[4] Such people generally live in small groups and move about a great deal. As a result they collect little property and tend to be egalitarian. Their movement is not unrestricted however,[5] but confined to specific areas. It is the area within which this movement occurs rather than permanent settlements which defines territory.

Group members share food as well as other possessions, and among aborigines articles have been traced through 134 persons.[6] This sharing creates friendship and social values are more important than economic ones. A web of different reciprocal bonds is expressed through laws, myths, song and ritual, binding people together.[7] This cultural elaboration becomes possible because obtaining food takes remarkably little time. Hunters and gatherers have much leisure time which is used for games and ritual; they are also remarkably well fed, contrary to general opinion.[8]

Hunters do not store food but *regard the environment as a store-house*. While each local group is associated with a geographic range there is considerable visiting among groups which do not maintain exclusive rights to resources but have flexible arrange-

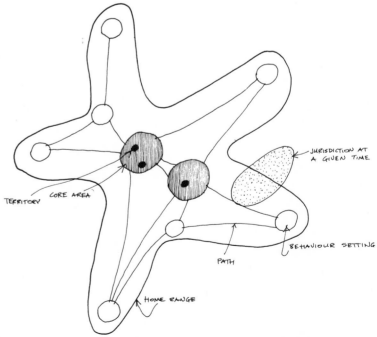

Diagrammatic representation of home range, core area, territory and jurisdictions derived from ethology.

38

ments. At the same time most groups have a home base or camp.

This generalised description of the way in which hunters and gatherers (including aborigines) use space can be expressed in terms of a set of concepts derived from animal studies.

Home range   The usual limit of regular movements and activities, which can be defined as a set of behavioural settings and linking paths.

Core areas   Those areas within the home range which are most used and most commonly inhabited.

Territory   A particular area which is *owned* and *defended* – whether physically or through rules or symbols which identify the area of an individual or group from others.

Jurisdiction   'Ownership' of a territory for a limited time only, and by some agreed rules.

Among animals the size of home range and core areas and their coincidence, and the times and duration of jurisdiction depend on the natural conditions (climate, rainfall, resources) on the one hand and the animal species on the other. In the case of hunters also the same physical factors play a role as do the values and life-style of the group.

THE AUSTRALIAN ABORIGINES

The social organisation of aboriginal Australia is very complex indeed, as are the legends, myths and art. The contrast of these with material culture is striking and provides another example of the general theme that symbolic elaboration occurs before material elaboration. The application of Western values based on material culture resulted in the evaluation of aborigines as particularly primitive and 'brutish'.

There is some controversy in the literature regarding the validity of generalising for the whole continent. Worms,[9] Birket-Smith,[10] Meggitt,[11] Hiatt,[12] Baldwin Spencer[13] among others discuss this issue. With regard to the symbolic representations of place it does seem possible to generalise, to accept that in spite of variations in some aspects of aboriginal culture, such as art,[14] certain features are sufficiently uniform for us to speak generally of 'aboriginal Australia'.[15]

ABORIGINAL SHELTER

It is generally thought that aborigines only had windbreaks but this is an oversimplification.[16] In fact aborigines had a considerable variety of dwellings although simple shelters were most common, at least in Central Australia.

Descriptions can be found of even more elaborate houses such as permanent huts plastered with clay over sods (Hutt River); beehive shaped log huts 4 ft. high, 9 ft. diameter (Hanover Bay); log houses 16 ft. long with recesses in walls for implements, entrance 3 ft. high and floor carpeted with seaweed. At Careening Bay there were dwellings with two stone walls 3 ft. high with saplings carrying bark and grass thatch.[17] This house, as well as houses with circular stone walls at White Lake with a central

Windbreak shelter, Argonga (Dr. Stephen Bochner) Central Australia.

Semicircular shade. 5–6 ft. diameter. Mulga branches arched over; leaf cover; floor scooped out to a depth of 3″–4″. Central Australia based on Gould; Thomas.

Cupola shaped wood frame hut with branch and leaf cover. Some of these are up tp 15 ft. diameter. Victoria and Queensland. After Thomas; Baldwin-Spencer.

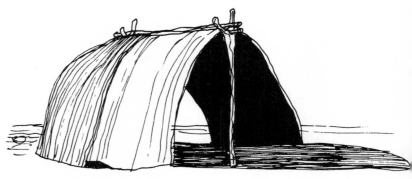

Hut of saplings and sheets of bark. (Australian Museum).

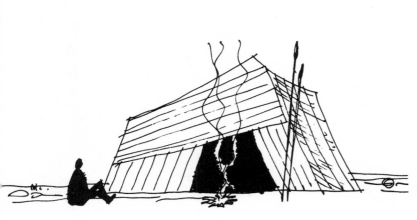

Bark hut, Central Australia. After Baldwin Spencer.

Two-storey hut, at Lynd River. Pole framework, bark floor and roof. After Thomas.

Hut of bent sheets of bark, (bent while fresh), 10–11 ft. long and 4–5 ft. wide. New South Wales. The open side is turned away from the wind.

House at Careening Bay. Two stone walls, 3 ft. high sapling roof thatched with bark and grass. After verbal description in Thomas.

upright carrying roof members covered with bark and grass coated with clay, and with a smoke hole, could have been influenced by Malay or Indonesian examples.[18]

At Lynd River there were two storey huts, while on Bathurst Island were found very large huts, some with windows, and descriptions exist of a wide variety of other dwellings.[19] The general point, however, is that aborigines had a much greater variety of dwelling types, and often much more substantial, than is commonly thought. At the same time their dwellings were less important than in most other cultures.

If we accept that dwellings have two functions,
(1) physical shelter and
(2) the provision of symbolic space and definition of space,
then the Australian aboriginal dwelling seems to fulfil mostly the shelter function although even this is minimal in spite of the often extreme climate. There seems no indication that dwellings fill any symbolic function. Whatever their nature, *dwellings do not seem to have much symbolic meaning or rules on layout and use,* other than the fact that each shelter or dwelling is for one family and outsiders do not enter without invitation – there are strong feelings of personal space and kinship avoidances. The residential unit, ideally, comprises a composite family of a man, several wives, unmarried daughters and uncircumcised sons.[20]

It is true that the hypothesis that aboriginal dwellings are devoid of symbolic meaning has not been demonstrated directly. The circumstantial evidence, however, is very strong and this may be the only evidence we shall ever have on the subject. As soon as we look at camps, for example, we find that they are arranged along well understood principles and rules differing in different tribes, but quite definite.[21] For example, when several tribes met, huts were grouped by tribes, the spacing between groups of huts being several times greater than between the huts within the group. The arrangement of camps according to phratries and classes reflected and helped to implement ceremonial rules regulating access of various classes to each other. All areas of Australia had specific, complex rules for positioning huts in the camp and while to the outsider the camp may give an impression of disorder there is a structure, such as a division into two parts reflecting kinship, (possibly emphasised by a natural feature such as a creek or hill) or the provision of special bachelors' and spinsters' camps.[22]

At large gatherings in Central Australia, to which some tribes travelled as far as 200 miles, the various camps were arranged so as to indicate roughly the locality of the owner – those from the south camping in the south, those from the north in the north. While camps were as impermanent as huts, the camp was laid out according to definite ceremonial rules.[23] Even a tribe as primitive as the *Kurna* arranged their camp so that huts were in certain directions and at certain distances from each other according to the relationships of the occupiers. The *Arunda* camp had eight groups of huts corresponding to the eight subsections into which the tribe was divided. Two neighbouring groups provided communal meeting centres for men and women respectively, restricted to the opposite sex, which could only be visited if approached from certain directions.

Camp divisions are still symbolic in this sense even today. For example, people in multi-tribal camps group according to the direction from which they come.[24] Within the camp fires seem to be more important than huts. Fires are built and kept going on nights when temperatures are 100°F and no cooking is done – it keeps spirits away.[25] Often, wherever an aboriginal will squat, he will build a small fire even though the main fire is close by, and this in the heat of the day, with no cooking to be done.[26]

These characteristics of the camps provide the first clue to the use of space by aborigines and helps clarify how socio-cultural and symbolic environmental functions are fulfilled. There does seem to be a set of places, but they are not in the dwelling. Some symbolic value and social and ritual rules seem to attach to the camp and the fire. The symbolism of place seems more related to the site and directions, i.e. to the *land* rather than the dwelling. In fact this will be the problem which will concern us for the remainder of this essay.

THE LAND

The physical environment of Australia is quite varied. Although most of it is arid, there are wet areas in the north and reasonably watered ones in the east and south east. There are forests, jungles, plains, mountains and deserts. Over much of the country, particularly its arid portions, there are common features – red rock and soil, purple hills, gums with grey-green foliage and white or light coloured trunks, scrub, waterholes, parrots and a number of unique animals and plants.

There are two questions which need to be considered.
1. How do the aborigines use this land?
2. How do the aborigines see this land?

HOW DO THE ABORIGINES USE THIS LAND?

We have already discussed the general use of land by hunters and gatherers. Aborigines live in groups each of which 'owns' a stretch of land and has as its basic unit the individual family which, in some tribes, has rights over a specific locality. Although authorities differ, tribes seem to vary from 100–1500 people, averaging 500.[27] In good areas tribal land may be as small as 50 square miles, in arid areas many hundreds of square miles.[28]

For example the *Walbiri* have an area of 40,000 square miles. They see themselves as one people who share a common culture and occupy a continuous territory with definite boundaries; they can draw maps of their own location and adjoining tribes.[29] Tribal borders are respected. Even friendly tribes do not have the right to enter each other's land at will; outsiders may enter an area uninvited only in an emergency (e.g. when starving) and have to recompense the owners. Strangers can enter through social sponsorship while ceremonial messengers and ritual novices with their guardians can travel more or less freely without the need for sponsors.[30] There are thus quite definite, recognised stretches of country and boundaries. These latter are often indistinct but can be fairly exact particularly when they coincide with a natural feature such as water, sand ridge, a grove of trees etc. These boundaries are fixed by mythology and aborigines can draw maps of their own and adjacent territories with relevant details and special features clearly marked.[31]

Different types of territorial understandings and types of demarcations exist and are related to definite sites.[32] They are clearest at totemic sites and other special sites and are less clear between other areas. These culturally defined boundaries do not imply exclusivity or sanctions against trespass. The same objective is achieved by having rules for accommodating people across boundaries.[33] The use of the European term 'boundary' suggests more precision than is the case. Normally identification was sufficient demarcation and the main interest was in the symbolic values of a particular place.

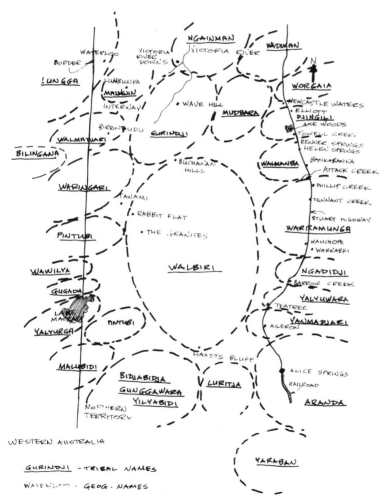

Approximate location of adjoining tribes, according to the Walbiri. Based on Meggitt. Tribal boundaries are notional and have been added for clarity; they indicate clear conceptions of tribal location.

Birth and subsequent residence in a locality occupied by a group and totemically associated with it was most important. There were various ceremonies which helped the conversion of non-members to members. Residence in itself only gave *economic – not ritual – rights* to the immigrant,[34] i.e. there was a distinction of the economic and ritual use of land with the latter more important.[35] It appears that each group had a ritual and social locus and an area whose main importance was economic. Both together formed the ecological life space.[36] The ritual areas had clearer boundaries than the foraging areas; the heartland areas were clear, the others interpenetrated and were more indeterminate.[37] There was usually a ritual tie between a clan and its estate, but also an emotional bond with the land itself. The boundaries of areas were demarcated by episodes in the sacred myths and hence were not subject to revision. All myths mention borders, limits beyond which a myth could not be told, nor song sung, nor ceremonies performed. Since boundaries were set down by supernatural beings they could not be questioned.[38] Each tribe thus knew the boundaries of the country in which it lived and identified with it.[39]

It is, in fact, possible to distinguish ten distinct types of areas among aborigines.[40]
1. Distinctive habitats
2. Named places and localities
3. Totem sites
4. Clan estates and ranges
5. Unused, shared and indeterminate zones
6. Regular camping places, including rock shelters and caves
7. Established ceremonial grounds
8. Networks of paths, fords and crossing places over natural obstacles
9. Places distinct from 7 where contiguous groups came together
10. Miscellany of capital sites such as watering places, fish weirs, raw material deposits, tool manufactories etc.

Thus there is a detailed and complex series of places which can be indicated on maps showing the mythological movements of Dreamtime heroes.[41]

HOW DO THE ABORIGINES SEE THIS LAND?

Many Europeans have spoken of the uniformity and featurelessness of the Australian landscape. The aborigines, however, see the landscape in a totally different way. Every feature of the landscape is known and has meaning – they then perceive differences which Europeans cannot see. These differences may be in terms of detail[42] or in terms of a magical or invisible landscape, the symbolic space being even more varied than the perceived physical space.[43] As one example, every individual feature of Ayer's Rock is linked to a significant myth and the mythological beings who created it. Every tree, every stain, hole and fissure has meaning.[44]

Thus what to a European is an empty land may be full of noticeable differences to the aborigine and hence rich and complex. Europeans may thus completely misunderstand the nature of the landscape because of their point of view. Messages only become meaningful when received and recognised. Signals and signs become perceptual or conceptual meaning through symbols.[45] Symbols thus change the biological and geographical world of signals and signs into a human world of meanings.

It is thus a likely hypothesis that aborigines *humanize* their landscape, that is take possession of it conceptually, through symbols – as we do. But whereas our symbols are material – buildings, cities, fences, and monuments – aboriginal symbols are largely non-material. They use, as I shall show later, natural features, myths, ceremonies and rituals, graphic and plastic symbols – and even monuments. For example, all people have sacred places. Most have then built buildings to stress the sacredness of the site. Aborigines stress this sanctity by returning to these places, by ritual and through mythological explanation of environmental variations.[46] In fact, of the total range of devices available, aborigines use all except written records, buildings and cities.

THE ABORIGINAL WORLD VIEW

Man may adapt to his environment mentally as well as physically. Through cosmology and cosmogony sets of concepts and categories of thought may be developed through which the world is understood. Categories such as time and space, identity and difference, causality, unity and multiplicity, appearance and reality, matter and spirit are different for people with different world views.

In aboriginal cosmogony the Dreamtime is central. Heroes come to a featureless world and transform themselves into natural phenomena, such as trees and rocks which have sacred meanings associated with the particular heroic figure thus creating the landscape.[47] The Dreaming, when things are made, is not just in the past but also in the present. 'All space is here, all time is now' – all appears symbolically and becomes operative through ritual.[48] Thus a sacred site is Dreaming, so are the actors in the ritual and the sacred symbols.

Besides having a different concept of time[49] aborigines also see space differently. It is not something measured – it is an area whose use is dictated by custom. *Every yard is known – but not its size.* Significantly different is the notion of ownership. Tribal lands are not owned even though groups of people had rights over it. Our concept of property ownership has no relevance to the aborigines' spiritual approach. More important to them is the fact that the people are 'owned' by the country – it knew them and gave them sustenance and life. Every person's spirit had pre-existed in this land in the Dreaming and no other land, no matter how fertile, could be theirs or mean the same. Men were permanently attached to their own country[50] and wanted to die in it.

This twofold nature of ownership characterizes all secret-sacred objects (*Churinga*) and sites of mythological and ritual significance (Dreamings). For example among the Aranda each individual had a personal stone or wood *churinga* kept in a secret 'storehouse' of the ritual group. The *churinga* is a lifeline to the spirit world and the Dreaming – and people belong to it. The 'storehouse' may be a hole in the ground (where the *churinga* is buried), a hollow tree, a cleft in a rock or a shed of branches. In any case it is concealed

from view and the whole area around it is forbidden to women, children and the uninitiated on pain of death.[51] Thus while the concept of a sacred storehouse resembles that of other cultures, it is not expressed by building, and, rather than being stressed, is hidden.

A similar relationship exists between ritual groups and natural or artificially constructed Dreamings – standing stones, rock masses, waterholes, trees or stone arrangements. These are permanent and symbolic assurances of the presence of the Dreaming which are the very ground of being and keep the world going. The whole world is a single entity the main characteristic of which is reciprocity.[52]

ABORIGINAL RELATIONSHIP TO THE LAND

From the discussion so far it is clear that the relationship between individuals and groups with their sacred object and sites, and the country generally, is more one of identification than ownership although there are elements of the latter. Boundaries seem to be important more with relation to totemic sites than food gathering areas and these boundaries are defined symbolically by means of legend, myth and ritual.

In terms of perceived environmental distinctions this means that:
a) with respect to the distinction between perceptual and associational aspects[53] aborigines attach many associational values to perceived features of the natural environment;
b) considering the distinction between physical and symbolic space[54] the importance of the latter is greatly elaborated.

Underlying the visible landscape there seemed to be a symbolic landscape which was more real and of which aborigines had a clear notion. This is similar to tribal art generally which expresses 'not aspects of the visible world but rather the invisible forces behind that world'[55] and also corresponds to Eliade's view that for primitive man the real world is the sacred world – the profane is unreal. Making the world real means making it sacred, and any feature of the landscape may manifest the sacred.[56]

What, therefore, needs to be considered is the relation of this symbolic world to the physical, the relation between symbolic and physical space. Aboriginal religion, mythology and symbolism need to be considered in relation to the physical environment. This can be done in terms of:
  i) the general relationship to the land and attachment to it;
  ii) the concept of the Dreamtime;
  iii) sacred places and totemic sites;
  iv) ceremonies, symbols, signs, monuments.

i) *GENERAL RELATIONSHIP TO THE LAND AND ATTACHMENT TO IT*

The land, no matter how arid, is home to the aborigines. They are aware of its problems but derive satisfaction from it difficult for the outsider to grasp '. . . to appreciate this sense of belonging to the land is to begin to understand the aborigines'.[57] When shown photographs of buildings, airplanes and cars they are unimpressed but show great interest in scenery, landscape, people and animals.[58] This close relation to the land is strengthened by the fact, already discussed, that hunters treat the environment as their storehouse. Aborigines have few tools or objects and rely on 'instant tools', that is they recognise potentially useful objects in the environment. If this object matches a 'mental template' or idea of a tool, for example a spear thrower, a concrete object results.[59]

Aborigines, like all primitive people, were not concerned with dominating their surroundings. Their view of life stressed the oneness between man and the rest of nature. Even their supernatural beings and immortals were not beyond human ken but in their midst and related to the land.[60] All writers on the subject seem to agree that aborigines were in balance with nature. They saw themselves as a part of nature rather than its antagonists. They cooperated with nature rather than trying to subdue it. There was no sharp line between man and the natural world, its animals and plants. Man did not differ in quality from other species but shared with them the same life essence.

A number of writers report that to keep warm the aboriginal adapted to conditions to the extent of controlling his blood circulation and metabolism. This enabled him to maintain body warmth from a very small fire; rather than building a large fire and sitting far from it the aboriginal built a small one and sat close to it. This lack of conceptual boundaries between the aboriginal and the world was reinforced by the lack of physical barriers such as clothing, houses or walls. While Western man relies on such barriers to keep out nature, reduce differences between seasons and times and defines places by manipulating these barriers, aborigines define places by *knowing* them and their distinctions. This knowledge is perceptual and 'real' as well as associational, mythical and symbolic; these basic attitudes also prevail all over the continent in spite of local differences.

ii) THE CONCEPTS OF DREAMTIME

Every publication dealing with aborigines stresses the central place of Dreamtime. As for most primitive people ritual is central – sacred and profane are intertwined. Religion is an inseparable part of every individual's daily life. Aboriginal religion is nothing less than 'the theme of existence and as such it constitutes one of the most sophisticated and unique religious and philosophical systems known to man'.[61] This religion therefore is essential for an understanding of any aspect of the socio-cultural life of aborigines.[62] Central to religion, and to all symbolic expression of it, is the Dreamtime.

This concept, existing in almost all aboriginal myths, deals with a period when great heroes and heroines travelled over the land which was flat and featureless – with no mountains, waterholes or living things. All these, as well as fire, laws and so on were created by the heroes whose paths and camping places are described in the myths and form sacred places. Usually the hero dies, turning into natural features which are also sacred.

These myths show how closely aborigines are bound to their surroundings, since every feature is mythically related to their origin. The group is linked to the land through the symbolism of myth. Myth is a symbolic statement about society and man's place in it and the surrounding universe.[63] It is an expression of unobservable realities in terms of observable phenomena,[64] in the case of the aborigines the features of their land. The first stories children would hear would explain the creation of natural features. The aborigines thus lived in a world dominated by natural features and the myths linking him with these were a central theme in his life. Most aspects of daily and ceremonial life were linked to the Dreamtime creatures and the local topography. Physical features of the environment were personified through the Dreamtime— rocks and trees were living evidence of the Dreamtime heroes.

The ties to these heroes and the land were kept alive by ceremonial, ritual and art.[65] The whole past history of the tribe was bound up with these ceremonies – and hence the natural features of the landscape as well as ceremonial objects. Often the dead were oriented towards their Dreamtime camping ground.[66] Thus aboriginal symbolic space is related to the Dreamtime and travel features of heroes rather than compass points. *The mythical landscape is superimposed over the physical landscape and they coincide at natural features.*

iii) SACRED PLACES AND TOTEMIC SITES [67]

Within the tribe or horde[68] there are ritual groups (clans) associated with natural phenomena or species. The tribe shares a cultural pattern protected by its boundary but clans are more closely related to special sites, identified with their totemic hero and his wanderings. These sacred centres (Dreamings) are more closely defined than the food gathering areas, and the sacred clan territory is very different from the relatively profane tribal area. The main tribal link is language[69] while the clan has closer links and a common ancestor. The tribal land is available to all members who share its animals and plants. The clan territory is only fully and freely accessible to initiated men who rarely left it except for special occasions. Married women often lived far from their own clan area but maintained spiritual and emotional ties with it. There is thus more sharing and less exclusivity to food producing areas (relatively profane) than to totemic areas (sacred).

The clan area is thus composed of a number of different totem sites linked by paths while the tribal land is a connected whole surrounding these sites.[70] The relationship of this to the model of space use seems quite clear.

The membership of a clan is explicitly expressed by referring to its totemic ancestors and implicitly to its *totem sites*.[71] Clan membership thus has a spatial component and a *special place*. Even the larger group is often identified spatially – with an area or camping site.

Some tribes have large numbers of clan territories which can be named and mapped[72] and this has been found in different parts of the country suggesting, once again, that there is some uniformity across Australia.

In these clan areas are a number of sacred sites and in each of these a particularly sacred spot – a life centre of natural phenomena, species or objects to which all clan members are intimately related. There are also cult lodges to which men belong. Their *churingas* are kept in caves, trees or underground and these sacred lodges have no buildings such as one might find in, say, the Sepik River area of New Guinea.

There is thus a clear distinction between sacred and profane, very much as Eliade suggests, even though there are no visible physical demarcations. For example when churingas were kept in caves, those entering to fetch them impressed palm prints near the entrance to establish *rites of passage*[73] indicating an awareness of a boundary between sacred and profane. In fact any place where churingas are kept becomes sacred, and the churinga is shown to initiates as a rite of passage giving rebirth into full membership of the clan. Similarly, ceremonial leaders frequently become such in special caves whereas other people who entered these caves would disappear forever.[74] There are thus a number of rites of passage related to environmental features.

Some sacred places are specially related to the conception of children.[75] When a woman conceives in a place where there are prominent features – rocks, boulders, ancient trees – one of the spirit children of the place enters her body and the totem of this place becomes the child's irrespective of the father's or mother's totem. This shows the importance of the place of conception and the individual retains a special relationship to the natural feature and would worry if the tree was to be cut down or the rock mined.[76]

Generally, then, the religious and social unit is defined through its relation to spirit beings and special sites. In fact their territory is defined by the sites claimed, which cannot be entered by others who may enter the food gathering area. The land itself represents *the most obvious, most enduring and most visible focus of the group*. In fact the complexity of the relationship between all social aspects of the group and various sites grows as one goes further into the subject but enough has been said to show the existence of a set of places of distinct levels of importance.

iv) CEREMONIES, SYMBOLS, SIGNS. MONUMENTS
These will be discussed later.

MENTAL MAPS

It has been pointed out several times that aborigines are able to map their 'countries', their sacred sites and the tracks of the Dreamtime heroes. In fact the link between the unseen, but very real, mythical world and the physical world is expressed through mental maps. Aborigines have such mental maps which have been studied, but have not been recorded systematically. Some data is, however, available.

Many of the decorations on the few objects which aborigines have, seem to be a series of watercourses along the track of Dreamtime ancestors. Other landmarks such as sandhills, rocky outcrops and saltlakes may be shown. But not all the watercourses of the region are shown, only those thought to have been created or visited by the particular mythological character concerned. They are, thus, not maps in a *practical* sense but mental mythological maps – mnemonic devices for recalling sacred traditions.

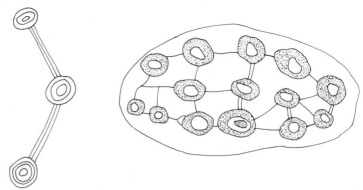

Designs by the Yiwara which appear to be 'mental maps', or conventionalized mnemonics for sacred places and tracks. After Gould.

Aborigines can make the most exact and complex maps of the journeys of their ancestral figures and they themselves re-enact the journey going in procession from sacred spot to sacred spot, following the divine route. If we remember the processions in tracing the boundaries of Roman (and other) cities[77] we find a similar way of defining place except that it was expressed concretely by building walls. In fact aboriginal areas where sacred objects are stored became sanctified and animals and people in them were safe – an early form of the city or house of refuge[78] but without physical construction.

THE DEFINITION OF PLACE

In general terms it appears that aborigines define place through sacred directions, routes of the Dreamtime ancestors and their stopping places which become sacred sites, landscape features and the like. Thus an apparently featureless landscape may become full of meaning and significance, legends and happenings – that is full of *places*.[79] The harsh environment is personalised through ritual and myth bringing its natural features into the realm of the familiar and friendly. Aborigines do not move just in a landscape but in a *humanised realm saturated with significations*.[80]

In this humanised realm physical features have a larger meaning which makes them part of the associational as well as the perceptual world; they exist in symbolic and sacred space as well as in physical space. This agrees with Eliade's view that sacred space is more real than profane space which is amorphous and formless.[81] Ritual orientation enables reference to some fixed points which are in sacred space. Rather than defining sacred space by building aborigines do it in other ways. By making each natural feature significant they obtain *the coincidence of the mythical and physical landscape which distinguishes places from each other and establishes a system of special places*. As I pointed out before the mythical and physical landscapes coincide at special features. More specifically, a number of ways in which aborigines establish places and distinguish between them can now be listed.

1. Space becomes symbolic through myths of the Dreamtime;

2. aborigines repeat the wanderings of the Dreamtime ancestors and re-enact various events at ceremonial grounds;
3. aborigines use sacred paintings and engravings on rocks or in caves and also construct temporary or permanent monuments including the use of body decoration;
4. they construct ritual and ceremonial sites laid out in a sacred order;
5. places become sacred by having the sacred *churingas* stored in them;
6. camp grounds in general are laid out in terms of symbolism and ritual rules;
7. fires are used to define place.

Some of these have already been discussed – the myths of the Dreamtime, storage of churingas, layout of camp grounds and use of fires. The others will now be described.

RE-ENACTMENT OF WANDERINGS AND OTHER EVENTS

Aborigines re-enact the wanderings of ancestor figures, stopping at specified places – trees, rocks, waterholes, special camp grounds. The paths are followed and acts repeated in a prescribed order. These pilgrimages can be described in quite considerable detail,[82] and the sites and tracks can be mapped.[83]

The re-enactments are complex; stereotyped ceremonies can be clearly described and the pattern of actor's movement can be drawn.[84]

Some of these ceremonies lasted for months and a strict temporal and *geographical* order was laid down.

These trips are intimately related to various features of the landscape. Every prominent and many minor landscape features are significant and become sacred places. Before initiation, novices are taught the routes of these Dreamtime beings which criss-cross the land in all directions. Through the pilgrimages and re-enactments of rites links to the land are set up and the aborigines temporarily re-enter the Dreamtime.

Places are thus defined by sacred myths which are made concrete through re-enactments. Since these re-enactments are of the creative wanderings they, in effect, repeat the cosmogony which fits Eliade's point that the ritual of constructing sacred space is efficacious in the measure in which it reproduces the work of the gods.[85] The purpose of re-enactment is to show the association between visible object and invisible power – it makes the unseen world visible. The events portrayed are also thought to be in the present as much as at the beginning of things. The time scheme is cyclic and re-enactments re-establish these cycles.

Accepting Eliade's notion that establishing of places involves making the profane sacred, re-enactment rituals do this through words, dance, symbolic objects and body paintings used. Intention precedes physical aspects; in fact, physical means in our terms are not essential. In many cultures much ritual symbolism presents the occult as located in the natural environment and its features – aborigines almost stop with this.

It has been suggested that in general there are nine characteristics of symbols with regard to religion, of which only *one* is the

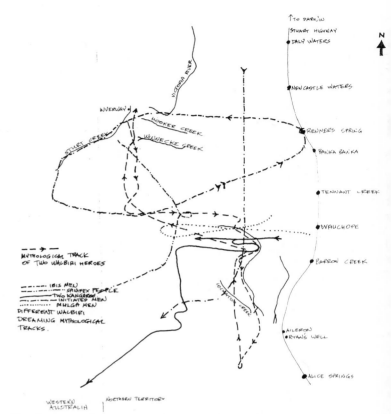

Sketch map of the mythological tracks of some heroes and Dreamings of the Walbiri. After Meggitt. See also Berndt; Baldwin Spencer.

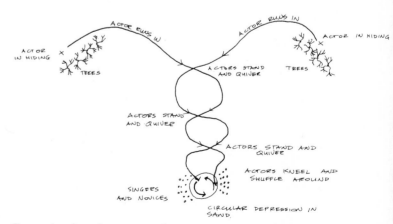

Conventional and stereotyped pattern of actor's movements in Walbiri ceremony. After Meggitt.

artefactual—actually fashioned and made.[86] Aborigines use all nine—including artefactual. In fact *only buildings are not used in the definition of place.* Their monuments are not buildings and other constructions *added* to the landscape but part of that landscape involving at most a rearrangement or reassembly of some of its elements.[87] Other cultures create a new physical landscape in keeping with creation myths. Aborigines structure their *existing* physical landscape mentally, mythically and symbolically without building it.

TEMPORARY AND PERMANENT MONUMENTS

Many descriptions and illustrations exist of ceremonies all showing the great variety, richness and complexity of the temporary 'monuments' used – body decorations, shields, poles, crosses and the like. Various markers may be erected, rocks emphasized by having blood poured on them or special bough huts built in which men spend much time during ceremonials.[88] During some ceremonials big fires are lit as 'temporary monuments'.

The various forms of body decorations are extremely complex involving painting, covering the body with down stuck with blood and so on as well as the use of extremely complex, elaborate and tall head gear.[89] People so decorated could be seen as 'temporary monuments' claiming a place by making it sacred through linking it with myth.

Various types of poles are erected as 'temporary monuments', for example the *Nartunja* poles which are symbols of natural or sacred natural objects.

Another example are the massive *Jelmalandji* poles used in rituals throughout Arnhem land, Roper River, etc.

Many other kinds are used and it is interesting to note that Eliade stresses the general importance of the erection and carrying of poles.[90] Other structures are also carried, for example, frameworks with crosses.[91]

More permanent monuments are also used. These include rock paintings, rock piles such as at Pukara described by Gould.

Among the largest and most complex are the rock alignments described by Gould[92] which are of a quite impressive scale.

Central Australian sacred poles (Nartanja; Kauana). After Baldwin Spencer.

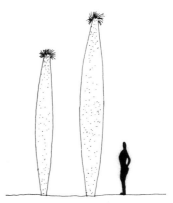

A pair of sacred poles from Arnhem Land (Jelmalandji). After Berndt.

Walbiri string cross. After Meggitt; see also Berndt and Baldwin Spencer.

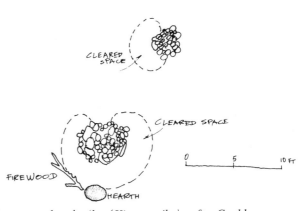

Plan of two sacred rock piles (Yiwara tribe); after Gould.

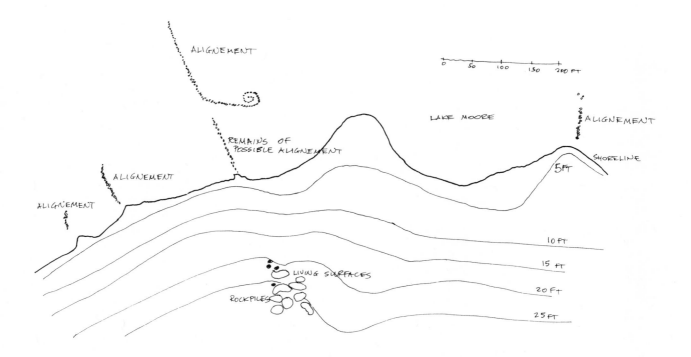

Series of alignments, including major serpentine alignment, approximately 240 ft. long. After Gould, who illustrated others.

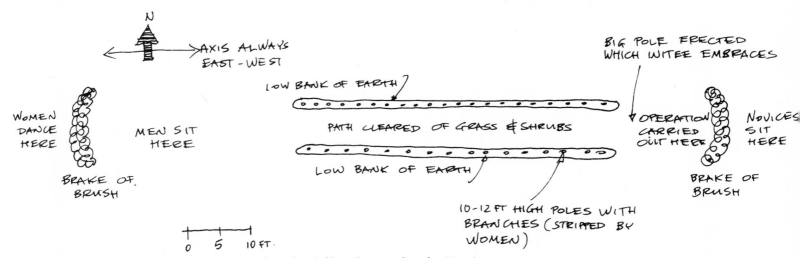

Ground for circumcision ceremony. Central Australia. After Baldwin Spencer. See also Meggitt.

CONSTRUCTION OF RITUAL AND CEREMONIAL SITES LAID OUT IN A SACRED ORDER

The ceremonies of various groups are associated with a particular spot. This may be marked by a prominent natural feature, for example, a great column of sandstone,[93] but in most cases rather complex ceremonial grounds are laid out.

For example, the ground for the initiation circumcision ceremony is placed out of sight of the main camp so women cannot see it and it is quite complex.

For the *Jirinda* ceremony at Yirrkala the ground is swept clear and on it are arranged mounds of sand (representing rocks) and an oblong depression at (a) representing a waterhole. The whole *Bugalub* ground represents a sacred *rajjga* emblem.

Another *Bugalub* is arranged with the sand mounds and depression arranged differently representing a sacred ritual ground used in certain circumcision ceremonies, but also a sacred site in Arnhem land, i.e. a definite geographical location.

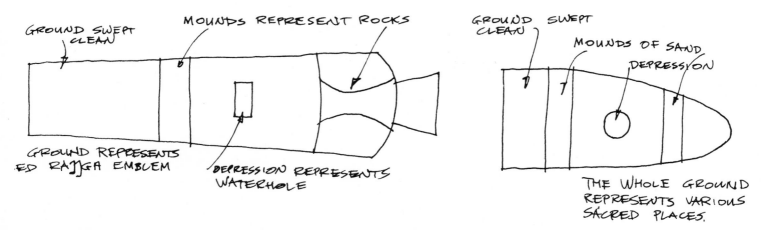

GROUND SWEPT CLEAN

MOUNDS REPRESENT ROCKS

GROUND REPRESENTS ED RAJGA EMBLEM

DEPRESSION REPRESENTS WATERHOLE

GROUND SWEPT CLEAN

MOUNDS OF SAND DEPRESSION

THE WHOLE GROUND REPRESENTS VARIOUS SACRED PLACES.

Two examples of grounds for sacred ceremonies in Arnhem Land. After Berndt, size not indicated.

CONCLUSION

In the largest sense the making of places is the ordering of the world, the clarification of the differences between places some of which are more significant than others. It is the making visible of a special space – in the case of primitive people sacred space which, according to Eliade constitutes a break in the homogeneity of indifferentiated space[94] and hence a *place*. I have tried to show that without building axes, sacred precincts, buildings or cities aborigines were able to make the world theirs through symbolic means and achieve a stable world consisting of places.

Our discussion of aboriginal place making is also a good illustration of Langer's concept of making visible an Ethnic Domain through the use of symbols. She stresses the importance of the congruence of symbols and whatever they are to mean.[95] By using natural features, the physical structure of landscape becomes congruent with mythical structure and hence humanised. If architecture is the mode of creating virtual space, making visible an ethnic domain and setting up a sphere of influence,[96] then aborigines create place by giving meaning to sites in terms of their culture – their ethnic domain. They do what architecture does in all the ways described but without the architecture.

Sorokin draws an implicit continuum between groups for whom shared spatial domains become an important symbol vehicle and those where they are not important – for example learned societies.[97] Aborigines are very much in the former category, which helps explain the rapid psychological and cultural breakdown of tribes when their lands and sacred sites were taken away. The link to these places was crucial because their title to the land went back to their very creation.

For the Aranda, all religious rites, art, poetry and drama were based on definite geographical centres. In the old days the complete ceremonial cycle could only be performed at proper sites and a man could only reach full social standing in his own area. Authority was based upon ties to the land. In Central Australia generally all art, song, myth, dance and so on was linked to the land. When aborigines lost their land they lost all. Losing their land meant more than economic loss – it was cultural and religious disaster.

To Europeans land meant buildings, crops, man-made artefacts, for aborigines it was a spiritual and emotional thing.[98] Because aborigines did not cultivate land or erect permanent dwellings, that is because they took possession of land in non-material ways rather than in European terms, the latter did not realise that aborigines owned, occupied and used land. They could thus appropriate such land without qualms.

The link can still be seen today, even if only among those aborigines who are not yet detribalized and already psychologically broken, i.e. those who still retain their culture. There are not many of these – in most cases their culture has been totally destroyed.

Among the few remaining groups with tribal culture more or less intact the traditional link to the land and specific places is still strong. The *Pinjandjara* in Central Australia still feel that the loss of their land to miners will lead to a destruction of their religion, culture and the tribe itself.

Starting in May 1970 eleven tribes at Yirrkala in Arnhem land have been pressing a claim for 50 square miles of land. Their case is based on the intense spiritual connection existing between themselves and their land. These close links, they claim, establish title and entitle them on declaration of ownership based on aboriginal law and custom. These aborigines claimed a timeless and inextinguishable relationship to their land much more significant than ownership in 'fee simple' which was the highest right recognized by the white man's system. Areas of land held by different groups could be accurately defined, they claimed, as could be the individual's rights. Among aborigines there were no disputes about who owned any particular tract, and boundaries were well established, often to within a few yards, and these were described in court.[99]

Aboriginal witnesses testified that the land had been given them by spiritual ancestors and their spiritual link with the land was proved by the churingas. The travels of the Dreamtime ancestors were described and the conflicts with proposed mining development stressed.[100]

The major case of this type in Australia receiving most publicity is that of the *Gurindji*. This case has been in progress since April 1967 and has become a *cause celébre* with political and emotional involvement leading to boycotts, sit-ins, public meetings, direct help and the like. This public involvement is strengthened by the fact that the Australian government refused to accept *any* traditional aboriginal land rights in 1971.

It is significant that the *Gurindjis,* who claim 500 square miles at Wattie Creek, refuse all offers of land, help and houses elsewhere in the same area. While the purpose of much of the action is to regain economic independence, cultural identity, dignity, confidence and self-respect, it is significant that, once again, the claim is based on the emotional and spiritiual ties to a specific area of land – a *place*.

It thus seems clear that the Australian aborigines were most definitely able to establish a sense of place which was independent of any buildings which they might have constructed. This suggests that in the larger sense the establishment of place is a symbolic process. The use of physical barriers is only one way of achieving this – although, apparently, an essential one in *our* culture and context.

NOTES

This article was written in April, 1971. A shorter and different version appeared in William J. Mitchell (ed.) *EDRA3,* University of California, Los Angeles, 1972.

[1] RAPOPORT, AMOS, *House Form and Culture,* Prentice-Hall, Englewood-Cliffs, NJ, 1969.
[2] RAPOPORT, AMOS, 'Some Aspects of the Organisation of Urban Space', *Student Publication,* School of Design, NC State University, Raleigh NC, Vol. 18, 1969.
[3] RAPOPORT, AMOS, 'The Pueblo and the Hogan: A Cross-Cultural comparison of Two Responses to an Environment', OLIVER, PAUL (ed.), *Shelter and Society,* Barrie & Rockliff, London, 1969.
[4] LEE, R. B., and DE VORE, I., (eds), *Man the Hunter,* Aldine, Chicago, 1968.
[5] CARR-SAUNDERS, cited in WYNNE-EDWARDS, V. C., *Animal Dispersion in Relation to Social Behaviour,* Oliver and Boyd, Edinburgh and London, 1962, pp. 21; 187.
[6] FALKENBERG, JOHANNES, *Kin and Totem* (Group Relations of Australian Aborigines in the Port Keats District), Oslo University Press, Oslo, 1962, p. 9.
[7] MOUNTFORD, CHARLES P., *Ayers Rock,* Angus & Robertson, Sydney, 1965, p. 17.
[8] See LEE, R. B. and DE VORE, I., 'Problems in the Study of Hunters and Gatherers' op. cit., pp. 11–12 and elsewhere.
[9] WORMS, A. E., 'Religion' in STANNER, W. E. H. and SHEILS, H., (eds), *Australian Aboriginal Studies,* Oxford University Press, Melbourne, 1963, p. 174.
[10] BIRKET-SMITH, KAJ, *Primitive Man and his Ways,* Mentor Books, New York, 1963, pp. 41, 50.
[11] MEGGITT, M. J., 'Marriage, Classes and Demography in Central Australia' in LEE and DE VORE, op. cit.
[12] HIATT, L. R., Ibid. p. 100.

[13] SPENCER, BALDWIN and GILLEN, F. J., *The Native Tribes of Central Australia,* (1894) Dover, New York, 1968.
[14] *Australian Aboriginal Art* (The Louis A. Allen Collection), Exhibition at Robert H. Lowie Museum of Anthropology, University of California, Berkeley, January 17–August 25, 1969, (Text by Albert B. Elsasser and Vivian Paul).
[15] This is also the conclusion of the Berndts. See R. M. and C. H. BERNDT, *The World of the First Australians,* Ure Smith, Sydney, 1964, pp. 23–24.
[16] I was guilty of just this oversimplification in *House Form and Culture,* (Ibid).
[17] THOMAS, N. W., *Natives of Australia,* Archibald Constable, London, 1906, pp. 71–72.
[18] Ibid, pp. 71–73; BERNDT, op. cit. p. 20, argues that aborigines did adopt stone houses which they knew from Malaya and Indonesia.
[19] THOMAS, op. cit., p. 74; BIRKET-SMITH, op. cit., pp. 34–35.
[20] MEGGITT, M. J., *Desert People* (A study of the Walbiri aborigines of Central Australia,), University of Chicago Press, Chicago, 1965, (Second Impression).
[21] THOMAS, op. cit., p. 74–75.
[22] MEGGITT, op. cit., pp. 75–76.
[23] BIRKET-SMITH, op. cit., p. 35.
[24] GOULD, RICHARD A., *Yiwara,* (Foragers of the Australian Desert), Charles Scribners Sons, New York, 1969, p. 173; L. R. HIATT, personal communication.
[25] GOULD, op. cit., p. 26.
[26] BOCHNER, Dr. STEPHEN, University of New South Wales, personal communication.
[27] BERNDT, *World of the First Australians,* op. cit., p. 35.
[28] STANNER and SHEILS, op. cit., p. 174.
[29] MEGGITT, op. cit., pp. 1; 30–32.
[30] Ibid, pp. 44–46.
[31] BERNDT, op. cit., pp. 34–35.
[32] MEGGITT, op. cit., pp. 67–73.
[33] Hiatt, Pilling, Lee, in LEE and DE VORE, op. cit., p. 157.
[34] MEGGITT, op. cit., p. 243.
[35] HIATT, L. R., 'Local Organisation among the Australian Aborigines', *Oceania,* Vol. 32, no. 4, June 1962, pp. 267–286; 'Ownership and Use of Land Among the Australian Aborigines' in LEE and DE VORE, op. cit., pp. 99–102.
[36] STANNER, W. E. H., 'Aboriginal Territorial Organisation: Estate, range, domain and regime', *Oceania,* Vol. 36, No. 1, September 1965, pp. 1–16.
[37] Ibid, p. 11. It is interesting that among animals also, home ranges for food gathering may be exclusive or overlapping, c.f. WYNNE-EDWARDS, op. cit., p. 100.
[38] STREHLOW, T. G. H., 'Culture, Social structure and environment in Aboriginal Central Australia' in R. M. and C. H. BERNDT (eds), *Aboriginal Man in Australia,* Angus and Robertson, Sydney, 1965.
[39] SPENCER, op. cit., pp. 7–8.
[40] STANNER, op. cit., p. 13.
[41] MEGGITT, M. J., 'Gadjari among the Walbiri Aborigines', *Oceania,* Vol. 36, No. 3, March 1966, p. 178; 196.
[42] RAPOPORT, AMOS and HAWKES, RON, 'The perception of Urban Complexity', *A.I.P. Journal,* Vol. 36, No. 2, March 1970, p. 107.
[43] RAPOPORT, AMOS, 'The study of spatial quality', *Journal of Aesthetic Education,* Vol. 4, 4 October 1970, pp. 81–95.
[44] MOUNTFORD, op. cit., pp. 13; 25; 30ff.
[45] FRANK, LAWRENCE K., 'The World as communication network'. in KEPES, G., (ed.), *Sign, Image, Symbol,* George Braziller, New York, 1966, pp. 1; 4–5; 8.
[46] FALKENBERG, op. cit., pp. 81; 84.
[47] ELKIN, A. P., 'Elements of Aboriginal Philosophy', *Oceania,* Vol. 40, no. 2, December 1969, pp. 85–98.
[48] Ibid, p. 88.
[49] Ibid, pp. 91–93. BIRKET-SMITH, op. cit., p. 23; MOUNTFORD, op. cit., p. 24; c.f. also ELIADE, MIRCEA, *The Sacred and the Profane,* Harper and Row, New York, 1961.
[50] FALKENBERG, op. cit., p. 48.
[51] SPENCER, op. cit., p. 11.
[52] BIRKET-SMITH, op. cit., p. 23.
[53] RAPOPORT, AMOS, 'Symbolism and Environmental Design', *International Journal of Symbology,* Vol. 1, no. 3, 1969, pp. 1–9.
[54] RAPOPORT, AMOS, *Journal of Aesthetic Education,* op. cit.

55 GOLDWATER, ROBERT, 'Judgements of Primitive Art, 1905–1969', in BIEBUYCK, D. P. (ed.), *Tradition and Creativity in Tribal Art,* University of California Press, Berkeley and Los Angeles, 1969, p. 32.
56 ELIADE, MIRCEA, op. cit.
57 GOULD, op. cit., p. 53.
58 Ibid, p. 73–74.
59 Ibid, p. 83–84.
60 STREHLOW in BERNDT, *Aboriginal Man,* op. cit., p. 144.
61 GOULD, op. cit., p. 104.
62 BERNDT, op. cit., p. xv.
63 MIDDLETON, JOHN (ed.), *Myth and Cosmos,* (Readings in Mythology and Symbolism), Natural History Press, Garden City NY, 1961, p. x.
64 LEACH in Ibid, p. 1.
65 See FALKENBERG, op. cit., pp. 85–86; MOUNTFORD, op. cit., pp. 17, 25, 197–199.
66 SPENCER, op. cit., pp. 119, 122, 497.
67 Most of this discussion is based on FALKENBERG, op. cit., specially pp. 7; 11; 16; 21–22; 114–117; 139; 271.
68 There is some disagreement in the literature about the presence of tribes, the meaning of horde, and their relationship. All agree, however, that some form of larger grouping exists.
69 c.f. ELIADE, op. cit.; GOULD, op. cit.; The Ancient Greeks.
70 For a diagram of this see FALKENBERG, op. cit., p. 21. Note the close resemblance of this to the home range, core area, territory model proposed earlier in this paper.
71 FALKENBERG, op. cit., p. 22.
72 MOUNTFORD, op. cit., p. 17 and Figure 3.
73 HAWKES, JACQUETTA and WOOLLEY, SIR LEONARD, *Prehistory and the Beginnings of Civilisation,* (UNESCO History of Mankind, Vol. 1), Harper and Row, New York, 1963, p. 212.
74 SPENCER, op. cit., p. 524.
75 FALKENBERG, op. cit., pp. 48; 234–240; 249.
76 SPENCER, op. cit., p. 124–126; 132–133.
77 RYKWERT, JOSEPH, *The Idea of a Town,* G. Van Saane, Hilversum, (nd).
78 SPENCER, op. cit., p. 133–135.
79 See for example, PORTEOUS, S. D., *The Psychology of a Primitive People,* Longmans Green, New York, 1931; PINK, OLIVE M., 'Spirit Ancestors in a Northern Aranda Tribe Country', *Oceania,* Vol. 4, no. 2, December 1933, pp. 176–186.
80 STANNER in BERNDT, *Aboriginal Man,* op. cit., pp. 227–311.
81 ELIADE, op. cit., pp. 20–22.
82 SPENCER, op. cit., Chapter X.
83 MEGGITT, 'Gadjari . . .', op. cit., pp. 178; 196.
84 Ibid, p. 212.
85 ELIADE, op. cit., pp. 29; 32.
86 TURNER, V. W. in HUXLEY, J. (ed.), *A Discussion of Ritualisation in Animals and Man,* (Philosophical transactions of the Royal Society of London, Series B, Vol. 251 (Biological Sciences)), 1966, p. 295. See also BOWRA, M. in Ibid., pp. 388; 390–91.
87 BERNDT, *First Australians,* op. cit., p. 247.
88 SPENCER, op. cit., p. 191.
89 For example see BERNDT, *Aboriginal Man,* op. cit.; BALDWIN-SPENCER, op. cit.; in fact any illustrated book on the aborigines.
90 ELIADE, op. cit., p. 32 ff.
91 SPENCER, op, cit., Figure 57, p. 307; MEGGITT, *Desert People,* op. cit., p. 76.
92 GOULD, op. cit., p. 137, ff.
93 SPENCER, op. cit., pp. 118–119.
94 ELIADE, op. cit., p. 37.
95 LANGER, SUZANNE, *Feeling and Form,* Charles Scribner Sons, New York, 1953, p. 27.
96 Ibid., p. 91 ff.
97 SOROKIN, P. A., *Society, Culture and Personality,* Harper, New York, 1947, p. 147.
98 BERNDT, *First Australians,* op. cit., p. 427.
99 *Sydney Morning Herald,* May 26, 1970.
100 *Sydney Morning Herald,* May 27, 1970.

THREE CITIES OF NEPAL

Jan Pieper

In the Valley of Kathmandu a peculiar urban culture has survived, which at one time was characteristic for the whole of India, and which in variations existed all over the East.

The Hindu township – the product and visual expression of this urban culture – is a settlement pattern, which can only be fully understood within the framework of religious beliefs, social organisations and power systems of the classical Hindu civilisations. The urban configuration of street pattern, buildings and quarters (*tols*) has a profound meaning to the townsman, and together with a very detailed schedule of seasonal religious activities and periodic ritual obligations, the spatial layout of the city rules and regulates his entire life. This makes the urban structure a major social stabiliser and an important element of support for the classical power systems of the Hindu world. For a full evaluation of the Hindu town planning principles we have to see the Hindu township from two different points of view: we have to see what it meant to the faithful townsman, and to the despotic ruler.

Elsewhere in the Indian sphere of influence this interpenetration of urban life and urban layout has gradually vanished through the processes of colonisation and modernisation. Though in some Indian cities the classical layout of the street pattern remains, urban life has changed completely, and the urban configuration has become meaningless.[1] Not so in Nepal, where a policy of complete isolation kept all foreign influence out. Only some twenty years ago this period came to an end, and the political system changed from an archaic Hindu kingdom into something more modern, though much of the old Hindu state survives. Since then the three Newar towns in the valley have hardly begun to change, and the colour of life is still much as it was as in the golden days of classical Indian culture.[2]

The Kathmandu Valley is an isolated amphitheatre – about 15 miles across – around the headwaters of the Baghmati River. Towards the North lie the massive walls of the Himalayas, and from India it is protected by the rugged Mahabharat Lekh. Due to this well-protected location, Hinduism, the Indian mode of production and Indian political institutions reached the Valley at a rather late stage. Before the Hindu era the Newar were a tribal

Taghupal Tole, Bhaktapur.

52

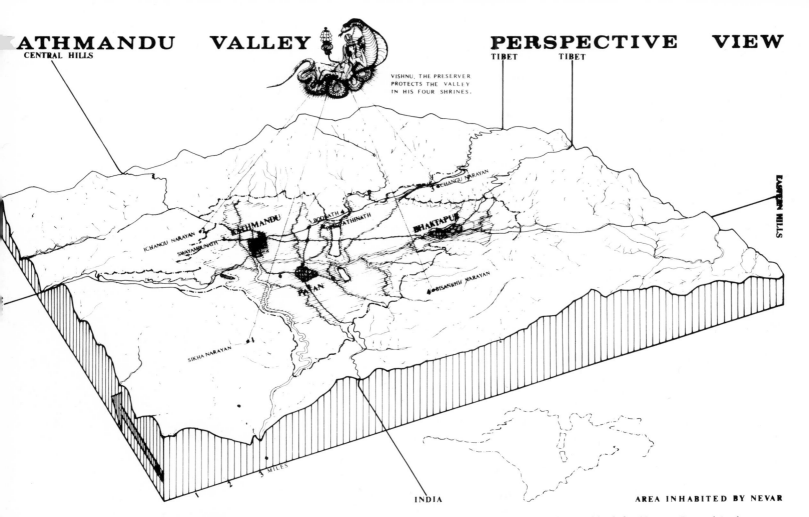

VISHNU, THE PRESERVER
PROTECTS THE VALLEY
IN HIS FOUR SHRINES.

CHANGU NARAYAN

KATHMANDU

BODHNATH
PASHUPATHINATH

BHAKTAPUR

ICHANGU NARAYAN

SWAYAMBUNATH

PATAN

BISANKHU NARAYAN

SIKHA NARAYAN

3 MILES

INDIA

AREA INHABITED BY NEWAR

The Valley of Kathmandu is one of the few wide high valleys in the Himalayas. This isolated amphitheatre is the world of the Newar. Beyond is the country of savage tribes and the abode of demons. The thick tropical jungles to the South, the rugged mountains around it, and the massive blocks of Ganesh Himal and Gosanthain to the North kept all human intruders out. Supernatural foes, however, had to be deterred and terrified with supernatural means: The four shrines of Vishnu in the four corners of the Valley form the outward ring of (the various systems of) protective constellations, which make up the mandala of the Valley. Similarly, the three towns, the tols *inside the towns and finally the individual* behals *and houses are safeguarded by* mandala *arrangements.*

people, organised in small warring kingships, which Percival Landon has compared to Scotland in the days of its warring clans.[3] These chieftains were unable to support a large non-agricultural population, and sizable cities, or even towns, did not exist.

But from the 12th century onwards, the Muslim conquest of Northern India drove groups of Rajputs into the mountain refuge. Of these, the Malla dynasty proved most successful, and they founded three petty princedoms in the valley. Under their reign, the country was soon Hinduised, the caste system introduced and strong, centralised political institutions established, modelled upon the despotism of the hydraulic states in India.[4] This provided the institutional basis for the systematic building of large cities, and large scale implementation of Hindu planning principles. The capitals of the three Malla princedoms, therefore, were the first urban settlements in the Valley, and they still are, up to the present day, the only cities in the country. The early Malla kings chose

three existing hamlets as residencies after the conquest of the Valley. They built palaces there, but no other spectacular planning and building was done during this first period of consolidation. The settlements grew slowly and irregularly. But the turn of the sixteenth century, well after the firm establishment of Malla power and well after the successful introduction of their social and economic innovations, saw large scale extensions of the three royal cities on a regular plan. The results of this systematic planning at a rather late stage, where settlements already existing on the site had to be incorporated into the overall layout, are the three very different towns of Kathmandu, Patan and Bhaktapur.

Kathmandu (Sanskrit 'Kantipur', Newari 'Yen') is located on a dry hillock between the Baghmati and Vishnumati Rivers, near where the old trade route from India to Tibet crossed the fords. Ancient sanctuaries dating back to the eighth century, like the temple of Lagan, stood on the site, as well as a small bazaar along

53

Aerial photograph of Kathmandu.

KATHMANDU

PLAN OF KATHMANDU.
A. Nuclear settlements to the North and South of the Malla town.
B. Rana period (1846–1950) development; low density Palladian villa-typ[e]
upper class housing and public buildings.

the road, when the Mallas chose the settlement as one of their residencies. But Mahendra Malla (1560–1574) turned the riverside hamlet into a royal city: he started the enormous wooden palace and the central Taleju temple, and settled a large number of people in the neighbourhood. They were accommodated in twelve oblong, rectangular wards: all the main streets run due north-east and east-west, and thus form a regular gridiron plan.[5]

The bazaar along the India–Tibet road, however, and the olde[r] settlements were not demolished, but they are still traceable on th[e] plan: to the north and south of what today is the urban core are[a] the street pattern is curved and crooked, and irregularly broken b[y] squares. These are the old nuclear settlements and the square[s] hold the oldest temples and monasteries of the city. The long straight road, which runs diagonally across the grid and extend[s]

owards the northeast and southwest into the open country is the
ld India–Tibet road, and the bazaars along the central sections
re still the major shopping districts of modern Kathmandu. The
ntersection points of this diagonal axis with the main streets of the
rid are triangular, small open spaces, with numerous temples and
agodas. The square plinths and pyramids of these sanctuaries are
ll, according to the Hindu planning ideals, orientated towards the
ardinal points, but their arrangement and location is extremely
aried, so that a walk along the bazaar and through this sequence
f irregular open spaces is a most fascinating experience.

The exact north–south orientation of the street plan – in spite of
he existing NE–SW axis of the old trade road – is indeed striking.
here is no functional explanation for this peculiar layout of the
ity – we must look at it with Hindu eyes. Cities were the largest
rtefacts man in the ancient East could make. Only the limitlessness
f earth and universe were of wider extent. Cities were understood
s an element of the cosmos; they were the manifest attempt to
rrange a very small sector of the universe according to the Hindu
nderstanding of the whole. That is why the Indian cosmology –
e. the esoteric knowledge of a universal order – can give us some
rst ideas about the intention and the meaning behind the lay-out
f the Hindu township.[6]

It is primarily one aspect of Hindu cosmology which is important
n this context: the whole universe is conceived as a huge, living
rganism, formed by the earth, the heavens and the hells. This
igantic construction is the manifestation of an ineffable world
pirit, and the creator god Brahma is the ruler of its permanent
hange. The cosmos passes through cycles within cycles for all
ternity. The basic cycle is 'kalpa', or one 'day of Brahma', and it
ill last for 4,320,000 earthly years. His night is of equal length.
60 such 'days' and 'nights' constitute one 'year of Brahma', and
rahma's life will last for a hundred years. After the cycle of these
undred years of Brahma the universe returns to the world spirit,
ho is the primeval cause of everything, until a new creator god is
volved and a new universe is formed. Each cosmic day,
rahma recreates the universe and absorbs it again. During the
osmic night he is asleep, and the whole universe is gathered up in
is body, where it remains as a potentiality. These are the two
spects of the universe: one is the manifested phase, where the one-
ess of the world spirit is split up into the multitude of things. This
s the world we see every day. The other phase is the non-manifested
here the multitude is dissolved in oneness, where the objects pass
rom their concrete forms into shapeless unity.[7]

This idea of permanent change, permanent repetition and the
ontinuous passing through cycles is one of the central elements of
Hinduism. In fact, it is the predominant aspiration of Hindu
eligious life to overcome these cycles and to achieve permanent
neness with the world-spirit Brahma. The various ways of
neditation are looked upon as vehicles which enable the yogi to be
nerged in unity with the world spirit for a limited period of time.
One of the favourite exercises of the Hindu is to contemplate over
graphic reproduction of the universe. These images of the cosmos
re taken as aids for deep meditation, and they are believed to have
ome purgatory effect on the meditator's mind. Such an object of
meditation is called a *mandala*. Mandalas can have various forms
and sizes. Most frequently they are painted diagrams but also large
houses, temples and urban layouts are based on the mandala idea.
Generally, all objects with some spiritual connotation can be
designed as mandalas.[8] This illustrates what the Hindu townships
were intended to be: they were large replicas of the universe which,
because of their diagrammatic layouts, were believed to have the
same cosmic-magic effect on the initiated town dweller that the
mandala had on the yogi.

The Hindu system of thoughts is so tight that it does not leave
much room for creativity in the design of these mandala layouts.
In fact, originality and imagination were not at all the intentions of
the Hindu planners: only the approved form was supposed to have
the desired effect, and all experiments were considered evil. Consequently, at a very early stage, these planning ideals were formu-
lated and laid down in a series of design canons, called the 'Vastu
Sastras'. The Vastu Sastras were in circulation all over the Hindu
world, and the National Archives in Kathmandu have a large
collection of Newari versions of the texts. The most comprehensive
collection of these canons is the *Manasara,* and it is also the most
accessible since it was completely translated into English by P. K.
Acharya in 1920.[9] The book contains detailed rules for the design
of virtually any object of everyday life. The architectural treatises
mainly are concerned with three subjects: location, proportion and
lay-out.

The town planning treatises of the *Manasara* deal with the urban
fabric mainly under two aspects: on the one hand the city is
described as a representation of the universe, or, in other words as
a micro-cosmos in itself, and the recommendations and directions
of the authors therefore aim to establish a set of rules, which would
make the lay-out a true replica of the whole. On the other hand,
the city is seen as an element of the whole, as a built object related
to a larger environment and to the overall organisation of the
universe.

To achieve the first object the Manasara establishes a canon of
design rules dealing with the arrangement of urban elements.
These elements are the walls, the streets and the temples. It is
significant that houses, and even palaces, are not mentioned in the
treatises. They were built on whatever space was left, and were not
regarded as chief objects of consideration. The Manasara mentions
eight possible systems in which these elements could be arranged.
They are shown in the diagrams and the plans. It appears from their
designations that at least some were modelled upon mystic symbols
and sacred objects. This is, however only evident in two of them,
namely the swastika layout, which derived its pattern from the
auspicious *Omkara* symbol, and *Padmaka* i.e. 'like a Lotus'. The
origin of the six other diagrams cannot be traced so easily.

There are, however, very few cities on the Indian subcontinent
which are exact reproductions of one of these diagrams, and most
of these few examples are not very old. Also the plans of the three
Newar cities are not based on any of the ideograms. However, the
builders tried to achieve precise orientation and geometric clarity
as far as possible. Geometric clarity, and hence a high degree of
artificiality, is certainly the major concern of Hindu planning, and

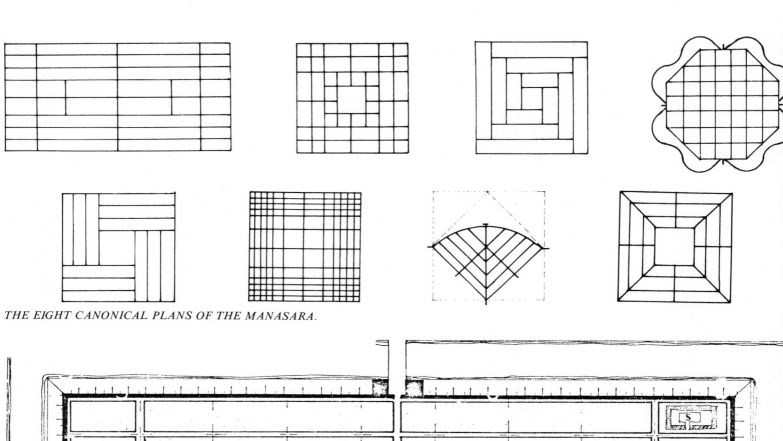

THE EIGHT CANONICAL PLANS OF THE MANASARA.

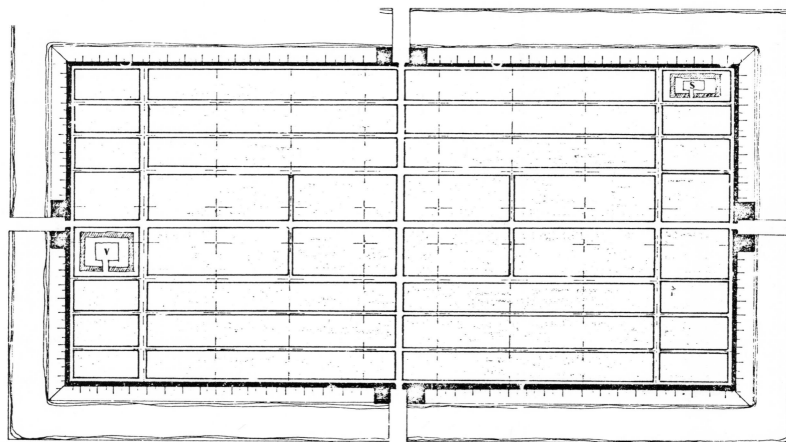

Dandaka

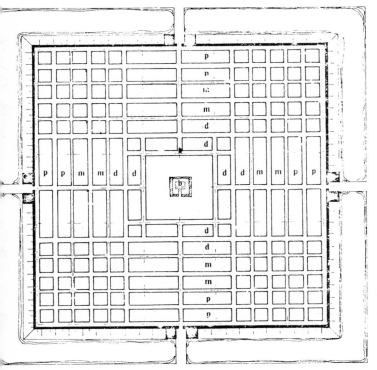

arvathobhadra.

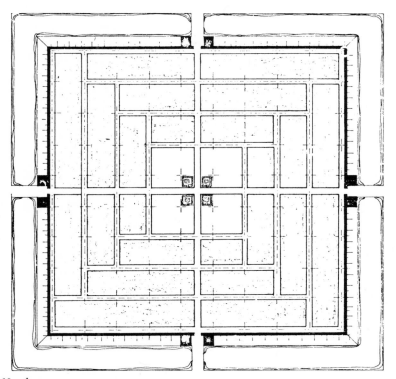

Nandyavarta.

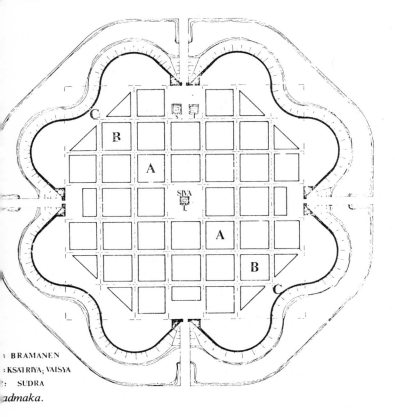

: BRAMANEN

: KSATRIYA; VAISYA

: SUDRA

admaka.

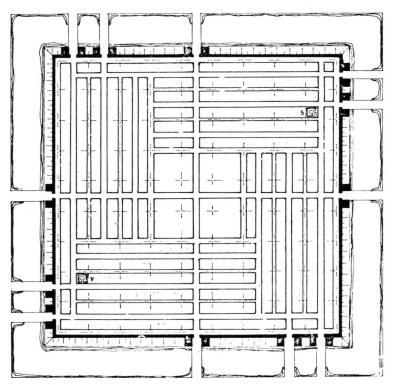

Swastika.

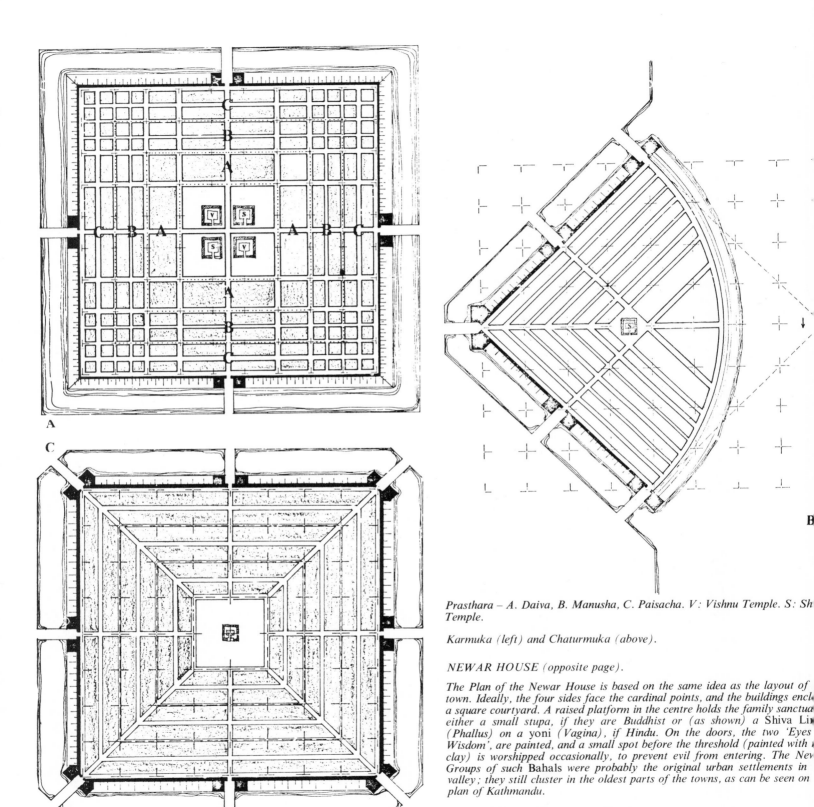

Prasthara – A. Daiva, B. Manusha, C. Paisacha. V: Vishnu Temple. S: Sh[
Temple.

Karmuka (left) and Chaturmuka (above).

NEWAR HOUSE (opposite page).

The Plan of the Newar House is based on the same idea as the layout of [
town. Ideally, the four sides face the cardinal points, and the buildings encl[
a square courtyard. A raised platform in the centre holds the family sanctua[
either a small stupa, if they are Buddhist or (as shown) a Shiva Li[
(Phallus) on a yoni (Vagina), if Hindu. On the doors, the two 'Eyes [
Wisdom', are painted, and a small spot before the threshold (painted with [
clay) is worshipped occasionally, to prevent evil from entering. The Ne[
Groups of such Bahals were probably the original urban settlements in [
valley; they still cluster in the oldest parts of the towns, as can be seen on [
plan of Kathmandu.

A typical Newar House, at roof level.

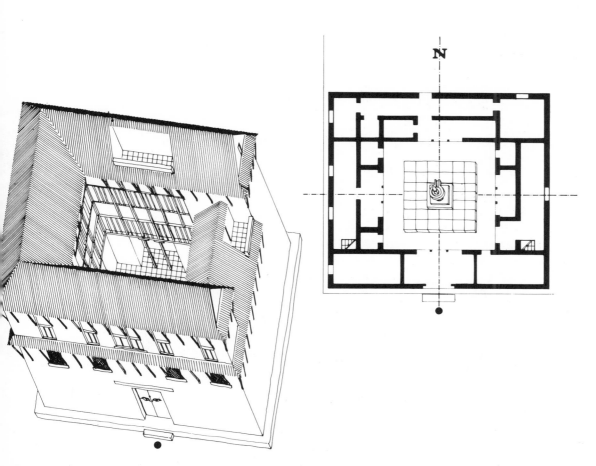

Aerial photograph of Patan.

in the Vastu Sastras this basic idea was expressed in an Aesopic language, which is typical for Hindu treatises, no matter on what subject. It is because of this geometric order that the Hindu towns could be read as diagrammatic replicas of the Indian concept of the universe.

The origin of Hindu planning in a cosmological concept is evident from the image of the city. Schematic inertness is characteristic for the plans of the canon, and the cities are such exact realisations of this idea that even the two-dimensionality of the ideogram was transferred from imagination into reality. The Hindu townships are merely flat configurations, entirely lacking the spatial dramatics of their Western counterparts. Formation of squares and piazzas, long flights of streets, towers, cupolas and impressive spaces – all this belongs to the vocabulary of the dynamic and expansive cultures of Europe and the Middle East and their overseas offshoots. The Hindu township is an evenly arranged flat area, from which even the towers of the temple hardly rise. The temples themselves are designed on the same principles: they are a condensed repetition of the urban plan and not envisaged to enclose large spaces. In fact, they only cover narrow, cave-like chambers, and their volumes compare unfavourably with the incredible masses of stones piled up to form them

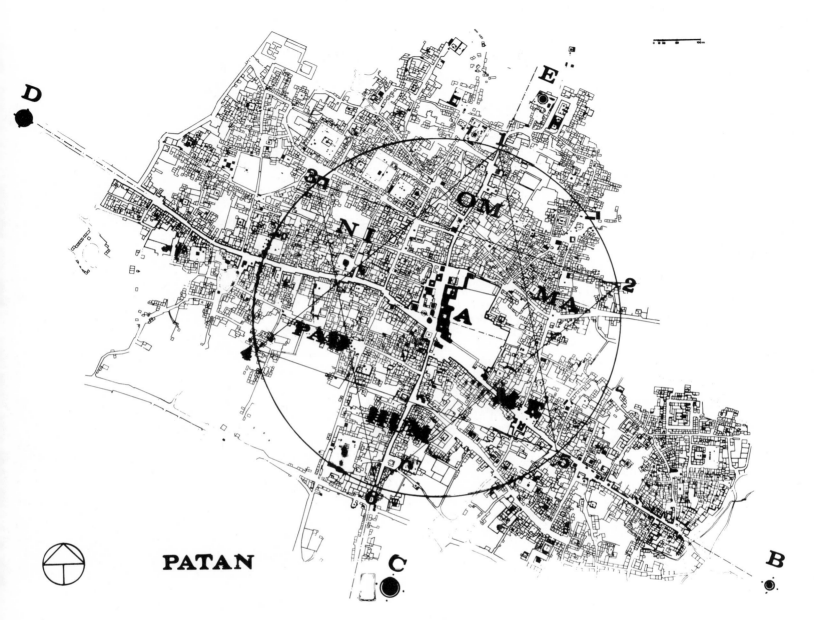

Plan of Patan.

PATAN

The architect restricted his efforts to model the temple surface, which was carved and sculptured even in hidden folds. Hence 'architecture', in a classical sense as the 'art of space', is a term unfit for Hindu buildings. More correctly they are 'walk-upon-sculptures', and it is significant that the Hindu architectural manuals do not differentiate between architecture and sculpture.

Even in Nepal, where (unlike in India) timber was preferably used, and this material could easily be employed to enclose con-siderable volumes, it was never used to that effect in religious architecture. The most original piece of Newar architecture, the pagoda, is characterised by its huge umbrella-like roofs, but they cover only very small, dark chambers.

Besides the establishment of design principles for the Hindu township as a microcosmos, the Manasara was compiled to assure an auspicious integration of the city as one element into the overall organisation of the universe. Great care was taken in the location

61

of the city. Buddha mentions architecture as 'a science the object of which is to ascertain whether the site for a building is auspicious or not.'[10] The Manasara provides all sorts of magic formulae for this purpose. Most interesting in this context, however, are the considerations which were given to the exact orientation of the city. The four main gates had to face the cardinal points, the streets were running cross-shaped north-south and east-west and all the main buildings had to be fitted into this framework. The determination of the cardinal points is a method of setting fixed reference lines in space, in a dimension where nature has not provided such constants. Time is measured by the constants of days and years, a rhythm which is determined by the movement of heavenly bodies through space. Thus, in the stars the dimensions of time and space unite. From their orbits' defining lines, the Hindu builders derive the basic cardinal points. The Manasara often refers to these lines as the 'magic cross'. To lay out a city on this 'magic cross' means to reconnect the man-made order of the city organism with the primeval order of the universe, to imbed it in the 'cycles of Brahma'. Thus constructed, the Hindu township becomes the combining element between man and cosmos, a mandala to walk on, a spiritual instrument to overcome the manifested world.

As a consequence of the canonical character of Hindu planning the majority of Hindu cities display the same geometrical clarity of the layout, the repetition of the same stereotypes and the same austere artificiality. In fact, artificiality is the principal aesthetic aspiration of Hindu design. Artificiality implies something metaphysical to the early inhabitant of the tropical regions, a lucidity which he does not find in the rampant nature around him. To the Hindu, artificiality is the expression of intellect, of non-nature, of the principle behind the manifested world: of the world-spirit Brahma. Artificiality is pure presence of Brahma. Life in an artificially arranged abode has a disentangling and clarifying effect on man. That is why the Hindu understands systematically organized spaces as a purifying adjuvant on his way through the cycles of metempsychosis into the unmanifested unity of the world-spirit.

The Hindus divide their settlement into various zones, arranged concentrically around their township proper. The degree of artificiality of these zones – and consequently their degree of cosmic-magic effectivity – intensifies towards the center. River, mountain, forest and swamp are the natural boundaries of the settled area. Beyond stretches the hostile world of savage tribes, and, even further beyond, the immeasurable extent of earth and universe. Within these demarcations range the better-known realms, the pastures and the cultivated fields of the surrounding villages. Immediately along the ramparts of the town extends a wide glacis, the funeral piles for the dead and the abode of spirits, demarcated by the pagodas and pavilions scattered in the fields. Then follow the town walls, the solid and distinctly built limits of the properly inhabited area. They round the magic diagram of the layout. There again the zones of the castes are arranged concentrically around the Brahmin plot, and the centre itself is an open square, holding the geometrically planned temple, a petrified display of the esoteric Hindu world.

The distinct contrast between the abundance of the world outside and the geometric clarity of the city has a deep meaning to the Hindu. His way from field and forest into town is more than just a transition from nature into a man-made environment: the passing through the gates signifies a step up to a higher stage of existence; it is the symbolic transmigration through the 'Mouth of Brahma'. This 'zoning' of the city proper and the land is striking in the Kathmandu valley. The neighbourhood of the three towns, and all low-lying areas are cultivated by Newar farmers. (The Newar also constitute the majority of the urban population). But on the dry hillocks and higher up the mountain slopes around the valley the ethnically different Parbate have settled. Their habitat starts from a certain altitude and the abrupt change is distinctly marked by a completely different cultural landscape: different crops, different people and a markedly different red and white painted house type. Further away live the Sherpas and Bhote with little contacts inside the valley. And beyond these hill tribes, the Newar believe, is the abode of demons and dragons.

This brief account of the Hindu planning ideals as rooted in the Hindu idea of the world explains why the streets of Kathmandu

Bhaktapur.

Bhaktapur from The South.

were arranged in a strictly geometric order against existing structures, and without any functional motivation.

Like Kathmandu, Patan ('Lalitapuri', 'Lalitapattana' in Sanskrit, 'Ela', 'Yala' or 'Yangala' in Newari) has a fairly regular, geometrical layout, roughly circular in shape, with the cross-like main streets pointing at four large stupas outside the gates, and a gridiron pattern of side streets. A fifth stupa[11] is located close to the central intersection, among an impressive massing of Pagodas and Shikara Temples next to the elaborately carved wooden structure of the Malla place. Nowhere else in the Valley is so much bygone splendour so close together as in Patan's Mangal Bazaar, and the city has always gained the unrestricted admiration of foreign travellers. 'It has the dignity and pathos which always tinge a city that has once been a capital, and in design and composition it is the noblest of the three.'[12] There are no older, nuclear settlements integrated into the regular plan of the city, though Patan was already famous as the major centre of Buddhism in the Valley during the reign of Ashoka. But the existing monasteries

and secular settlements were completely destroyed by a small Islamic force of Sultan Shams-ud-din of Bengal, in the year 1347.[13] The Malla of Patan, then the most powerful dynasty in the Valley, took the opportunity to reconstruct the city entirely on a regular plan.

The four stupas were taken as points of reference for the new city. Local tradition explains the plan as a representation of the Buddhist Wheel of Life, the Buddhist diagram which corresponds to the famous mantra of the benign Bhoddisattva Avalokitesvara *Om Mani Padme Hum,* and as such is believed to have the same beneficial effect as the mandala of the street pattern has for the Hindu townsman.[14]

Not all Hindu towns are laid out on a geometrical mandala plan. In such a case, the lay-out had to be ritually corrected so that it would again be suitable for the residence of high caste Hindus. A great variety of bizarre theories for these rearrangements exists, and for all possible deficiencies peculiar planning operations are recommended as ritual remedy. The third town in the Valley,

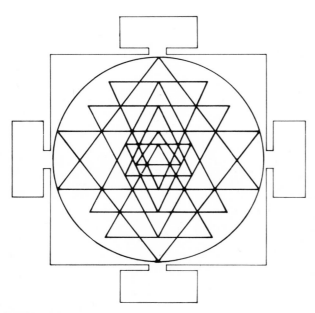

BHAKTAPUR MANDALA.
The graphic design is a corruption of the Sricakra Mandala ('The Mandala of the Wheel of Sri'). This is a Hindu mandala of the Siva and Sakta schools, known as mandala of the sakti, i.e. of the divine, female power, by virtue of which Siva can manifest and display himself in things. The diagram is composed of nine triangles; the four downward facing triangles represent the Satki, the tendency of manifestation and fulfilment, whereas the five upward triangles symbolize Siva, or the phase of return. Therefore, in these nine triangles is expressed the process of divine expansion, which proceeds from the One to the Many. 31. The iconographic composition of the Bhaktapur mandala corresponds to this basic idea. The central triangle – apex directed downwards to indicate the tendency towards manifestation – holds the Supreme Sakti, Siva's female component, here represented as Kali, Taleju (i.e. an incarnation of Parvati) and Durga.

Bhaktapur, ('Baktapuri', 'Badgaon', 'Bhaktagram' in Sanskrit, 'Khopa', 'Khvopa', 'Krmprm' in Newari) is a typical example of a city which was treated in this way. The settlement grew up around a junction of a branch of the old India–Tibet trade route (via the Chalung pass) and the highway into the eastern provinces. From this junction the road follows the curved edge of a dry plain over the Hanumante River, and then leads to Kathmandu and Patan, some nine miles towards the west. Ananda Malla made this junction town his residence (in the 13th century) and he built a palace on a site called 'Old Durbar Square' by the locals. The settlement continued to grow irregularly, until the reign of Yaksha Malla (1428–1482), who moved the palace to the present site and built a new town towards the south of it. This extension – commonly called the 'Lower City' – was not laid out on a mandala plan, though far more regularly than the older 'Upper City': the old east-west trade route (which looks like a 'W' on the Plan of Bhaktapur) was taken as the spine road of the 'Lower City', with a number of perpendicular side streets.[15]

This arrangement does not at all comply with the canonical layouts. Undoubtedly, the Hindu mind will see a defect in this, since a street plan not based upon the mandala theory would leave

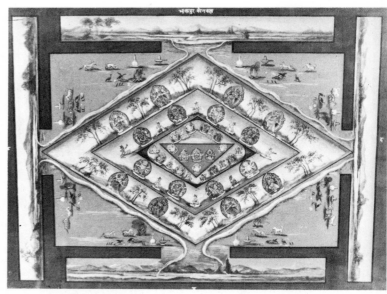

Mandala of SRICAKRA.

the city open to the harmful activities of every unclean and evil spirit – as widely and vividly depicted in the Vastu Sastras. The desired mandala effect therefore had to be achieved by some other means. In Bhaktapur, a constellation of eight deities – *Matrikas*, i.e. mother goddesses – was laid around the city. Each goddess has a sanctuary outside, where she resides – usually in an unimpressive structure on a small hillock, and completely hidden in a thick grove of trees – and another house within the town where she is worshipped. This building is called *dyocchen* and is usually elaborately carved, and has a guilded façade. A city with such a superimposed 'iconographic' mandala will appear just as safe and ritually pure to the Hindu as a city with a 'structural' mandala, composed of streets and lanes. The theoretical foundation for this is a peculiar feature of Indian iconography.[16]

The Indian pantheon is nothing else than a representation of the universe: each of the gods represents one small aspect of the cosmos, and together they form the whole. This again is just another variation of the basic theme of Hinduism, the Unity of All Being. The specific aspect, for which one deity stands, or for which a family of deities stands, can also be indicated by a symbol, an element or a colour. And from a graphic arrangement of such attributes it is only a small step of further abstraction to the pure, geometric diagram of a linear mandala. In Bhaktapur, the *Matrikas* form only the outward, though the most important, ring of protective and benign deities. Other gods are arranged closer towards the centre, like the group of Ganeshes. On the plan, their location does not indicate any geometric lay-out, but when the mandala of Bhaktapur is shown on a Tangka or other religious paintings, it is always drawn that way. The mandala here belongs to the Taleju temple, and shows an old interpretation of the arrangement.[17] The deities demarcate concentric zones, and these are roughly identical with the hierarchy of the town's social topography. The central triangle, demarcated by the three Ganesh sanctuaries,

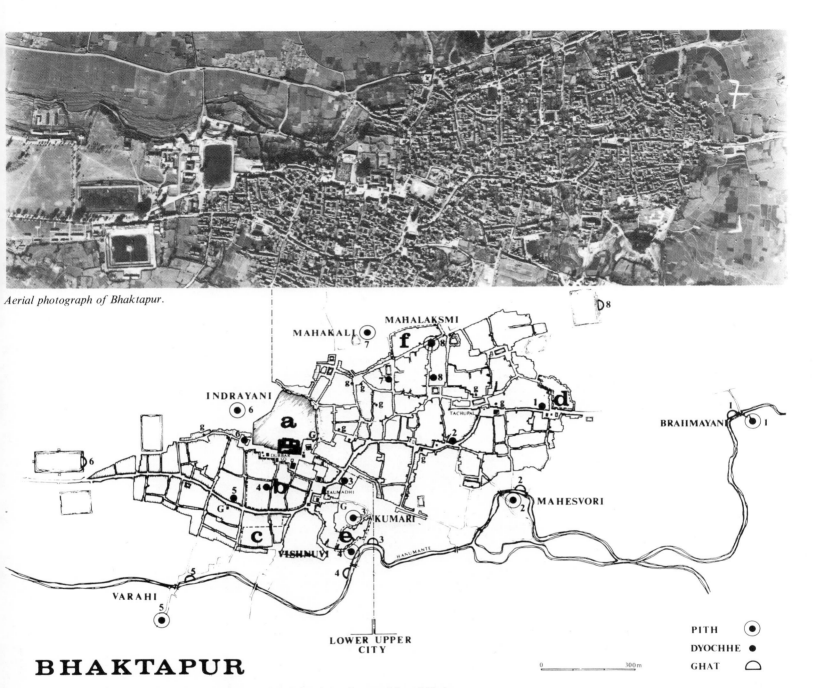

Aerial photograph of Bhaktapur.

MAHAKALI ⊙ 7

MAHALAKSMI

f

INDRAYANI ⊙ 6

a

BRAHMAYANI ⊙ 1

VARAHI

MAHESVORI

b

c

G

KUMARI

e

VISHNUVI

LOWER UPPER
CITY

PITH ⊙

DYOCHHE ●

GHAT ⌒

0   300m

BHAKTAPUR

The layout of Bhaktapur corresponds in all iconographical details to the mandala of Bhaktapur.
The old Malla palace (a) holds a sanctuary of the Supreme Sakti, the Talju temple. Talju and not the generally more important deities of Kali, Durga or
Parvati was chosen since she is the protectress of the Malla. To the south of the palace are the Brahmin quarters (b). They inhibit·an area roughly
identical with the central triangle of the mandala: the three Ganesh in the apices represent the Bhalaku, Mulaku and Chalaku – Ganesh temples, marked on the
plan. Hence it seems the hierarchic allocation of the castes within the urban system is a variation of the same idea of divine expansion, as expressed in the
mandala: it proceeds from the central position of the twice-born to the marginaal of the Sutras, who yet have to go through many cycles of metempsychosis.

encloses the residential quarters of the Brahmins. Significantly these are located in the planned extension of the 'Lower City', and next to the Malla palace, which indicates the strong affiliation of these two groups in the old system. Other groups are placed similarly, according to prestige and status in the Hindu hierarchy, and closeness to the central triangle is indicative of high rank. The 'outcastes' – butchers, scavengers and menials – are located outside the inner city, and some even outside the city proper, i.e. outside the protective ring of the Matrikas. Their quarters are easily discernible since their huts are smaller and – different from the substantial, tiled and half-timbered houses of the higher castes – mud-built and thatched.

Like everything else in the Hindu world, this spatial representation of a social hierarchy is religiously motivated. But here, more than in the esoteric planning ideals and the pious arrangements of sanctuaries, it is evident that the reason for the sacred layout is not only religious zeal. So far I have investigated how the layouts of Hindu towns are rooted in religious beliefs, how the street plans developed from the mandala ideas, and how, therefore, the city is

Shrine in Bhaktapur.

regarded as an object of devotion. Now let us see how all this fitted into the power structure of the classical Hindu states; what it meant not to the faithful, but to the ruler. Esoteric town planning where entire cities were laid out as large scale objects of devotion and religious meaning, flourished only in one power system: in oriental, despotic, managerial states. K. A. Wittfogel has termed this 'great, non-western system' the 'oriental despotism'.[18] The natural homes of this system are the arid countries of the Orient with heavy periodic rainfalls. If these rains are to be productively employed, large hydro-engineering works are necessary, which in turn require a strong, centralised administrative apparatus. This apparatus provides the institutional basis for the unlimited power of the central figure, the 'oriental despot'. In this system of 'oriental despotism', the privileged caste of officials and managers will be the ruling class, and not a feudal class of landowners.

Nepal, with its frequent, moderate rainfalls all the year round is not a natural home of such a system of total power, and here it did not evolve from earlier tribal societies as it did in neighbouring India. But from there it was imported by the Indian Malla dynasty and they, characteristically, started large-scale irrigation works[19] and the typical large-scale building of palace cities. They also imported the caste system from India, where it had a long history as the major social stabiliser and a safe foundation for the despotic power. The system is characterised by a fixed distribution of roles, honours, duties etc. typical for a specific rank in the social hierarchy. It is extremely stratified and need not be described here in detail.[20] However, the important features are that it consists of four main groups (*varna*), of which the lowest and largest is considered to be contaminating and only fit for doing manual work. Since the earliest days, the two upper groups have shared power in a unique way: the nobility holds all secular sway, but its position depends largely upon the sanction and the ritual assistance of the priest caste. This assistance was very costly, since it had to be compensated by large donations, usually gifts in kind, or prebendal foundations. The majority of all preserved Indian inscriptions deal with these prebendal foundations, which gives an idea of the regularity of this practice.[21]

The Sudras, the lowest *varna* in the social hierarchy, form the bulk of the population. Almost all of them are peasants, since in classical Hindu states agriculture is the cornerstone of the economic system. In the most recent census of Nepal, less than five per cent of the population is classified as urban, and except for the modern city of Biratnagar (near the Indian border) all of them live in the three Newar cities of the Kathmandu Valley.[22] As in all other oriental, despotic states, the cities of the Valley did not primarily function as market towns, with a wealthy merchant bourgeoisie but were artificially created by an act of the sovereign to cater for the needs of his court. The Hindu social system reserved the possibility to accumulate wealth exclusively to the Raja's palace, or to the Brahmin's temple. The despot, his priests and his privileged officials were the only consumers of sophisticated goods, of works of art and luxury merchandise. They alone could employ large numbers of skilled artisans. These craftsmen did not flock to the cities voluntarily – they were systematically settled there. The

Street scene in Kathmandu.

Kite flying on Bhairar Temple.

artisans and merchants were the only concentration of a large number of non-agricultural population in the country. The peasant masses lived in little, isolated villages scattered all over the Valley, in little half-independent 'beggar's democracies', which were too small to do any harm to the ruler, and which were left alone as long as they paid their taxes.[23] But the masses of the urban population constituted a real danger to the despot. In fact they were the only possible internal enemy for the ruling class. The three cities of the Kathmandu Valley – like any other Hindu township – were designed as devices to control this critical massing of people, as 'ruling machines'. The esoteric connotations of the mandala layout, the ritual bonds, the contamination laws, the immobility which the zoning imposed on every member of the community, and all other religious implications described above are part and parcel of the enormous, repressive construction that supported the total power of the Hindu rulers.

The urban culture of the Newar reflects the typically Hindu interpenetration of the sacred and the profane: a city structure rooted in an esoteric world of ideas and beliefs interferes with, and even shapes and schedules all important aspects of urban life. This helped to support the classic power system in many subtle ways. I shall relate a few examples from Bhaktapur, where the old culture is still most vital, though its political meaning has become insignificant – the Malla rulers have gone, and modern states have different ways.

It is possible that the most important aspect of Hindu town planning is that it kept the urban masses – in spite of spatial closeness – in small, often rival communities, which were as isolated as the scattered villages in the open country. A communal feeling of misery and oppression could never arise in these quarters, and nobody would think of fraternisation. Barricades have never been built in any Hindu city.[24] Though the political usefulness of such an atomisation of the urban masses is only too obvious, a Hindu would hardly accept this interpretation. He would have a purely religious version at hand, and within his own system of thoughts, this would, amazingly, make sense. He would point out that since the mandala plan of the city is a true representation of the cosmos and its hierarchy, where each caste has its specific place, they must have the corresponding place in the replica, if the whole is to be beneficial.

One important aspect of the marked zoning of Hindu towns is that it paralyses caste mobility. Social systems may change quickly, if conditions are favourable. They are mobile and dynamic. But urban systems, and especially the heavily built-up core areas of the Newar towns, are comparatively static. The impact which this can have on social development is very apparent in Bhaktapur. The Nepalese Panchayat constitution of 1962 abolished the status of untouchability, but the social topography of the city has not changed at all. The untouchable's place in the town is still marginal, their quarter despised and their hutments are still thatched.

The great events in the life of the Newar community are the festivals. These festivals are always connected with the city, and the whole urban scenery is used for their staging. But the streets and squares are not just a background for the processions, ritual dances and sacrifices – it is through these festivals that the towns-folk communally operate the great mandala. Primarily, these festivals are most spectacular events and real highlights of life in the Valley.[25] Every festival has a distinct atmosphere of its own. There are scenes of tranquil beauty in Divali, when thousands of butter lamps light the city for a brief hour like a huge Christmas tree. More common, however, are dramatic events, like Durga Puja, when many thousands surround the Matrikas, and offer their donations, or the Great Carriage Festival, when the Upper and Lower City compete in pulling a huge temple carriage along Bhaktapur's spine road.

These mass festivals and ritual processions are staged at enormous cost. Besides their religious meaning, their importance is mainly economic. The Newar consume communally whatever wealth they have been able to accumulate. It is hard to imagine for a Western mind, which values private well-being and individual wealth almost as the sole purpose in life, how happily poor and rich alike contribute. Usually, these contributions are not financial but in terms of services. The amount and nature is minutely stipulated for each caste or *guthi*.[26] This practice explains partly why the Newar cities are so rich in temples and public resting places (*patti*) and votive structures, for the construction and maintenance cost was raised from similar contributions. They had to be paid periodically all through a person's economically active life, and burdened all social strata. The wealthier classes, however, especially the rich merchants, are financially drained in addition by unscheduled sacrifices, private festivals and public banquets, which they are forced to give from time to time if they want to maintain their social status. I was present on such an occasion, when a wealthy merchant of Bhaktapur donated new ceremonial dresses to a group of temple dancers. This was taken as an occasion for an extra festival, which was celebrated with a large ritual procession, an enormous animal sacrifice in front of the merchant's house, and finally a communal banquet in the main street. All this was paid by the merchant, and he spent over £500 on that occasion, an amount which is considered big money by the Newar middle classes.

Thus, through these occasional public entertainments at the expense of the rich, individually accumulated wealth is communally consumed. The impact which these spending habits had on the power structure of the old system can hardly be over-estimated. In 16th century Europe the accumulation of enormous wealth in the hands of the merchant class meant the end of the old feudal system. In the Newar towns this drainage mechanism is still working, though nobody benefits from it any longer. Instead, it now has very negative consequences for the country's economic development, since apart from that in the hands of the state and a few ruling families, there is no capital available for productive investment.[27] Here again, the traditional meaning of the city and its physical structure is most important, since it is the traditional ritual manipulation of the 'great mandala' through mass festivals which requires enormous sums and hence perpetuates the classical situation of unproductive capital consumption.

The city was a device to secure the status quo through social atomisation and economic manipulation of the urban masses – never had this been possible without that nimbus of magic and spiritual fear which rests upon them. In Hindu towns the gods are alive!

Bhaktapur's eight *Matrikas* are alive in the Naua Durga: each year, during Durga Puja, masks of the mother goddesses are given to a family from the caste of temple dancers. From that day on, the group takes part in all important communal events, and also in private ceremonies of prominent personalities. They are no longer looked at as ordinary humans, but are believed to be endowed by Durga with great Tantric powers. They are entitled to take possession of all cattle which cross their way, and people treat them with great fear and veneration. In animal sacrifices they fulfil the key ceremonies. In particular they represent the goddess and drink the blood from the throat of the victim while it is still alive. After nine months the masks of the Matrikas are returned to the temple and destroyed. The goddesses are no longer resident in the city and cease to protect it. For three months, when the Matrikas have gone, the mandala is ineffective, and the people of Bhaktapur believe that this is the time when cholera is prevailing and evil spirits haunt the city. During Durga Puja, when new masks are handed over to a different group of dancers, the Matrikas return, safety is re-established, and the harvest can begin.

Another divine incarnation is also residing in the city, the 'Living Goddess'. The 'Living Goddess' is chosen from the goldsmith caste. She is a little girl, with remarkably grown-up behaviour and unusually stern features. She will be 'Living Goddess' as long as her body is not hurt and bleeds. When she has her first menstruation, or if she has any injuries before, a new 'Living Goddess' is chosen to be carried around the city's ceremonial paths in fantastic processions, with huge purple umbrellas, amidst a gay crowd who all want to touch her. The suggestive power of the little serious girl being carried around as the 'Living Goddess' is enormous, and leaves a deep impression even on the casual, rationalist foreign observer.

The gods are alive in the city in many forms, in people, in temples, in houses and even in the very stones of the pavement. It is believed that a goddess, Chowasa Ajima, who takes everything unclean and spoiled, dwells under the city and is manifest in the pavement. Black stone slabs with various ornamentations are placed in the brickwork of the street surface to mark her body, and people take their leftovers and their household waste as sacrifice to these stones.

It is hard for us inhabitants of an urban environment not rooted in an esoteric world of ideas to understand the importance which the Hindus attach to the supernatural of their cities. The townsfolk live in a strange mixture of veneration and fear, and this made the Hindu urban culture such a suitable foundation for the classical oriental system of total power.

Of all Western scholars who studied the Hindu civilisation and its interpenetration of the sacred and the profane, it was Nietzsche who was most deeply impressed. To him it was clear that this was not accidental but designed – a system of 'Sacred Lies', as he termed it,[28] and he was fascinated by its perfection and complexity. It is, indeed, amazing how well this system of 'sacred lies' worked, and how long it lasted. Urban unrest – so common all through European history – never occurred in India before 1857,[29] and is still an impossibility in the three cities of Nepal.

NOTES

[1] Such Indian cities are, e.g. Mathura, Jaipur, Tanjore, Madurai.
[2] SPATE, O. H. K., India, Pakistan & Ceylon, London, 1972, 2 vol., p. 465.
[3] LANDON, P., Nepal, London, 1928, 2 vol., Vol. I, p. 33: 'The conditions of this mountain region must have been somewhat similar to that of Scotland in the days of its warring clans. And unless the distant authorities of India or Tibet thought it worth their while to maintain the international highways which passed through Nepal, it seems unlikely that even as a means of communication with India did any importance attach to the collection of small, warring kingships that established themselves and were in turn destroyed in and around the little valley of Kathmandu.'
Landon's work is still the best comprehensive account available, though somewhat out of date. The more recent book by HAGEN, T., Nepal, Bern, 1971, 2nd ed., is comparatively superficial, and rather a nice pictorial introduction than a scientific investigation. Older works are still worth reading, especially Colonel Kirkpatrick's Account of the Kingdom of Nepal, Edinburgh, 1819, and H. A. Oldfield's, Sketches from Nipaul, London, 1880. A very good book is the Physical Development Plan for the Kathmandu Valley, prepared by C. Pruscha and K. Pandey, and published by H.M. Government of Nepal, Dept. of Housing and Physical Planning, Kathmandu, 1969 (On sale in Kathmandu). A good general introduction is H. Seemann's, Nepal, 1969, available through the German Embassy, Kathmandu.
[4] For the history of Nepal see WRIGHT, D., History of Nepal, Cambridge, 1877, PETECH, L., Mediaeval History of Nepal, Rome, 1958, LEVI, S., Le Nepal, Paris, 1905, and REGMI, M. C., Study in the Economic History of Nepal, Kathmandu, 1971. The big work, History of Nepal, Kathmandu, 1970, and the older additions of 1952 and 1960 by D. R. Regmi, are very unsystematic and almost useless.
[5] The regularity is now broken, since the earthquake of 1934 destroyed the SE portion of the Malla city, and it was rebuilt in a modernistic manner.
[6] The literature on Hindu cosmology is enormous, and unfortunately often of very low quality. The most comprehensive work is certainly the systematic comparative analysis by KIRFEL, W., Die Kosmographie der Inder, nach den Quellen dargestellt, Bonn, 1920. The relation between cosmology and architecture is brilliantly dealt with by KRAMRISCH, S., The Hindu Temple, University of Calcutta 1941, Not so brilliant is DUTT's, B., Town Planning in Ancient India, and SHUKLA's, D. N., Vastu Shastra, University of the Punjab, Chandigarh, no date, but unfortunately they are almost the only sources on the subject in English. A. Volwahsen has tried to make the best out of this, and his book on Hindu architecture (Weltkulturen und Baukunst – Indien, Hirmer Verlag München, 1968) is certainly worth reading.
[7] For Hindu philosophy and religion see: GLASENAPP, H. v., Die Religionen Indiens, Stuttgart, 1943, and Die Philosophie der Inder, Stuttgart, 1958. A good general presentation of Hindu culture is BASHAM, A., The Wonder that was India, available as a Penguin.
[8] See TUCCI, G., The Theory and Practise of the Mandala, London, 1961.
[9] ACHARYA, P. K., An Encyclopaedia of Hindu Architecture, 7 vol., Leiden, 1920.
[10] Dialogues of the Buddha.
[11] This stupa is now hardly visible, but a photograph taken in 1914 in Landon's Nepal, Vol. I, p. 209, shows the building in good condition.
[12] LANDON, 1928, Vol. I, p. 209.
[13] PETECH, 1958, p. 119.
[14] See LAUF's, D. I., essay on Mahayana Buddhist symbolism, in Tibetica 22, p. 13, published and edited by Einrichtungshaus Schoettle, Stuttgart, 1968.

[15] For all details on the architectural history of Bhaktapur I am obliged to Mr. Krishna Prashad Shresta, Director of the National Galleries in Bhaktapur.
[16] Compare BHATTACHARYYA, BENOYTOSH, The Indian Buddhist Iconography, Calcutta, 1958.
[17] The painting belongs to the High Priest of the Bhairav Temple, TAUMADHI, TOLE, Bhaktapur. It is undated, measures about 48 × 30 cm, and is said to be painted by a former priest of the temple. The background is grey-green, the landscape is painted in a naturalistic manner, and the deities show their characteristic colours.
[18] WITTFOGEL, KARL AUGUST, Oriental Despotism, Harvard, 1957 (German edition Die Orientalische Despotie, Köln, 1962).
To everyone who is familiar with Wittfogel's theories it is clear how much my approach in analyzing the Hindu planning principles is indebted to his ideas.
[19] Their outstanding achievement is the construction of the great Bhaktapur irrigation canal. See: 'The State Owned Bhaktapur Canal', an article in a Newari weekly, which is partly translated and quoted in REGMI, M. C., 1971.
[20] WEBER, MAX, Gesammelte Aufsätze zur Religionssoziologie – Die Wirtschaftsethik der Weltreligionen, Bd., 'Indien und China', Tübingen, 1922, 3 vol., English, The Hindu Social System, Glencoe/Ill., 1958.
[21] WEBER, 1958.
[22] Source: The Physical Development Plan for the Kathmandu Valley, Kathmandu, 1969, p. 78.
[23] For the various Malla and Gurkha taxation systems see: REGMI, M. C., 1971.
[24] This policy has produced some bizarre urban patterns in Northern India, most notably in Allahabad, where the different sectors (muhallas) of the city are enclosed and separated from each other by high crenellated walls, with only a few gates (which used to be closed for the night), thus forming individually fortified cities within the city.
[25] A brief description of the most important festivals can be found in Seemann's little brochure, Nepal, and a list is given in the Kathmandu Valley Plan.
[26] The Guthi is a typical Newar social institution, probably a leftover from previous tribal organisations. There are two forms of guthis: Sana Guthis, and Devali Guthis. Sana Guthis originated in the custom that a dead person must not be touched by his own relatives. Therefore members of the same caste form socio-religious institutions for the mutual assistance in case of death or illness. Eventually, the Sana Guthis developed into a very extensive organisation with many different branches for specific purposes. Most important for the urban development of the Newar towns became those guthis which were founded to build and maintain temples. They owned and administered a substantial part of urban land, and since these estates were tax free and could not be confiscated, they had a considerable control over the building activities.
Devali Guthis are of lesser importance. A Devali Guthi comprises all male descendants from the same male ancestor, and on ceremonial occasions the guthi plays a role far superior to that of the member's family. See: Seemann, 1969, p. 4.
[27] For this very important aspect see: KAPP, W., Hindu Culture and Economic Development, Bombay Asia Publishing House, 1961.
Also the 'Village Monographs' of the Census of India, (1961) are quite illuminating, since they give statistical details on the chronic indebtness of villagers (Published by the States of the Indian Union).
[28] Nietzsche sketched his views on India in a few notebooks, which were published in 1906 as part of his assets under the title, Wille zur Macht (Zeal for Power), GLASENAPP, H. v., has commented these papers in his Indienbild Deutscher Denker, Stuttgart, 1962.
[29] This is the year of the Great Mutiny in the Indian Army.

A great cloth painting owned by the monastery at Kharsha, unfurled by the lamas. Minutely embroidered in gold and coloured threads on an orange cloth, it depicts Buddha surrounded by his tutelary deities.

ARCHITECTURE AND SYMBOLISM IN TIBETAN MONASTERIES

Romi Khosla

Tibet is one of the most inaccessible countries in the world. The phenomenal advances in transport and communications had by-passed it until very recently. Both geographical and political factors have been responsible for this isolation. The Tibetan plateau is dissected by valleys which run north east to south west and their altitude varies between 11,000 to 16,000 ft. above sea level (3,500–5,000 m.). The population density is meagre, the land completely undeveloped and desolate and the distances are enormous. As recently as ten years ago, the journey from Lhasa to Peking took eight months of hard travel. The country is surrounded by massive mountain ranges several valleys deep to the north, south and west. The north-eastern part of Tibet is relatively flat, desolate and un-inhabited. In the north-west the Kun-Lun ranges naturally separate Sinkiang from Tibet and thus over three-sevenths of the country is a freezing desert where only occasional herds of wild animals are to be seen. The centres of Tibetan life lie in the south where the intricate river networks of the upper Yangtse (flowing to China), Salween (flowing to Burma), Mekong (flowing to Cambodia) and the Tsangpo (flowing to Bangla Desh) irrigate the land and allow most of the $2\frac{1}{2}$ million Tibetans to subsist at a basic level as farmers and herdsmen.

The nomadic life which is still characteristic of some of the Ladakhi tribesmen in the west is a remnant of their origins which go back several centuries to the Ch'iang tribes which roamed the pastures of Central Asia. Fragments of these tribes broke off from the main body at some stage and drifted south, eventually to settle into agricultural communities, while others of them continued in their nomadic way moving across the country from pasture to pasture with the changing weather. Thus, very early in the history of Tibet, long before Buddhism came in the seventh century, two basic ways of life had been established which relied on each other for their survival. This fundamental division in their occupation came about for climatic and physical reasons. Most of the year round the severe climate of the country restricted movement of the cattle and people. In the late spring and summer, the whole country burst into a spasm of activity which meant that the land had to be tilled, the cattle grazed on fresh grass and the sheep sheared before the winter set in again. The pastures for the cattle are generally located on the slopes of the passes above the tree line whereas the agricultural land lies along the valley floor irrigated by the waters of the melting snow. So while the peasants dug and ploughed the earth, the nomadic herdsmen packed their tents and moved their yaks and goats up the mountain slopes and passes which were green with the first grass of spring.

To this semi-nomadic land, there came a wholly alien force which transformed its life completely. This was Buddhism, which was introduced to Tibet in about 640 A.D. Prior to the introduction of Buddhism, the local inhabitants were bound up in a totemic religion called Bon. Buddhism succeeded very rapidly because it transformed the Bon totemic classification into a Buddhist one. Thus one complete system of classification was substituted for another with the aid of clever links which took elements in the Bon myths and introduced them into the Buddhist pantheon. Buddhist deities doubled up as Bon ones and in their Buddhist roles they established links with animals and other personified natural forces which had Bon origins. The people were, therefore, able to regard Buddhism as a natural extension of their awareness in the context of Bon.

At a basic level Tibetan society remained the same despite the advent of Buddhism. The nomadic and semi-tribal element continued in the same way whereas the agrarian community settled into a firm feudal pattern. The economic foundation thus continued to be agrarian. Buddhism completely altered the superstructure of Tibetan society by setting up a new pattern of institutions (the creation of a 'church'); organisation and hierarchies of authority (a new class of Lamas) were established.

The most powerful tool in changing the superstructure was the monastery. It was the physical manifestation of the symbolic link between Man and his origins, his reason for existence, his inevitable destiny. Buddhism taught that life on this planet is a perpetual cycle of suffering of enormous scale and power which results in a circle of birth-death and rebirth. Death is the termination of the tangible elements which compose man and it disintegrates the link between visible and invisible elements just as rebirth establishes this link. It is this cycle of disintegration and reassembly which must be broken to create a total harmony which finally prevents the cycle from reforming. The monk, *arhat,* must follow the way of Buddha and guide himself to harmony through the teachings of Buddha. The faithful following of this procedure leads to *Nirvana,* which literally means 'blowing out' or 'exploding'. The walls of the

monastery are covered in frescoes which symbolically illustrate this complex process of realising Nirvana through both the *Sutra* and *Tantra* schools.

Like all religions, Buddhism too propagated right from its introduction into Tibet the elitist nature of its message. It started off as a court religion in the reign of Songtsen Gampo who died in 650 A.D. and was the thirty-second king of the Yarlung dynasty. He married the princesses Wen-ch'eng, daughter of the Chinese Emperor T'ai-tsung of the T'ang dynasty and Bhrikuti, daughter of King Amcuvarman of Nepal. Both princesses came from Buddhist families and their arrival in the Tibetan court was followed by the building of the first Buddhist temple in Tibet to house the Chinese and Nepalese images of deities which the girls had brought. This temple came to be called the *Jo-Khang* – the most sacred temple in Tibet. It remained a temple and was never converted to a monastery although its present size and shape has considerably developed since its founding.

Royal patronage for the new religion continued in abundance during subsequent reigns. The only exception was King Lang Darma (836–842) known to Buddhists as a persecutor of their faith. This patronage in the form of wealth and land gifts enabled

The pastures for the cattle are generally located on the slopes of the passes above the tree line. Here the nomads pitch their tents and spend the summer collecting butter from the rich milk of the yak. These grasslands also feed the herd of horses, which monasteries own and use to transport their share of the grain from the surrounding villages. Pensi Paso in Ladakh.

Tibetan Buddhist culture is polarised between the elite of the educated lamas living up in the monastery and the peasants and herdsmen who live a precarious life in the village below. The lamas concentrate on religious and spiritual matters while their peasant brothers look after the crops grown sparsely in the hostile landscape. Kye monastery and village. Spiti.

Built away from the village, Rizong, a monastery of the later period in Ladakh, forms the centre of monastic life in the region. The hierarchical organisation of the complex can be seen with the temples with large windows on top, supported by the communal assembly areas with the cells of the individual lamas below and along the outer edges.

Maps of the Indian subcontinent. The area enclosed with a dotted line indicates the region of Ladakh.

73

Buddhism to spread to the far corners of Tibet. The origins of the complex hierarchy of *lamas* that ran the administration of government lie in these early beginnings, when it became imperative to create an elite which was initiated, disciplined and organised enough to spread the message throughout the land. The monastery developed as the headquarters of this campaign and gradually a social system emerged whereby potential monks were recruited in childhood. They were plucked away from their villages by force of social custom and introduced to a completely secluded life which concentrated on religion. The rest of the family meanwhile produced the surplus to support them in the pursuit of knowledge. Patronage of these monasteries gradually spread in Tibet to the rich landlords and aristocratic families who, by letting out their lands to tenants, were able to amass fortunes and share it with the monasteries. This close liaison between the lay and religious leaders of the land was important in establishing the effective government of Buddhist Tibet.

The size of the monasteries varied enormously and some of the biggest ones, like Tashilumpo, had over 5,000 lamas. There was, of course, only a minority of these lamas who actually practised and meditated upon gaining the higher truths. Others were concerned with the production of texts which involved printing, translating and copying. Still others were specialists in painting and carving while some kept stores, cooked and played music. About half of the lamas were scholars and hence familiar with the five branches of non-Tantric literature which were:

Logic
Doctrine of Universal Truth
Doctrine of the Middle Way
Treasury of philosophical notions
Monastic discipline.

The sacred spaces contained by the temple walls are inevitably the topmost buildings. Below them are built the communal eating spaces and them come the individual cells of the lamas.

Alchi monastery is the oldest temple complex in Ladakh dating back to the eleventh century A.D.

Ground floor plan of Alchi temples in Ladakh. The remains of the boundary wall indicate the line that separated the sacred within from the profane without.

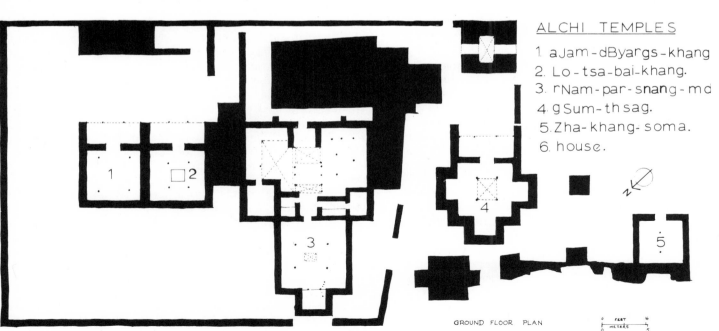

ALCHI TEMPLES

1. aJam-dByargs-khang
2. Lo-tsa-bai-khang.
3. rNam-par-snang-md
4. gSum-thsag.
5. Zha-khang-soma.
6. house.

GROUND FLOOR PLAN

0   FEET   16
0   METERS   5

The few lamas who solely pursued the path to Nirvana then went on to study Tantric disciplines and these took them beyond the fifteen years of study required to become a lama. These lamas who were able to confine themselves within the spiritual aspects of their existence, were able to elaborate further and deeper into the teachings of Buddha. Gradually, enormous volumes of texts dealing with the interpretations and experiences of these lamas were built up and the size of libraries in each monastery grew. With the proliferation of these experiences came the development of the various schools or sects in Tibet. Each monastery, and thus each lama and family, belonged to one of these sects. Of these sects, four are the most prominent and they are distinguished in essence by their varying emphasis on the different lines of teachers who gave relative importance to different deities. It becomes immediately obvious to the trained observer on entering a monastery or temple to which sect it belongs, not only because the lamas of each sect dress differently, but also by the selected deities represented in the frescoes and by the lay-out of the altar. The schools are as follows:

1. *Nyng-ma-pa* – the Tantric school of the Ancient Ones founded in the ninth century A.D.
2. *Kargyu-pa* – the school of 'Whispered Transmission' founded in the eleventh century A.D. This school is further divided into eight sub-schools, four of which are counted as great while the other four are considered as lesser ones.
3. *Sakya-pa* – founded in the eleventh century A.D.
4. *Gelug-pa* – the school of 'Virtuous Ones' founded in the fourteenth century A.D. Both the Dalai Lama and Panchen Lama belong to this sect which is popularly called the Yellow Hat sect. The present Dalai Lama *Tenzin Gyatsho* is the fourteenth reincarnated spiritual leader of this sect.

The monastery or *Gompa,* as it is known in Tibetan, is the centre of all religious teachings of Buddha. On entering it, one is overcome with the wealth of creativity that abounds on the walls and altars of the various temples. Each painting, each image, decoration and feature has a symbolic meaning which requires profound knowledge to interpret. When the first monasteries were built by the Buddhists in Bon-believing regions, a powerful effect upon the non-believers was inevitable. There was nothing typically Tibetan about the early monasteries. The first one, that of Samye, was built in 755 under the guidance of Indian *gurus.* It was laid out in a symmetrical form consisting of a central temple surrounded by four smaller temples and eight smaller ones beyond that. The whole complex was enclosed within a circular wall. Samye was said to be a copy of the Odantapuri Buddhist monastery in India. Its plan was based on a *mandala* as were those of subsequent monasteries and temples. The symbolic connection between the mandala and the temple is an important one to understand.

A mandala is a diagram of the universe. Visual representation of spiritual and natural forces forms a crucial part in Tibetan iconography and the mandala is at the centre of them. More than just a diagram, the mandala is a symbol of a consecrated region. The outer line which delineates the first layer of the mandala is the line which separates the terrestrial from the celestial. Nor is the

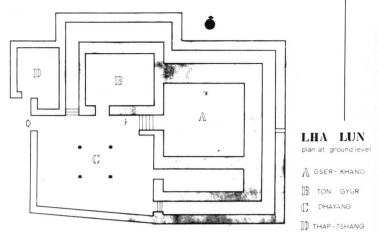

LHA LUN
plan at ground level

Ⱥ GSER - KHANG
ℬ TON GYUR
C DHAYANG
ⅅ THAP - TSHANG

Before the disciple can enter within the sanctity of the altar room (gSer-Khang) he is required to circumambulate in a clockwise direction around the perimeter of the temple. Here in Lha-Lun, Spiti, a special passage has been constructed for the purpose.

mandala a static diagram because it also represents the cosmos in constant motion pivoted around the central point known as *meru.*

The initiated *arhat* seeking to realize the mandala is compelled to concentrate upon it and enter within it so as to eventually merge completely with the central deity within. The Tibetan temple within the compound of the monastery is also a mandala. Just as the disciple mentally enters the spiritual realm of the diagram through concentrated meditation, he too, by physically entering the temple, arrives within a spiritual realm.

The plan of a typical temple has physical features each of which corresponds to some spiritual discipline. Before the disciple can enter within the sanctity of the altar room, he is required to circumambulate in a clockwise direction around the perimeter of the temple. This process of circumambulation goes back to the earliest Buddhist times when the first *stupas* were built to house the remains of Gautama Buddha. The number of rounds can be 1, 3 or 108 depending upon the intensity of belief and the urgency of the need to enter within. The mandala too has a circle around it which has openings on four sides each leading to the inner sanctum.

Having performed the circumambulation, the disciple enters a porch which is the transitory realm between the profane and sacred realms. Here he is confronted with the first of the many frescoes of the temple. Inevitably each set of frescoes has symbolic meaning. The porch always has the images of the four guardians. The Tibetans call them *rgyal-cen-bshi* and they represent the guardians of the four cardinal points who dwell on Mount Sumeru at the gates of Paradise. Within the complex hierarchies of Buddhist deities, these guardians inhabit the lowest compartment of the celestial world and they guard the sacred realm from the wicked elements and spirits. Each of these guardians is a king and, besides riding an immortal elephant, has an army of demons commanded by eight generals. Their images were originally placed by the Buddhists on the four sides of the *stupas* and their function was to guard the relics of Buddha. From this origin, they have developed a sophisticated role which they perform in the Tibetan temple. They

The porch is the transitional space between the outside and the inner temple, and always displays four guardian deities. These flank the doorway on either side and are each identified by their posture and dress. Symbolism and architecture are inseparably merged. The columns are capped with lotuses while the joists are decorated with auspicious symbols. Hemis monastery, Ladakh.

are grouped in pairs and placed on either side of the main door leading within.

Alongside the guardian deities one inevitably finds the Wheel of Life painted on one wall. This reminds every visitor of the unending cycle of death and rebirth. The Wheel of Life, known in Tibetan as *srid-pahi-kor-lo*, is one of the commonest and yet most profound symbols of Buddha's teachings. In it the six realms of the 'samsaric' world are illustrated showing how the various forms of existence on this earth are conditioned by illusion and the ego. Each segment illustrates how the ego gathers only those forms and forces around it from which egotistical satisfaction is fulfilled. In the centre of the circle, three animals (a red cock, a green snake and a black hog) chase each other showing how three root causes detract the ego from enlightenment. These are as follows:

Red cock — passionate desire and physical attachment.
Green snake – hatred, enmity and aversion which are the poisons of existence.

Black hog — darkness of ignorance and the delusion of ego which provides a motive force for the perpetual circle of birth and death.

The second circle illustrates the six realms of existence into which most beings can be classified. These are as follows; starting from the top and moving clockwise:

1. The realm of the gods. This is the realm where a carefree life is led and the pursuit of pleasure and aesthetics provides the motivating force for delusion.
2. The realm of Titans. Here the language of force and strife makes its inhabitants hungry for power and their delusion comes from believing that power is a real force.
3. The realm of Pretas where the beings of unfulfilled desire and perpetual craving are being constantly frustrated in their search for true satisfaction.
4. The realm of hell which is full of beings suffering from infernal pains which result from their egotistical deeds.

Of the four guardian deities. Kuvera *(rNam-Thos, Sras) is the most popular as he is also the guardian and giver of endless wealth. He is identified by his yellow colour and the mongoose vomiting pearls in his left hand.*

5. The animal realm is dominated by blind passions and uncontrollable instinctive desires. Here even the faculty of speech is missing, so liberation is doubly removed.
6. The realm of man is the sixth realm. He is conscious of the need to seek liberation but needs guidance from the teachings of Buddha.

Liberation from all these realms can be effected if the individual seeks the teachings of Buddha and follows them. The image of the deity Avalokitesvara is painted in each realm as he descends into the wheel of life and liberates the minds from their inescapable traps.

The painting of images on the walls of the temple, both on the porch and within the inner sanctum, is highly symbolic. Tibetan architecture is inextricably bound up with the illustrations and use of colour on its elements. Thus, to discuss the images and their symbolism is synonymous with discussing the architecture. The single most important aspect of Tibetan architecture is the presence of the painted image inside the temple. The evocation of the mystical atmosphere of a Tibetan painting is not the creation of the painter's mind. The painting does not seek to represent the fancy of the painter or his own interpretation of events and experiences. It is a record of visions, mystical experiences and teachings which are laid down in texts or personally interpreted by lamas. All the paintings, and indeed all the contents of the Tibetan temple, are concerned with the triple aspect of our existence – death, life and after life. They represent, symbolically and visually, the spiritual planes of our existence, and in order to do this accurately, it is necessary for painters to comply to rigid rules of geometry and technique.

The general name for a Tibetan painting (frescos and the cloth paintings are known as *t'ankas*) is *Zin K'ams* which literally means 'realm' and implies the partaking of the realm of Buddha. The realm of the painting and that of the temple is inextricably mixed up and to discuss one is to discuss the other. The functional name of the painted image is *Mtongrol* which means 'liberation through sight', implying that the person viewing the painting and understanding it (or for that matter entering the temple) will be liberated through his vision of the spectacle. Hence the figures represented on the paintings are not bodies or even representation of bodies, but rather 'essences' which have taken a bodily form defined by the line that surrounds them and a terrestrial home defined by the walls that enclose them. The line of the painting and the wall of the temple cuts into the void and extracts from it the 'essence' which is the visible form. The Tibetan name for the act of painting is *vi mar bkod pa,* which literally means 'to dispose into lines' by the artist who, through meditation, has reached the plane of experience at which the painting is conceived. Thus the two fundamental principles which compose the painting are evocation and line and those that compose the temple are evocation and wall.

Tibetan temple architecture and all its elements are completely subservient to the religious and spiritual aspects of Buddhism and they cannot be viewed in isolation. The role that an image of a deity plays in the interpretation of Buddha's teaching is essential to understand as it is totally identical to the function of the temple. The arrangement of figures, their identification and their relevant symbolism which gives the paintings on the walls their deeper meaning, are full of complexities.

In plan both the temple and the painting (whether it is a linen one or a fresco) follow the Tantric mandala where a central deity (on the altar) dominates by its size and importance. Inevitably, the central figure in a painting or on the altar sits on a lotus throne which is, in essence, a symbol at two levels. At the exoteric or uninitiated level, the flower represents the creation or the physical blooming of beauty. At the esoteric or initiated level, the lotus symbolises the blossoming of full 'realisation' in the centre of the heart. It is the complete experience of the 'universal truth'. As it is pictorially represented, the lotus displays the first row of petals opening outwards while the other rows are closed inwards and

The Tibetan name for the act of painting is vi-mar-bkod-pa, *which literally means 'to dispose into lines'. The line of the painting or fresco cuts into the void and extracts from it the 'essence' which is the visible form. The grid lines give the sacred proportion to the drawing and are laid down in the text.*

linked under the throne, holding in their centre the secrets of full initiation. The open first row, folding outwards revealing its inner colour, symbolises the point of arrival of the mind seeking initiation. It is a glimpse of what full initiation involves. The colour of the lotus throne is either red or white. Red stresses the solar symbolism and the active nature of the deity seated on it; and generally accompanies the *Dharmapalas* or defenders of the faith. A white lotus seat emphasises the lunar aspect of the deity, its passive, meditative and preaching attitude.

The Dharmapalas known in Tibetan as *Chos-skyan* are eight in number and act as the guardians of Buddhism. They can easily be identified by their terrible aspect, in menacing attitudes surrounded by flames which consume the enemies of the faith. Their location both on a painting and on the temple walls has symbolic meaning. The whole of the region represented within the temple or painting is sacred and has to be guarded closely so that these eight guardians perform a more intense vigilance than the four guardian deities of the porch. Very often the image of a Dharmapala is placed above the door of the central temple and its function is to fight away the ignorance which may try to enter into the sacred realm.

The temple room itself, known commonly as *Lha-Khang* is the real dwelling place of the various deities. Symbolically it is not on this earth and this is expressed all around the painted walls by a rainbow band which runs three feet above the ground, below which images are not painted. The chapel itself can be of various sizes depending on the size of the monastery and its age and importance.

If the plan is rectangular, then the altar is placed in the centre of the shorter wall, though removed from it, very often to allow a passage behind for circumambulation. The room inevitably has two or more rows of columns with the central portion having the wider span, unless the room is small and square. In arranging the furniture and layout of seating, the pattern seldom corresponds to the symmetry of a mandala. The main chapel room known as a *Du-khang* is essentially used for performing religious ceremonies. The arrangement is thus more functional than symbolic, although no aspect of the temple is completely devoid of symbolism. Monks sit in two or more rows, facing each other across a central nave. They have low seats and small tables in front of them on which are placed the religious objects and the tea cups. The head lama, or leader conducting the particular service sits on the right of the image on a raised divan. He either faces the central door or else sits alongside the monks, depending upon his superiority and local custom. Once the lamas are gathered in the Du-khang, they are not to be disturbed as they are communicating with the deities that dwell within the chapel.

Most monasteries have a number of chapel rooms beside the Du-khang. These rooms are set aside for special deities and unusual functions. The *Mgoyen-khang* is a sacred room that contains all the images of the Dharmapalas in their most frightening and awe-inspiring forms. The disciple does not normally enter this room as it is considered highly inauspicious. Before entering for special purposes (such as lighting the lamps) he knocks three times so that the deities who dwell inside can be warned of an alien presence. To surprise them with an unannounced entrance would be to invite their fury upon oneself. Another sacred room is the *Mani Lha-khang* where an enormous prayer wheel is housed and disciples go in and give it a turn and help spread the message of Buddha, which is printed inside the wheel. The *Gzim-chung* is the personal room of the incarnate lama and it has its own private altar and a collection of paintings and books. It is the private

The spiritual head of the religious community is often an incarnate who is recruited in childhood as a sacred born. He is brought in to the seclusion of the monastery and carefully nurtured to spiritual maturity. Kye monastery, Spiti.

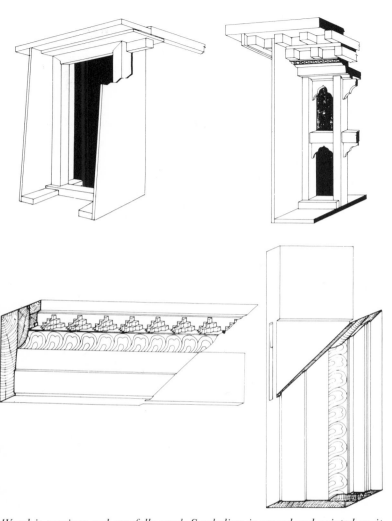

The entrance porch to the monastery is seen from the courtyard where the religious dances are held. Above the porch is the gzimchung *where the incarnate lama has his own private altar and collection of books. He sits and supervises the dance at the annual festivals. Likir monastery, Ladakh.*

Wood is precious and carefully used. Symbolism is carved and painted on it wherever it forms the frame of a window or door (below). The opening petals of the lotus leaves can be seen in the lower drawing which open out to receive the initiated into the inner sanctum of the temple beyond.

meditation chamber of the most senior lama and visitors are generally not permitted within.

It is a characteristic of all Tibetan monasteries that they form a loosely-knit collection of rooms performing various functions. These individual temple rooms are tucked away in a random manner which is dictated more by the topography than for any symbolic reason. Their inter-relationship seldom has any meaning because each sacred room is the separate dwelling place of some deity. After the room is built, elaborate ceremonies are conducted to invite the deity to inhabit its own dwelling place. The room can only have a religious function if the deity is considered to be present. If the deity chooses to depart from its dwelling place then the senior lama is compelled to rebuild the temple. He may get to

know of the deity's departure by a number of signs and omens which are usually reflected in the structural cracks that appear in the mud construction. Once it is felt that the deity has left, the temple is demolished and re-erected on the same site.

This process of demolition and re-erection had been going on for decades in Tibet. Nothing is considered permanent in the unending cycle of life and death and the temples too undergo the cyclical change. The destruction of frescoes to create new ones is not considered to be a profane action. Indeed, frescoes which are no longer inhabited by the deity automatically become worthless and must make room for a new dwelling place. Thus, the entire architecture of the temple is wholly subservient to the presence of the deity in the fresco image on the wall. The flight of the deity leads

Once the head lama feels that the deity has left, then the temple is demolished and re-erected on the same site. This process of demolition and re-erection had been going on for decades in Tibet. Nothing is considered permanent in the unending cycle of life and death, and the temples too undergo the cyclical change, Lamayuru Monastery, Ladagh.

Often built in impossible locations, the Tibetan monastery commands a vast landscape around it. Its dominant position symbolised its religious and political supremity. Shashur monastery, Ladakh.

A Ladakh lama blows a traditional long horn in the porch of a temple. Guardian spirits are painted beside the entrance.

to the end of the old architecture and the creation of a totally new architecture. Inevitably, the rebuilding process involves changes in the shape and content of the room, depending upon the type of personal guidance given by the head lama. Tibetan painting and architecture has developed through time due to this process of the 'life' and 'death' of the temple room.

Tibetan architecture and its symbolism belong to a deeply religious age. To understand both one has to seep oneself into the highly complex meanings that the Tibetans give to life. It was an intensely active religion until very recently and the material from it is still too fresh to have been studied objectively by scholars. In the years that come, we may be able to study their culture more comprehensively and interpret their beliefs in a scientific language that can be understood in the industrial age of today.

HOUSE DECORATION AMONG SOUTH ASIAN PEOPLES

Tore Hakansson

Throughout man's known history he has decorated his body with signs and symbols in the form of ornaments, tattooing, costumes and dresses. In particular the orifices had to have magic protection from demons and evil spirits.

This need for magic protection was also extended to man's dwellings and homes, and especially to their entrances. In Burma, Thailand and China the architectural style demands that the roofs of all sacred and important buildings are curved at the corners – because there is a belief that demons and evil spirits can only fly in straight lines.

Protective symbols, signs and figures are used outside holy places in all cultures to ward off demons. As examples we need only mention the gargoyles of Notre Dame in Paris, the Dvarapalas, protective deities outside the entrances to Buddhist temples, lions and eagles – power symbols – on royal palaces and the Gorgon's head over entrances to official buildings. Our common horseshoes nailed with open end up to catch the devil are still in use in many homes. The designs on old iron stoves served not only as decoration or trademarks, but were also reminders of the importance of guarding the fire. The traditional Hindu house is guarded by *alponas*, the geometrical designs made from white and coloured riceflour, which the housewife applies in front of the doorstep to the main entrance as well as in the shrineroom. Another type of geometrical design is used in the Voodoo rites in Haiti. These *vèvèrs* made from cornflour are placed around the sacred centrepole in the house where the ceremonies are taking place. The gods descend on this pole and take possession of their devotees.

For the purpose of this article, sign refers to a signal or communication with a single meaning, understood by all concerned. A symbol can have several meanings, it can have exoteric and esoteric meanings, and the meaning can be concealed or forgotten or vary from one group to another.

A symbol can also have an emotional connotation: a dried flower can be invested with an emotional value which is known and felt only by its owner. National flags have a strong emotional appeal to the people concerned with these symbols.

In this chapter we will describe some signs and symbols found in community houses, dormitories or youth houses among certain tribes in South and South-east Asia and especially those among the Gonds and Saoras in Central India. Actually, such institutions as these can be found in all parts of the world and they are sometimes only men's or bachelors' houses. They should be viewed as expressions of public life which unite the different groups in a community to common action for common interests. They are educational institutions where the young are instructed in the social and religious life of the tribe, the avoidance of evil spirits, the promotion of fertility – including good harvests, hunting and fishing, and also children, family life and sexual happiness.

A few examples of communal dormitories in different parts of the world might be cited.

The Kiwai Papuaus of British New Guinea, according to G. Landtman, have a youth house called *darimu,* which is used as a dormitory and also for initiation ceremonies and instruction in agriculture. A wood carving of a naked woman which is believed to ensure a good supply of sago is shown to the initiates. The building is supposed to contain magical heat and is dominated by great carved posts representing erotic figures with blood smeared upon them. A darimu building has magical powers even at a distance.

Raymond Firth describes the *ravi* in New Guinea as a huge thatched house, fifty yards or so in length, built on piles and having as its most characteristic feature a high, overhanging open gable which yawns like the gaping mouth of some primaeval crocodile. The raising of the heavy main posts which bear the weight of the gable demands concentration of effort, organisation of labour and engineering skill, and the owners of the house take pride in their size. A new post is decorated with flowers and palm branches before it is set up.

Going to India we find first the dormitories in the North-east frontiers, in Nagaland. C. von Furer-Haimendorf writes, 'There can be no doubt that the men's house system is a very ancient institution. The role which the *morung* plays in the villages of the Konyaks shows how deeply it is rooted in their social organisation . . . it appears that the morung belongs together with the log-drum to the oldest cultural stratum of the Naga Hills.' The morungs serve as dormitories – separate for boys and girls, although they may visit each other in the night after previous appointments. They are not only used for sexual initiation preparatory to marriage but also as training centres for warriors and storage houses for skulls of enemies, and for drums and weapons. The posts and

Alpona patterns in chalk (or flour) drawn by the womenfolk on the threshold of their front door or gate to compound. Erode Tamil Nadu State, South India.

beams are fantastically carved. The Konyak Naga's morung is specially fine – a great house on carved pillars with sexual motifs and containing a large xylophone. The sexual motifs do not refer to sexual activities only, but also to fertility and agricultural work, as well as serving as stimuli to male aggressiveness and fighting.

Further east in Indo-China, in the mountains east of the Mekong river live the Lamet. Their community houses, *cong ying,* are built in every village. According to Izikowitz there are two village gates, hung with magical instruments which prevent evil spirits from entering the village. In the centre of the village lies the community house cong ying. It is a gathering place for the men of the village, and some men cook their food in the *cong,* as the cooking hearth in their dwellings are taboo for them. The cong is also a work centre

for all kinds of implements, baskets, musical instruments, arrows and cross bows, also objects used in religious ceremonies. The cong is also a hunting centre where the hunter takes his prey and has it butchered. Izikowitz writes that 'the skull of prey from the hunt is cleaned thoroughly and decorated with a number of magical ornaments and is then placed under the roof of the cong together with the bamboo spear that killed the animal. This head is a sacrifice to the spirit of the forest, which gives the Lamet good luck in hunting. At the sacrifice one prays also to the forest spirit, who is then supposed to come and live in the skull.'

The roof of the cong is covered with leaves of cane palm and supported by heavy poles. The walls are of splintered bamboo, loosely braided. 'There is not a single nail to be found in the whole

Youth dormitory, with steeply pitched 'boat-shaped' roof. After a photograph by Parkinson.

Carvings inside a morung, N.E. India. After a photograph by C. Von Fürer-Haimendorf.

Morung in a semi-Naga village, North-East India

Member of a semi-Naga morung.

The *ghotul* is the village dormitory of the Muria Gonds, who live in a mountain and jungle area on the borders of the States of Madya Pradesh, Orissa and Madras. The great Indrawati river and its tributaries flow through the hill and forest land and in the rainy season make the land of the Murias impenetrable. They live in such a difficult and mountainous area that they have been saved from the influences of 'civilisation' and thus to some extent have retained their ancient institutions, dances and customs.

The ghotul is the centre of the social, religious and artistic life of the Murias. W. Elwin writes that it is 'an institution, tracing its origin to Lingo Pen, a famous cult hero of the Gond, of which all the unmarried boys and girls of the tribe must be members. This membership is carefully organised; after a period of testing, boys and girls are initiated and given a special title which carries with it a graded rank and social duties. Leaders are appointed to organise and discipline the society. Boy members are known as *chelik* and girl members as *motiari*. The relations between chelik and motiari are governed by the type of ghotul to which they belong. Two distinct types of organisation are recognised. In the older, classical type of ghotul boys and girls pair off in a more or less permanent relationship which lasts till marriage. They are often 'married' and cohabit in the dormitory for several years. In the more modern form of ghotul such exclusive associations are forbidden and partners must constantly be changed.'

The religion of the Murias is greatly influenced by Hinduism,

Carving on ghotul *pillar, Muria Gond.*

Modelling on a clay wall in a Muria ghotul, *the original only 6″ high.*

house, everything is fastened with strips of bamboo. Each opening has a double door of roughly hewn planks of dark, hard wood. A high relief in the form of a buffalo head decorates the inside of the door. The ornament is divided in two, half on each half-door. A crosspiece is thrust in the nose of the sculptured head to lock the doors.' Buffalo horns and the ancestral spirits have some connection with each other, since it is the skull of a buffalo that is hung on the altar of the ancestors.

In the plan of the house can be seen a smithy and a forge with a sacrifice pole. On the other side hangs the big village drum, which is moved to the village even before the houses are built. During the sacrifices, which are made once before rice sowing begins and once when the rice has reached a certain height, the big village drum is beat upon incessantly to ward off evil spirits. The drum is also used at ceremonies for the forest spirit – for good hunting and as a means of signalling. It is a double-headed drum, made of a hollowed-out tree trunk, about 1–2 metres long. On its side is sculptured an iguana lizard in high relief probably related to the most important ancestral spirits. Inside the cong are also huge sacrifice poles and at the base of these are stones driven into the earth smeared with blood of a pig sacrificed to the village spirit, who was supposed to live in the earth under the cong. The religious cults and symbols in the cong may be seen as a kind of 'social activator' (Izikowitz) 'which stimulate the manifestations of unity and activity in the whole community'.

but it has its own great pantheon of gods: first and foremost Lingo Pen, the founder and protector of the *ghotul*. Then there are the clan gods, the Earth mother, the marriage god and local gods. The village mother is, in spite of the name, an evil spirit causing illness and accidents – a sort of witch. For all the various gods there are temples in the villages; some mud houses, some open sheds with courtyards and pillars before the entrance. Inside they are decorated with symbolic carvings and objects relating to the gods: chains, spears, axes, shields and brass images. Generally there is a central pillar of wood at the foot of which there is a flat stone, a seat for the god, and on the pillars may be carved phallic symbols, or a vagina with clitoris and labia or representations of the sun or the moon. In the temple may also be found the decorated dancing sticks used in ceremonial dances and the hunting horn used to summon the people to festivals.

The marriage ceremony is one such festival with both sorrow and

View of Markabera ghotul, *with members dancing in the main ground.*

The Markabera ghotul *showing central round-house in the dancing ground.*

Motiari, *girl member with drums, in Markabera ghotul.*

y – sorrow for the parting from the ghotul – 'the paradise of the unmarried' – and from lovers and friends of youth, joy for the new atus, home, parenthood etc. A small shelter is built as a marriage booth on nine poles placed in a square with a centrepole on which a representation of the vagina is often carved. Then the married airs are placed in a ceremonial bed while friends and relatives hout 'penis' and 'vagina' and sing and joke about sexual functions. he booth is further decorated with strings of green mango leaves, oconuts, sheaves of grain and flowers, symbols of the fruit of the arth – for the woman is earth and the man is the gardener who ust plough and sow.

The position of the ghotul building is always outside the main illage, and generally a place of natural beauty is chosen. The hotul of Markabera, where I was staying in the spring of 1952, is tuated near a large forest full of silk cotton trees with large red blossoms, and the view over the mountains and valleys on the other side is breathtaking. The drawing shows the plan of the ghotul which at that time housed about forty boys and girls. It has four buildings of which three are for sleeping while the open round house is used for plays and games, making of ornaments and carvings. The courtyard is used for dancing and games. The ghotul is fenced in by upright poles to keep out the animals, and within the fence the ground is sacred. It enjoys the protection of the gods and no evil can enter or take place, neither can guilt and shame enter into the minds of the youths who live there, nor can unwanted pregnancies occur within the fenced compound. The ghotul is built by the cheliks themselves but with help and advice from older men. 'The motiari bring grass for the roof, stones and earth for the floor and when the walls are ready plaster them with mud.'

The large outer verandahs are delightful for sleeping in the hot

Group of Motiari, *girls of the ghotul.*

The peacock is a fertility symbol among the Konds; this carving is in a Kond ghotul.

Another ghotul *carving, with sexual attributes emphasised.*

nights, and the inner rooms are comfortable in the rains. The wooden pillars which support the roof, and the doors, when there are any, are the main places for decorative and symbolic carvings. There is no furniture in the simple dwellings; mats woven of straw are rolled out on the ground for sleeping. Headrests of wood are often carved with suggestive figures of boys and girls, breasts and other sex symbols. They are generally 3–4 feet long and big enough for a couple to rest their heads on.

The clan system among the Murias is very confused and totem-animals may vary from one village to another. There are ghotul pillars decorated with tortoises, or hooded snakes, or birds, or elephants. One pillar can have carvings of a boy with a large penis, a bow and arrow, and a snake. Elwin writes: 'Phallic symbols are

Drums are a standard interior decoration of the ghotul, and are suspended from the roof of the building. Chelik, a Muria boy member of Markabera ghotul plays one of the drums.

ery common. In nearly every ghotul there is somewhere a represen-
ation of the vagina, often about two feet from the ground on the
entral pillars. In the small Kobur ghotul there is one slender
illar covered with carvings of the vagina, as always showing the
litoris, but here there was a double clitoris and a clitoris upside
own. Often a chelik may be seen with an enormous penis, a
otiari in his arms. The boys say that these carvings are very useful
s an approach to girls. It may be that the vagina in the central
illar is a relic of a custom now forgotten of initiating smaller boys
y pressing them against it.'

From Markabera ghotul Elwin quotes one of the boys about sex
ducation: 'A little boy doesn't need to be taught anything. Does a
oung crab have to be taught to dig earth? But the older boys
enerally tell them how to do it. When the little boys tell them their
ecrets and how they tried but failed, the older chalik show them
he best way. The older girls do the same for the little girls. Some
mes older girls who get fond of little boys teach them themselves.
ut we learn everything by being in the *ghotul*. How can the little

boys check themselves? Who doesn't feel a desire to eat when he
sees people enjoying a feast in his presence?'

At festivals branches of the silk-cotton tree *Bombax mala-
baricum,* called *simul* or *semur* by the Murias, are placed by the
ghotul buildings or carried in processions. This majestic tree
carries huge red flowers in the spring, before the leaves have
opened. The forests round the ghotuls look as if on fire and it is no
wonder that this tree has given name to the first ghotul, Semurgaon,
according to the legend founded by the god Lingo Pen himself.
The semur branches are placed on little platforms of mud, which
are covered with white clay and decorated with figures of boys.
There are many legends about the semur tree. According to ghotul
rules no girl has complete sexual relations before the menarche,
before 'the red blossom has opened', a metaphoric reference to the
semur blossoms. The tree has got large thorns or spikes on its
trunk, and there is a tale about its origin, which shows how the
symbolism of the universal Vagina Dentata legend also appears in
the ghotul:

91

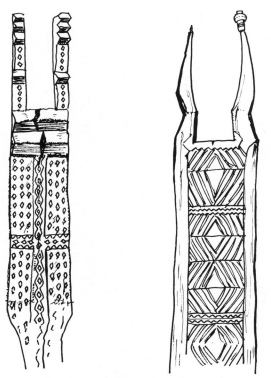

A Kond pillar, a replica of a pillar used for human sacrifice. Five foot high it has a fork in which the head of the victim is pulled back.

Another Kond sacrificial pillar.

In the old days there were teeth at the back of the vagina. The penis was also very long, but the teeth cut it when it went in until it got its present length. But one man got angry at this and took a stick of wood, drove it in the vagina and broke off the teeth which then got stuck in the wood. He threw away the stick and it grew up and became the first semur tree with thorns.

In central India there are many tribes who have managed to retain a little of their past heritage of symbolism in art and dance. But all these poor jungle tribes are under great pressure from powerful Hindu neighbours, missionaries and social workers all of whom, in different ways, try to force their own ways of life on these people. It is, therefore, only a question of time, and these traditions will disappear altogether.

We shall first turn to the Saoras, a hill tribe living south of the Gond area. Reference has already been made to the custom of making designs on walls and floors of houses and shrines all over the world – the *alpona* of India, *vèvèrs* of Haiti and so on. The motives for most symbolic decorations are of common concern to all men: birth and death, fertility and love, sickness and accidents. The ghotul was a closely knit, cooperative community. The Saoras and other neighbouring tribes have not got this institution, but they use much the same symbols. Thus the Konds carve a peacock as a fertility symbol on doors, and it is also a charm against snake bites. Actual peacock feathers are used by the *shaman* as a fan

when he goes into trance. The peacock is also associated with the cult of the dead and wooden peacocks are often placed on top of shrines for funeraries. The elephant is another important symbol, not only for strength but also for luck and riches. The white elephant, associated with the birth of Buddha, and the elephant god Ganesh in Hinduism testify to its importance in religion. Carvings and drawings of elephants are very frequent in Saora houses. Animals are generally shown in full figure, otherwise a common method of symbolisation is to show a thing by its parts: a woman can be suggested by breasts or vulva. Carved fishbones, like an X-ray photograph, suggest a fish and stand for fertility. They can be found on door panels – each panel having a different motif, either incised or carved out in low relief. Often the designs appear to be purely geometrical but on closer view one finds that the tribal artist indicates anatomical details of men or animals. The Swedish ethnologist Herman Stolpe stated as early as 1890 that geometric form could be derived from progressive modification of natural objects. Woodwork is made by men, but wall decorations in mud or clay are made by women, even while the house is being constructed – with the exception of the Saoras among whom the wall-paintings are made by men.

There remains a last remnant of the ceremonies connected with the Meriah, the human sacrifice, as practised by a neighbouring tribe, the Konds, in the past; surviving Konds can be found in Central India and Orissa. Replicas of the pillars to which the victim was bound are still made in traditional Kond houses, dedicated to the house gods and placed in the middle of the building supporting the grain bins above the kitchen. At the foot is a small earthen altar with bones of buffaloes – nowadays used as substitutes for human beings. The pillars are 5–6 ft. high and forked; when the victim was tied to the pole his head was pulled right back through the fork. In some places a wooden clapper is attached to the pillar; when a priest pulls the cord to sound the clapper during a sacrifice it signals that the god possesses him. Some of these pillars are fairly old. Whenever the Konds move to a new village they take their pillars with them and erect them in their new homes. When a son marries he gets a new pillar made and maintains it all his life. The carvings are of different patterns, mostly geometrical 'so long as it pleases the god'. Only good carvers are engaged for the work and the design is said to be revealed in a dream by the Earth mother, to whom the human sacrifice was dedicated in the past.

It has already been mentioned how Hindu mythology has more and more penetrated into the tribal beliefs and ceremonies mixed with them. Gonds in certain districts celebrate Krishna's birth by making wall paintings, offering gifts before them and sitting down together for a feast. But instead of picturing the religious aspect of the Hindu god the aim of these paintings is aphrodisiac. In Hinduism the milkmaids following Krishna's flute symbolise the souls of men being drawn to the supreme god. The Gond youths on the other hand offer milk and curds to the picture and pray: 'As the seven hundred milkmaids followed Krishna, so let the girls of this village follow me.' Girls pray: 'As Krishna loved the milkmaids and never left them, so let the youths of this village love me and never leave me.'

The Saora pictographs resemble those of the Gonds in being made ceremonially, and in certain points of style 'both use the same medium, the wall of the house: both overcrowd this simple "canvas"; both insert casual and unrelated details as they occur to them; both affect the frame, drawn either with multiple straight lines or of parallel lines elaborately enhanced. But the Saoras carry the practice far beyond anything imagined by the Gonds. . . .' The Saora pictures, which are called *ittal* have as a central theme a 'house', represented by a circle or rectangle. The artist, called *ittalmaran,* begins by the outlines, then, starting from the bottom and working upwards, he fills in the outline. 'In drawing a human figure he first makes an outline of the body, either with a single triangle or with two opposed triangles which meet tip to tip. He whitens in the triangle and adds the arms, legs and head. . . . A horse is made with two opposed triangles similar to those of the human figure but turned on their side. Legs, head, tail and finally rider are then added. Great care is taken to indicate the hair by small strokes along the neck and tail. Similar attention is paid to the skin of a bear, a peacock's tail, a deer's horns or a porcupine's quills.'

A shaman is called in when the artist has finished the first draft of the picture and 'proceeds to complicate the course of true art by fussy religious inspirations. He worships before the picture and calls on the ghost or god in whose honour it was made to come and inspect it. He falls into a trance; the spirit comes upon him and offers its criticism through his lips. He takes a lamp and makes a minute examination of every figure. The unseen spirit is seldom backward in suggesting improvements. "You have not given me a comb", he may complain, or "there are not enough *chaprasis* (watchmen) sitting at my gates", or "when I was alive I once rode a bicycle; have you forgotten it?" This is one way in which some of the pictures get so overcrowded; ghosts do not seem to like blank spaces; every inch of wall-space must be filled with tokens in their honour.'

When the shaman is finally satisfied with the picture the artist receives his payment in form of rice and liquor. If it is a special festival friends come in procession with gifts and the shaman hangs a dedicated pot in front of the painting. The ittal is now regarded as a little temple within the house. These pictures are, in fact, the one-dimensional homes of the dead, the heroes and the gods. 'A spirit sits in his ittal as a fly settles on a wall. Offerings are made before the picture on every ceremonial occasion, and branches of fruit or ears of grain are hung round the pot at harvest festivals. In certain cases the ittal is repainted every year.'

The paintings can be divided into several categories according to their symbolism and purpose. First comes the ittals for promoting fertility of the crops. There is a ceremonial bringing out of the seed for sowing and at the same time an ittal is made on the wall in the priest's house. A fowl or a pig is sacrificed and the blood sprinkled over the seed. An ittal shows these fertility symbols – a farmer and his son with a bullock, cow and calf out to plough. Behind goes a pregnant woman with a bundle of seed on her head, then a potter and his wife with loads of pots on head and on a yoke, and lastly two gods on an elephant. The elephant is a symbol of

Girls of the Mishmi tribe carrying water in bamboo tubes, Asam.

luck and riches; the pots to be filled with food and the pregnant women carrying seed are all designed for promotion of fertility. Before sowing begins each kind of seed is offered with prayers in front of the ittal. In another ittal we see Labosum, the Earth God, also with ploughing, pots, women in the field and the sun and the moon as favourable signs.

The second type of ittal deals with origins and curing of diseases. The origin is always the result of interference from gods or ghosts or evil spirits – a god can be insulted by neglect or insufficient attention and takes revenge by sending an illness; a ghost seeks comfort from his family or friends and if he doesn't get it he brings illness or accidents. The protection and cure consequently is based on security measures like correct and timely sacrifices to the gods and appeasement of the family ghosts and other spirits by proper ceremonies. The Saora priest *Kuranmaran,* finds out who is the offended unseen power and by going into a trance in front of an ittal he guides the painter into making the right drawings which, together with an animal sacrifice, satisfies the ghost or god so that he withdraws the illness. Elwin gives the complete background and analysis of the ittal by Tissano, a Kuranmaran who went with his wife to work in the tea gardens in Assam. (Tribal people are often taken by unscrupulous labour contractors to far-away places where they have to work for subsistence wages.) Tissano's wife died and he himself became very ill. Another Kuranmaran told him that his illness was caused by two spirits from his home village. An ittal was made on the wall of the hut in the tea garden and Tissano recovered and returned to his Saora home village. But after a year he fell ill again and now the local Kuranmaran declared that the two spirits were very angry because Tissano had left them behind sitting like flies on the ittal of his hut in far-away Assam. 'We had to get two aeroplanes', they said, 'and fly after him and now when we have got here, there is nowhere for us to stay!' Tissano made an ittal in his house exactly like the one he had made in Assam. It shows one spirit on an elephant, his clerk on a horse and his watchmen in a row. Below can be seen the other spirit with his guard. These are two trees with monkeys. When the picture was ready the spirits complained through the Kuranmaran that it did not include the two aeroplanes which they had taken at great expense. Two planes were painted on the ittal and Tissano recovered.

The third type of ittal is associated with the dead and the underworld to which they go and where they are ruled by gods or 'spirit-helpers'. They have frequent relations with the living and there is even a system of marriages between this world and the underworld. Elwin records that 'every Kuranmaran takes a wife from among the spirit-helpers, has children by her and calls on her for inspiration in his sacred duties. Similarly the Saora priestesses have their unseen husbands who visit them in dream and trance.'

It has already been mentioned that fertility of the crops is an important subject for ittals. The dead have an important function here which can be seen from an ittal. At the time of taking out the seed, the ghost of a man named Jamburu who had died five years before began to pester his widow for attention. He gave her fever; he made noises at night among the pots; he visited her in dreams. One night he showed her a house – 'That's the kind of house I live in; make me one like that on your wall.' He then showed her men riding on elephants and horses. 'That's how the other dead come to visit me.' He showed his potter and his lizard (which is kept as a pet in the homes of the dead) and concluded: 'Draw all these things before you take out your seed; otherwise your crop will be ruined.' Early next morning the widow hurried to the shaman and found that they had each had exactly the same dream. The ittalmaran drew the picture under their direction; its central feature is the substantial two-storeyed house, with three rooms crowded with the dead Jamburu's wives and other dependants.'

The Saoras understand and use the symbols of their ittals as an integral part of their dwellings. The peacock and the snake are guardians of the ittal house which is indicated by rows of hatching over a square. The inhabitants, their guards and spirit helpers are all depicted to show their importance in the underworld. The sun is indicated by concentric circles, and, with a stylised representation of a copulating couple, indicates fertility.

The account of signs and symbols in this article shows how intimately architecture, art and religion are connected and how important they are for preserving the social order among the tribal people. They are directly related to their cults and myths as well as to their everyday life. Their dreams, hopes and fears are directly expressed in the planning and use of their dwellings, their carvings and paintings, their rites and dances. Without these elements of culture their whole social structure collapses. However crude and childish their symbols and art forms are, they are a necessity for all, a condition for their physical and mental health and survival. Can that be said about the signs and symbols in the art and architecture of our civilisation?

BIBLIOGRAPHY

BOAS, F., *Primitive Art*, Oslo, 1927.
BOWER, GRAHAM U., *Drums behind the Hill*, New York, 1950.
ELWIN, V., *The Muria and their Ghotul*, London, 1947; *Tribal Art of Middle India*, London, 1951.
FIRTH, R., *Art and Life in New Guinea*, London, 1936

FÜRER-HAIMENDORF, C. von, *The Naked Nagas*, London, 1950.
HAKANSSON, T., 'Sex in Primitive Art', in *Encyclopedia of Sexual Behaviour*, New York, 1960.
KIZIKOWITZ, K., 'Community House of the Lamet', in *Ethnos*, Stockholm, 1943.
LANDTMAN, G., *The Kiwai Papuans of British New Guinea*, London, 1927.

ANOTHER THICK WALL PATTERN: CAPPADOCIA

Suha Ozkan and Selahattin Onur

THE CAPPADOCIAN WAY OF MAKING SPACES

In the architectural design process, space is generally conceived under the determining effects of the definitive boundary elements. The prevalent materials, the methods of construction and the specific purposes and ways of utilisation of these elements constitute the major set of concerns in the process of design and are decisive in the formation of spaces.

When designers speculate on 'order', they always base the argument on the order implied by the space-defining elements. They are not interested in the order of the diverse aspects of the phenomenon for which the design is aimed and specified. Order is realised in terms of the institutionalised perceptual qualities and meaning of the elements of form and abstracted concepts that serve as the tools for arranging these elements in accordance with the specified purposes.

Although entrusted with the technical and artistic aspects of the phenomenon, designers, consciously or not, are at the same time involved with an inexhaustible variety of activities – technological, economic, political, ideological, theoretical – which comprise their activity at all its different levels. The choice and the determining effects of the definitive boundary elements on order rest on issues beyond and, on the whole, not consciously related to the act of designing. This hypothetical abstract state of the design activity is manifest in the formal ideas and arguments based on functional and metaphysical rationalities.

The designer, as the giver of spatial form to established social concepts and ideals, plays through the mediatory role of his product an intermediary role between the system of relationships that sustain these social concepts and ideals and the immediate level of everyday life. Operating for the different, yet essentially linked, levels of established system of relationships and values, design activity mediates the specific modes of social existence determined by these relationships and values. This mediation is progressively pervading all spheres of life, while, at the same time, the gap between what is mediated and everyday life widens.

The space-defining elements and the order imposed by them are mediators and in all their aspects cannot be separated from what is mediated. The mobility, flexibility and availability of these elements, and the dynamism and responsiveness of the orders they can bring

about, may be considered to be symbolic of freedom in choice of elements and formation of spaces. Yet these concepts are developed and the order these elements presuppose is constituted within the institutional framework which absorbs the full implications of their intentions at the level of reality at which they are introduced. These intentions in their abstract or circumscribed state are utilised in the intermediary role of the design activity to which they belong.

In the formation of spaces the system of defining elements, among the aspects of which the technical, economic and legal dominate, play a decisive role. The defining of space lends itself to the determining effects of a lower order which become the predominating concern of the designer, technically and aesthetically. This is logical and can go on if space is a product of the values behind which are those of exchange and efficiency.

The liberation of decision affecting the formation of 'form' from the order imposed by space-defining elements by removing these elements from the design process has a potential symbolic significance. This suspension can bring about a more radical understanding of their role and is symbolic of a possible state in which for everyday life there is obtained the chance to try out ways towards its rational organisation. By the rationality of such organisation is meant the extent to which it presupposes for man that there is the chance to change himself through social practice, by testing alternatives for and experimenting with different ways of living and working with others, as well as of organising his relations with nature. There are no more pre-formed space-defining elements or static and irreversible spaces produced by decisions made in a given reality. There is, instead, the essential process of making spaces that is to be sustained through some means – very few, and simple enough to be handled by anybody. Space is no longer conceived under the determining effects and constraints of the definitive boundary elements and the structure and methods of construction which are to be sustained at their own level of importance. These are accommodated by a 'superstructure' which has the potential to lend itself to the free formation of spaces.

One may come to think of a soft carveable material which would maintain structurally the spaces hollowed out – a soft superstructure immediately responsive to man making his personal/

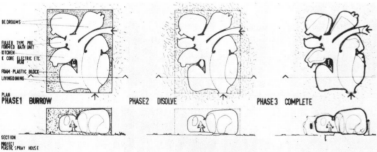

vary, as it does, from the baobab trees and earth formations to such ideas as the use of plastic blocks. David Greene in his 'Spray Plastic House'[1] demonstrated a process of carving out one's own house into a body of foam plastic block with the outcome fixed with spray plastic. The process is known to be practised in earth's formations over various parts of the world which are treated, more or less, like what one could call naturally available spaceframes. The Cappadocia region of Turkey is just one of them.

Christopher Alexander utilised the process less emphatically, in composite order with the traditional methods of building in considering the personalisation of environments as opposed to the standardised provisions of the industrial society. His 'Thick Wall Pattern'[2] consists of a hand-carveable space-frame as the walls of any dwelling where the inhabitants, with the freedom of carving into them, are offered a chance to personalise their dwellings.

Dichotomising the process of adaptation into two categories, mass adaptation and personal adaptation, Alexander states the problem as mass adaptation, dealing with widely shared general characteristics and provided by technological means, crowding out personal adaptation.

He discusses and criticises five different solutions, proposed for the provisions of a high degree of personal adaptation, which would be compatible with the modern means of production as well. The five different solutions are presented as: universal space, custom-made houses, do-it-yourself houses, architectural variety built in by a designer and flexible interchangeable components.

Sorting out the tendencies, he concludes that the way houses are constructed should invite incremental personal adaptation and changes which will be permanent and, therefore, accumulate as different life styles pass through. Thus, the stock of houses available would become progressively more differentiated. This differentiation and variety will become real, since it is specific to the real variety of people in the society.

Assuming that large parts of the house were built from mass produced components, he limits this process of differentiation to the zones 3–4 ft. in or near the surface of the space defining elements which, he says, carry most of the personal identity and character of the building. It is where people keep most of their belongings.

The making of environment well-adapted to its inhabitants can go far beyond that provided by personal belongings, moveables or the nooks and niches of Alexander's 'Thick Wall Pattern'. The process of carving out the spaces to be lived in from an amorphous continuous mass defies the assumption about the space-defining elements and its limitations acknowledged by Alexander. One can mould the total space lived in, subtract from the mass more, thus adding to the differentiated space or filling in those spaces not desired.

This process is already practised in the troglodyte settlements found in various parts of the world. In Cappadocia, Central Anatolia, it has been the most characteristic mode of providing space for the activities people have been engaged in for over fifteen hundred years. The earth formation which serves as the inherently structural mass is tuffa rock.

Tuffa is basically unhardened calcium carbonate. Quite soft for

Massive tuffa rock into which town of Uchisar has been carved.

David Green's 'Spray Plastic House' project.

communal environment. The surfaces appear and forms take shape at the limits of the carving, at the limits towards which genuine human knowledge, demand and expression tend.

This process of cutting into and hollowing out from an amorphous mass is the reverse of the prevalent space-forming process of building up the space. The material of the amorphous mass may

Cappadocian landscape with Uchisar in the distance.

carving, the surfaces exposed get hardened as the product of the chemical reaction with the carbon dioxide of the air. i.e. $[Ca(OH)_2 + CO_2 \rightarrow CaCO_3 + H_2O]$ – apparently calcium hydroxide is the basic composition of the soft tuffa. The origin of the tuffa rock is volcanic dust which, drifted by southern winds from a nearby volcano, Erciyes has settled down and formed a thick layer. Development of bonds among the particles of volcanic dust, due to compression of its own weight and precipitation has formed a soft tuffa layer all over the region. i.e. $[CaO + H_2O \rightarrow Ca(OH)_2]$. Precipitations through ages, in their own pattern of flow, washed some away and formed valleys, canyons, rock faces and cones (fairy chimneys). Each of these varieties in the landscape has provided different potentialities for carving the spaces for habitation or other purposes.

Throughout its history this particular area of Cappadocia has been inhabited by agrarian people who, making use of its peculiari-ties, have been able to remain intact and independent from the direct effects of the wars and the authority of centralised powers. The geography of the region has permitted it to remain off the main routes of movement, and mountainous tracts of land have facilitated protection and seclusion for people seeking a place of refuge or religious retreat.

During the period sixth century B.C. – 17 A.D. when the land changed hands between Greeks, Persians and Romans until it became a Roman province, the ruling native dynasties could retain their autonomy to a great extent. Roman concern with the control of strategic routes left the natives still intact in this un-penetrated land while channelling the building activity of the Romans to the plateau region and the towns occupied by the ruling classes – military and landed aristocracy – and organisations. There are only a few exceptions, for example, a Roman tomb in classical style of which only the remains are left.

'Fairy Chimneys' used as dwellings.

There are no traces left of the native settlements prior to the Early Christian and Byzantine period. This is largely due to the irreversible process of carving into the same rocks previously carved and thus progressively obliterating or changing the previous spaces and the whole settlement pattern. The same techniques used perennially, in both carving and decorating, add to the difficulty of identifying and dating the different stages.

One form of rock dwelling is the use of some cavity in the rocks. Another form, or transfiguration that a cave dwelling may undergo, is the actual carving and organising of spaces and furniture – tables, seats, wash basins, nooks and niches – to meet permanent and changing needs and demands. This activity, to be found in the later form of rock dwelling, has taken place in reciprocal relation to the forces eroding the land. Therefore not all that appears to be a multi-storey arrangement of spaces, for instance, can stand as witness to a multi-storey pattern of settlement in general. Carving

activity has come down to ever lower levels as the valley bottoms have become eroded, sometimes leading to the abandonment of the upper levels. Yet, on the other hand, stairs have been carved in or ladders, mainly of rope, used to reach the valley bottom, or paths were carved along the sides of the cliffs interconnecting the different levels and other valleys.

Anatolia was a place where the Greek and Eastern worlds met and had to live side by side. The complexity and richness that stem from the symbiosis of the Greek and the Eastern worlds set the background for an understanding of Anatolia. The mythical reality that the people created through their sympathetic relation to the world and the condensation of its meanings in symbolic forms were predominantly based on the experience of the divine in things. Any experience or expression was essentially spiritual or religious. Gnosticism, mystic cults and the cult of the divine ruler were the influential trends. All of them have been more of Persian or Oriental origin than Hellenistic.

Cappadocia has been symbolically as appealing to the mystic cults and the Gnostics who, in their search for truth through the practice of asceticism, were seeking salvation from the toils of material existence, as to the newly evangelised communities and the evangelisers who saw in this extraordinary land the image of another world fit to be the bedrock of a new society with new spiritual ideals. The introduction of Christianity, which polarises the everyday spiritual experience by concentrating it in the symbol of a single God, encountered difficulties in spite of the fact that Judaism had already made its way into Anatolia.

In spite of the teachings of the Gospel and the uncompromising and polemical attitude of the evangelists, gnostic philosophy and mystic trends have been assimilated into Christian thought and can be seen in practices like asceticism. Nothing represents this better than the influx of certain symbols into Christianity. Pagan imagery came to be used for the purposes of Christianity.[3]

Uses of various formations of tuffa.

View of the town of Uchisar and the characteristic Cappadocian landscape from above.

In the communities newly established the monks lived side by side with the peasants. Monasteries, their refectories, churches, chapels and hermitages, are found integrated in the settlements. During the 4th century A.D. many churches have been carved into tuffa. Unlike their contemporaries of masonry construction, they have survived earthquakes, though they have been affected by erosion. Till the end of the thirteenth century more than a thousand religious establishments were carved into the rocks.

Reflections of the official authority of the Byzantine church, of orthodoxy, are to be found in the architecture of these religious establishments. Carved in tuffa, they are basically the adaptations of the typical models that are built in the Eastern Christian world.[4] The symbolic disciplining that runs through the architectural forms and decoration is based on a philosophy which has institutionalised the religious meanings of form from those of individual elements to the basic plans of churches. The articulation of the exteriors as well as of the interiors reflects the established styles. Arcaded façades with columns that define the narthex, or the tops of natural cones that house the church, giving the shape of the typical pointed roof are examples of such treatment of the exteriors. In contrast, there are examples of masonry-built dwellings where the exterior has been constructed in the shape of cones.

In the interiors of the churches, which are based on accepted layouts, elements like pillars and columns are structurally redundant as the material that is carved makes it possible to do without them; this can be observed in the cases where these elements have fallen down or have been taken away. In the latter cases extraordinary spatial effects are produced, though accidentally, that could not have been dreamt of by those who were following some official or conventional canon. On the other hand, geometrical

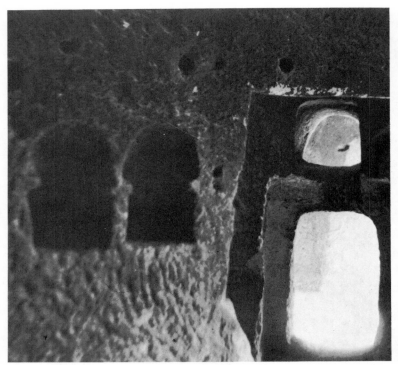

Above, details from the refectories of churches at Goreme.

A classical Roman tomb carved into a cone at Avcilar (Matiana).

A staircase to valley bottom.

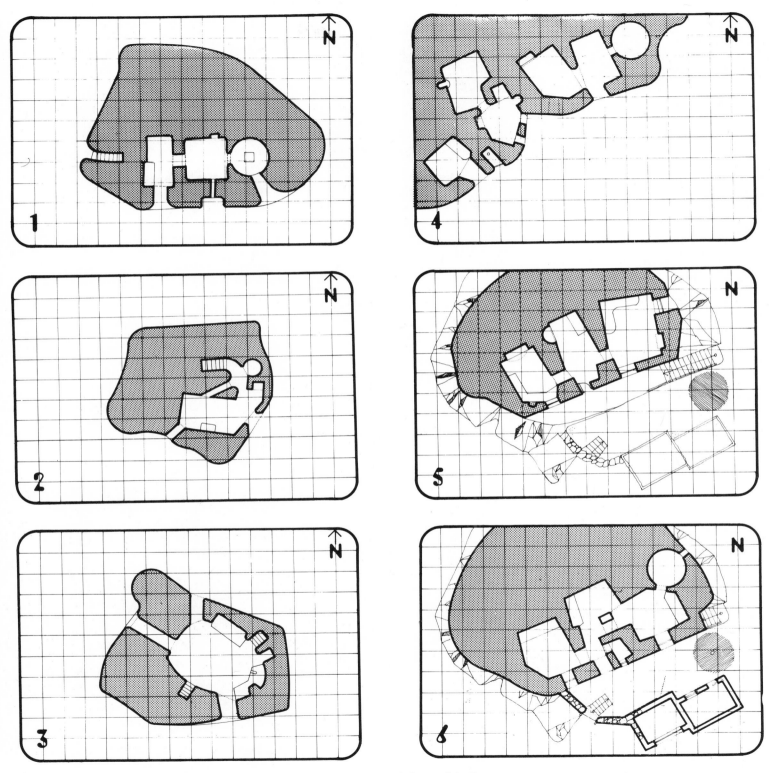

Plans of some dwellings carved into cones and rock-faces, as surveyed by S. Ozkan and S. Onur.

Dove-cotes.

aberrations in reproducing certain accepted forms, whether accidental or intentional, testify to the awkwardness of the attempt to transpose the geometry achieved in a different medium with different techniques. The tendency to geometricise or regularise, observable in the plans, becomes more thought-provoking when one sees the reconstruction drawing of one of the underground cities by a contemporary expert who has reduced the whole thing to a quite orthogonal framework of wall-slab construction.

The proliferation of images, which came to be more and more associated with idolatry and magic, was reacted against by those whose spiritual needs did not match with such tendencies, and by those affected by Moslem and Jewish religious thought that contested idolatry. Another consideration of prime importance was the increasing number of monks and the power of the orthodox church over the ruling of the Byzantine Empire. The feelings of the common people against the monasteries and the monks, due to the social imbalance caused by their increasing numbers and influence, were manipulated and used by the ruling imperial power in a way that resulted in the persecution of monks who favoured image-worshipping, and in the closing down of the monasteries. This is the iconoclastic movement that started by the beginnings of the eighth century and lasted till the beginnings of the ninth. Though it is presented as a reaction against the images, iconoclasm involves such diverse, yet related conflicts as the ones mentioned.

It was during this period of iconoclasm that most of the well-developed churches of Cappadocia were carved into the tuffa. The prohibition of decorative imagery led to the use of geometrical patterns made by lines of red paint, which is characteristic of this period, as well as to the covering of the frescoes and paintings in the churches with stucco. Nothing but the cross could be used as a symbol. It was also during this period that Arab invasions took place, increasing greatly the troubles of the monks, who found their refuges in the cliffs of Cappadocia, now more precious than ever. The solution for the common people living on the plains to the Arab raids, on this battleground that stood between the Arabs and the Byzantine Empire, was the underground cities built on as many as eight to ten levels, like Kaymakli and Derinkuyu.[5] The end of this period is marked not only by the end of these raids, but also by the end of the persecution of the monks and monasteries that stood against iconoclasm. The power of the church and of monasticism over imperial rule was restored. Though a rebirth of imagery took place, it did not last long before the monasteries

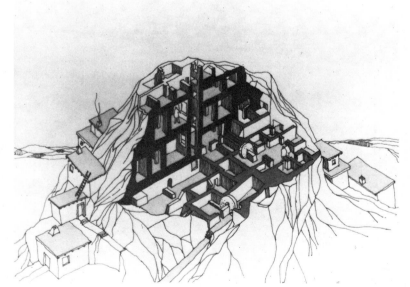
Axonomatric projection of the underground city of Kaymakli (Sondos) as surveyed by M. Akok.

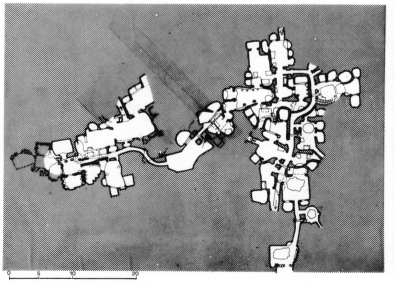
A partial plan of the underground city of Kaymakli as surveyed by M. Beken.

102

A Multi-storey house carved into a 'fairy chimney' at Avcilar.

The composite order of the carved-in and the masonry-built, Avcilar.

A road-side souvenir shop.

were brought under the effective authority of the Byzantine Church.

With the occupation of Anatolia by the Seljuk Turks, from the 12th century on, there were large numbers of Turkish settlers in the area who became involved with agricultural production and carved into tuffa mainly for domestic purposes, much in the same way as the early communities. Seljuks, like the Romans, were oriented to the main routes and large towns in their building activity, which was comprised mainly of institutional and public works. During the Ottoman period which followed there was a dwindling of the Christian population in this area which greatly decreased during the early years of the Turkish Republic.

The sympathetic and direct relation of these self-sufficient agrarian communities to this environment has affected the continuation of gnostic trends throughout, as much as has the indirectness of the official authority of the Byzantine Church. This very relation has generated sound ecological principles upon which their productive and building activity is based. Agricultural land, which is mainly in the valley bottoms, is quite scarce. The fertility of the land is augmented with the collected droppings of pigeons for which they have carved pigeon-coops painted red to attract these birds. On the façades of some of these pigeon houses blind arcades have been carved. The production and the making use of available resources were maintained at a proportionate level and in direct relation to demands.

Space, like the rest of the fruits of their labours, was not a

A Cappadocian village.

commodity. It could, instead, be described as conditioned by past cultural values, beliefs and habits. The medium, tuffa, they chose and the techniques they devised presented a novelty, yet this discontinuity in the means did not go without cultural continuities in meaning – not only experienced, but institutionalised meaning – which dictated the forms carved into the rocks.

The region exhibits the work of the adaptive processes which have resulted in differentiation, not only in space-defining elements, but of spaces and their juxtaposition. The irregular, and the approximations to the regular, as well as the images of their culture constructed through traditional means, exist together in what could be described as a multi-layered lattice. Inbuilt at the same time is a relaxedness and an unselfconscious attitude which, no doubt, was also augmented by the conduciveness of the medium. The product of this attitude is a diversity and a juxtaposition of spaces making up this multi-layered lattice in which no one layer dictates the spatial organisation of the other. This quality is also enhanced by, and in turn, enriches, a way of life which does not compartmentalise

Detail from the lobby of the rock-cut 'Kaya Hotel' at Uchisar, carved in 1966.

A souvenir shop at Goreme valley.

A shop.

and segregate functions, though it differentiates the spaces required for them.

Growth and accummulation took place through the irreversible process of carving since, in physical terms, once a space is carved it cannot be uncarved,[6] though it can be transformed into something else through the same or any other process due to changing aims and techniques appropriate to their realisation.

Thus the process of carving into the body of rock is determined by an intentional response to the motives, the influence of the activity and diverse forces of the situation. The acquired space is the initial state, a given for further developments or extensions into the superstructure, or a given to be refuted. The process can be exemplified by the generation of the two underground cities, or the response of the first monks to tuffa. Any set of decisions about the particulars of an extension is determined by the previous set of decisions and particular environmental conditions.

$$D_t = D(S_t, H_t, V_t) \qquad t = 0, 1, 2, 3, \ldots, n^7$$

Yet decision is not a mere resultant of vectors like the combined effect of natural forces that wear down and shape the land. The impacts of human intervention and natural forces are subtractive processes with qualitatively different results. The latter are continuous and are exerted over the whole land, while the former displays discontinuities and has been at work only in parts of the region.

Although it is sufficient to hollow out in order to accommodate a multitude of activities in varying forms of expression, the most prevalent practice today is a composite one. A 'fairy chimney' could appropriately be the basic structure for a multi-storey dwelling, while rockfaces at ground level are hollowed out for storage, or can also be made to provide all the spaces needed by a Cappadocian family whose main involvement is the cultivation of vines and related extracts of grape.

However the composite technique, that is the juxtaposed and superimposed uses of two different modes, the traditional masonry construction and the carved-in, is more extensively employed. Spaces are generally carved for the purposes of storing their agricultural produce and in the form of dove-cotes and nesting places for collecting droppings to be used as fertilisers.

The transposition of the 'masonry look' of the primaeval forms inherent in masonry structures to the hollowed out openings has become the basic symbolic disciplining which sustains a visual homogeneity in the totality of the environment.

More and more, in the consumer societies propelled by industrial production, specifically in the urban context, discontinuities in the means (rather than the continuities of cultural symbols or imitation of past images or preconceptions) dictate the forms through which, though it seems paradoxical, old ways, habits and mystifications are perpetuated.

Space has become a commodity for exchange. Space is private space or public space. Making it involves decisions and practices, however rational they may be, based on the dichotomised existence of the individual and the social in the form of institutionalised relations which bring about their mutual destruction.

The order of the space-defining elements is the embodiment of these relations. This order varies at different levels of activity which are essentially linked. Along with the conceptual relations that are reflected, it is necessary to suspend the structures that hold or reflect them in order to understand their relation to the making of spaces. This becomes crucial in the case of an interpretation which demands the recognition of environment as the perceptual and ephemeral work of its inhabitants. The order of the permanent structure and static forms only denies the need and possibilities of this recognition.

In the case of Paolo Soleri's *Arcology*[8] the recognition of the dynamic process of life and its relation to its environment is purged out of its context and caged in static imagery. In 'Arcologies' super-structures with thick walls are proposed, but quite different from those of Alexander, or those of Cappadocia. These walls are, as far as one can trace, non-responsive, i.e. not carveable.

From the points of view both of the manifested image and required technology, Soleri's utopia implies modern – or otherwise – technology comparable to the present mode of producing spaces in Cappadocia and with similar potentials in responsiveness. The present and past structures of Cappadocia fully satisfy the 'Arcological' concerns of Soleri, especially ecologically.

NOTES

[1] COOK, PETER, *Architecture: Action and Plan*, Studio Vista, London, Reinhold, New York, 1967, p. 6, David Greene's 'Spray Plastic House, 1963' project published previously in *Archigram 3*.

[2] ALEXANDER, CHRISTOPHER, 'Thick Wall Pattern', *Architectural Design*, July 1968, pp. 324–26.

[3] Some examples of the pagan imagery and symbols that were reinterpreted by the Early Christians and used extensively in the frescoes and decorations found or uncovered in the religious establishments of the Cappadocian region follow:

Fish is a symbol recurrently used in pagan myths. The first Christians took this widespread use of it for granted and made it into a secret code to elude the Romans who kept a close watch over their activities. They used the word 'ichtus' which, in Greek, meant 'fish' and, at the same time, corresponded to the initials of the message they were passing around: Iesous CHristos hYios Soter. This earliest Christian symbol also stood for the necessity of baptism for man – as necessary as water is for fish.

Rooster, in Partians, symbolises prophecy. In Zoroastrianism, the rooster is believed to keep away the evil spirits, White Rooster, used in Cappadocia, is the symbol of good luck while Black Rooster is considered to be a Satanic creature. In Greek mythology, rooster belongs to the underworld. In Christianity it signified alertness and was used as a symbol to repel Satan.

Rabbit, which is a mystical and magical symbol, belongs to the Satanic cult. It has frequently been associated with Venus for the quality its meat is believed to have in enhancing beauty and sexual desire. Rabbit, the Easter bunny which lays eggs, has its pagan origins in this cult of fertility.

Stag, which was the sacred animal of a god worshipped by the Hittites, prevailed in the various mystic cults and myths as a symbol of immortality. It is usually depicted together with a plant of immortal life that gives it this quality. In Christianity, such a plant is given to the stag by Christ whom it carries across a river. For Christians it represented a yearning for God, as well as Christ Himself – the stag with a cross on its forehead.

Lion is one of the most common motifs that recur in pagan myths. The early Christians expressed their novel ideas about salvation through this motif.

Peacock, in antiquity, represents immortality according to mystic cults. In folklore there is an ancient myth about the incorruptability of the peacock flesh. Christian reinterpretation made it into a symbol of resurrection and preservation of the body.

Of the pastoral scene, Palm Tree stood for immortal life and paradise while Pine, which belonged to the cult of fertility, promised man health and growth with its branches that were believed to keep away the evil spirits. These symbols have been used by the archaic and the Christian world alike. Vine, the Dionysian symbol, is an icon that stands for Christ and also means Salvation and Eternal Hope.

The pagan Dove of the cult of fertility is a symbol of good-nature, peace, love and chastity. In Christianity, it is believed to embody the souls of martyrs and saints besides being a symbol of honesty, good-nature, innocence, peace and salvation. It has also been used as an icon of Christ.

This symbolism was used to convey the new religious idea to the initiated. Not only the imagery of the mystics cults, but also of the Imperial rule, the cult of divine rule has played a role in Christian imagery, like Christ Enthroned. The Emperor himself, for some period, was regarded as a mediator between God and the mortals. With Christianity becoming the religion of the State, the pomp and pageantry of the Empire at that period affected Christianity.

[4] The following church types summarise the modes of ordering that were widely employed in the organisation of spaces. Churches, unlike the religious buildings of pagans, are places of congregation where ceremonies take place. Their form has been modelled more after the pagan public buildings than pagan temples. Their general planning and structure were determined by the liturgical canons which gave shape to these ceremonies.

The Archaic type is composed of a rectangular nave with either flat or barrel vaulted ceiling. There is a semi-circular apse where the ceiling gets more shallow. No iconostasis or side nave exists.

The Classic Basilica type with altar, gallery and atrium can be found in Eastern and Western Christian worlds alike. The semi-circular apse, which is a couple of steps higher than the barrel vaulted nave, has niches on its periphery. The side aisles, which are separated from the nave by four or eight columns, have flat ceilings.

Another variation of the basilican type is the Barrel Vaulted church with rectangular nave and three apses – the middle apse being larger.

The Central Plan type exists in the form of a cross-shaped church, with a dome in the middle. Usually, there are no columns.

Of the latest type known are the Cross Vaulted churches with more than one dome and no columns. An iconostasis is located in the front of the middle apse.

[5] *vide*, BROOKE, MARCUS, 'An Undergound City Seven Storeys Low', *Illustrated London News*, June 1971, pp. 51–53.

[6] COWAN, PETER, 'On Irreversibility', *Architectural Design*, September 1969, pp. 485f.

[7] Where: S_t is a-priori structural state vector, H_t is historical state vector, V_t is environmental vector, D denotes a decision function, Cowan, P., op. cit.

[8] SOLERI, PAOLO, *Arcology, City in the Image of Man*, M.I.T. Press, Cambridge, Mass., 1969.

BIBLIOGRAPHY

GEERKEN, SIGRID und HARTMUT, *Goreme Kilavuzu, Fuhrer durch Goreme*, TTOK Yayini, Istanbul, 1968.

GIOVANNINI, LUCIANO (ed.), *Arts of Cappadocia*, Nagel, Geneva, Barrie and Jenkins, London, 1971.

GRÉGOIRE, H., 'Rapport sur un voyage d'exploration dans le Pont et la Cappadoce', *Bulletin de Correspondance Héllenique*, t. 33, 1909, pp. 1–170.

JERPHANION, G. de, *Une nouvelle province de l'art Byzantin, Les eglises rupestres de Cappadoce*, Paris, 1925–1942.

RAMSAY, W. M. and BELL, G. L., *The Thousand and One Churches*, London, 1909.

ROTT, H., 'Kleinasiatische Denkmäler aus Pisidien, Pamphilien, Kappadokien und Lykien', *Studien über Christliche Dankmäler*, 5 und 6 Heft, Leipzig, 1908.

THIERRY, NICOLE et MICHEL, *Nouvelles Eglises Rupestres de Cappadoce, Region du Hasan Dagi*, Librairie C. Klincksieck, Paris, 1963.

THE BOAT AS AN ARCHITECTURAL SYMBOL

Ronald Lewcock and Gerard Brans

The influence of boats and boat building on houses and religious shrines can often be seen in the maritime societies of the world. In its most direct form this influence ranges from the re-use of old boat timbers, producing unusual curves in the roofs of buildings, to the utilisation of complete boats, or copies of them, as shelters on land. In a technologically developed culture the influence of boats on buildings conflicts with the development of houses or communal buildings as integrated structures; in the latter the demands of use and construction at a more sophisticated level take precedence over the secondary use of old materials from boats, or reconstructions of them as roofs. In such circumstances, where a society's traditional links with the sea still extend to the urge to express them in buildings, conscious resort to symbolism is made. The architecture remains essentially integrated and simple, dictated by efficiency and structural logic, but incorporates changes, usually in form, to acknowledge the primacy of boats in the heritage of the people. Any subsequent change in values would often be accompanied by a growing awareness of traditions, leading to their reinforcement and reinterpretation in symbolic terms. Eventually the symbolism itself may be lost, as indeed it seems to be in much of the architecture of China and Japan, but the forms remain to serve as important clues to the sources of their cultures.

SOUTH-EAST ASIA

The coastal communities of a large region extending eastwards from South India to the Pacific, and northwards to Formosa and Japan, share many common characteristics in the design of their boats and their methods of fishing. The possible sources of these common traditions will be discussed below. Many of the coastal societies have communal ceremonies involving the use of large boats; the ceremonies range from formal visits to neighbouring villages to mark the commencement of peace or war, to ceremonies placating the ocean – reminding one of such ceremonies that were held in Genoa and Venice. The communal boats were larger versions of ordinary fishing boats, with variations which suggest survivals of earlier extinct designs. A large boat is shown stored in the accompanying illustration. (This example is from Ceylon. Its form is characteristic of the whole region, although in the eastern Indonesian islands and Indo-China the prow and stern have a more

pronounced curve.) In storage the boat is raised on a framework of posts driven into the ground. The boat rests on this frame the right way up, necessitating a temporary roof of palm leaves to protect the interior from the weather as long as it is on land.

It is clear that such a boat stored in the middle of a village retains its importance in the eyes of the community. It is still the communal boat, symbolising the unity of the society, and retaining all the special powers it assumes when in ceremonial use. It is not difficult to understand its eventual influence on the design of buildings of symbolically related function and importance.

THE INFLUENCE OF BOATS ON BUILDINGS

1. *The Building in the Form of the Stored Boat*
If we compare the stored boat with the spirit houses and communal rice stores of the Toraja people in the Celebes Islands, the resemblance is immediately apparent. Not only is the form of the building extended at the ends to represent the stern and prow of the

A large boat stored during the monsoon on the shore near Galle, Ceylon. It is raised on a platform of four posts and a frame, and protected with a pitched roof of cadjan leaves.

Detail of gable of a house of the Toraja, Celebes Islands, Indonesia.

Interior of a Celebes spirit-house.

Communal rice stores of the Toraja, Celebes Islands, Indonesia. Archipelago (Grubauer).

Gable front of a spirit house of the Toraja, Celebes Islands, Indonesian Archipelago (Grubauer).

ceremonial boat, and decorated as these features usually are in Indonesia, but the whole is raised on a simple framework like that supporting the stored boat. Furthermore, the interior of the building has a raised 'gunwale' around the edge, from which people step down into the sunken plank floor of the building. This runs unbroken from one side to the other, disturbed only by the posts – masts – of the roof construction.

An important feature of this type of building is that the huge overhanging gables at front and rear are not usually supported by poles direct to the ground (even though the prow and stern of the stored boat frequently are). As though to emphasise that the superstructure is a complete form supported only on the platform at its base, the gables are often braced in a series of kingpost trusses, linked by one diagonal member in each gable. The latter is frequently ornamented to recall the horse, the hornbill or other bird or animal motif used as the finial ornament of the prow or stern of

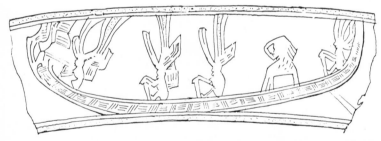

A typical Indonesian 'proa', or ceremonial boat, represented in a bronze drum of the Dongson culture. Museum F. Volkerkunde, Wein.

Houses of the Kambot, Sepik in North West New Guinea (Gardi).

the ceremonial boat. Alternatively, freestanding woodcarvings of hornbills or other birds or animals perform the same function. The remainder of the gable is elaborately decorated with carved patterns.

Where, in very large buildings, a supporting pole does stand on the ground under the gable, it is noticeable that it does not do so at the end of the overhang as in the stored boat, but near the main platform as though similarly to emphasise the integrity of the roof form.

2. *The Building in the Form of a Boat's Hull*
In other parts of South-East Asia the roof, which naturally in the Sadan-Toradja examples begins to look like a boat itself, has a curve which is further exaggerated so that the resemblance to the ceremonial boat with upcurving stem and prow is more marked.

Pasemah house, Sumatra, Indonesia.
Tanimbar house, Eastern Indonesia (Vroklage).

Communal house of the Washkuk, Sepik in North West New Guinea (Gardi).

109

In these cases this seems to have been all that was necessary for the roof to symbolise a boat.[1] Many examples of this kind of house are found in Sumatra, especially among the Batak and Pasemah people. Roofs with less pronounced curves, but seeming to achieve their symbolism from the resemblance of the roof itself to a boat, are found as far east as New Guinea.[2]

3. *The Building in the Form of a Boat in Full Sail*

In the Lio district of Flores, in the East Indonesian archipelago, the whole building is seen as a boat. The two main posts which support the ridge are called 'masts', the flanking sides of the high roof are compared with sails.[3] It is remarkable how different the roofs of these houses are from those in the same island that represent hulls or stored boats.[4]

In the Naga district of Flores the main posts supporting the ridge are called masts, and the wall (screen) between the first and second spaces when houses are divided, is called the 'sail'.[5]

4. *The Building in the Form of a Platform Carried on Two Boats*

A typical type of South and South-East Asian ceremonial boat is made up of two boats joined, with a flat platform between them. The boat example from Ceylon has a similar form, made by giving two protecting keels to the hull. (The ordinary fishing boat has two hulls as well, one for the boat and one as an outrigger. There is often a woven platform between the two for the catch of fish. Both the hull and the outrigger are hollowed-out logs, as are the keels in the Ceylon boat.)

Buildings representing this type of ceremonial boat are found in middle Flores Island, near Timor, and in other parts of the

Houses in the Lio district of Flores Island, Indonesia. The inhabitants view the houses as boats, and the flanking sides of the high roofs are compared with sails (Vroklage).

Illness house in central Flores Island, Indonesia. This is shown in a partly demolished condition, with the framework remaining (Vroklage).

Beam end from a spirit house, central Flores Island, Indonesia.

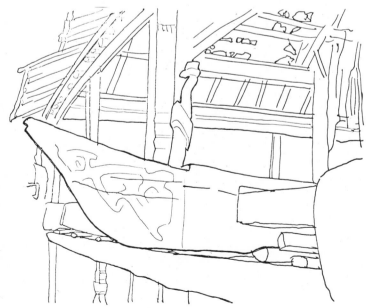

Indonesian archipelago. The illustration shows the decayed framework of a partially demolished spirit house, while detail of the end of the beam of another building of this type is also illustrated. The ends of the beams are upturned and decorated like the ends of the ceremonial boat, the *proa*. Such a treatment occurs not only in 'spirit houses' but also in 'sickness houses', the dwelling houses and grain stores of the chiefs of the villages.

5. *The Building with a Boat placed on its Ridge*

In areas where the tradition of roofing with a hipped roof was strong, alternative means of invoking the sacred form of the ceremonial boat were evolved. One was the construction of a woven basket in the shape of the boat on top of the ridge of the house. In the example shown a model boat is placed there. This model boat may contain ornamental chains and pendant ear-rings made out of leaves; these are an offering to the spirits for the protection of the newborn child.[6]

House of the Nage people, Flores Island, Indonesia. It has a woven representation of a boat on the ridge (Vroklage).

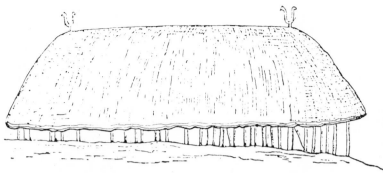

House of the Manggarai, West Flores Island (Vroklage).

6. *The Building with a Ridge-Piece in the Form of a Boat*

In Tanimbar, one of the most easterly of the Indonesian islands, the ridges of the buildings are concave, with upturned projections at the ends decorated with carvings of birds, animals and reptiles, so that the large ridge-piece itself represents a boat.[7]

This type of expression of the dominant symbol of the boat is widespread throughout South-East and East Asia, as far, indeed, as China and Japan. In the northern areas, however, its provenance has been forgotten.

Its symbolism remains pertinent to many peoples throughout Indonesia, as is shown by the importance of the boat in the culture of the communities where it occurs. For example, each village of Tanimbar characterises itself as belonging to a ceremonial *proa*, and those along the coast or the rivers still maintain such a boat. Similarly, further west in the Ende district of Flores Island the ridges of the houses represent boats, and the main posts which support them are called 'masts'; the high attic under the roof is known as the 'sail'.[8]

7. *The Building with a Roof in the Form of a Boat Upside Down*

In many societies, especially those of Oceania, such as the Maori, the distinction between the nature of sea and shore is visually expressed by turning ceremonial boats upside down when they are stored on land. Such upturned boats become the pattern for another interpretation of the roof of a house, and one which is closer to the direct hipped form, such as the houses built by the Manggarai, West Flores Island.[9] The points of the hips are here crowned by a pair of carved wooden rafter ends which project above the roof to represent protecting buffalo horns, a feature apparently originating in India, but rationalised by the boat-centred cultures who say that they represent crossed oars.[10] This feature survives in traditional Japanese architecture in the temples of Ise. The use of buffalo horns to afford magic protection is still practised among the Toraja of the Celebes, where the skull is fastened to the gable which represents the stern of the proa.

8. *The Village in the Form of a Boat*

Wherever boat-centred cultures occur it is usually possible to find whole villages patterning their shape and organisation on the form of the ceremonial proa.

A village in Flores Island has its houses built in two semicircles facing each other, which Arndt believed referred to the 'boat'. The clan who lives in the middle is called 'the mast and sail'.[11] In one district of central Flores the village names are associated with boats. One is called 'sail', another 'rudder'. Vroklage explains this as possibly due to the splintering of an original village which represented a proa.[12] In another village the village head is called 'the beginning of the high mast' and 'the end of the big *prauw*', which is equivalent to 'leader of the *prauw*'. Elsewhere the village head is called 'steersman'.[13]

Villagers of this type think of themselves as living in boat communities. A man who, after his marriage, goes to live with the family of his bride, is called 'someone who gets into another boat'.

The villages of Tanimbar discussed above follow the belief that each community exists both on land and on sea in a boat. Therefore the stem of the ridge of their main buildings is always turned towards the sea.[15]

In the plan of a Todo village on Flores the determining feature of

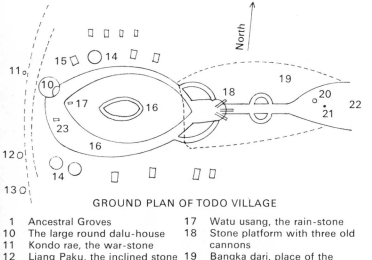

GROUND PLAN OF TODO VILLAGE

1	Ancestral Groves	17	Watu usang, the rain-stone
10	The large round dalu-house	18	Stone platform with three old
11	Kondo rae, the war-stone		cannons
12	Liang Paku, the inclined stone	19	Bangka dari, place of the
13	Lolo bali, the wedge-shaped		original settlement and the
	stone		resting-spot for the earth- spirits
14	Round houses	20	Large trees
15	The rectangular house of the	21	Toto-stone
	ruler's mother	22	Graveyard of Todo
16	Stone-covered ovals	23	House for the gong

Plan of Todo village, Manggarai, West Flores, Island (Van Bokkum).

layout is the focal position of the ancestral graveyard, itself shaped like a boat. An encircling area of earth and a framing path in stone follow the same form, around which the houses are grouped, with the 'dalu-house', the spirit house and residence of the chief, at the stern. The village is entered across the site of an earlier village, past another graveyard, through an elaborate formal arrangement of curving paths.

In middle Flores, the head of one village compares his community with the crew of a proa, and the man who leads in prayer is called the 'captain'. In the Kei Islands the word for ceremonial boat, *belan*, also means 'community under a chief'.[16]

9. The Meeting Place in the Form of a Boat

In Ambon, in the Moluccas, the megalithic meeting place is called the proa.[17]

On the Kei Islands, according to Drabbe, 'the village community is often called *sori*, the common word for boat; the village square, the dancing place, where all important affairs were carried out, was often shaped like a sori. One of the most important parts of the great ceremonial boat . . . was the four plank beds, on which the people felt as much at ease as in their own homes. The [owner of the village] was called *riribum réréngjar*, which is the term for the plank beds of the large communal boat.'[18]

On Tanimbar, the chiefs, several dignitaries and the common people have definite positions in the ceremonial boat. These are repeated around the meeting place. Every village has such a meeting place, and where several villages have become joined there are as many meeting places as there were separate communities originally.

Each is in the form of a proa. Even where the meeting place is perfectly round, one side is called 'the stem' and the other 'the stern'.[19]

THE ORIGIN AND MEANING OF BOAT SYMBOLISM IN SOUTH-EAST ASIA

Decorated buildings of almost identical appearance to those of the Toraja in the Celebes (type 1) are depicted on two thousand-year old metal drums used by the Bronze Age culture of South-East Asia.[20] This culture, known as the Dongson culture, spread from the mainland of Indo-China to many of the islands of the Indonesian archipelago, Formosa, and perhaps to Japan as well, apparently in the period c. 700 B.C. to c. 300 B.C.[21] It possessed bronze but possibly iron as well. Its spread was not uniform, but took the form of scattered settlements existing side by side with older megalithic societies. It was clearly a predominantly maritime culture spread by people travelling in small groups in big boats. The Dongson communities apparently believed that the souls of their dead travelled back across the sea to the land of their ancestors. Accordingly, to judge by the surviving cultures which appear to be related to the Dongson, the dead were laid in state in funerary houses designed to look like ceremonial boats, (even the sickness houses were symbolic proas), and the coffins, whether of stone or wood, were shaped like boats and actually called proas.[22] The practice may thus be seen as a form of concrete symbolism and as a means of achieving sympathetic magic.

The village community, the descendants of the original ancestors who came by proas, also wanted to live on land in a proa which represented the type of unity that once came over the sea to the island. This type of social order and its symbolism has survived in communities widely spaced apart, and often no longer related to the sea. The focus of such villages is sometimes a group of ancestor stones, or a boat-shaped 'spirit-house' in which the souls of the ancestors are respected and worshipped, reminding the members of each village of their origin. In other tribes the same memory is preserved in those meeting and dancing places which take the form of proas.[23] Occasionally the whole shape of a village is done in the form of a boat, or the house of the chief, the grain stores or the houses of all the members of the village symbolise boats.

A wide range of supporting evidence may be adduced to confirm the existence of the maritime Dongson culture. In particular its decorative patterns, spiral curves, especially in opposed pairs tangentially linked, may be found wherever the symbolic boat roofs occur. Similarly, spirit houses may contain boat models with a male crew represented by small cylindrical stones. These imply the ancestors who came across the seas and took local women as wives. (Women are depicted by smaller stones in rectangular boxes, and not in boats.) Ceremonial drums and gongs, often of great antiquity, and usually cast in bronze, are used by some of the societies who build boat roofs. Many of the drums found in Eastern Indonesia show animals and birds which are unknown there, so that either the drums or the people who made them originated elsewhere. Other ancient bronzes include models of ceremonial boats about two feet long, and a wide range of jewellery in bronze and

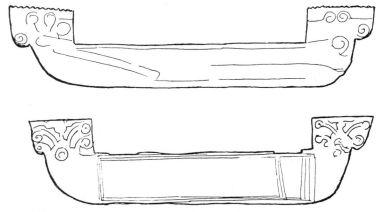

Stone doorsteps in the form of boats, Flores, Indonesia.

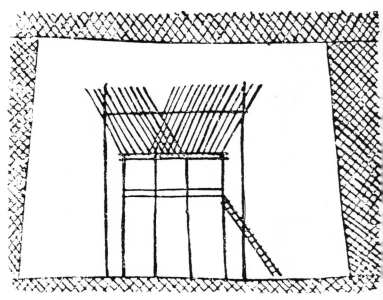

Clay tomb model of a building, Japan. Of a type typical of the period 2nd c. B.C. to 3rd c. A.D.

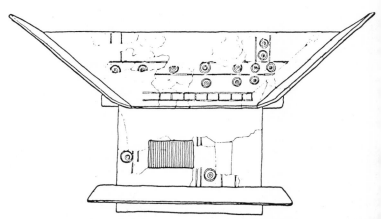

Representations of a building on a bronze bell, Japan. c. 2nd c. A.D. (Ohash collection).

copper is in boat-derived shapes. Many of the communities build sacrifice poles with model boats at the top, usually made of stone, in which offerings are placed; the spirits of ancestors are believed to take these offerings, and are conjured up by the presence of the boat.

In some places, temporary ceremonial boats are made to be used at the sacrifice feast to initiate the making of new gardens. They have oars, rudder, mast and sails, and in them are placed stones and food for the ancestors, and grass and treebark from the site. This ensures that the ancestors will protect the garden against all sorts of disaster. Finally, in some societies, symbolism extends from the representation of the whole house as a boat to the depiction of boats in small parts of the building, as in ridges, floor beams and, in houses in Flores, stone doorsteps.

THE EVOLUTION OF BUILDING FORMS AWAY FROM DIRECT REPRESENTATION OF THE SYMBOL

Fusion of the 'boat symbolism' culture with more ancient cultures in which strong architectural traditions already existed probably led to the adoption of characteristic forms of the former in combination with the building practice of the latter. This process may quickly have resulted in the suppression of direct boat symbolism, and even to the elimination of the memory of the origin of these symbolic forms from the minds of the people. Such a process would explain the lack of conscious boat symbolism in the explanations of the Chinese and Japanese for the characteristic form of many of their buildings. Yet the links with the Dongson culture are strong, particularly in the case of the Japanese, whose early bronze bells (c. 1st or 2nd century A.D.) have representations of buildings which show them to be closely related to those we have been discussing in Indonesia. Further evidence is to be found in the clay tomb models (c. 1st or 2nd century A.D.) and in the oldest temple forms, those of Ise and Izumo, which although continuously renewed, are believed to date from the 3rd and 6th century A.D.

The bronze representations, and the buildings of Ise all have straight ridges, but other features confirm the links with boat symbolism. The ridge poles project far beyond the roof forms, and the end rafters extend several metres into the sky; Vroklage[24] believes that the straightening of the curved ridge and, in particular, the reduction of the raised ornamented stem and stern to plain projections of the straight ridge, are symptoms of 'decline and decadence' – they are developments which also occurred in Indonesia. But it seems more likely that they represent an approximation of the symbol to contain it within the simple forms of direct building construction, a step made possible because it was such a clearly

114

Shrine building at Ise, Japan, c. 5th c. A.D.

House from Kabaena, Celebes (Vroklage).

understood symbolism; also, ironically, a step which would eventually lead to the complete loss of symbolic meaning.

THE LIVING SPACE OF A HOUSE AS A REFLECTION OF BOAT SYMBOLISM

The plan of Celebes buildings, in which the plank floor is surrounded by a raised sleeping bench, has already been discussed. The analogy with an ocean-going boat is further exemplified by the design of the fireplaces; in the spirit houses they are wooden trays covered with earth and set into the raised sleeping bench at the front and rear near to the steps. In type they closely resemble the cooking trays at the stem or stern of a boat used during a long voyage. Similar patterns occur in most of the communities in which boat symbolism is found in building or village form. The house is not divided into rooms, but remains one space, although on Palau special rooms for childbirth may be created by erecting temporary screen walls in the houses. Otherwise low mat screening is the most that ever occurs. Only priests have in their houses a specially separated place.[25] Sleeping takes place on mats spread on the raised sleeping bench around the edge of the house. Open attic floors for storage are often used, usually over only part of the plan.

Throughout Indonesia such houses tend to be extended family dwellings, with several adult males and their wives, rather than single family units. The unified nature of the plan, emphasizing a need for cooperation between all the inhabitants, is thus all the more significant. Activities which are felt to warrant privacy, such

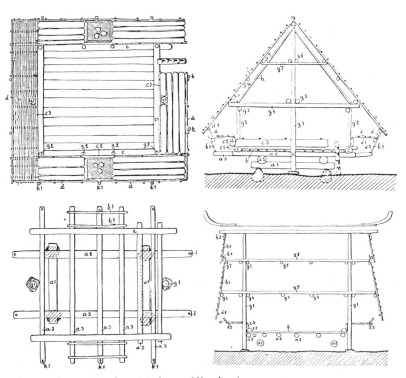

Plane and sections of a spirit house (Kaudern).

as courtship, would usually take place away from the house within the jungle.

SYMBOLISM IN THE HOUSE AS EXPRESSION OF A CONCEPT

The boat as a shelter implies a very tight social organisation, as on a ship. It is characteristic of what Lévi-Strauss has called the *pensée-concrète,* the symbol giving expression to an idea, a phenomenon he finds in many non-western cultures, and one which undoubtedly has a role in the western world as well. This is clearly exemplified by the use of the boat as a symbol. Here there is represented a distinct way of thinking and conceptualising about social organisation and the pattern of living, from birth to death. The symbol is not merely a visual analogy, but is integral with the very concept of the village and the dwelling.

The people of these communities do not build 'symbols', they build houses according to an inviolable tradition of which symbolism is the generator and the essence.[26] Sometimes, indeed, it may eventually happen that its symbolism is no longer understood, but the tight social and cultural organisation will continue giving expression to its forms. This phenomenon may explain architectural characteristics in many cultures, not only in the case of the apparent boat symbolist influences in China and Japan already cited, but also boat symbolism in Scandinavian and early Buddhist architectures in India.

Shelter can be symbolised, and made more important in the process. As well as physical shelter, the symbol may provide psychological shelter.

Formerly a distinction was made between spiritual and material culture. This was useful on an abstract level, but led to the neglect of the all-pervading nature of spiritual influences. The symbol of the spiritual sphere often sprang in the first place from the material culture. Empirically, the two cannot be divorced.

In the examples we have been considering there is a very intimate connection between shelter and symbol. Symbolic relationships between sea and land, man and community, the individual and his ancestors, death and the perpetuation of life and so on, are given expression in buildings, meeting places and even in the layouts of villages. Ordinary shelter has been used to express spiritual ideas.

NOTES

[1] VROLAGE, B, A. G., (1).
[2] c.f., TISCHNER, H.
[3] VROKLAGE, (2), p. 263.
[4] VROKLAGE, B. A. G., (2).
[5] VROKLAGE, B. A. G., (2).
[6] VROKLAGE, (2), p. 267.
[7] VROKLAGE, (1), Figure 3a.
[8] VROKLAGE, (2), pp. 265–6.
[9] VROKLAGE, (1), Abb. 5.
[10] VROKLAGE, (1), p. 754, (2), pp. 266–7.
[11] VROKLAGE, (1), p. 728 & (2), p. 198.
[12] VROKLAGE, (2), pp. 266–9.
[13] VROKLAGE, (2), p. 269.
[14] VROKLAGE, (2), p. 270.
[15] GEURTJENS, v. VROKLAGE, (1), p. 712.
[16] VROKLAGE, (2), p. 196 and VROKLAGE, (1), p. 717.
[17] RÖDER, v. VROKLAGE, (2), p. 195.
[18] VAN WOUDEN, p. 31–2, referring to the Kei Islands, taken from Drabbe.
[19] GEURTJENS, v. VROKLAGE, (1), p. 714.
[20] PARMENTIER, HEINE-GELDERN, (3), 190, 191, Figure 25.
[21] HEINE-GELDERN, (3), p. 176.
[22] VROKLAGE, (1), p. 755; HEINE-GELDERN, (1), p. 149; (3), 207, 208.
[23] VAN WOUDEN, pp. 31–32.
[24] VROKLAGE, (1), p. 714, 722.
[25] TISCHNER, p. 113–4, referring to Palau, from KRAMER, A., Vol. 111, p. 205f.
[26] c.f., CUNNINGHAM.

BIBLIOGRAPHY

ARNDT, PAUL, *Gesellschaftliche Verhältnisse im Sika-Gebiet,* Endeh, 1933.
CUNNINGHAM, CLARK E., 'Order in the Atoni house', in *Bijdragen tot de Taal, Land-en Volkenkunde,* Vol. 120, 1964, pp. 34–69.
FRASER, DOUGLAS, *Village planning in the primitive world,* New York, 1968.
GARDI, RENE, *Sepik,* Baarn, 1958.
GRUBAUER, A., *Unter Kopfjägern in Central-Celebes,* R. Voigtländer Verlag, Leipzig, 1913.
HEINE-GELDERN, R. von, 'Prehistoric Research in the Netherlands Indies', in *Science and Scientists in the Netherlands Indies,* the Board for the Netherlands Indies, Surinam and Curaçao, New York City, 1945, pp. 129–167.
HEINE-GELDERN, R. von, 'Das Tocharerproblem und die Pontische Wanderung', *Saeculum,* II, No. 2, 1951, pp. 225–255.
HEINE-GELDERN, R. von, 'Some tribal art styles of South East Asia: an Experiment in Art History', in FRASER, DOUGLAS (ed.), *The Many Faces of Primitive Art: A Critical Anthology,* Prentice-Hall, Englewood Cliffs, New Jersey, 1966.
HORNELL, JAMES, 'Boat construction in Scandinavia and Oceania', in *Man,* Vol. 36, No. 200, 1936.
HORNELL, JAMES, *Water Transport, Origins and Early Evolution,* Cambridge University Press, Cambridge, 1946.
KAUDERN, WALTER, *Structures and Settlements in Central Celebes,* Elanders Boktryckeri Aktiebolag, Göteborg, 1925.
PARMENTIER, H., 'Anciens Tambours de Bronze', in *Bulletin de l'Ecole Française d'Extrême-Orient,* Vol. 28, 1918, pp. 1–30.
STEINMANN, ALFRED, 'Les Tissus a Jonques du Sud de Sumatra', in *Revue des Arts Asiatiques,* Vol. II, 1937, pp. 122–137.
TISCHNER, HERBERT, *Die Verbreitung der Hausformen in Ozeanien,* Verlag der Werkgemeinschaft, Leipzig, 1934.
VROKLAGE, B. A. G., 'Das Schiff in den Megalithkulturen Südostasiens und der Südsee', in *Anthropos,* Vol. 31, 1936, pp. 712–57.
VROKLAGE, B. A. G., 'De prauw in culturen van Flores', in Cultureel Indië, Tweede Jaargang, 1940, pp. 193–99, 230–34, 263–70.
WOUDEN, F. A. E. van, *Types of social structure in Eastern Indonesia,* translated by R. Needham. Koninklijk Instituut voor Taal-Land-en Volkenkunde. Translation Series II, Martinus Mijhoff, The Hague, 1968 (Original title: *Sociale Structuurtypen in de Groote Oost,* J. Ginsberg, Leiden, 1935), 1935.

ART AND MAGIC IN THE SOUTHERN BANTU VERNACULAR ARCHITECTURE

James Walton

The first Bantu peoples to enter southern Africa all built beehive-shaped huts; either frameworks of saplings covered with thatch or corbelled stone structures. But a curved surface of reeds or thatch or of rubble masonry afforded little opportunity for the display of artistic talent and it was only with the introduction of the cone-on-cylinder dwelling that the Bantu love of colour and pattern could find expression on the smooth clay-smeared walls. It is very probable, therefore, that mural decoration was first practised by such Sotho-Tswana tribes as the Tlapin, Hurutse, Koena and Pedi, who built cone-on-cylinder huts, and from whom the art spread to the Nguni and the earlier Sotho when they also adopted the cone-on-cylinder hut form.

NATURALISTIC PAINTINGS

The Sotho-Tswana homestead consists of one or more huts set in a courtyard, *lapa,* bounded by a wall or reed fence. The fronts of the huts, the inside walls, the floor of the lapa and the wall surrounding the lapa are all decorated with patterns which originally comprised chevrons, triangles, rectangles, diamonds and a variety of curved shapes. Animals and other naturalistic subjects are also sometimes depicted on the inside walls. Campbell, who visited the Tlapin capital of Likatoo, near Kuruman, in 1812, observed that 'the huts were not only larger and more carefully constructed than those of the Nguni, but that the walls were painted and adorned with various patterns. The wife of Chief Salakutu had decorated

Hurutse wall painting in Chief Sinosee's hut, Kurrechane.

117

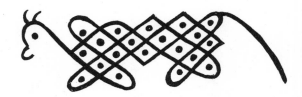

Lunga wall paintings from north-east Angola (after José Redinha).

118

Ila-Tonga wall paintings, Zambia.

Zoomorphic wall paintings from Farmerfield, Salem, Eastern Province, South Africa.

Decorated Kalanga granary, Rhodesia (after J. Theodore Bent).

the walls of her house with a series of paintings, being rough representations of the cameleopard (giraffe), rhinoceros, elephant, lion, leopard and steenbok done in white and black paint.'

On his second journey, in 1820, Campbell went farther north to the extensive Hurutse village of Kurrechane, where the houses were of considerable size. One of these, belonging to Chief Sinosee 'was neatly finished; it was circular like all the others, having not not only the wall plastered both within and without, but likewise the inside of the roof. The wall was painted yellow, and ornamented with figures of shields, elephants, cameleopards, etc. It was also adorned with a neat cornice or border painted of a red colour. In some houses there were figures, pillars, etc. carved or moulded in hard clay, and painted with different colours, that would not have disgraced European workmen'.[1]

In the centre of the house was a circular room with a conical roof reaching up to the apex of the thatch. This was the private sleeping room of the chief himself, and its wall was also decorated with delightful representations of elephants and giraffes. Campbell also saw a house in Lesotho which was ornamented with the figures of animals in like manner. This led Stow to comment, 'As these cases are unique in the several tribes where they occur, viz. among the Batlapin, the Bahurutse, and the Bakuena of Moshesh, all widely separated from each other, and whose national mode of painting, when they indulge in it, is confined to the representations of lines, spots, lozenges, curves, circles and zig-zags, it becomes an interesting subject of speculation whether the attempt to represent animal life in these isolated cases was a spontaneous development in the artists whose handiwork they were, or whether, as was frequently the case in those days, these men had taken Bushman wives, or were half-caste descendants of Bushman mothers, and thus the hereditary talent displayed itself in their new domiciles among people of either the Bachoana (Tswana) or Basuto (Sotho) race.'[2]

The portrayal of animal figures on the walls of the huts is not

Mosaic patterns on Taung hut, Lesotho.

VENDA

c. EARLY SOTHO
1877

after Stow

SOUTH AFRICAN
BANTU
WALL PAINTINGS

SOTHO

TAUNG e

HLUBI f

THEMBU g

Walton

South African Bantu hut patterns.

onfined to those Sotho-Tswana tribes mentioned by Stow. The
la-Tonga, who live in the angle formed by the Zambezi and its
ributary, the Kafue, also decorate their huts and grain stores with
olourful abstract designs and schematic motifs. Their most artistic
ecorations, however, depict trees, animals and human figures,
ften in amusing situations, such as a painting of a man fleeing
rom a charging goat to the safety of a nearby tree. Closely related
s the Lunda mural art recorded by José Redinha from the north-
ast corner of Angola.[3] There the paintings include masks, a wide
ange of mystical signs in which continuous interlacing patterns
redominate, stylised human and animal figures decorated with
atterns associated with initiation rites and ceremonial dances, and
n assortment of everyday subjects such as plants growing in pots,
eroplanes and match-stick figures.

Theodore Bent, when he journeyed to Mashonaland in 1891,
recorded Kalanga paintings in the Sabi valley. He described two
huts from 'Mtigeza's kraal which were 'as yet roofless, but substantial huts being built in the *kraal* entirely of mud, which is a
new departure for the Makalanga. The insides of these were
decorated with squares of black and white, like those one sees in
Bechuanaland [Botswana]. Inside the huts were big household
granaries for the domestic stores, also made of mud and decorated
curiously with rims, and rude paintings in white of deer, birds and
men. One represents a wagon with a span of six oxen.'[4]

Interesting and unusual paintings were found in huts in the
vicinity of Farmerfield, near Salem in the Grahamstown district of
the Eastern Cape Province. The large cone-on cylinder huts of
these people have simple patterns on the outside but the interior

121

walls are decorated by friezes of zoomorphic forms which appear to represent a combination of plants and human figures. The family occupying the huts claimed to be Xhosa, but their paintings are so foreign to those of the Xhosa that some other influence was evident, and eventually they stated that the grandfather of the family was a Mosotho who had moved into the area and married a Xhosa woman. Unlike most wall paintings, these were executed by men, and although the owners asserted that they had no special significance, they give the appearance of serving some purpose other than that of mere decoration.[5]

GEOMETRICAL PATTERNS

Although many examples of naturalistic mural painting have been recorded, geometrical patterns provide the usual form of hut decoration. The earlier designs were all-over patterns of shapes filled in with solid masses of colour or with coloured bands, which were either straight or wavy. Until recently all the pigments used were derived from the ground, which yields quite a wide range of colours. Light and dark grey, ochre and reddish-brown, black and yellow or black and white are the most common combinations. Such patterns have persisted among the Sotho-Tswana, and they are still found in association with other forms of decoration among the Pedi, Venda and Transvaal Ndebele.

A particularly local form of decoration is common among the Sotho of Lesotho and neighbouring territories. In this, the shapes are filled in by parallel grooves, engraved in the soft clay be means of the fingers, a piece of stick, or sometimes with the prongs of a table-fork. Such patterns are referred to as *litema* patterns, *litema* being the name given to the furrows of a ploughed field, which so resemble the wall patterns created by the Sotho housewife. These patterns probably originated after 1870 when the plough was first introduced, and no doubt some woman, when smearing the walls of her hut, noticed the patterns which her fingers left in the wet clay and decided to extend such form of decoration to the shapes which had previously been painted.

Decorated Sotho homestead in the eastern Orange Free State, South Africa.

the usual litema patterns, but the space around the windows, the door frame, and often the border around the façade are emphasised by moulded relief patterns picked out in richer colours. The wall surrounding the lapa is the canvas on which the housewife chiefly lavishes her artistic talents, abandoning the traditional patterns and depicting farmyard animals, parts of houses, human figures, or whatever else captures her imagination. Similar fashions have spread to Lesotho, where their expression assumes a more sober form.

The Sotho housewife does not confine her artistic activities to the exterior of the hut. The inside walls are frequently decorated with all-over patterns, patiently applied unit by unit, and low-relief decoration is also common. The greatest care is bestowed on the wall above the *mohaoloana*, the raised platform at the back of the hut, where pottery and other treasured possessions are stored and

...w relief decoration on the interior of an old hut on Thaba Bosiu, Lesotho.

Clay screen in a rectangular Sotho house, Masianokeng, Lesotho.

Once the idea of litema patterns was conceived it would quickly ...read, as is evident from the rapid distribution of another form of ...coration introduced by the Taung. The Taung are a Tswana tribe, ...ted for their skill as potters, who, after extensive wanderings, ...timately settled in south Lesotho. They build cone-on-cylinder ...ts and, as is usual in Lesotho, the wall on each side of the ...trance is smeared with coloured clay and decorated with litema ...tterns. The remainder of the wall surface, which faces the ...evailing wind and rain, is smeared with mud in which small ...nes are embedded to prevent it from being washed away. These ...nes are arranged in delightful mosaic patterns which, it is ...imed, are based on the bead patterns formerly decorating the ...ung warriors' shields.

The Sotho living on farms in the eastern Transvaal and the ...stern Orange Free State have largely adopted the flat-roofed ...ctangular dwelling with a central entrance and a window on ...ch side. The front wall is smeared with clay and decorated with

Pedi homestead, northern Transvaal, South Africa.

123

Pedi wall patterns, northern Transvaal, South Africa.

protected by the medicated twigs of *mofifi* wood buried beneath it by the medicine man. With the introduction of rectangular dwellings the mohaoloana has often been replaced by a clay wall-cupboard or sideboard, which is usually of fretted clay work moulded around a framework of reeds. The screen which separates the living-room from the bedroom is also built up from a series of scrolls and fretted panels.

From Lesotho, the eastern Free State and the eastern Transvaal the cone-on-cylinder hut, and with it mural decoration, crossed the Drakensberg and spread to the Nguni tribes living in Natal, the Transkei and the Ciskei. Externally the Nguni restrict their hut

decoration to borders surrounding doorways and windows, b within these limits they achieve a wide variety. Close under t Drakensberg, where inter-marriage between Sotho and Nguni h taken place, Sotho litema patterns are frequently associated wi the traditional Nguni decoration.

Among the Pedi, who live in the northern Transvaal, mur decoration is concentrated largely on the walls surrounding t lapa. Some of the patterns show a distinct affinity with those of t Tswana and these probably represent the earliest Pedi mural a More commonly, the walls are divided into a series of pane executed in grey, ochre and reddish-brown. Each panel contains ecorative motif, which may be a series of concentric circles, a symbol from a playing card, or even a painting of a donkey or other animal.

Still farther north in the Transvaal the Venda and Lemba have adhered to the simple geometrical patterns of the earliest Bantu settlers. The walls of their cone-on-cylinder huts are decorated with bold bands of colour, sometimes broken by solid triangles. The more interesting line patterns decorate the curved clay seats which flank the entrance, and these seats bear a striking resemblance to those fashioned by a number of tribes in West Africa and the Congo, from where the Venda originated.

The first Nguni to live in close contact with the Sotho were the Ndebele of the Transvaal. They not only followed the building traditions of their neighbours but they also decorated the walls of their huts and lapas with similar patterns. The Ndebele settlement unit consists of a hut surrounded by a lapa which is enclosed by a boundary wall and which is divided by a low wall into a front lapa and a rear lapa; the former serving as an outdoor living space and the latter as a cooking area. Along the length of the hut and front lapa wall are clay benches arranged in tiers. These benches and the side walls of the hut and lapa are decorated in traditional Sotho-Tswana fashion, being covered with an arrangement of triangles filled in by a series of straight or wavy parallel lines executed in greys, browns and black. The pigments are mostly natural ochres but slaked lime is employed for the white background. Soot mixed with clay provides the black pigment, and grey is obtained by mixing soot with lime.

The Ndebele housewife, with her marked appreciation of colour and pattern, developed a form of decoration which may be regarded as peculiar to the Ndebele. To the façades of the huts and lapa she applies richer colours and more varied designs in the form of panels which appear to have been derived from beadwork. The colour range was extended by the inclusion of washing blue and later by the use of commercial pigments. The lavish and colourful

Transvaal Ndebele lapa *wall, with early type of patterns on the benches.*

Transvaal Ndebele, lapa *entrance with stylized human figures making up the pattern.*

Transvaal Ndebele wall patterns, Transvaal, South Africa.

Transvaal Ndebele lapa walls.

Lapa, *Southern Sotho, Eastern Free State.*

decoration of the front walls is consciously planned to contrast with the sombre hues of the side walls, thus accentuating the vivid patterns of the front walls. In some of the later designs pictures of human figures and buildings are skilfully arranged as panels in the façade, and European-style furniture, motor car registration letters and other features of twentieth-century urban life all find a place. Nor is the decoration confined to the painted panels. The entrances and lapa walls are often elaborately enriched by moulded clay decoration, including urns and ball finials and quite intricate pediments.[6]

Mural decoration among the southern Bantu is a vital, living art form which has spread rapidly during the present century. Contact with modern ways of life has given it an added interest instead of destroying it, as has so often been the fate of peasant art in many other countries. It is essentially a changing art, for the designs have to be restored or replaced annually after the rains.

STRUCTURAL PATTERNS

In Rhodesia, the Limpopo valley, Botswana and Angola an entirely different type of mural decoration was often employed. This decoration is an integral and structural part of the wall, and can be divided into two broad groups:

1. Structural patterns – resulting from the arrangement of the bricks or stones or by leaving gaps in the walls. The building material is the same throughout and there is no variation in colour.
2. Material patterns – resulting from the use of stones of different geological character and colour arranged in bands or geometrical patterns. The patterns are produced entirely by the use of stones of different colour which are all laid in horizontal courses.

Structural patterned walling first attracted attention in Rhodesia, where it was studied by Hall and Neal, who published a full list of

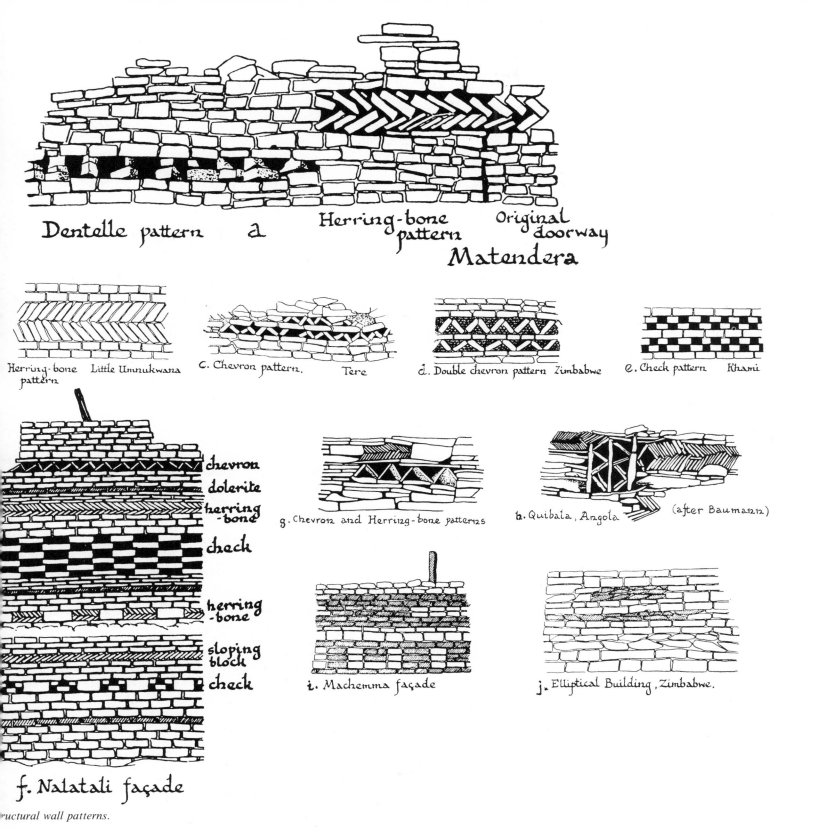

Dentelle pattern   a   Herring-bone   Original
                                         pattern   doorway

Matendera

Herring-bone   Little Umnukwana   c. Chevron pattern.   Tere   d. Double chevron pattern Zimbabwe   e. Check pattern   Khami
pattern

chevron
dolerite
herring
-bone

check

herring
-bone

sloping
block
check

g. Chevron and Herring-bone patterns   h. Quibala, Angola   (after Baumann)

f. Nalatali façade   i. Machemma façade   j. Elliptical Building, Zimbabwe.

ructural wall patterns.

127

all the examples which they had discovered, and which formed the basis of later lists.[7] The structural patterns can be classified as:

Dentelle: Formed by placing the stones of one or two courses such that one corner comes to the front, flush with the wall. This pattern is rare and occurs only in the eastern ruins of Zimbabwe and Matendera.

Chevron (Zigzag): Is widely employed throughout Africa, and Schofield has pointed out that the Shona call it *chikubga* and consider it appropriate to women. 'This', he adds, 'may throw an unexpected light on the statement of De Barros that the sixteenth century Monomotapa kept his womenfolk at Zimbabwe'. The gaps between the stones composing the chevrons may be open or filled with rubble.

Double Chevron: This pattern consists of two rows of chevrons separated by a horizontal course of thin stone slabs, and is largely confined to the eastern ruins of Rhodesia, where it is known from Matemba, Zimbabwe and Tere, but a peculiar vertical arrangement has been recorded from Quibala in Angola.

Herring-bone (Arêtes de poisson): Formed by two rows of stones arranged obliquely to the wall courses and at right angles to each other. It is widely distributed and is found in association with all the other patterns.

Sloping-Block (Cord or Girdle): Consisting of a single course of sloping stones, inclined either to the right or left. Usually associated with chequer pattern.

Chequer (Check or Trous d'hirondelles): This is formed by leaving gaps between the stones and exhibits a number of variations. It is found on Rozwi-Venda sites in the south-east of Rhodesia and in northern Transvaal but later examples also occur on lapa walls in Botswana.

Patterned walling in northern Transvaal and in northern Botswana is directly linked with that in the south-western part of Rhodesia. In Botswana, apart from the unverified record of dentelle pattern at Lipokoli, herring-bone is the only pattern represented on the ruined sites. The Limpopo valley examples are generally simple and crude and consist of short lengths only. Chequer pattern is the only pattern found at Haddon and Verdun, at Maryland herring-bone and sloping-block patterns have been noted, and at Machemma Kop all three types of pattern occur.

In Rhodesia patterns resulting from the use of different coloured stones are confined to darker or lighter coloured bands in a grey granite background, as at the Zimbabwe Elliptical Building. Similar horizontal bands occur at Nalatali (Naletale) and Dhlo Dhlo, where they are of dolerite, and at Bala Bala, where a single band of white quartz is introduced into the granite courses. The finest patterns of this kind are those at Machemma Kop, in the northern Transvaal, where a unique façade is produced by the use of white quartz motifs in a dark grey dolerite wall.

In other cases, as at Khami and Mshosho, the monotony of the grey granite is relieved by the irregular introduction of occasional blocks of pink granite, or of a darker igneous or metamorphic rock. An interesting variant of this is provided from Khami, where blocks of granite have been recovered on which diamond and

Patterned stones from Khami, Rhodesia.

chevron patterns have been engraved. Their position in the w[all] does not indicate any special significance and they give the appe[ar]ance of having been re-used. It would almost seem that the patterned stones were used by people inhabiting the site bef[ore] the present walls were built, but the designs on the stones a[re] definitely the same as those found on Rozwi band-and-pa[nel] pottery.[8]

Referring to the banded pattern at Zimbabwe, Caton-Thomps[on] writes, 'I should like to draw attention to the fact that mu[ral] decoration of alternate courses of horizontal bands of a stone brick of a different colour is characteristic of Saracenic architectu[re] and I am inclined to think that some such fount of inspirati[on] accounts for the appearance of this decoration at Zimbabwe'.[9]

A consideration of the distribution of the structural patter[ns] reveals a certain two-fold division. The chequer pattern is confin[ed] to the Rozwi-Venda, where it is usually associated with herrin[g]-bone, but also with sloping-block and chevron patterns. Frequent[ly] as at Dhlo Dhlo, Khami and Nalatali (Naletale), the entire wa[ll] face is patterned. On the other hand, the dentelle and doub[le] chevron patterns are confined to the eastern Rhodesian sites, whe[re] decoration is not so evident. This regional division may well ha[ve] resulted from occupation by different but related peoples. T[he] chequer and associated patterns are certainly attributable to t[he] Rozwi-Venda, who came from the Congo or Angola towards t[he] end of the seventeenth century. The dentelle and double-chevr[on] patterned walling is usually associated with an earlier culture whi[ch] may belong to pre-Rozwi peoples from the Congo. There we[re] doubtedly migrations from the Congo into Rhodesia before that of the Rozwi. Some of the Chewa-Maravi elements reached Zambia by the beginning of the sixteenth century and there are Portuguese references to such an invasion by peoples from the Congo who overthrew Monomotapa in A.D. 1560. It is probable, therefore, that the existence of patterned walling in Rhodesia, northern Transvaal and norther Botswana is the result of influences from the Congo; influences also established through tribal traditions and through such cultural features as the double iron gongs, which also had a Congo origin and which are found in association with structural patterned walling.[10]

The West African origin of structural patterns is supported by the discovery by Baumann of such patterns on graves in an extensive graveyard on a granite mountain south of Quibala (Kibala) in Angola. The graves are covered with herring-bone and chevron patterns, and Baumann ascribes them to the Jaga. He contends that by the discovery of these patterned graves the connexion with Zimbabwe becomes so evident 'that any doubt is impossible', and he suggests that structural patterned walling was carried to Rhodesia in the seventeenth and eighteenth centuries by the Rozwi, who migrated from the Lunda region.[11]

Farther north, Théodore Monod reported patterned stone walling in the Berber ruins of Mauretania, notably at Ksar el Barka (Tagant) and Tichit (Aouker). At Ksar el Barka the patterns are structural and comprise double chevrons separated by a single horizontal course, as at Tere and Zimbabwe in Rhodesia, and herring-bone patterns with the two rows similarly separated. At Tichit the patterns are material and include not only dark bands and isolated stones but also complex patterns similar to those at Machemma. Monod concludes that 'the evidence presented, without pre-judging its eventual significance, is as follows. Four decorative elements of the dry-stone architecture of Rhodesia: horizontal chevrons (herring-bone) (Matendera, Dhlo Dhlo); vertical double chevrons (Zimbabwe); horizontal layers of dark stone (Zimbabwe, Dhlo Dhlo, Khami); and the irregular incorporation of isolated dark stones in a clearer background (Mshosho), are found again in the Berber dry-stone architecture of the western Sahara'.[12]

Between Mauretania and Angola, Tor Engeström recorded chequer pattern and chevron pattern on the *ginnas* of the Dogon at Sangha, in the bend of the Niger. The Dogon build their walls in clay but Engeström suggests that the patterns had their origin in a more durable material such as stone or burnt brick, and that they are, directly or indirectly, the results of Berber influence prior to the time when the Dogon moved to their present locality.[13]

Whilst it is true that the patterned walling found in Africa could have originated independently in a number of different places, the distribution pattern and the uniformity of the designs themselves, in both form and construction, indicate that the various examples rose from a common origin. Monod suggests that the patterned walls of Rhodesia, northern Transvaal and northern Botswana and Mauretania are the most marginal representations of an early Berber architectural style; 'the faintest resonances farthest removed from the source.' Engeström similarly looks to an early Berber origin for the patterns on the Dogon *ginnas*. Terrasse regards South Morocco and Arabia as representing the two terminations of the spread of Berber architecture.[14] If the patterned walling is of Berber origin, as Monod and Engeström suggest, then Arabia and South Morocco would be the starting points for the subsequent diffusion of this architectural feature – along the east coast of Africa on the one hand and down through West Africa to Angola on the other. The patterned bands on a minaret in Zanzibar and the patterned mihrab wall of a mosque at Kota Kota on the western shore of Lake Malawi are the results of the east coast spread, whilst the patterned walling of Mauretania, Sangha and the Angola graves are the products of the westerly diffusion. Subsequent migration of the Rozwi and earlier tribes from Angola resulted in the patterned walling of Rhodesia, northern Transvaal and Botswana.[15]

The purpose of the patterned walling has been the subject of a considerable amount of speculation. Many of the earlier workers in Rhodesia were particularly concerned with the orientation of the decorated sections of walling with a view to establishing a solastral association with the ruins, but no uniformity has been demonstrated. In several cases, as at Zimbabwe, the patterns occur only on the most imposing walling, suggesting that they designated the chief's quarters. This is supported by the occurrence at the old Venda settlement of Verdun, in the northern Transvaal, of a short length of pattern behind the chief's seat in the wall, and by the elaborate patterned wall at Machemma Kop, which bounds the chief's quarters. Such evidence indicates that the patterned walling of the Rozwi-Venda was employed as a symbol of chieftainship and was used to designate and possibly protect the chief's quarters. The patterns on graves in Angola may have had a similar significance.

PROTECTIVE SYMBOLS

Whatever the origin of the patterns so far discussed, today the majority are only decorative. Some symbols, however, are still considered to have a protective power or to ensure fertility. Among the Nguni and Sotho-Tswana the entrance to the hut is protected by forked twigs buried by the medicine-man under the threshold. The Sotho use *mofifi* wood for this purpose; *mofifi* meaning darkness, and this wood is believed to have the power of enshrouding the hut in darkness so that evil spirits cannot find the entrance. Should they by chance manage to find the doorway then they will be unable to see anything inside the hut.

The Venda of the northern Transvaal formerly had carved wooden doors covered with protective symbols. Today such doors are rare, but a number are still scattered among the various museums, the finest I have seen being one of a group of three obtained from Sibasa and preserved in the Transvaal Museum, Pretoria. This door, *vhoti,* which measures 137.5 cm. by 50 cm., was adzed from the outer rings of a tree trunk, thus avoiding the use of the sap wood, and it retains the curvature of the trunk. It was hung by means of two projections, the upper one passing through a hole in the lintel and the lower one rotating in a depression in the threshold. This method of harr-hanging was known in ancient and Etruscan times and it occurred in the Near East as far back as

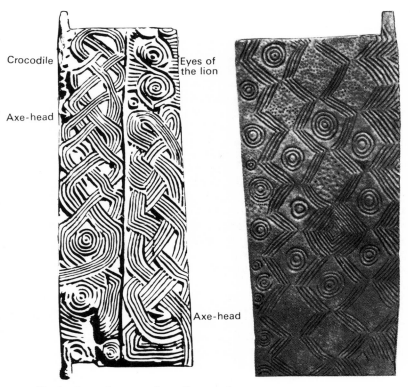

Crocodile

Eyes of
the lion

Axe-head

Axe-head

Venda doors from northern Transvaal.

highly prized possessions which are handed down from father t
son.

The Sibasa door is richly carved with a series of interlacing band
of grooves, enclosing a number of sets of concentric circles, whic
are found on all the doors and are prominent on a door photo
graphed by Stayt at Tskikobakoba's Kraal, where he discovere
three examples. These concentric circles are referred to by th
Venda as the 'eyes of the lion', and they are inscribed on the door
as a protection against evil intruders. The only other decorativ
motif is an axe-head, which appears twice on the Sibasa door.

Farther north the Hera fashion similar harr-hung doors fron
mashuma wood, and an example from Buhera, north-east Rhodesi:
is preserved in the National Museum, Bulawayo. This is rathe
larger than the Venda doors, measuring 150 cm. by 60 cm., and :
is decorated with a series of triangles and diamond patterns. M
K. R. Robinson has recorded similar doors from the Sabi Reserv
together with doors that have no other decoration than a pair c
protruding bosses, probably representing breasts.

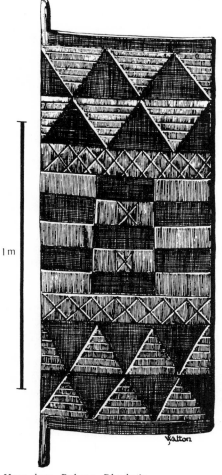

1 m

Hera door, Buhera, Rhodesia.

4000 B.C.[16] William Fagg has pointed out that harr-hung carved
wooden doors are in common use among most, if not all, of the
Sudanese tribes of the Guinea Coast and the Western Sudan, some
of the finest in point of artistic ornament being found among the
Dogon, Bambara, Senufo, Baule, Yoruba, Ibo and Balumbo
tribes.[17] This substantiates the connection of the Venda with West
Africa, a connection suggested by the similarity of the structural
wall patterns of the Rozwi-Venda and those of the Dogon. Such
doors do not exist among the Sotho-Tswana and Nguni or any
other tribes south of the Venda.

The upper harr projection of the Sibasa door is decorated with a
carving of crocodile's teeth, which have a protective significance.
Writing of the Venda chief, who alone was entitled to use a carved
wooden door, Stayt says, 'His sleeping hut is sacred and used to be
protected by a stuffed crocodile. The presence of this creature was
kept a close secret, and it was never seen by any but his nearest
relatives. It is said that today the sleeping quarters of one or two
chiefs are still guarded in this way. The true significance of this
crocodile could not be ascertained, but the crocodile is closely
associated with Venda chiefs, and is regarded by them as a sacred
object.[18] Stayt further says, 'In speaking of or to the chief many
curious euphemistic expressions are used, his most ordinary actions
and possessions being described in a peculiar and roundabout way.
His door or hut is called the "crocodile".' Such carved doors are

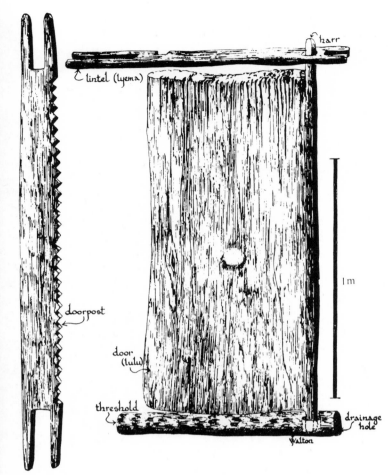

Mambwe door and door frame, Kawimbe, Zambia.

of a goat, the householder was told that when he built his hut he had neglected to call in the medicine-man in order to save the fee and consequently the hut had been wrongly sited. He had actually built his hut over the top of a lightning bird, he was told, and the bird was struggling to free itself, so causing the hut to be damaged. Once the medicine-man had determined a new site and the hut was rebuilt no further misfortune befell him.

The belief that lightning is a bird is widespread but the bird revered as the lightning bird varies from tribe to tribe; among the Venda it is the bird of prey, Raluvimbi; among the Southern Sotho it is the hamerkop, and among the tribes of north-west Transvaal it is the flamingo. In 1951, when travelling through the Dilli Dilli valley in south Lesotho, I came across a homestead of medicine-man, and around the lapa wall were ten tall poles, each surmounted by a carved wooden bird. The owner of the hut said that these wooden birds were intended to keep away the lightning bird, for,

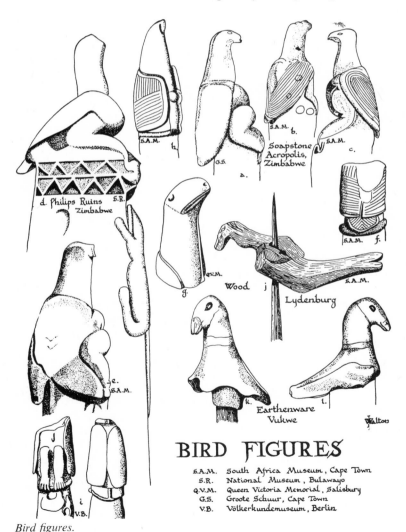

Bird figures.

BIRD FIGURES

S.A.M. South Africa Museum, Cape Town
S.R.   National Museum, Bulawayo
Q.V.M. Queen Victoria Memorial, Salisbury
G.S.   Groote Schuur, Cape Town
V.B.   Völkerkundemuseum, Berlin

A group of tribes living in the north-western parts of Zambia came from the south-east of the Congo basin and, because of their origin, are referred to by other Zambian tribes as 'the people of the west'. A Mambwe door from that area is preserved in the Transvaal Museum, Pretoria. It measures 140 cm. by 63 cm. and is decorated by a single raised boss. The lower harr rotated in a hole in the threshold, which was provided with a drainage hole to permit the escape of collected rain water. The upper harr passed through a hole in the lintel, *lyema*. The door frame was completed by two door posts, slotted at each end to accommodate the threshold and lintel. These door posts, made from *namunsi* wood, are toothed along one or both edges and represented the jaws of a crocodile protecting the entrance, thus providing a parallel belief to that of the Venda in regarding the crocodile as a protective symbol.[19]

Protection of the entrance of the hut is not enough to ward off lightning, fear of which is common among the Southern Bantu. Some years ago the hut of a Mosotho, living near Maseru in Lesotho, was twice struck by lightning, and at last the unfortunate man sought the advice of the medicine-man. After paying the fee

when it saw these birds on the poles, it would imagine that the hut
was already visited by other lightning birds and so it would pass by.
In 1918 J. S. Trevor found three similar wooden birds and a carved
animal mounted on poles, 5.5 m high, surrounding an enclosure
belonging to headman Moraba of the Roka tribe, in the Lydenburg
district of the Transvaal. The Venda place an effigy of a bird on the
top of the hut roof, and Miss Earthy has collected from Moçambique a wooden bird which had four legs for securing it more safely
to the roof. At Vukwe, in the Tati Concession of northern Botswana, Wieschoff discovered two complete earthenware birds and a
fragment of a third in a midden near the western wall, and each
had a socket underneath suitable for mounting the figure on an
upright pole. Wieschoff concludes, 'it is certain that the Vukwe
birds, like those of Zimbabwe, once crowned the top of a wall'.[20]

The soapstone birds from Zimbabwe are the most famous of
such carved birds, and were first described by W. Posselt, who
reached Zimbabwe in 1888. He recorded that, 'there (on the
"Acropolis") in an enclosure which served as a cattle *kraal*, I saw
four soapstones each carved in the image of a bird and facing east;
one stone shaped like a millstone and about nine inches in diameter;
and a stone dish, broken, about eighteen inches in diameter, with a
number of figures carved on the border. The "bird" stones were
planted in an old ruined wall within the enclosure.'[21] After considerable opposition from Chief Andizibi, who was then occupying
Zimbabwe, Posselt eventually managed to obtain one specimen,
now preserved in Groote Schuur, Cape Town.

Three years later J. Théodore Bent recovered four birds on
pillars, one fragment and two miniature birds. 'From the position
in which we found most of them', he wrote, they 'would appear to
have decorated the outer wall of the semi-circular temple on the
hill'. He added that, 'though they are different in execution, they
would appear to have been intended to represent the same bird;
from the only one in which the beak is preserved to us intact, we
undoubtedly recognise that they must have been intended to
represent hawks or vultures'.[22]

Discussing the four birds, R. N. Hall stated that they, together
with another beam which had previously supported a bird figure,
'were standing more or less erect and fixed in granite cement on the
Eastern Temple of the "Acropolis".'[23] Three stood on a raised platform on the west side of the interior immediately on the left-hand
side on entering at the western entrance, and the fragment of
another was found by Bent among the loose stones surmounting a
small platform on the left-hand side of the eastern entrance. It
would thus appear that these six birds stood on platforms on the
inside of the boundary wall of the 'Eastern Temple'. In 1902–3
Hall discovered the upper portion of another bird on the 'Acropolis', and in 1903 he found, 'on the east side of a high and massive
wall and at the south side of a small conical tower in the north-east
Enclosure of Philips Ruins', the very fine soapstone bird which has
since become emblematic of Rhodesia.

In all cases where any association can be proven the bird figures
on posts served as protection against lightning, and invariably
surrounded the lapa of a medicine-man or chief. At Zimbabwe,
where they were found in association with phalli and soapstone

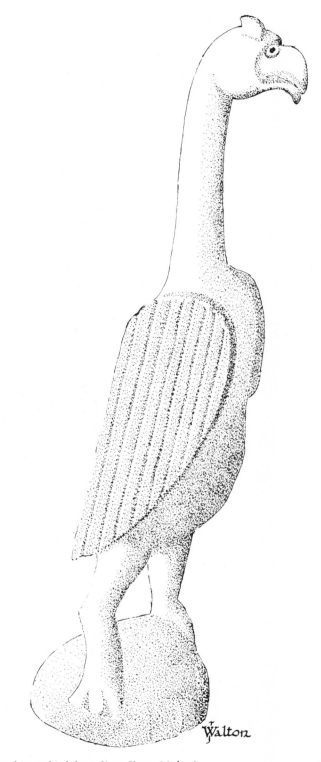

Carved ivory bird from Kota Kota, Malawi.

bowls, they no doubt fulfilled a similar function, and the 'Eastern Temple' was probably the lapa of the medicine-man. The agitation caused by Posselt when he attempted to remove one of the figures suggests that they were still regarded by Andizibi and his followers as having some important significance.

The soapstone birds from Zimbabwe represent two distinct species which were probably the lightning birds of two different peoples. One is a naturalistic representation of a bird of prey of the hawk or eagle type, and Schofield stated that the natives in the vicinity of Zimbabwe still regarded the Bateleur eagle as a sacred bird, and greeted it with hand clapping whenever it was seen. The other bird is a more conventionalised bird with a fan-shaped tail and square-cut wings, resting on a raised ring. No complete example of this type is known, but a head and neck found by Hall seems to belong to one of the fan-tailed bodies. A noticeable feature of this type is the pronounced flange or ridge down the front and back, exactly as one would find in a metal casting, and Masey has already suggested that it 'is evidently a copy of a bronze original, the jointing of the metal and the back and front being carefully reproduced, whilst the treatment of the eyes, mouth, etc., is distinctly a metallic one'.[24] It would appear that the soapstone carvers reproduced the eagle type from nature, and later, when another tribe appeared on the scene, the carvers carved the lightning bird of the second tribe from a metal model. The uniformity in treatment of these birds and the universal presence of the ring indicates that they were all copied from the same model.[25] In 1955, at Kota Kota, on the western shore of Lake Malawi, I came across several ivory carvings of birds very similar to those of Zimbabwe. The carver said that he didn't know what bird it represented but that local carvers, who worked in soapstone, wood and ivory, 'had always carved such birds'.

Among the Sotho and Nguni other methods are also employed to protect the hut from lightning. The Sotho put a forked twig of mofifi wood in the apex of the thatch, and when a storm is approaching longer forked branches are taken out of the hut and placed on the thatch. The Nguni also put medicated sticks on the thatch, but the Cape Nguni often use another protective device. Around the crown of the thatch they place a plaited wattle ring and fill it with soil into which a number of small stones are embedded. According to So3a, a plant i-ntelezi, is often grown in this soil as a protection against lightning. 'Here it grows undisturbed, and conveys to the inmates of the hut a feeling of security.'[26]

FERTILITY SYMBOLS

Granaries are not only protected from theft and other misfortunes but they are frequently adorned with symbols to ensure that the seed will produce an abundant harvest. Bent recorded Kalanga granaries from eastern Rhodesia which were decorated with breasts and cicatrisation patterns, thus representing the female form. 'This is the favourite pattern in Chibi's country and with the neighbouring dependent tribes for female decoration, and they admire it so much that they put it also on their drums, on their granaries, and on their pillows, and on their forges. The "breast and

Kalanga granary with 'breast and furrow' pattern (after Bent).

Budjgu iron smelting furnace with 'breast and furrow' pattern, Rhodesia.

133

Budjga dura *(granary) with painted lion, Rhodesia.*

Mambwe grain store with wooden arms carved with 'crocodile's teeth', Zambia.

furrow" pattern, one might technically term it, and I fancy it has to do with an occult idea of fertility.'[27] The Kalanga iron smelting furnace is actually modelled in the female form, with breasts in relief and cicatrisation patterns, and the *fuyère* represents the male element.

The *dura* of the Budjga headman, in which he stores the threshed beer grain, is sometimes decorated with a lion, which not only protects the grain but also ensures that the beer brewed from the grain will endow the drinker with the strength and bravery of a lion.

The Mambwe of north-western Zambia build great granaries, and on each side of the opening to the granary are fixed two curved beams carved with 'crocodile's teeth' to protect the crop in the same way that the crocodile door posts protect the entrance to the hut.

NOTES

[1] CAMPBELL, JOHN, *Travels in South Africa*, 1815 and 1822.
[2] STOW, G. W., *The Native Races of South Africa*, 1905.
[3] REDINHA, JOSÉ, *Parades Pintadas da Lunda*, 1953.
[4] BENT, J. THEODORE, *The Ruined Cities of Mashonaland*, 1892.
[5] WALTON, JAMES, 'Mural Art of the Bantu', *South African Panorama*, April, 1965.
[6] WALTON, JAMES, op. cit., 1965; *African Village*, 1956.
[7] HALL, R. N. and NEAL, W. G., *The Ancient Ruins of Rhodesia*, 1902.
[8] WALTON, JAMES, op. cit., 1956.
[9] CATON-THOMPSON, G., *The Zimbabwe Culture*, 1931.
[10] WALTON, JAMES, op. cit., 1956; 'Iron Gongs from Central Africa', *Man*, LV, 1955; 'Some Features of the Monomotapa Culture', *Third Pan-African Congress on Prehistory*, 1957.
[11] BAUMANN, H., 'Steingräber and Steinbauten in Angola', *Beiträge zur Kolonial-forschung*, Tagungsband I, 1943; 'Die Frage der Steinbauten und Steingräber in Angola', *Paideuma*, 1956.
[12] MONOD, THÉODORE, 'Sur quelques détails d'architecture africaine', *Acta Tropica*, 1947.
[13] ENGESTRÖM, TOR, 'Contributions aux connaissances des styles de construction au Soudan Français', *Ethnos*, 1955; *Notes sur les modes de construction au Soudan* (Statens Etnografiska Museum, Stockholm), 1957.

[14] TERRASSE, HENRI, *Kasbas berbères de l'Atlas et des Oases*, 1938.
[15] WALTON, JAMES, 'Patterned Walling in African Folk Building', *Journal of African History*, 1960.
[16] WALTON, JAMES, 'Carved Wooden Doors of the Bavenda', *Man*, 1954.
[17] FAGG, WILLIAM, footnote to 16.
[18] STAYT, H. A., *The Bavenda*, 1931.
[19] WALTON, JAMES, op cit., 1954.
[20] WIESCHOFF, H. A., *The Zimbabwe-Monomotapa Culture in South-east Africa*, 1941.
[21] POSSELT, W., 'Under the Mashona Kings', *Sunday Times*, Johannesburg, 17 August, 1924; 'The Early Days in Mashonaland and a Visit to the Zimbabwe Ruins', *NADA*, 1924.
[22] BENT, J. THEODORE, op. cit.
[23] HALL, R. N., *Great Zimbabwe*, 1905; *Prehistoric Rhodesia*, 1909.
[24] MASEY, F. A., 'Zimbabwe: An Architect's Notes', *Proc. Rhod. Sci. Ass.*, 1911.
[25] WALTON, JAMES, 'The Soapstone Birds of Zimbabwe', *S. Afr. Arch. Bull.*, 1955; op. cit., 1956; op. cit., 1957.
[26] SOGA, J. H., *The Ama-Xosa: Life and Customs*, 1931.
[27] BENT, J. THEODORE, op. cit.

DECORATED HOUSES OF PYRGHI, CHIOS
Eugenia Politis

Usually Greek things grow upon you little by little. But from the moment you face Pyrghi, at any time of the day, you are absorbed by its mystery. It is like one off-white stone that has rolled through the centuries and is now resting quietly forgotten in the middle of a plain. It is the first thing you see as you turn the last bend of the road leading to it from the town of Chios. As you approach across the plain through fields, surrounded by low hills, things become clearer. The off-white houses are joined together like a chain in much the same way as the hands of the peasants are joined when they dance the Dhetos – their traditional circular dance of the carnival season. And as you enter the village you feel that you enter the unfamiliar world of another century, where people do not run after time but breathe an air of peace, health and diligent service.

There, the tension you find in the face of the modern city dweller is missing. For the inhabitants of Pyrghi the world is very narrow, it is as large as their village.

Physically and economically the north of the island of Chios differs greatly from the south. The north is mountainous, rocky and barren and the soil is shallow and infertile. The houses of this region are interesting because of their extraordinarily primitive nature. The south, on the other hand, is revealed as an area of relatively luxurious abundance and among the villages of the region Pyrghi is the richest. Here the soil is fertile and the mountains of the north give way to low hills which facilitate both cultivation and transport.

The principal crop and source of wealth to Pyrghi and the south is mastic, an edible gum which oozes from the trunk of the lentiscus

Pyrghi, Chios in the 1920's.

shrub. Nowhere else in the world is this crop produced on a commercial scale. Enriched by the production of mastic the villagers found the way to overcome the struggle to meet basic needs and so could afford to exercise their interest in cultural activities. The relatively economically advanced state of Pyrghi and the geographic position of Chios however meant that they had to submit to the raids and occupation of many invaders; Byzantine, Genoese, Venetians and Turks. But it was during the Genoese occupation of 1346–1566 that Chios was developed and became one of the richest and most beautiful islands of the Eastern Mediterranean. The traveller Olivier wrote that when he passed through the narrow passage between Chios and Asia Minor he felt that he had passed into another world. He reported that in Chios he found people who enjoyed freedom, who were virtuous, kind, brave, cultivated and rich. No other city of the East, he said, enclosed so many people liberated from prejudice, so full of common sense and logic and endowed with better organised minds.[1] Fustel de Coulanges wrote: ce qui faisant le plus d'honneur à la Grèce'.[2] And de Nicolai wrote: 'I did not see in any other place a people so amiable and civilised who tried with honesty to gain the sympathy of foreigners'.[3] Generally the people of Chios were called by foreigners 'Les garçons du Levant'.[4]

The noble Genoese Justiniani monopolised the mastic trade, becoming extremely wealthy and building magnificent buildings and fortifications throughout Chios. To safeguard their interests in the mastic trade they organised the building of several fortified villages in the southern part of the island. These fortified entrenchment villages were established in order to protect the vulnerable and scattered villages from the attacks of pirates and brigands sailing the narrow waters between the island and Asia Minor. These new mastic villages were built far from the sea shore, as were most of the old towns of the Aegean. It was during the period between 1346 and 1415 that they must have organised the building of Pyrghi, concentrating the scattered populations of the neighbouring villages of Chalkios, Callikados, Sosoda, Managros, Fana, Ceros, Dhotia, Galatis, Strofili, Eborios and Megalagros, to become its first inhabitants.[5] It seems that these villages which became the kernel of Pyrghi were Byzantine. The word Pyrghi, meaning tower, as well as the names of the villages and the areas around them, are Byzantine and are mentioned in documents dated before the arrival of the Genoese. The church of Sts. Apostles, a remarkable little Byzantine church built in the thirteenth century and now hidden by the houses off the main Pyrghi square, should be mentioned here. The historian Zolotas believed that around this church was formed the first Byzantine village of Pyrghi.[6]

In 1422 the geographer Christophorus Bondemondius reported and marked on his map the fortified village of Pyrghi.[7] Other travellers describe Pyrghi at this time as a fortified village, large, well populated and as a Genoese establishment.[8] In 1566 Chios was occupied by Piali-Pacha, and the Turkish occupation, which lasted until 1912, began. Chios suffered two terrible blows in the nineteenth century. In 1822 the Turks destroyed the island; Pyrghi, among other villages, was plundered and the people massacred. The

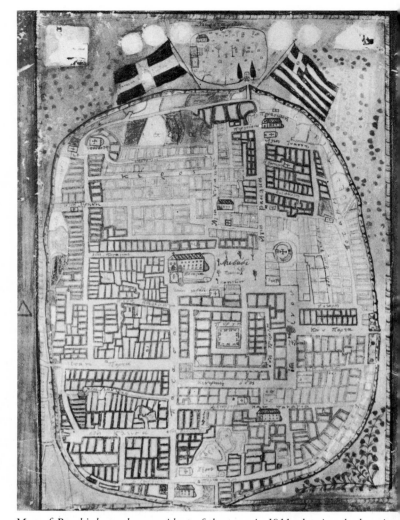

Map of Pyrghi drawn by a resident of the town in 1911, showing the location of the tower, main square, streets and town entrances.

second blow was the earthquake of 1881 when most of the villages in the quake area were ruined, only parts of the old houses surviving. Pyrghi however, along with two other villages in the quake area, survived almost undamaged. An eyewitness wrote: '. . . while curiously enough, the villages towards the south, Mesta, Olymbi and Pyrghi were hardly affected at all'.[9] As a result Pyrghi remains one of the most vital mediaeval villages on the Mediterranean.

We can reasonably assume that Pyrghi was built in a short time. W. Eden remarks: 'The poleodomic system and the way of entrenchment demands on the one hand a specific size of the village and on the other, an "act of foundation".'[10] But it is remarkable that although the village was built by a foreign power, an authentic Greek system was adopted. This system, which formed the village wall by building the houses in an unbroken line, is found on other islands and in other cities, e.g. the neolithic dwellings of Salliagos,

The main square, Pyrghi, as it was in 1928. The tower is to the right.

south-west of Chios,[11] and on Rhodes in the seventh century B.C.[12] We also find this method employed in the building of Byzantine monasteries, e.g. Dafni and Mount Athos.[13] This poleodomic system is also in evidence in the design of archaic Ionic cities built before the adoption of the Ipodamion system. And both Thucydides and Plato mention its use in the construction of Platees and other ancient Greek cities.[14]

Pyrghi exists today because of its closely integrated poleodomic system and the method employed by its builders when constructing it. Despite a general erratic asymmetry, all neighbouring houses share a common wall which effectively interlocks them at one or more points, making demolition and replacement difficult. A further reason for its preservation was that the people of the village kept their beliefs and a substantially unaltered way of life through many centuries. Pyrghi survived not only the onslaught of time but the effects of several foreign occupations; what is remarkable is

the manner in which the foreign influences were absorbed. The people of Pyrghi displayed a natural reluctance to copy foreign elements but they appear to have observed and ingested them, allowing them, eventually, to emerge in altered forms which were harmoniously interwoven into the fabric of their lives.

Although initially Pyrghi may have been built in a short time what we see today does not reflect the work of a moment but rather gives us the impression of flexible adaptability sufficient for the village to have been able to fulfil the needs of its people through the centuries.

On entering the village of Pyrghi one immediately feels encircled by its fortification. The rear walls of the outermost houses present a high unbroken line, at the corners of which small round towers mark changes in its general shape. The only openings into this outer ring are in the fronts of the inward facing houses. Unfortunately today it is difficult to determine how many entrances into the

The first floor coffee-house seen to the right of the main square in the previous photograph, and in its South-East corner.

village were incorporated in the outer wall, because of latter-day building outside it. It is probable, however, that there were two, both hung with iron doors and always guarded. These doors were closed at sunset and were not opened until sunrise.

Once inside the village wall one is confronted by a labyrinth of twisting narrow streets, which lead to the village square in the centre of the complex. This street pattern is subdivided by three main and slightly wider streets which run from the outer wall to the central square.

Separated from the square by two lines of houses is the large central tower dominating the whole village with its size. It is rectangular in plan – 20.95 by 17.80 m – built of stone and surrounded by a smaller wall. It consists of a ground floor and two upper floors, the ground floor being used for storage only, with the house on the first floor reached by a removable outside staircase.

The tower was sited in the middle of the village in order that it might quickly and conveniently be reached by the villagers when the presence of raiders was signalled from the coast. On their approach signal fires were lit on round watch towers, *vigles*, on the coast, and when the villagers had all safely reached the tower the staircase was drawn up and the tower became a fortress.

Unfortunately, the tower has not been preserved entirely. Several houses have been built inside it, making it impossible to see how the doors and windows were arranged on the two floors. Today only the shell remains; most of its stones have been used to build the wall around the village school.

Man in this place creates and at the same time he destroys. If he finds something to be of no further use to him – it does not matter how beautiful it is – he destroys it and replaces it or turns it into something useful.

Once relieved of its defensive purpose the tower began to decay and it, along with other ruined sites about the village, became the focal point of a superstitious tradition among the villagers. It became related in their imagination with ghosts, *vourvoulaki*.

Believing that 'their blood roars' the vourvoulaki are held by the villagers to be the ghosts of men who died violently, unblessed by a priest. Fearful of these ghosts, which are invariably described as pipe smoking Armenians or Arabs, the village women prepare a special gift, called *canissia,* as a token of appeasement. The canissia are made up of a little money, cigarettes and especially prepared sweets, inedible by mortal man. The small canissia packages are placed at night near the 'sighting' along with a jug of water which is broken on the spot. The breaking of the filled jug is an ancient gesture aimed at washing away evil spirits. If in the morning the canissia are gone appeasement is certain – the cigarette-smoking youths of the village have long been the source of relief for the canissia bearers.

Today the square has replaced the tower as the centre of village life. In it are gathered the church, the principal shops and three of the coffee houses. It is in the coffee houses that the men congregate, there to play table games while discussing local events and problems, the tobacco and mastic prices and to exchange news from relatives abroad, with international events only rarely supplanting local issues as topics for conversation. Quietly chatting women sitting in doorways fringe the edges of the square which is filled with the gay voices of children darting like birds across its open expanse. On feast days the square is in its glory, echoing with songs of the season and, in February, with the traditional music of the weeks of Carnival. To see these people on feast days is to understand why there is a pan-Hellenic saying about them. It goes:

'All Chiotes (people of Chios) are crazy,
some more, some less.'

The great event of the year is the fiesta *panigiri* – the celebration of the 'Falling Asleep', held on 15 August. It is the big festival of the village that is awaited by everyone all year long. They dance for three days and three nights: *Paramoni* – Eve, *Giorti* – Main Day and *Paragiorti* – The Day After. The orchestra, with folk instruments, is placed in the middle of the square and the villagers dance non-stop around it. All the villagers are gathered there drinking, eating, singing, dancing, being together, merry and happy.

But if the square is the place in which the villagers are concentrated, the house is the place which concentrates the family. The streets link the square (the community) with the house (the family).

There are three streets which start from the square and end at the village wall. From them, other, narrower streets start which serve the houses between, and finish in dead-ends. The main streets are 2.00 m wide and the alleys are about 80 cm. Until recently the streets were paved with stone; water was concentrated in the central drainage channels of the main roads and was carried outside the village walls. Today the streets are covered with cement.

Over the streets there are many rooms supported by semi-circular vaults; these rooms firmly link opposite facing houses. This practice has the advantage both of saving space and of strengthening the village as a whole against the action of earthquakes to which the area is prone.

A prime factor in both the defences of the village and its fundamental construction is the system employed to link all the houses

Arches spanning one of the narrow streets. Originally these were at roof level and permitted rapid access to the tower in times of seige.

distil the raw sunlight into a sweet optical wine. At night, with a full moon, shadows create images of a cubist painting. The high narrow houses with their small windows, their balconies, sky-lights, the slim, engraved wooden doors and the flat roofs with their extraordinarily shaped chimneys, within a single building type do not produce monotony. On the contrary they strike a balance between unity and individuality; every house stands, as it were, on its own, with its own independent identity, yet at the same time, it is unified with the whole village. Each house is an individual fortress, and part of the common fortification which is the village itself.

In building the house as a castle the builder consciously employs materials which are available in the vicinity and which contribute to and reinforce his aim. The basic construction used in practically all the houses is that of stone vault supported by stone walls. Because of limited ground space the height of the houses developed vertically, some being two storeyed, some three.

The ground floor is used as a stable occupied by animals, and stores for hay and agricultural products. The barrel-vaulted stables are not fitted with windows and are lit only through the open separate doorways. From the front door stairs lead straight up to a landing which in turn leads to a vaulted mezzanine, halfway between the ground and first floors, and used as a hay loft. The first landing is called, in the dialect of Pyrghi, the *parapoundi,* while the hall at the top of the stairs is called the *poundi.* Usually being higher than the rooms on either side, it is often lighted by clerestory windows. Generally in the upper and lower halls lunettes are let into the sides of the barrel vaults above the doorways and sometimes all round the hall. Off this hall is the living-room, called in Pyrghi the *spiti,* which literally means house, the bedrooms, called *spitakia* (little houses) and the kitchen, where the bread oven is situated. There are rarely any big windows in the kitchen. This, combined with the fact that the centrally-placed cooking fire was not provided with a chimney – only the bread oven had one – caused problems of smoke ventilation. This problem was resolved by the simple traditional methods employed in houses of ancient Greece of making a hole in the kitchen ceiling.

with each other and with the central tower. This is achieved by narrow, arched stone bridges spanning the streets from house to house at roof level. These bridges, which still stand, permitted the villagers when under attack to reach the tower without having to set foot in the streets.

Today, as in the past, a large part of the people's lives takes place in the streets. During the day children run up and down playing games, the old women sit outside their doors cleaning mastic in flat straw baskets as others put together tobacco leaves, occasionally singing some slow, familiar old song. At night the scene changes and love songs replace the lullabies of the day. During the day the narrow, gently curving streets with their spanning arches

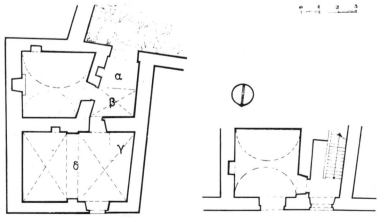

Plan of Pyrghi house, indicating its poleodomic structure. The ground floor (top left) has access to an enclosed garden; the smaller first floor.

139

The staircase which connects the ground floor with the parapoundi is always steeply inclined and is made of stone. The staircase which leads from the parapoundi to the poundi is made partly from stone and partly from wood. This was done in order to use as little space as possible and also to facilitate defence; the people, when pursued, could climb to the poundi and pull up the wooden staircase behind them. Another small wooden stair or ladder leads to the roof which today is cemented over and is used for drying various crops, the washing and as a gathering place.

Mention should be made of smaller details of the architecture of these houses. Semi-circular heads top the doors of most of them and small fan lights are incorporated in the tympani. Similar fan lights, *zamilikia,* often occur above main windows. These windows usually have decorative semi-circular heads constructed with bricks, in the Byzantine style. The majority of the windows are small but they are charming with their white, hand embroidered curtains. The fan lights are of the same type and construction as the larger windows found in many of the churches. Their tracery is of plaster. Between the plaster ribs are placed little pieces of glass; they are mostly of clear glass but with some of the important central pieces of design in various crude reds, blues, yellows and greens, all simply arranged. Many of the larger windows have seats let into the walls beside them, from where it is a custom to sit and watch the activity in the streets below. Outside they always find a place for flowers.

The chimneys have a simple but extraordinary shape and variety, as though each villager was trying to surpass the other. They use amusing combinations of materials, stone, tiles, cement, tin and glass. Of the engraved wooden doors few now remain, but they were certainly the best ornament of the house. The favoured position for carved stone is over the lintel of the front door, where many of even the smallest houses have some little device. This might take the shape of a cross or a wreath with the name of the person who built the house, and sometimes a date as well. Because of their belief that every house has its spirit, for luck and to keep the house spirit friendly they place either a horseshoe or a black-handled knife behind their front doors.

A common feature of interior walls is the niches let into them. These niches are adorned by either sculpted, complex plaster representations of flowers and/or other designs, which are colourfully painted, or by naïve paintings. The niches are also used to hold family icons. Stone sinks and basins are sometimes interesting for their engraved stone and marble backs but of the furniture there is very little to note. A piece which is worth comment is the family trunk. Made of wood and engraved with traditional designs which include flowers, cypress trees and the old monastery, it is used to store the costumes of great-grandparents which are brought out on every big occasion for the youngsters to wear.

But the most unusual and striking feature of all to be found in Pyrghi is the decorative plaster-work, called by its inhabitants *xisto.* The larger part of the façade of the house is almost always covered by a wide variety of simple geometric forms, creating patterns described in horizontal rows 15–30 cm wide. Each row is separated by a narrow, plain white strip of plaster 3.5–5 cm wide.

Street corner in Pyrghi showing xisto *decorated façades, iron balconies and coloured glass fanlights in the spandrels.*

The decoration descends in most instances to within 1–2 m of ground level. The geometric patterns give way, around windows and doors, to the softer lines of curving, flowery designs; while on church walls crosses and religious emblems appear.

Both the method of executing this work and the work itself is called by the villagers xisto, which means scratched surface. It is a comparatively simple technique. A mortar mixture is prepared of sixty per cent sand and forty per cent cement and lime is added little by little until the mixture becomes like a thick cream. To ensure the use of only the finest materials both the sand and lime are separately sieved beforehand. Working in bands across the house, from the top downwards, an area is covered with mortar to a depth of two centimetres. (The amount applied is calculated on

Xisto – *decorated/façade showing the scratches of the sgraffito technique. Built in 1680 this house was re-decorated in 1948.*

the basis that one man can work three square metres a day). The mortar is then smoothed with a trowel until the lime rises to the surface as a whitish 'cream'. This cream is left for two or three hours to stiffen, then the area is painted with two or three coats of white or coloured distemper. Once painted the surface is laid out in bands of two different widths, one of 15–30 cm, followed by one of 3.5–5 cm. This is done with the use of a straight edge and a long nail or with the help of a stretched thread. The inside of the wider band is then decorated. With no fixed design to copy, the craftsman proceeds to freely draw, with the nail or compass and rule, geometrical patterns of semi-circles, rhomboids and triangles. Then while still damp, the white top surface within the design is scratched away with an ordinary table fork, thus revealing the dark mortar underneath.

Until 1955–8 black sand was used in the mortar mix. This sand was gathered from a beach called Focki, one hour's ride by donkey from Pyrghi. Since the ban on the use of the Focki sand, plain fine sea sand has been substituted. To overcome the loss of the traditional black sand the craftsmen of today employ the darkest cement available in Greece, itself a dark grey in colour. The craftsmen are not worried by the change of materials because they have found that, although when first done the contrast is not great, with time the dark areas deepen. The use today of coloured distemper, as it was sometimes used in the past, has largely been discarded. They explain: 'When we used colour distemper it did not last long, the sun absorbed the colour until finally it became white. So why not paint them white, right from the beginning? . . . The sun wants to make everything like his colour, like his face, white. "Hey over there", the sun says to the houses, "you are going to be like me who watches over you, you must resemble your master".'

It is common for the work to be carried out by a team of four men, each of them involved in different tasks, following one another. The leading craftsman lays down the design inside the wide bands. In doing so he does not calculate in order that the

141

whole design fits the zone symmetrically. 'I don't worry if there is not space to finish my flower or geometrical design, I think it is beautiful to let it go out of sight, to lose it for a moment, then see its end reappear. It shows that it continues, it gets lost, it's there but we cannot see it', the leading craftsman explains.

The origins of xisto have puzzled many authorities, leading to the expression of widely differing opinions. F. Koukoules considers the decorative Pyrghi façades to be remnants of Byzantine art; he claims that when not employing façades of carved stone, houses of the Byzantine period were decorated instead by the xisto method in simple geometric designs, examples of which can still be seen on the buildings of the Melanikou and Tekfour Serai in Constantinople.[15]

This view had been accepted as the most likely explanation until recently, when the comprehensive essay 'Xista – Sgraffiti in the Anonymous Architecture of Chios' by Professor H. Bouras was published. In his essay Professor Bouras points out that Mr. Koukoules' explanation is not a persuasive one because it does not take into account the chronological distance between the two examples, i.e. that of Pyrghi and Constantinople. Nor does it take into account the basic differences between the two examples, or embrace the differences in the spirit of the decoration and the detail of expression. Another opinion that xisto came from the East seems unacceptable and the weaknesses of this argument are well elucidated by Professor Bouras.

The opinion that the origin of xisto is Byzantine was first expressed to me in 1964 by the oldest artist then alive, Nicolas Koudouris-Vates, who was teaching me the technique that year. He told me that his father George, who was an artist in xisto in Constantinople, brought it to Pyrghi in 1889. But the xisto, which is found on a wall in Cambos (the remains of a big house destroyed by the earthquake of 1881), seems to refute Mr. Koudouris' claim.

In my research on the island I found, in the same year, xisto on the exterior wall of a house in Vrodatho, a few miles North of Chios Town. Later, searching for more information in the Corai Library of Chios, I found an old photograph showing the town of Chios before the 1881 earthquake. The houses in the photograph had scraffiti façades. This photograph, together with the few other examples I have mentioned, provide evidence that xisto existed at places in Chios other than Pyrghi.

Mention must be made of an album of photographs held by the library of Chios.[18] These photographs, taken the day after the 1881 earthquake, reveal the presence at that time of xisto in Chios town. It also seems possible that the form was employed as much in the town, Cambos, and other villages as in Pyrghi. But we must keep in mind that Pyrghi was one of the few places that survived the 1881 earthquake. And that when the town of Chios and the other destroyed villages were rebuilt new fashions were adopted which excluded xisto. The above mentioned photographs together with other examples given by Professor Bouras lead us, as he says,[19] to the conclusion that the craftmen of xisto in Pyrghi probably used the examples of Chios town as prototypes for their work. But from where did xisto come to Chios and when?[20]

Bearing in mind that the technique is the same as that of the scraffiti of the Byzantines I suspect that its origins lie with them.

The Catholic church of St. Nicholas, Chios, after the 1881 earthquake. An Xisto-*decorated wall can be seen at the right.*

Yet in 1965 I found scraffiti in Switzerland (St. Moritz) and in Spain (Barcelona). This suggests the possibility that scraffiti came to Chios from the west.

There is a similarity also between the Pyrghi façades and examples built by Italian craftsmen in central Europe. This coincidence is mentioned by A. Vanalopoulos in his *History of Contemporary Greeks*. This hint led Professor Bouras to an exploration of the possibilities it suggested. His comprehensive study reveals that his suspicion was justified. In his essay he propounds the theory that xisto travelled to Chios from Italy during the 15th century – a period of remarkable artistic and architectural activity by the Genoese Justiniani.[21]

The technique of scraffiti xisto was employed in Italy from the Renaissance onwards. In Italy, however, the craftsmen limited themselves to merely imitating the regular system of carved-stone

Sgraffito *of similar character to* xisto, *San Moritz, Switzerland.*

masonry construction. This practice in its simple form spread widely outside Italy. It is difficult to ascertain precisely when xisto arrived in Chios or on which building it was originally used. But there is no doubt that it must have been incorporated along with other Italianate features that formed the architectural character of the island.[22]

On the oldest houses of Pyrghi there is not a great variety of design but merely imitation of the regular system of carved-stone masonry construction. Those of more recent times, however, reveal growing variation and intricacy of design.

If few features of the façades of the houses reveal their origin, it is obvious that new designs were added to the repertoire of the Pyrghi workmen. It seems that when the craftsman was working he was reluctant to continue to imitate the structure of a stone wall. He extemporised instead and new indigenous designs were created. It is obvious that his visual experience was the food of his inspiration.[23] He adopted simple geometrical shapes and themes, already familiar to him in embroidery, woven articles and jewellery. The relationship between the geometrical patterns of the familiar domestic articles and those employed in xisto is quite clear. 'Actually the achievement of artistic imagination could be described as the finding of new form for old content, or as a fresh concept of an old subject'.[24] In some of the oldest houses the edges of the lowermost band of decorations are finished with the representation of a fringe of tassles as are found on the edges of carpets. This brings to mind the old Byzantine custom of hanging large expensive decorative clothes from windows and balconies on feast days. It is possible that the memory of the Byzantine custom reached the people of Pyrghi.[25]

The above mentioned thoughts were largely supported by details of an interview I had in 1973 with George Bollas, the leading craftman of Pyrghi. He was proud to tell me that he often adds new designs to his work. He does not specially think of them or design them previously. 'I may have seen a decorative design that I like

Hand-made lace curtain in Pyrghi windows showing stylized geometric fret and decorations, and tasselled fringe.

on a blanket or a sheet at home. It stays inside me, I remember it and I do it while I work on the wall; there it gives birth inside me.' He prefers to divide the wall into narrow zones, 15–20 cm wide and 3.5 cm high. 'From a distance it looks like a carpet. . . . It is more fun', he says.

Different craftsmen extemporise in different ways. They may keep some of the old designs and combine others in their individual way. They even add new elements according to their own visual experience and artistic imagination. The Pyrghi people are not bound in their work by formal considerations other than those of the technique. They are free to use, in whatever way they choose, variations of the basic abstract shapes, the circle, the square, the triangle and the rhomboid. These shapes in combination form the basis of all their designs however simple or complex. The characteristics of the old simple wall structure are retained even in the

143

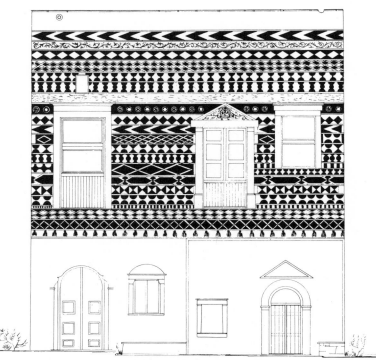

Drawing of the village hall, Pyrghi, showing tasselled fringe (Professor Bouras).

portions show that the craftsman shapes the parts with a view to their final place in the total pattern. The four basic shapes he uses are themselves simple: complexity lies in the sum of the whole. Undoubtedly these shapes once had symbolic significance; the circles may have represented the sun, or the moon; the triangles, water or fire. Today they are symbols that have lost their meaning through the centuries, and to the artists are now only decorative geometrical shapes to which they may attach figurative associations as in the examples collected from George Bollas. Yet these shapes are not simply decorative even now.

Although today we cannot identify their original meaning and symbolism, they still retain a deep significance which closely relates them to the village and its people. The geometrical shapes are essential to the house; they give it its special character. Each house

Costumes of Pyrghi women with richly embroidered overblouses and plain white skirts. Coloured glass fanlights can be seen behind them.

more complex patterns. Thus the patterns are arranged in horizontal zones as the steady ascent of stone or brick.

The prime element of the craftsman's work is the line. He employs lines when laying down the design and the prongs of the kitchen fork he uses when cutting out the positive from the negative describe lines and help to create both texture and depth.

The enclosed black scratched surfaces stand out as figures while the enclosing white ones appear as the continuous surface of the ground. The flowery designs of the windows are not just decorations. They are a way of framing the window. They confirm the figure character of the opening and provide a protusion beneath which the ground surface of the wall can end.

The white ground stands still while the black enclosed figures monopolise the movement and the tension. They are charged with energy. The movement of each detail fits logically in the movement of the whole. Thus results a successful composition with mutual interactions.

A total comprehension of the demands of harmony and balance of abstract forms is certainly the most remarkable achievement of the Pyrghi artist. In every example of his work there lies strikingly revealed a total understanding of the elements of design and of the limits of his materials. This is all the more remarkable when the speed at which he must work is considered. Thus it may be argued that his is not the 'primitive' expression of a simple peasant but a highly refined and, in a sense, sophisticated abstract art form.

The symmetry and unity of the whole and the planning of pro-

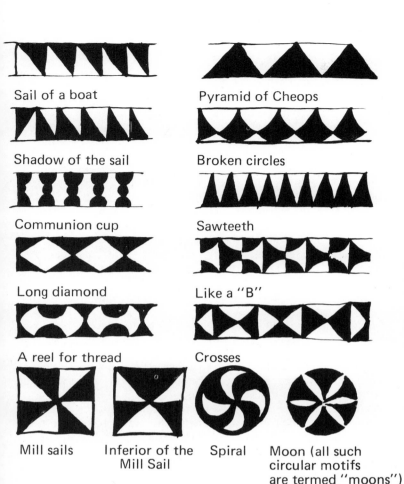

Sail of a boat

Pyramid of Cheops

Shadow of the sail

Broken circles

Communion cup

Sawteeth

Long diamond

Like a "B"

A reel for thread

Crosses

Mill sails

Inferior of the Mill Sail

Spiral

Moon (all such circular motifs are termed "moons")

Symbol shapes as they appear to, and were identified by, xisto *artist George Bollas in 1973.*

is part of the unbroken chain which creates the whole wall-village. In their horizontal zones the designs help to keep the continuity, the symmetry and the unity of the village.

But as an entity these patterns on the houses have a close relationship with the people themselves. If one happens to meet a woman in her traditional costume outside a house in the village square, one finds that the house and the costume are similar in many ways. Lifting one's eyes upwards from the ground one sees the same white, plain area in the skirt and suddenly, after this undecorated surface, a brilliant combination of embroideries, patterns and bright colours united in the overblouse. At the top the oddly shaped hat, embellished with decorative pins and pieces of glass, is similar to the chimney, which itself is a peculiar, gay crown to the house. But the close relationship between the symbols of xisto, the houses and the people does not lie only in their appearance. It goes deeper. I believe that in the symbols of xisto their music can be seen engraved on their walls. It is difficult to imagine visual symbols which better illustrate the particular qualities of their music. Its cruder, wilder, staccato moments are perfectly displayed in the rough black angles of the triangular and diamond shapes standing

deep and sharp in the clash of black and white. In turn these isolated angular shapes in their rows give way, as in the music, to a smooth slow dance, of circles and curves moving under a balcony, evoking the sadness of a plaint. At other times the flow of the notes becomes delicate and fresh as though specially composed to follow the movement of the flowery patterns around the windows. I think it is worth mentioning here what the well known musicologist P. Petridis says about a Pyrghian song: 'I find it difficult to remember another melody, folk or arranged, Greek or foreign, which, with such limited means, manages to express such wealth of inner feelings and high-flown sentiments in such a reserved, almost spartan, way.'[26]

Decorated wall with characteristic signs. The circular 'moons' can be seen beneath the surface of a balcony. 1969.

The close relationship between the people, their life, their work and everything that one sees and hears in Pyrghi is best felt and seen in the big feast day of 15 August. It is when one sees the villagers dancing in the square that one feels the way they express themselves and begins to understand that one cannot say – this is a piece of music, this is a costume, this is a house. They are all united in a whole. You feel everywhere the necessary, the indispensable, the synthesis of which engenders sincerity and harmony.

It is sad to note that the people of Pyrghi do not share the visitor's admiration of their work. Now that the difficulty of communication no longer exists, influences from the outside world affect it more easily.

Some years ago they started to demolish the old plaster work and imitate the painted houses of people in the present-day Chios

Town. Fortunately in 1938 Mr. Philip P. Argentis financed the redecoration of the façades of the houses in the square, insisting that they should all be remade. Recently the National Tourist Organization which, rather belatedly, took over the care of the place, arranged that the façades of the square houses be again redecorated in the old style. Although a few changes have been made, we can still admire today the art which characterises Pyrghi.

During the past few years it has become clear that the village built in the fourteenth century can no longer serve the needs of the twentieth century villagers. External fashions and technology have begun to influence the attitudes of the villagers to the extent that they have begun to copy many of the aspects of life in the town of Chios. Until recently they rapidly replaced the beautiful engraved wooden doors with those made from wrought iron and glass. They painted over the frescoes under the balconies with plastic paint and were demolishing the unique xisto, overpainting it with bright plastic colours. Unfortunately the drive to follow fashion is stronger than any inclination to appreciate the art they themselves have created.

The law has stepped in, in all its subtlety, to protect the village from the villagers by obliging them to maintain it in as near an original state as possible. If they don't obey the work is stopped by the police and they are taken to court. 'Why do they want to impose on us?' they protest; 'When we built our houses, in the past, it was fun. Now it is a regulation.'

While the decline of Pyrghi's customs and traditions has obviously set in and their eventual destruction is almost certain, there seems here to be a special case for conservation. The quality of people's lives must be the first consideration but it seems obvious that to legislate the spontaneity out of their creative instincts is a foolhardy and purpose-defeating gesture. The people of Pyrghi should be encouraged to go on adapting their village, as they have for centuries, under guidance which does not interfere with the creative processes.

Façade of a small house. The plaque on the first floor, by the steps that lead to the roof reads 'Re-done in memory of George Theotakas and Michael Theotakis, 1951'. Above the crosses is the inscription 'Love Thy Neighbour'.

NOTES

[1] PACHNOS, ALEXANDRE, 'Chios', *Great Greek Encyclopedia;* vol. KD, pp. 604–622, 1934.
[2] Ibid.
[3] Ibid.
[4] Ibid.
[5] AMADOS, C. J., *Chiakon Lefkoma* (Album of Chios), G. Tsima & P. Papachrisanthaki, Athens 1930.
[6] THEOTOKAS, GEORGE, *Neoellinika Grammata*, no. 148, 30 September, 1939.
[7] ARGENTI, PHILIP P., *I Chios para tis Geographis ce Perigites,* Vol. 1, p. 13 and picture No. II.
[8] Ibid.
[9] PAGANELLIS, SPYROS, *Othiporike Symiossis – I Sismi tis Chiou* (The Earthquake of Chios) 1883, p. 24.
[10] EDEN, W., B.S.A. (Athens 1950), p. 16.
[11] 'C.B.', *Architectonika Themata,* (Architecture in Greece), 1970, p. 84.
[12] KINCH, K. F., *Vroulia*, Berlin, 1914, p. 112; DEMARGUE, J., *Les ruines de Goulas où l'ancienne ville de Lato en Crète,* B.C.H., 1901, p. 282 and *Fouilles de Lato en Crète,* B.C.H., 1903, p. 206.
[13] ORLANDOS, A. K., *Monastiriaki Architectoniki,* B' Publication, 1958, p. 12.

[14] THUCYDIDES, *Plataika* II, 3–4; PLATO, *Laws* (Law 779), Plato suggests the entrenchment of the city in such a way.

[15] KOUKOULES, F., E.E.B.S., vol. IB, p. 85.

[16] BOURAS, H., *Xysta – Sgraffitti stin Anonymi Architektoniki tes Chiou* (Xysta – Sgraffitti in the Anonymous Architecture of Chios), Polytechnic School – University of Salonika, 1970, vol. E, p. 5.

[17] Ibid., p. 6.

[18] Album, *Les Ruines de Chio*, Castania Frères, Phot. Smyrne, 1881.

[19] BOURAS, H., op. cit., p. 8.

[20] Ibid., p. 10.

[21] Ibid., p. 13.

[22] Ibid., p. 14.

[23] Ibid., p. 14.

[24] ARNHEIM, RUDOLF, *Art and Visual Perception*, Faber and Faber, p. 141.

[25] BOURAS, H., op, cit., p. 14.

[26] PETRIDES, P., *Tragoudia tes Chiou* (Songs of Chios) *Proia* (Newspaper) 23 June 1934.

BIBLIOGRAPHY

AMADOS, C. J., *Symvoli is tin Meseonikin istoria tis Chiou*, School of Philosophy, Athens University, Vol. E.

AMADOS, C. J., *Chiakon Lefkoma* (Album of Chios), G. Tsima & P. Papachrisanhaki, Athens, 1930.

AMADOS, C. J., *Ta Mesaionika Choria tes Chiou* (The Medieval Villages of Chios) in *Arthra ce Logoi*, Athens, 1953.

ARNHEIM, RUDOLF, op. cit.

CANELAKIS, C., *Chiaka Analecta*, 1890.

ARGENTI, PHILIP P., *I Chios para tis Geographies ce Perigites*, Vol. 2, Athens, 1946.

ARGENTI, PHILIP P., *The costumes of Chios*, Batsford, 1953.

BOURAS, H., *Xysta – Sgraffitti stin Anonymi Architektoniki tes Chiou*, (Xysta – Sgraffitti in the Anonymous Architecture of Chios) Polytechnic School – University of Salonika, Salonika 1970, vol. E.

CATLA, C. M., *Chios under the Genoese*, Vol. I, 1908.

Chiaka Chronika (review) Volume B, 1914.

CORAIS, A., *O Papatrehas*.

COWBURN, WILLIAM, 'Popular Housing', *Arena*, September–October, 1966.

FISHER, ERNST, *The Necessity of Art*, Penguin Books, 1963.

GIALOURIS, N., *Architectoniki Diakosmisi sto Pyrghi tes Chiou* (The Architectural Decoration in Pyrghi of Chios) in *Nees Morfes*, 3, 1962, pp. 27–30.

GIELDION, SIEGFRIED, *The Eternal Present – The Beginnings of Art*, Oxford University Press, 1962.

LOUKATOS, DIMITRIOS, *Laographika Cimena*, (Folklore essays), pp. 303–314.

LAMBAKIS, A. and BOURAS, H.: *Ta Mesaionika Choria tes Chiou*, 1956–1957, (The Medieval Villages of Chios) Vol. A, edited by Michelis, P., Greek Metsovion Polytechnic, Athens, 1960.

ORLANDOS, A., *Monuments Byzantine de Chios*, (Planches), Athens, 1930.

PACHNOS, ALEXANDRE, *Great Greek Encyclopedia*, Vol. KD, pp. 604–622, (Chios).

PAGANELLIS, SPYROS, *Odiporike Symiossis*, (A' The earthquake of Chios), 1883.

PERNOT, HULBERT, *L'Ile de Chio*, Paris, 1903.

PERNOT, HULBERT, *Melodies Populaires de l'Ile de Chio*, Paris, 1903.

PETRIDES, P., *Tragoudia tes Chiou* ;Songs of Chios) *Proia* ;Newspaper), 11, 16, 25 June, 1934.

PERILLER, *Chio l'Ile Heureuse*, Athens, 1930.

PSICHARIS, J., *Nea Estia*, 1954.

PSICHARIS, J., *To Taxidi mou* (My Trip) 1888–1926.

RUDOFSKY, BERNARD, *Architecture without Architects*, New York, 1965.

SMITH, ARNOLD C., *The Architecture of Chios*, London, 1962.

THEOTOKAS, GEORGE, *To Pyrghi tes Chiqu*, (Pyrghi of Chios) in *Neoellinika Grammata*, No. 148, 30 September, 1939.

THEVENOT, *Relation d'un Voyage fait au Laivant*, Paris, 1665.

VIOS, STELIANOS, *E Gynaika tes Chiou apo tes Archaeotitos eos Simeron* (The Woman of Chios from Antiquity till the Modern Time) in *Phone tes Chiou*, Athens, November, 1930; 1st year, No. 2, pp. 8–9 and No. 2, December 1930, pp. 11–12.

VIOS, STELIANOS, (edited by ARGENTI, Ph. P.), *The Folk-Lore of Chios*, 2 vol., London, 1949.

VIOS, STELIANOS, *I Sygchronos Chios ce i Pallea*, (Modern and Antique Chios), Chios, 1937.

VLASTOS, A., *Chiaka* (History of the island of Chios), 1840.

ZOLOTAS, G., *E Istoria tes Nisou Chiou* (History of the Island of Chios), Vol. A.

ACKNOWLEDGEMENTS

I would like to thank for their help, information and understanding: The people of Pyrghi; Mr. Haralabos Bouras, Professor of the History of Architecture in the Polytechnic of Salonika; Mr. Labakis, Architect; Miss Angelike Vios for lending me the unpublished manuscripts of Mr. S. Vios; Mrs. Alivisatos and Mrs. Theotokas for letting me have the information, photographs and designs from the archives of the writer Mr. Theotokas; Mr. Petros Petridis, musicologist, Academy of Athens; Mrs. Agiotandi and Mr. Anninos from the Folk Music Archives for letting me record the music of Pyrghi; Miss Leslie Abdella for translating into English the French book *L'Ile de Chio* by H. Pernot: Mr. Alekos Calabokas, Head Librarian of the Corai Library, Chios; Mr. Mark Edwards and Mr. Paul Oliver for advising me on the draft.

REFLEX-MODERNIZATION IN TRIBAL SOCIETIES

Fritz Morgenthaler

Representations of the inanimate as well as of the animate objects of our environment are not, emphatically, the same as the objects themselves. We give subjective or collective meanings to objects. The flag of a nation or a fetish in an animistic culture express, for instance, such a meaning which collectively is understood. The significance represents a symbol, whereas the object as such is a sign for this symbol. A culture is based on systems of laws which, among other factors, reflect themselves in signs and symbols. Languages too are based on these laws; they consist mostly of symbols and signs and play an important part in the culture. The emotional meanings, connected with a lifestyle, ambitions, wishes, goals and interests on the one hand, and the emotional and symbolic significance of the objects on the other hand – all these become an organic entity in an intact society. This entity may change or may be disintegrated. In periods of cultural change, fluctuations may be observed between a progressive trend to change and a conservative one to maintain traditions. These alternative movements have emotional sources and correspond to swings around an hypothetical median, difficult to characterise. The important point is that the link between symbol and object does not show rigid connections. Within a culturally determined frame of reference the relationship between symbol and object may change, although the inner coherence of this relationship remains intact.

If a Saharan nomad grows up in a tent and later on comes to live in a new modern building at Dakar, this fact alone would not mean that the inner coherence between shelter and symbol is disrupted. On the other hand, the persistence of the wish of an Italian business man to live in a mediaeval Tuscanese tower is not enough to prove the presence of this same inner coherence. Disintegration in the organic entity occurs when the circumstances of life make the hitherto integrated meaning of an object lose its significance. It is therefore essential that the deviations from the traditional culture-immanent symbol remain within the limits of integrative capacity. It is not the deviation as such that would represent disturbances of the cultural equilibrium. The failure to maintain the median level constant (around which the progressive and conservative swings take place) or a widening of the margin for the swings would bring about an upset of the culture.

It is an interesting phenomenon that we are generally intuitively aware of the degree of assimilation that is, or was, at work in a process of cultural change. There are signs, signals so to say, indicating the nature of a disturbed or undisturbed cultural equilibrium. For me, for instance, the skyline of Manhattan is a well-integrated sign of a change in the rapport between shelter and symbol. The increasing split, however, between sleeping and working cities in the same town, seems to me a terrifying sign of lack of assimilation. The architectural productivity along the Spanish Mediterranean coast realised in the last two decades under the increasing pressure of the tourist industry, is for me a sign of distintegration with most important destructive effects on culture. The incessant destruction of the city where I am living reflects, in my opinion, a definite sign of lack of assimilation of the civilisational process, actually in action. My personal opinion, however, is not relevant: nor yours, nor that of any isolated person. It is strange enough that a huge mass of population, which may be understood as the very victims of the disruptive cultural development, rushes into the sterile lodging compounds along the Spanish coast and spends its vacation obviously without visible signs of psychic discomfort. The big city centres of the world continue to attract millions of people every year, notwithstanding the fact that the living conditions in the slums and in new rectangular blocks forcibly create an ever-increasing general uneasiness.

I would like to bypass the romantic, sentimental trend, which often comes to the fore in the concept of saving the ancestral heritage as if in a museum. I also disregard the assumption that a lack of sufficient and appropriate architectural conceptions, or the impotence to carry them through, might be the source of the present-day crisis. My purpose rather is to focus on the dynamics, i.e. the mutual interchanges, that are at work between expanding civilisational processes and the cultures which are transmutated by these means.

The monstrous civilisational process in the western world is reflected in the manifold aspects of the increasing influence of advanced technology and industrialisation. The consequences of such an overwhelming process in socio-cultural changes on the one hand, and of the psychological impact that these socio-cultural changes produce in each individual on the other hand, are complex and difficult to investigate, because the incongruities provoked by the collision of cultural patterns and western influences, occurring in the initial phase of such processes, belong already to the past. These difficulties, however, appear in a different light if one considers that the western societies are technically the most developed in the contemporary world. Having integrated their industrial development by themselves they created an evolutive acceleration (Ribeiro). In such an evolution the above-mentioned incongruities, although certainly present, undergo a discrete and largely concealed successive secondary adaptation. In this article I hope to elucidate some shapes of the mutual interchanges between the civilisational processes and cultural changes, by focusing on certain underdeveloped societies. For my examples, socio-cultural aspects from West African cultures and from Papua New Guinea are chosen. Considering such aspects, one is confronted with phenomena, showing interesting incongruities at almost all levels and activities of social life. In this connection Darcy Ribeiro's book *The Civilisational Process*[1] helps for a better understanding. He shows with clarity the influences a higher developed civilisation exerts on an underdeveloped one. Backward peoples are forcibly subdued to more highly evolved technological systems with the consequent effect of 'reflex-modernisation', which inflicts loss of autonomy and the risk of ethnic disintegration on the incorporated groups. From the viewpoint of the civilisational process an incorporation, or 'actualisation' (Ribeiro), of the underdeveloped group occurs. This much is certain; the cultural level is not characterised by these processes. Ribeiro says that one has to overcome the tendency to view the most highly developed societies of today as the ideal socio-cultural system and the objective towards which all peoples are moving. Viewed within this framework, the developed and the underdeveloped peoples of the modern world do not represent distinct and unequally advanced stages of cultural evolution. Whereas the developed societies show an evolutionary acceleration, the underdeveloped ones are those, that were drawn in by historical incorporation as "external proletariats", which are destined to provide not only the necessities of life, but prosperity for the developed peoples to which they are related.'

Summarising Ribeiro's statements for my purpose to confront West African and New Guinean cultures with the intruding civilisational process of the western world, I am emphasising the process of reflex-modernisation which is one of the most significant signs in underdeveloped societies. Along the developmental lines of reflex-modernisation certain pathways are generally selected by which the undermining of the traditional culture spreads.

My first example concerns the Dogon (Mali, West Africa) and is based on insights gained in an extended ethno-psychoanalytical research work conducted by Paul Parin, Goldy Parin-Matthey and myself in 1960 and 1965.[2] In my vignette the Islamic world plays the role we attributed above to the intruding western civilisational process.

The Dogon live in a mountainous area, situated in the south of the Niger-knee. They are animists with a highly differentiated spiritual world, and their carved-wood artefacts, as well as their mask-dances, are of worldwide renown. Although in the last decades the surrounding Islamic cultures exercised an increasing influence upon them, the Dogon mostly preserved their own cultural autonomy. Our psychoanalytical and socio-cultural studies of the Dogon society made it very clear that the Dogon culture could maintain its inner coherence and autonomy as long as the extended family, the fundamental unit of the society, would be able to fulfil the basic socio-economic, as well as the emotional, needs of its members. The architectural setting in a village expresses the inner coherence and the symbolic connections of one form of shelter to another. A corresponding harmony exists between the shelters, tools and all the objects of daily life on the one hand, and the emotional inner psychic conditions of the Dogon on the other.

This became particularly impressive when Dommo, one of my Dogon partners in psychoanalytic dialogue, wished to show me his house in his village Audioumbolo. Having climbed the hill where the village was situated, Dommo took me on an extended tour of, successively, the shelter of the old men, the house of the chief, the court of the magician and the *Ginna Bana* (housing compound of his own extended family) with all the granaries belonging to it. Finally, at the end of our tour, Dommo stood in front of his own shelter, a twin house, in which his father already lived together with his two wives. I remembered that we had bypassed this place at the beginning of our tour, since Dommo's home was situated just at the entrance of the village. Dommo could not show me his house before having integrated it, and himself, and his visitor again and again in the whole unit of shelter, sign and symbol, that is one of the basic representatives of his personal identity, which is at one and the same time a group identity.

The Dogon personality displays a high degree of flexibility, because, for distinct reasons, the psychic organisation generally develops in a direction that perpetuates constant oscillations between one form of gratification and another. Sometimes one object is exchanged for another; at other times the relationship to one and the same person is altered. A Dogon can feel simply like a comrade of all those of his age and sex. Or he can be integrated in the hierarchical line of his younger and elder brothers, extending up to the fathers and the dead ancestors of his whole people, he himself being subordinated to his elders and ranking above those younger than himself. The tendency to identify is, from childhood on, the basis for the eminent capacity for social cohesion possessed by the Dogon people. Resentment attitudes, greed or envy hardly ever appear in the behaviour of adults. The urge to appropriate is often mitigated by the wish to distribute. Working together and participating in communal activities and singing and dancing, pacify instinctual demands, which could endanger the whole cultural formation.

The main village in Dogon land is Sanga. The chief of the village, Ogobara, belongs to a big family of great social and political importance. Its influence obviously moulded many of the adaptational movements that were unavoidable in the last decades, but also guaranteed the further autonomy and the maintenance of the Dogon culture. Among Dogon people, Ogobara is an uncommon personality: for many he is a model, for others a stumbling-block. Although he was the leader of the mask-dancers, and by this means one of the important supports of the traditional

The village of Sanga, Dogon territory, Mali. On the right side of the open space Ogobara's mosque was built.

customs and rituals, Ogobara was Mohammedan. Inclining towards an Islamic way of living and thinking, he expressed what he meant by being a modern and civilised Dogon. Some five years after having realised our research work with the Dogon, we again visited Sanga and were impressed by the relevant changes that had taken place meanwhile. Many people, but almost exclusively those of the younger generation, declined to wear the traditional clothing and show themselves in the modern dress usually found in the Islamic towns of the neighbourhood. Above all, a mosque was built up in the centre of Sanga. The mosque, however, did not show the typical signs of Islamic styling, but was almost completely integrated in the traditional setting of the Dogon architecture. Ogobara was the initiator of the new building, and he wished to have it built very close to his own house. In fact it was not so much Ogobara's personal claim. The pressure to erect the mosque came from the communist centralistic government. Although it should have been a revolutionary step towards more appropriate integration of the different cultures into a homogeneous entity of what could be 'the people of the Mali Republic' it was obvious that the enterprise represented already an effect of the reflex-modernisation in action. Ogobara probably identified with these trends and became an instrument of the powerful centralistic leaders. Since industrialisation and sophisticated technology have not yet reached the remote area of Dogon land Ogobara met severe difficulties in realising his plans. The fact must be emphasised that no opposition came from the powerful representatives of the traditional animistic society to Ogobara's intrusive and obviously culture-destructive trends. Unattainable technical assistance, the lack of supplies and facilities were at the root of Ogobara's problems. He finally asked the advice of the traditional council of the oldest men at Sanga who deliberated, as they had been used to do, whenever the Dogon society applied for the traditionally relevant solution to a problematic situation. In the case of Ogobara's mosque enterprise, the council of the old men decided to resolve the present problem in the same way as would have been the case if a new Ginna Bana (the housing compound of a big family), a fetish house for the priest or a shelter for the old men were to have been constructed. In the traditionally co-operative way all men of the village worked together, singing, drinking and dancing in between. They participated in the communal fulfilment of something of general interest, because the old men, those who are nearest to the ancestors, and therefore predestined to watch to see that the right things are done, told them to do so.

This vignette shows that even strong elements of a most penetrating civilisational influence could be almost completely integrated within the still stable framework of a traditional culture. The example is typical for a transitory period of a civilisational process in motion. The question however remains open as to whether this process will succeed in a culture-adequate evolution, or whether the culture will endure the disastrous effects of an uneven reflex-modernisation.

Mauretanian nomad tents in the savannah south of the Sahara before modern technology invaded the country (1958).

My second example concerns Mauretania, the independent republic of south-western Sahara. Inappropriate technology, imported from the west, has not only destroyed many natural resources of the country, but has also provoked deep cultural changes. Notwithstanding these facts, the isolated individual seems to be somehow reluctant to follow completely his highly directed wishes for modernisation and evolution.

The small population in the huge territory – nomadic cattle herders, living in tents and following the tracks between the few water holes in the southern Sahara – passed for an underdeveloped civilisation. Aiming to advance modernisation in the country the government caused the savanna regions of the southern part of the country to be riddled with artificial bore-holes, enlarging by these means the available sources of water. The consequence of this action was that the cattle herds increased explosively. Soon the forage supply in the savanna became insufficient for the herds, and therefore within a few years, widespread devastation of the scanty vegetation took place. The whole area of the oasis culture in the South-Mauretanian Savanna underwent a secondary transformation in a sandy, barren country. The nomads were compelled to sell their cattle herds, and since the socio-economic conditions of their life had changed, they preferred to exchange the camel with a motor car, and to settle down in villages, or, at least, in the new city-like centres, which had been artificially enlarged.

At the remote oasis of Chinguetti, situated in a mountainous area of the Mauretanian Sahara, we observed a transitory phenomenon of the civilisational process in motion. Nomads, coming from the south, have settled down in the oasis. According to the traditional laws of living patterns in the oasis, they built new mud houses with an additional court behind the shelter, carefully enclosed by mud walls. Whereas the original Chinguetti population are used to laying out their gardens in this court, the nomadic immigrants pitch their tents there. Already accustomed to quite a different way of life – as traders of gasoline for instance – they organised the housing for daily life quasi-normally in their newly built mud shelters. Visitors, however, are welcomed in the tents in the courtyards. The traditional symbol of the original shelter is still alive, although the sense of such a reception seemed to have lost its content. In the vast desert area the tent of a nomad is the unique shelter for anybody coming across the wastes. It is a sign and a symbol in one, for the traditional hospitality that plays an important role in the culture of the Saharan nomads. The tent in the court of the mud house represents a relic of the symbolic nature of a shelter in the traditional sense.

This example hints of the emotional forces in each individual, which are put to the service of the coherence between the objects and their symbolic values. Something of fundamental importance seems to happen if this coherence definitively breaks down.

My third example concerns the Agni, a West African culture, which was, in 1965 and 1970, the object of our second ethnopsychoanalytical study.[3] The following vignette shows the reverse of the coin, so to say, of the effects of reflex-modernisation. It exemplifies how unintegrated trends versus modernisation select

pathways along the lines between the weak points in the social structure, undermining the traditional culture.

The Agni, an Akan people, live in Ivory Coast near the frontier with Ghana. They are involved in an industrialised, agrarian production of coffee and cacao, mainly supported by foreign labourers, who settled down in special districts of the Agni villages. Their employers, the aristocratic Agni, are gentlemen out of service, rather than leaders and principals of their business. The old traditions and the dreams about a great past impair an efficient economic management of their activities. The society shows a matrilinear organisation, but such an institution does not mean a simple antithesis to the patrilinear one. The family system of the Agni consists of a multitude of functional circles, which are often contradictory. The individual's social life fluctuates between and orientates itself along the lines of institutionalised settings for ritualised patterns of behaviour. Agni society is characterised by these inherent contradictions: the personality of its members is complex, tense and full of conflict. Proud and suspicious, they dis-

Two young men of the Agni society at Béou, Ivory Coast. Though they live in the high forest they think of themselves as urban.

152

trust everybody. One of their most relevant proverbs says: 'Follow your heart and you perish.' In social contacts they avoid stable relationships; their love affairs are superficial and several divorces are common in the lives of almost everyone.

These characteristic personality-traits are reflected in the architecture of their 'cities'. An Agni village is conceived like a town – a micro-Manhattan. Rectangular 'streets' divide the housing complex, and each compound is centred around a court with several entrances and exits. By these means one of the most pronounced identity feelings of the Agni personality is enhanced – the conviction to be a city man. He enjoys walking about the streets and through the courts, not anonymously, but uninhibitedly doing what he likes. 'I do not know him who does not interest me. I like my friends, but if one offends me, I do not know him later on. He is again one among many others.' An Agni, who leaves his country, would never go to live in a typical African village. He would go to town, to Abidjan, the big capital of Ivory Coast, dreaming of finding there happiness and inner fulfilment.

The ambiguity of the Agni personality leads to a frightful self-destruction. They destroy their own 'cities' from time to time, intending to rebuild their shelters in a better way. Reality proves, however, that they cannot realise what they hoped to do. The decadent aspects of the Agni culture reveal themselves as an ideal field for reorganisation, modernisation and civilisation. Under the heading of a governmentally centralised target, development by means of the import of foreign material goods has only one purpose in mind, namely to overcome the low status accorded an underdeveloped society. In the case of the Agni, governmental credits enhanced architectural productivity. Inappropriate buildings were erected, following the models of the cheapest French worker's lodgings. Villages rebuilt and modernised in this way were by no means adapted to the Agni personality-structure. The Agni moved away, and the monotonous row of *beton*-shelters was occupied by socially uprooted emigrants, who came as workmen from abroad.

Although the need for social structure proved to be stronger than the attractive trends toward modernisation, one may see in this example how uncohesive and unstable was the relationship between the shelter and its symbolic content. This incoherence was due to an intra-cultural process and must be understood as a specific moulding of the Agni culture itself. In this case the rupture of the coherence between the object and its traditionally-based symbolic signification has not been the result of an intrusive reflex-modernisation. Nevertheless, it must be emphasised that inner cultural transmutations may be predisposed to become weak spots within the frame of differentiated cultural bodies, which still show enough inner resistance to postpone the loss of their autonomy and the destruction of their ethnic values in the early phases of the civilisational process.

In Papua New Guinea I met a different form of cultural self-destruction. While the Agni in West Africa destroy their shelters because restless instinctive demands call forth conflicts with reality, the population of Masantoni, a remote village in the Korowori district of the middle Sepik, do so with inner con-

viction. In New Guinea the civilisational process of modernisation and the use of advanced technology is still in its first stages. In spite of many efforts to create a reflex-modernisation, access seems to be difficult. Only a few centres, mostly along the coast, represent isolated spots of western civilisation. In Papua New Guinea, however, the missionaries are the very pioneers of the expected reflex-modernisation. Among the different missions, the Seventh-Day Adventist missionary organisation is one of the most penetrating and invasive, although it is not the most important in the country. The missionaries settled down, for instance in Masantoni, and brought new ideas, modern ones. They forbade smoking, sexual activity before marriage, eating the traditional pork meat and, above all, the exercise of the traditionally institutionalised rituals, as well as the artistic representation of native fetishes. In an ecstatic and intrusive way the natives were forcibly convinced that the Seventh-Day Adventists' thinking and beliefs must be the best and the only valuable ones for Masantoni's population. The missionaries succeeded and built up a church. The building material

Tambaran house at Palimbei, Middle Sepik, Papua New Guinea.

reminds one of the cultural meaning of the traditional shelters, but the use of the sago-palms, as pillars and walls, was no more than an ornamental attribute put on a sterile scanty shelter. Following the advice of the missionaries the population of the village destroyed their symbolically-loaded houses, threw away the idea of the traditional Tambaran-house, and rebuilt their village in the new style, situating the houses in two rows with a kind of no-mans's land space between.

In this case the reflex-modernisation took place by means of a spiritual penetration on the basis of direct seduction. The main effect was that the individuals seemed to be profoundly convinced of having reached a state of modernity. With this conviction in mind, they propagated similar modernisation and evolution among their still animistic neighbours. In personal contacts the people's

The rear of the ancestor's seat, as it is found in every Tambaran house. Palimbei, Middle Sepik.

affective reactions were as open and differentiated as are generally met in villages of the middle Sepik, where the traditional, animistic culture was still alive. When entering, however, in discussions on religious or political themes the people changed their attitude almost abruptly, adopting the typical sectarian behaviour that in such instances is encountered all over the world. Defensive attitudes then came to the fore in Masantoni, as well as in the New Guinean Highlands, where similar conditions are to be found. But if the affective contact was once re-established – their reluctant attitude being only superficial – impressive melancholic traits appeared, when, with aroused emotions, they sang the old traditional songs or timidly showed an old stone-tool of their ancestors, hidden in a dark corner of a shelter.

This vignette shows the artificial disruption of the animistic representational world. The force of this process was suggestion and seduction. As magic-thinking processes play an important role for the psycho-economic equilibrium of native, animistic societies, seductive and suggestive tendencies, coming from abroad, find in the cultural setting a particularly vulnerable area. The 'cargo-cult' in Melanesian cultures is a spectacular example. Although an effective cultural change is generally the consequence of relevant changes in the means of production, one must not underestimate the undermining influence a preliminary spiritual penetration might exercise on a traditional culture. My example, however, is not typical for the middle Sepik cultures. I saw more villages, like Tambanum or Palimbei, where all aspects of social life, and above all the architectural setting, are expressive signs of a still coherent traditional culture. There, the congruence between the functions of the objects and their emotional and symbolic meaning is fully evident.

The evaluation of the four vignettes I have presented above has to take into consideration that the most important point of our investigation focused on the conditions under which an appropriate integration of new symbolic patterns, especially those connected with the representations of shelters, is enhanced or impaired.

I think that the great capacity for integration of the Dogon society is evident. In the astonishing integration of Ogobara's mosque enterprise, the essential fact is the tendency of the Dogon people to maintain, above all, good personal relationships with one another. One has to stress two points: first, the fact that Ogobara could not separate himself from the social group and finally called for advice in the traditionally institutionalised way; second, that the mosque was required to be built in the very centre of the village, close to the chief's house. Both facts enhanced integration. In trying to generalise the dynamics of this process, I would say that the more the society as a whole is actively involved i.e. not passively seduced, and the more a civilisational innovation appears in the centre of cultural life, the more the capacity for integration is enhanced. In applying this to our western world, the Eiffel Tower in Paris – for me – and the skyline of Manhattan may be good examples.

Evaluating the Mauretanian vignette, I would say that in an already far-reaching disruption of the cultural organisation, strange behaviour patterns may come to the fore, which isolated individuals or small social groups may develop. These incongruities might be signs of a healthy apprehension over the conflict of regressive tendencies versus cultural collapse. In trying to generalise the dynamics of these phenomena, I would suggest that in a socio-cultural period of crisis, one should focus on seemingly incongruent eccentric attitudes arising in social life. They could be important, especially for architects, who have to look for better conditions, i.e. for a better understanding of possible integration processes. In adapting these views to our western world, numerous activities of the young generation may provide good examples.

The vignette concerning the Agni culture shows that conflicts of ambivalence play an important role in personal relationships. In contrast to the Dogon, who greatly value good social rapport, the Agni are constantly involved with their personal problems. Such predispositions create in West-African cultures weaknesses in their social cohesion. Along these pathways civilisational innovations are often imported, infiltrating, for instance, an isolated area of a destroyed Agni village, which, after the devastation, seems to be culturally irrelevant. Thus, a foreign body is placed like an erratic obstacle somewhere in a peripheral part of a culture and interferes later on with the assimilatory processes of the whole society. Therefore it is in principle a conceptual mistake to exile a civilisational innovation in an area of a country where parts of the society are living in a possibly transitory social crisis. These conceptual errors are often encountered in the Western world too, when, for instance, huge industrial compounds are displayed in remote valleys, to give the still 'underdeveloped' cattle farmers the opportunity to become factory-worker proletariat.

In evaluating finally the Masantoni vignette of New Guinea, I would like to stress how important the ideological precursors of civilisational innovations may be, first of all in their confusing effects, impairing appropriate integrational processes later on. For our socio-cultural environment, the monstrous advertising and propaganda industries may articulate similar effects on us, as the sectarian indoctrination affected Masantoni's population.

In evaluating, conceptualising and generalising my few examples, which are in fact only a pale reflection of all the manifold experiences we had during our research work, I am compelled to report a further experience in West African societies. It concerns a special form of identification, which must be understood as a psycho-pathological form of relationship. It generally occurs if a foreign person, highly invested with prestige, enters into an emotionally strong relationship with a native. We called this form of relationship 'identification with a patron'. It happens if one partner becomes highly idealised and represents a model figure for the other. If the idealised partner neither realises nor understands the affective cathexis at work, and if, therefore, nothing is done to unmask and annul this confusing tendency, the idealising African partner expects more and more the full gratification of all his urges and instinctual demands. His new idol becomes the representative of the projected self-esteem, while he, simultaneously, loses his formerly present inner psychic autonomy. As this autonomy is intimately linked with the culture-immanent representational world, one can see how disastrous may be the collapse of the autonomy of the personality. In complete submission, the native presents himself as the only valuable present to the idolised partner. If the 'patron' accepts this role, it does not last long but

Old pillars of a broken down Tambaran house at Palimbei.

155

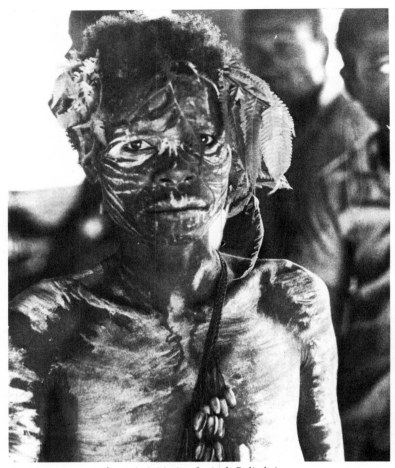

Dancing women at the main initiation festival, Palimbei.

obviously had an overwhelming effect, summoning in the chief's mind, and that of the population, the expectation of great rewards. The danger that overnight we would be involved in an intense 'patron-relationship' with the whole population of the village took on a dramatic aspect when we were asked to assist an ill woman, who had lost consciousness some three days before. We could anticipate that an injection of an antibiotic would probably cure the obvious epidemic meningitis. In trying to avoid an unpleasant issue, we asked the chief to assist personally in our medical intervention. The chief sent his eldest son, whom we involved in the procedure. He had to clean the skin with alcohol, to hold the syringe and so on. A lot of people of the village, of course, were present. The following morning the treated woman felt healthy and walked about in the village. Immediately our prestige grew into gigantic dimensions. The chief came in a submissive attitude, adolescents demanded to join us, wishing to live in our country, children were brought as presents, and people were already standing around our cars, in anticipation of what they could probably seize when the big fusion between us and them took place. Using

Two girls from Faranah, members of an animistic culture, Guinea, West Africa.

only until the unrealistic, fusional relationship ends in a dramatic upset. The African, victim of an involuntary seduction, requires with ever-increasing aggressiveness his rights to be protected and cared for, whereas the naive patron begins to argue, speaking of lack of gratitude and needs for further education. Heavy aggressive impulses come to the fore on both sides, and only the fast departure of the 'patron' might avoid a sometimes dangerous outcome.

One evening we arrived at Faranah, a village in West-African Guinea, and decided to stay there overnight. According to the custom, we presented ourselves to the chief of the village, who accepted the guests with the honours provided in the culture for those events. His speech, however, both for the assembled village population and for us, was too long and overloaded with emphasised statements of our high prestige, and how this prestige would last to the village's profit. Our two fully equipped Land Rover cars, and above all, the fact that we were medical doctors,

156

our prestige, we commanded the chief to set up an adequate council with all the traditional rituals, which custom demands such an event calls forth. We ordered that the whole population of the village should be present. The chief suddenly gave up his former submissive attitude and organised, at great speed, what we asked for. Then we made long speeches, emphasising again and again how everything that occurs within this village depends on the strength and the spiritual emanation of the personality of the chief. We made clear that we could never have cured the ill woman if the chief had not asked us to do so, and had not agreed that his son should show us the shelter where she slept. After all, the eldest son of the chief had assisted the procedure of the injection, and nobody would know if the healthy effect had not been connected, in some way or another, with these circumstances. We did not tell a lie. We rather tried to conceptualise their way of thinking and reality-testing. In fact, we transferred our prestige back to the personality of the chief. The chief replied to our speeches with re-established self-esteem. Everybody again followed his instructions: when we loaded our cars, the population helped us carefully. Nobody asked for further unrealistic assistance. We left Faranah in the same state of affairs as that in which we had arrived the day before.

What did we do?

May I be permitted to express it in terms, using the context of the vignettes, presented above. We acted like the Dogon, incorporating the foreign body, i.e. ourselves, within the traditional cultural frame. We centralised our purpose on the person of the chief. Involving the chief's son, rather eccentrically, in our medical activities, we introduced the traditional object into the modern environment. We did what the nomad did at Chinguetti. We restrained ourselves from acting like the Ivory Coast Government dealt with the Agni, and avoided giving good advice or futile European objects as presents. We had no missionary goals in trying to convince them that our way of thinking might be better than the culture of the population, but we enhanced, through adaptation, the integrative capacity of the chief.

What could have happened at Faranah can be summarised as follows: as representatives of the highly idealised modern civilisation, we could have become the idol, from which lasting gratification of all instinctual demands might have been expected. The danger of a possible failure of the chief's capacity to maintain the culturally determined prestige in his role was due to the fact that he himself was inclined to enter into a 'patron-relationship' with us. Thus, a disturbance of the socio-cultural equilibrium of our hosts could easily have been provoked.

Introducing this example in my context, I hope one can better understand along what lines a loss of autonomy and disintegration of ethnic distinctness may develop. In the case of a 'patron-relationship', these symptoms concern psychic reactions of individuals, and one must not equate such phenomena with apparently similar occurrences in socio-cultural changes of whole societies, which develop under the pressure of civilisational processes. I am aware that comparisons between psychology and sociology are questionable, such simplifications generally being conceptual

errors. It has not been my purpose to confuse; my aim was simply to indicate that within socio-cultural changes a disintegrative process could develop that would remind us, in its phenomenological aspects, of the worst issues of a relationship along the lines of an identification with a patron. To be sure, again, the comparison is wrong. Socio-cultural changes do not occur by psychological means. They are induced by changes in the means of production, and these changes occur under the pressure of technical revolutions.

Whatever the real socio-economic conditions in civilisational processes may be, if a distintegrative development occurs and the ethnic distinctness of the culture collapses, signs are observable that are very similar to those I have described above. (In these instances, however, only one individual, or at most a small group of persons, are involved.) Thousands and thousands of daydreaming people then demand modernisation of their style of life, as if all their conflicts would be resolved, and all the urges and instinctual demands would be satisfied by these means. From the psychological viewpoint, the most relevant effect of these emotional swings of the masses consists in the fact that each individual who might be most interested in maintaining the traditional, creative patterns of his material, as well as of his spiritual environment, becomes counter-active to his most prominent interests. Seen from the socio-economic and practical viewpoint the rush of the culturally disoriented masses into the big industrialised centres, the ever-increasing claim for further technological and civilisational evolution together with numerous other aspects represent a gigantic peripheral pressure on all governmental and socio-economic activities of public interest. In my opinion, this aspect is still underestimated. Among many other fields, the architecture of today is subjected to this pressure. As architectural products are visible and tangible objects, they best externalise the hidden laws of these processes at work. It is simply not true that the empty, tedious new shapes of the big African cities, or of the new centre of Djakarta, or of the Mediterranean Spanish coast, or of the row of new buildings in the town where I am living are only the result of the doubtfully creative intuition of the architects who conceptualised and built them. The devastation of the cities and the architectural jungle in these countries are, much more, the unavoidable consequences of a passive subjection under the hypnotic peripheral pressure of the masses.

The masses are not conscious of their historical situation. They are satisfying needs, leading the architects to bëlieve that these needs are really their own. They do not perceive that not only their productive capacities but their entire lives have turned into merchandise. In their function as merchandise they only serve capitalism. They do so as renters of a flat in a housing compound, as purchasers of automobiles to transport them to their place of work, as commuters between leisure and labour. Their claim for modernisation of their lifestyle has been shaped by socio-psychological processes which underly the pressures of the same economic and power-structures which have first contributed to a disintegrative development of their culture, and then in a second step have produced a psycho-social outfit which helps to complete exploitation.

People of Faranah, Guinea.

158

...can Village.

Socio-economic factors are the causes of the disrupture of the culture-relevant link between the object representations and their symbolic values. The integrative capacity is overwhelmed. In the case of claims for civilisational innovations, uncontrollable instinctual demands come to the fore and initiate the peripheral pressure, to be seen not only in the societies with underdeveloped civilisation, but also in the most developed ones. Within the stream of these pressures, relics of symbols flow along. Unexpectedly they may appear as ornamental attributes on the walls of the uniform, rectangular lodging-compounds, industrial buildings, etc. Sometimes they are even interwoven, as eccentric splinters, into the architectural concepts.

Is it true that the creative originality of signs and symbols, in the realm of what a house, a village, a town could mean for a man living today is lost – or have we, by the ornamental attributes civilisational innovations sometimes show, perhaps to be reminded

of the nomad at Chinguetti, who pitched his tent in the court behind the mud-house? Is the symbolic significance in both instances really the same? I doubt it, but I do not know. If it proves to be the same so much the better. We could then look forward with trust into the future.

NOTES

[1] RIBEIRO, DARCY, *The Civilizational Process,* Smithsonian Institution Press, Washington, 1968.
[2] PARIN, PAUL, MORGENTHALER, FRITZ, and PARIN-MATTHÈY, *Die Weissen denken zuviel,* Psychoanalytische Untersuchungen in Westafrika, Kindler Taschenbucher, Munich, 2079.
[3] *Les Blancs Pensent Trop,* 13 entretiens psychanalytiques avec les Dogon. Payot, Paris, 1966.
[4] *Fürchte deinen Nächsten wie dich selbst,* Psychoanalyse und Gesellschaft am Modell der Agni in Westafrika. Suhrkamp Verlag, Frankfurt am Main, 1971.

159

PATTERNS OF CHANGE IN AN AFRICAN HOUSING ENVIRONMENT
Julian Beinart

'And the Black Man keeps moving on, as he has always done the last three centuries, moving with baggage and all, forever tramping with bent back to give way for the one who says he is the stronger. . . . They call it slum clearance instead of conscience clearance – to fulfil a pact with conscience which says: never be at rest as long as the Black Man's shadow continues to fall on your house'.[1]

Ezekiel Mphahlele's writing, that of the poet and participant, is, if less anodyne than official statistics, no less accurate a description of a centrifugal process that has given a special shape to contemporary cities in southern Africa. The constant shifting of Africans and other non-white peoples outward from the centre of the city has kept them on or close to the periphery, pushed out from a position of enclosure to one of isolation; from a condition of choice, however limited, in the private market to the optionless environment of authority housing. While epidemics and civil disturbance were often the raisons d'être for immediate action the process has proceeded at a rate dictated by the pressures of a white electorate on the one hand and the weight of African urbanisation on the other. Throughout, the process has been underpinned by a constant belief by authority in the value of geographical separateness, which if naïve at first – a minute of the Johannesburg City Council of 1904 suggests that 'the advantages of keeping the native quarters completely away from the white population will be obvious to everyone, whether one considers the interests of the Native or those of the poorer class of European' – attempted a more sophisticated rationale[2] later.

Black urbanisation and white reaction not only produced new methods to explain old attitudes, but changed an administrative framework from one characterised by a lack of regulation to one which superintends over almost every aspect of non-white, urban life; and saw to the application of these laws with increasing rigidity and efficiency. A lecture by the Chairman of the Non-European Affairs Committee of the Johannesburg City Council in 1966 blandly lists ninety-six separate acts passed since 1945 'affecting the administration of Non-European affairs' and adds that 'in addition to the Acts, knowledge is required of the regulations framed under the various Acts'.[3] In sum, at the cost of their being kept outside the matrix of urban life and without having taken part in the making of any of the decisions that shaped the process, non-white people have been provided with hundreds of thousands of new houses on vacant ex-urban land, and inner-city slums have been cleared.

CHANGE: THE URBAN SCALE

In Johannesburg, the core city of Southern Africa, the process can be seen more clearly than in any other.[4] Built in 1886 as a mining camp, it soon attracted Africans as mining and domestic labourers and Malays, Coloureds, Indians and Chinese to provide other services. The town grew fast and ten years later half the population of 102,000 within three miles from Market Square were non-white. Apart from those houses by the mines, Africans spread themselves all around the centre but already the tendency to be located separately and to the west showed itself in the position of the Native, Kafir and Coolie locations (Zone 1).[5]

The first thrust out of this zone is commonly attributed to the plague of 14 March 1904 which caused the City Council to burn the Coolie location the same night and shift Africans to a site (later called Pimville) adjoining a large sewerage works, about ten miles from the city centre (Zone 3). The decision to move so far is partially explained by the Council: 'We are convinced that the public interest requires not only that the location should be placed outside the town but that it should be as far as possible removed from any neighbourhood inhabited by the Europeans'.[6] On the top of a small hill temporary huts were built and land leased for private house-building. Pimville remained a problem for the City Council: in 1929 the infant mortality rate was reported to have been 958 per 1000.[7] Its history is a rich one, however, and among its products the singer Miriam Makeba is still affectionately known as Pimms No. 1!

For a long time Pimville remained an isolated village separated by mine workings and dumps from the inner city, and its attractions, whatever they were, were not enough to prevent Africans from returning to the inner city. But the city was spreading and in the last years of the South African Republic, the owner of a farm called Sophiatown, about five miles from the centre of the city, offered his land to the Government for use as a 'location'. Although the lease was cancelled after the Boer War and some white people settled there, its natural attractions – it also adjoined a municipal sewerage and depositing site – caused it to become an

160

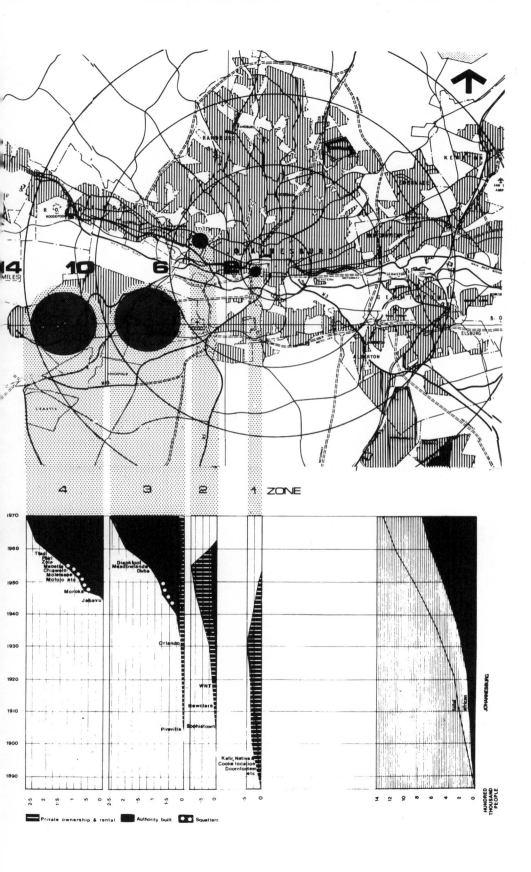

*Johannesburg – Distribution of
African population 1886–1970.*

161

Aerial photograph of the Western Native Township, showing Sophiatown, Newclare and Coronationville.

be recognised as a non-white suburb. Here, and later to the south in Newclare adjoining the railway line, Africans became land-owners and others tenants of privately built housing and back-yard rooms (Zone 2).

It took the high mortality rates of another disease – influenza – to stimulate the City Council once again to try to clear the inner-most area. In 1918 it established its first municipally built township for Africans, Western Native Township, between Sophiatown and Newclare, thus consolidating what became known as the 'Western Areas'. Zone 2 was now established as a permanent area of African residence and here between the mid-thirties and fifties the synthesis of a new African urban culture took place: one of physical poverty but intense community, of crime and deprivation, but one cele-brated with a new music, journalism and writing. It had, in

Nathaniel Nakasa's words, 'a heart like Greenwich Village Harlem'.[9]

Zone 1 was still full, Zone 2 filling and Zone 3 had Pimvil Alexandra, a freehold area, and Eastern Native Township, smaller version of W.N.T., had appeared in the east but the ne development was again in the west. After a long period of ind cision and inactivity during which Maud claims that 'in fact, tl annual expenditure on Natives and on the zoo had roug coincided',[10] and with the backing of the Natives (Urban Area Act of 1923, Orlando and with it the permanence of Zone 3 a later Zone 4, was established. Slum clearance in Zone 1 could nc proceed but this put pressure not on the other zones, as the Coun may have hoped, but on the intermediate zone. If poor peop have to move they will move as short a distance as possible, espec ally if this move coincides with their preference of the private market over the discipline of municipal housing. Africans in Zone 1 diminished and Zone 2 swelled.

But the war soon made choice academic. Industries stimulated by war production needed labour and now even W.N.T. and Orlando were packed. For the first time a squatters' movement appears as a spontaneous exodus of sub-tenants from crowded houses in Orlando and Pimville, and to a smaller extent also at Newclare and Alexandra. Riots followed and the Commission of Enquiry appointed to investigate these interpreted the position of movement leaders such as James Sofasonke Mpanza as follows: 'By applying the segregation provisions and not setting aside any land on which we (the Africans) may build ourselves, the Municipality has taken on itself the duty of providing us with houses. But it has not carried out that duty; there are no houses for us. Very well, then, we shall go and sit down on municipal land and wait for the Municipality to come and put a roof over our heads.' The City Council responded by screening squatters (there were 60,000 in one camp alone) and transporting them back to camps of 'controlled squatting' provided either with breeze block shelters (Shanty Town) or with elementary services only (Moroka). The latter, erected on an area of 1,534 acres adjacent to Jabavu[12] established Zone 4 at a distance of twelve miles from the centre city as a place of African urban residence.

Now the movement to get rid of all Africans (later all non-whites) from the inner zones gained momentum. Africans in Zone 1 were disappearing and now only Zone 2 remained. Already in 1939, as a result of agitation by white ratepayers in the neighbourhood, Councillor S. J. Tighy 'had begun vehemently to urge the total removal of all Non-European settlements in the Western Areas as a solution to the problem.'[13] But while previous removals were of a scale small enough to be coped with by municipal funds and an attitude of laissez-faire, new resources of determination, capital, organisation and labour were now needed. They emerged after the 1948 general elections, the first to be won on an open 'apartheid' ticket. Lassitude was replaced by religious resolve. Some of the capital came when 'Sir Ernest Oppenheimer was invited to visit Moroka and was so aghast at what he saw that he arranged with his colleagues in the mining industry to loan the City R6 million (about $8\frac{1}{2}$ million dollars) repayable over twenty years, interest being changed at $4\frac{7}{8}\%$'.[14] The organisation came in the form of a separate Housing Division in the City Council solely for the purpose of building houses for Africans; and the labour through one of the many Acts that had followed Nationalist rule – the Native Building Workers' Act which now made it possible to train and use Africans to build houses in proclaimed African townships. (Job reservation had of course ensured that they could not build for anyone else anywhere else.)

Vigorous house building took place in both Zones 3 and 4 and first Sophiatown (replaced by a white suburb grotesquely called Triomf) and Newclare were cleared and their inhabitants removed to Meadowlands and Diepkloof; and finally in 1961 the people of W.N.T. were shifted to a rebuilt Moroka (the end of squatting) and Chiawelo. Eastern Native Township and Alexandra, domestic servants and a few others remain as temporary anomalies but to all intents and purposes Johannesburg was now all white and the inner circles cleared.

CHANGE: THE COMMUNITY SCALE

It was only in the later years of this process – after the Second World War – that the effects of institutionalised racial discrimination really began to distinguish the pattern of residential location in Johannesburg from that of a similar size North American city. There are certainly no parallels for the planned establishment of such vast areas for a single racial group as have grown since the War and are still growing at not much more than suburban densities, on the outskirts of South African cities. Pimville and Orlando foreshadowed this pattern but the housing areas of Zones 1 and 2 were different. Compared with some of the classic early American generalisations, these inner zones coincide closely with Burgess' zones of 'transition' and 'working men's homes'; and the wedge of non-white housing to the West has much resemblance to Homer Hoyt's 'low-class residential' sectors. (In fact, a Johannesburg Municipal survey in 1951 recognised this sector phenomenon and suggests that the Western sector be planned as completely non-white.)[15]

Sophiatown, Newclare and Western Native Township were the focal inner-city ghettoes of Johannesburg. Each had its own character ('W.N.T. was the place to go home to, Sophiatown a place to have a ball')[16] but the whole was a viable mixture: the relatively peaceful W.N.T. in the middle between the 'inflammable' Sophiatown on the north and the 'lusty' Newclare on the south, Indian and Chinese shopkeepers along the seams between them and the 'prim and pretentious'[17] Coloured people's township of Coronationville on the east. For those that came to live here, particularly for those straight from the country, it was where they learned the urban life: where they were fashioned by what was around them and where they in turn responded by matching their surroundings to their own developing physical and spiritual needs.

It is difficult to distinguish which qualities or which combination of qualities of time, people and ghetto place itself could account for the generation of such response; but nowhere was it as energetic and organised, at both personal and social levels, as in Western Native Township. Certainly a generally benevolent municipal administration, individual home rentership and reasonably secure tenure marked W.N.T. from Sophiatown and Newclare, and are all given by residents themselves as reasons for having been satisfied there. People called the place 'Thulandisville' (O.K., I heard you) referring to the fact that the Municipality responded to their requests; they sang a song about a city councillor, Mr. Ballenden:

'Siya mbongu Ballenden   (We thank Mr. Ballenden,
Ngokusikhuph'e dolbeni'   for having taken us out of
                       town.)

They also mention liking the ethnic composition ('a gay mixture of all tribes'), the low rent, the low costs of transportation to

Land use and growth of the Township.

Space changes in various house types.

SPACE CHANGES

- Municipal Additions
- Private Additions
- Porch Enclosures
- House Type A 2-room
- B
- C
- D 3-room
- E
- F
- Single Rooms

Land use and growth.

LAND USE AND GROWTH

- ● Shops
- ○ Coal and Wood Suppliers
- Beer Hall
- Shebeens
- Garage and Taxi Services
- Library
- ■ Churches
- □ Schools
- Creches
- Municipal Offices, Clinic, etc.
- Communal Hall
- ⊠ Old Age Home, Hospital, Girls' Home
- Sports Fields
- △ Communal Bath Houses
- – – Pedestrian Paths
- Bus Terminals
- Growth : Stage One 1918
- Stage Two 1919 -1920
- Stage Three 1924
- Stage Four 1925 - 1928
- Stage Five 1930+

164

Air view of the Core area of the Western Native Township with central facilities and demolished Sophiatown on right.

town, the inexpensive and wide range of goods ('from a candle to beer') available from the many stores in the area, and all the social amenities within walking distance.

The table below attempts to summarise some of the patterns of action and response that occurred over the four decades of Western Native Township's existence. The first was a period of immigration and organisation of a village environment that must have resembled in many respects the rural background with which the residents still had an active intercourse. The thirties faced the community with the problems of ordering a society suddenly swollen and made more complex by the filling of the Western areas; and if the response was still tentative, by the fourth stage when a generation had already been born in the township it had become confident enough to challenge authority wherever the community felt threatened. Time had replaced the residents' natural insecurity of rentership with a sense of permanence and optimism which the alteration of their houses and the symbols on them reflected. By the last years of the township's life, the community, with a constantly increasing commitment to urban life, had changed a limited and impersonal environment into one which, if still overcrowded,

dangerous and poor, nevertheless contained much that was rich and special.

CHANGE: THE DWELLING SCALE

Although the organisations housed by them might have been sponsored by groups within the community, all communal facilities in Western Native Township were built by the Municipality or other outside agencies. Thus the efforts of the community to change its physical environment were limited almost entirely to adapting their dwelling units and the immediate surroundings of these.

(a) *Changes of space and function*

There were only three ways in which tenants could achieve more space inside their houses. Choice of any of these depended on the amount they could afford and the method of payment; all required scrutiny by the authority and were almost invariably a source of friction between tenants and authority.

The first method, the enclosing of the front porch of the house either with temporary or permanent materials, was the most

165

STAGE ONE 1918–1930	STAGE TWO 1930–1940	STAGE THREE 1940–1950	STAGE FOUR 1950–1962
HOUSING Township established but little demand for houses. About 2,000 houses built in five stages: first single rooms, huts and 2-roomed houses, and after 1930 3-roomed houses (See Fig. 2). Houses have no plaster, ceilings, floors or internal doors. Houses built at costs ranging from $156 to $226 per unit; house rents from $3·50 per month upward.	Population pressure builds up (population about 12,000 in 1933) and township crowded. Municipality allows residents to house sub-tenants on application but demolishes outbuildings and shacks built by tenants in back yards. Municipality recognises pressures on space and at end of this stage adds an additional room for tenants who request more space and are willing to pay increased rental.	Municipality considers temporary porch enclosures health hazards and orders them removed after fires. Building of additional rooms by Municipality suspended until after war: tenants may still do so at own expense. Illegal outbuildings still being removed by Municipality. Municipality first adopts resolution to remove W.N.T.	Rents increased: now range from $2·50 to $9·00 per month. Municipality acts against permanent porch enclosures but after test court case and in loco inspection allows such construction on approval of plans by superintendent. No more municipally built room additions after 1957. Municipality begins negotiations with tenants about removal but refuses to compensate tenants for any improvements.
Tenants use cowdung on floors, mud on walls, hessian for ceilings and curtains as interior doors. First decorations by people of Bakwena tribe consisting of patterns and animals scratched in mud and dung.	Tenants build shacks in yards and enclose front porches with wood or metal ceiling panels (Mr. Duda the first of these builders) to make more enclosed space). Tenants try painting decoration on brickwork (Ben Ngqaza the first). Tenants complain and rents reduced.	Tenants build porch enclosures (Mr. Stahlo) the first builder, generally for living space but sometimes for shops. First decorations (family Sithole) on permanent porches and front walls. A few tenants make major alterations to houses at own expense.	Demonstrations against rent increases. Decorations on plaster walls become very popular with many variations on limited number of themes. Agitation about removal and especially lack of compensation begins but by 1962 township almost completely removed and 'Coloured' people move in.
SERVICES: People walk, cycle or use horse-drawn public transport. Municipal tram service extended to W.N.T.: fare 3c to town. Houses have no individual water supply; only two communal taps per street and bucket sewerage. Municipality erects fences and plants some trees around township and in three streets.	Street-lighting installed and later electricity also available to tenants at own expense (20 years later only 5% of households had installation). Municipality erects fences around individual house plots. 1937: African newspaper calls W.N.T. "dinghy, dirty, and ill-kept but is impressed by what some of our people are doing to improve their conditions that are anything but conducive to noble living".	Tram fares increased to 4c and after tram boycott, service is withdrawn. Railway extended to Newclare (within walking distance of W.N.T.). Individual water supply and waterborne sewerage installed. Roads improved and stormwater drains installed.	Public Utility Company Bus Service introduced with terminus in centre of W.N.T.: fares now 4c to town.
Women form organisation to prevent women from throwing dirty water into streets.	Tenants plant trees and hedges in front of houses.	Strikes, riots and boycott of trams after fare increase. Space in front of house developed as outdoor living space with decorated gateposts and letter-boxes.	Residents boycott buses because of fares. A few cars appear in township, often derelict, and taxi and car repair service in vacant lots adjoining certain houses.
COMMUNAL FACILITIES AND SOCIAL ORGANISATION: Municipality builds administrative offices and police station. First schools (American Board Mission and Wesleyan Methodist Mission) opened. First churches (Presbyterian and Congregational) built. Municipal clinic and later first private hospital built (Nokuphila hospital).	Communal Hall built by Municipality. Two more schools (one high school) and six churches erected. 'Talitha House' girls' reformatory opens. Municipal Beer Hall opens after continuous police raids on houses where women brew beer illegally in back yards.	First African library built. Two more schools (second high school) opened. Two more churches built. Old aged home and Y.M.C.A. opened. Playground equipment installed by Municipality as well as additional sports fields. Co-operative society goes bankrupt and replaced by seven privately owned shops including 'Abyssinian Fish & Chips' shop. Municipality offers prize for best gardens at W.N.T.	New creche opened by Native Council of African Women from money raised from residents. At end of this stage, W.N.T. has seven schools, ten churches and ten shops.
First residents arrive either from areas nearer city centre or from country: wide variety of tribes take up residence. Occupation of residents almost all unskilled or domestic workers: average annual household income about $170. Witch-doctors provide some medical and magical services. Before 1923, control of village in hands of 14 men, 'Iso Lomzi' (Eye of the Village) replaced by Advisory Board and Vigilance Committee, with chairman considered as mayor, to work with Municipality: annual elections with parties choosing colour, e.g., the blue party, to distinguish themselves.	Economic level of residents remains static: average annual household income about $180. First African co-operative society founded with 166 members and four shops (tearoom, grocer, butcher and baker). Wide variety of social, sporting and entertainment organisations formed: W.N.T. Ladies' Civic Society, Unemployed Young Men's Club, Hungry Lions Benefit Society, Philharmonic Society of W.N.T., W.N.T. Pioneers' Club, Children's Picnic Committee, etc. Sporting Clubs: Transvaal Jumpers Football Club, baseball, tennis, cricket, etc. Jazz and dance bands: Merry Black Birds, Harmony Kings, Jazz Maniacs, Japanese Express Band, etc. 1937: first report of crime at W.N.T. to appear in 'Banty World' newspaper.	War stimulates growth of new industries and average annual income rises to about $340. 'Rising tide of lawlessness' and hooliganism (tsotsis) reported in African newspapers. Civic guards and later Civic Protection Society (C.P.S.) formed to combat thugs and gangs. Gangs: 'Corporatives' and 'Young Americans from New Orleans' said to have been formed and stove pipe trousers worn after showing of film 'Orchestra Wives' in local cinema. Shebeens: 'Green House' and 'Shepherds' offer illegal liquor and 'Stokfels' system instituted (rotating parties who supply liquor). Saloons in houses offer illegal gambling particularly 'fah-fee': lady decorates her house with lucky horse symbol. Political parties active: mayor of W.N.T. decorates his house with African National Congress symbol.	Population still almost entirely working class with small percentage of professional and clerical workers: average annual household income now about $560 but still far below Poverty Datum line (about $700). Fairly static population with high proportion of widows as female heads of families and pattern of interchange with rural areas less frequent than before. Riots at Municipal Beer Hall because of police raid. Boycott of schools organised by African National Congress and residents open their own school, Mohlomo Community School: Mayor expelled from A.N.C. after having been accused of sabotaging boycott. Gang warfare between W.N.T. 'Corporatives' and Sophiatown 'Berliners'; also clashes between 'Russians' and Civic Guard. Jazz singer Dolly Rathebe stabbed and famous reporter Henry Nxumalo killed by thugs. Witch-doctors ('nyangas') still operating and consternation caused by appearance of 'tokolosh' (magic animal) in W.N.T. After failure of continued representations to Municipality, people accept being moved out: Mayor addresses residents: 'This is the saddest day of this township . . . this is the oldest township of Johannesburg and people of this area in Johannesburg have made the greatest contribution in building Johannesburg'.

W.N.T. family belongings awaiting removal.

The standard 2-room house in its original state.

167

Improvised gate to a W.N.T. house.

Porch enclosure of temporary materials.

obvious and cost the least. The idea of providing a front porch in the design of the house seems to have come from a desire by the authorities to reproduce the outdoor sitting area apparently common in tribal dwellings.[18] The reasons the porch seems to have satisfied residents in townships are somewhat different however: a survey in Orlando showed that over 90 per cent of residents wanted one because 'a house doesn't look like a house without a *stoep*, Europeans generally have verandahs and people like to sit on stoeps in the evenings and during the weekends.'[19] Certainly the porch was a luxury in Western Native Township: in almost all the houses it occupied approximately one-eighth of the area of the rest of the house and in the earliest two-roomed houses as much as three-fifths. Consequently over 80 per cent of tenants altered their porches, almost all enclosing them completely to make additional interior space which they used either as sitting rooms (about 60 per cent), bedrooms (about 30 per cent) or kitchens. (A handful

were used as storerooms and in a few cases as either tailors' or cobblers' shops.) The porch also had to serve as an entrance, houses in W.N.T. having been equipped with only one door and this always opened onto the porch.

The addition of the porch was too small to make a fundamental difference to the life-style of the family: in almost all the houses a family size of six (the average for the township was higher) still meant that every room was also a bedroom sleeping at least three. To get a significant increase in space tenants had either to build themselves or have the Municipality do it and pay an added quarter to their rents. The Municipal addition was always at the back of the house and this together with the enclosed porch meant an additional area half again that of most of the houses. An existence below the Poverty Datum line however meant that few could afford the increased rent and only 5 per cent of tenants availed themselves of the Municipality's offer. Even fewer (about 1 er cent) could afford to make permanent structural alterations themselves but those that did spent an average of $650 on these, about four times the original cost of the house itself. Sometimes these alterations expanded the existing rooms (from 9 ft. by 9 ft. to 12 ft. by 12 ft.) instead of adding another room, this being a solution which favoured the arrrangement of furniture over the need for privacy. A letter from a tenant to the superintendent explains this preference: 'Now, Sir, if I have one extra room it will mean that I must divide my bedroom suite as well as my dinning room suite according to the number of rooms. As for instance, I will have to store few chairs in this extra room, and other furniture for the bedroom too, which is no good. . . . I cannot put the whole Dinning Suit in, and I have two pieces of three pieces of Chesterfield Dinning r. Suit left at the store for want of space. Organ and piano are also in the kitchen, all which things ought to be in the Dinning Room.'[20]

This method of expansion was allowed only in the case of the few three-roomed houses standing on bigger plots; in all other cases four-foot side spaces had to be maintained. As houses had no back doors and the kitchen was always in the front, the area at the back of the house was seldom used and never improved. The space in front of the house however was treated with as much concern as was the house façade itself. Here was an opportunity to make an outside living area to replace the enclosed porch, to furnish it with gardens, paving and pergolas and surround it with hedges, gates and sculptured gate-posts cum letter-boxes (see axonometric drawings).

If the amount of space that these people could add for themselves was limited by their poverty, it achieved size for them through being so indistinguishably connected with their general struggle. Thus when the Municipality refused to compensate them on the grounds that they had been warned that they had improved their houses at their own risk and that they were being given indirect compensation through better housing in the new townships, it did not satisfy them. Neither did it when they were allowed to take the improvements away with them or sell them to the new

4 W.N.T. family at the porch of their house. The porch area has been bricked in and an extra room gained.

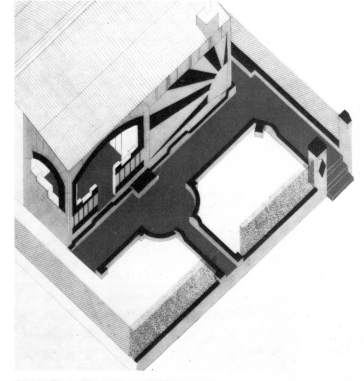

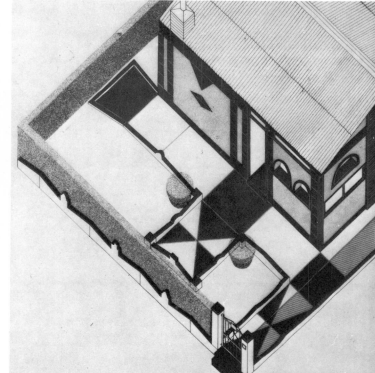

'Coloured' immigrants. One of the officials understood the problem when writing in a memo: '. . . It must be remembered that the sentimental value of their houses is really more important than the intrinsic value . . .'[21] A resident of twenty years in W.N.T. understood it even better: '. . . originally we were handed these houses in their base and barren constructions and structures, in consequence of which all of us started from scratch, plastering, rounding the floors and pulverising the walls, as well as applying some paintings . . . this incredible decision of "penalising" the Natives against compensations is that WE HAVE MADE USE OF THE GROUND AND DERIVED COMFORT OF THESE IMPROVEMENTS.'[22]

b) Decoration

Indigence having prevented them from making alterations, which would change substantially the way they could live inside the house, residents discovered a way of making it look different from the outside. In 1961 three-quarters of all the houses in the township had street-facing façades which were either plastered and decorated or plastered alone.

The original house was built of cheap red bricks and residents considered the appearance so 'unfinished' that it forced them to do something to make it look 'beautiful'. In the first days of the township, residents did this by mixing cowdung with red clay soil and scratching *litema*[23] patterns in it. These early decorations were attributed to the first decorators, people from the Bakwena tribe, who drew animals and figures 'like the Bushmen paintings' or the chevron and grid patterns common in tribal mud-wall decoration. Then the township was still empty and cows grazed among still unoccupied houses.

By the 'forties and 'fifties however the decorations had changed as much as the township. The materials were now bought in the hardware stores of Sophiatown and the designs complex enough

A group of five axonometric drawings of the original house, and altered houses (opposite).

Builder working on the facade of a single room.

171

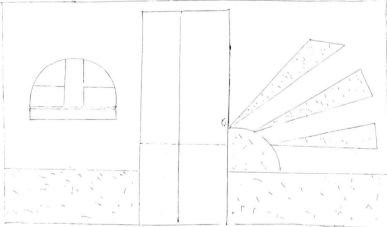

Photograph of House No. 1347.

Drawing of house No. 1347 by the ex-tenant as remembered after three years and builder's drawing of the same house.

to warrant the commissioning of a builder. There were over twenty such builders working in W.N.T. and each claimed that his work carried his own stamp. The builder of house no. 1347 (see photograph) described his way as follows: 'I plastered the whole wall first, smoothed it, left it to dry for about two days. Then I used a string dipped in oxide powder with a nail tied to one end, knocked the nail in at one end of the wall, and then stretched the string (I asked somebody to hold the other end taut) and then proceeded to mark the straight lines by pulling the string in the middle, leaving an imprint on the wall. Then I chipped out the marked area with a hammer. I sprayed the chipped part and while wet, applied the rough-cast by hand, using a trowel to even it out. Having done

the solid portion at the bottom and the sun's rays I then worked on the sun by drawing a circle with an ordinary food plate.'

Only the street-facing façade was treated in this way. A few tenants claimed that it was too expensive to do the rest (the average cost of a decoration was about $50 or one month's household income) but most felt anything else would not be seen. For some the façade was a way of indicating their position in the community ('I was a school teacher and so wished to enhance my status') but for most it had to do with a less specific extroversion: 'wanting my house to be admired' or 'wanting to please my neighbours.'

In a highly other-conscious community the façades were thus a way of both satisfying outsiders and at the same time receiving the

Plan showing proportion of decorated and plastered houses.

DECORATION
● Decorated Houses
○ Plastered Houses

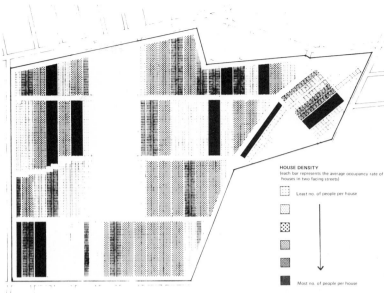

House density.

HOUSE DENSITY
(each bar represents the average occupancy rate of houses in two facing streets)

□ Least no. of people per house

↓

■ Most no. of people per house

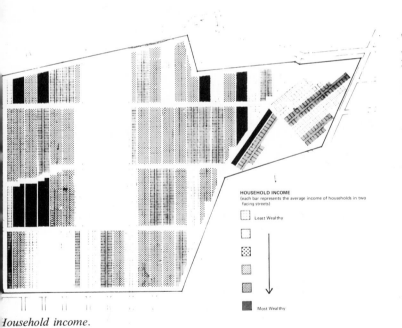

Household income.

HOUSEHOLD INCOME
(each bar represents the average income of households in two facing streets)

□ Least Wealthy

↓

■ Most Wealthy

Intensity of decoration.

INTENSITY OF DECORATION
(each bar represents the ratio of decorated houses to all houses in two facing streets)

□ Least intensively decorated

↓

■ Most intensively decorated

gratification of their approval. Never stepping beyond certain tacitly approved norms ensured against displeasing others and trying your best to be different within this framework meant maximising your own well-being. Herbert Gans suggests a similar process of competition within conformity in Levittown: 'I heard no objection among the Levittowners about their similarity of their homes ... Aesthetic diversity is preferred, however, and people talked about moving to a custom-built house in the future when they could afford it. Meanwhile they made internal and external alterations in their Levitt house to reduce the sameness and to place a personal stamp on their property.'[24] But while Levittowners could move out when they could afford it, W.N.T. residents could not. It is one thing waiting until you can achieve goals, it is another when you know you can never achieve them. Then you

Decorated houses showing use of 'razor-blade' motif.

ave to compress your frustrated ambitions into what you have ow and you make your possessions look like those you will never ossess. Thus the houses of W.N.T. are imagined versions of houses n white suburbia – decorated W.N.T. houses were called 'Park- own', the wealthiest suburb in Johannesburg – decorated with all he intensity necessary to sustain such a myth.

Certain areas within the township seem to have been regarded s better than others and people moved within the township to uit their environment to their position. The area of three-roomed ouses in the north-east corner was considered the best and the ldest houses on the southern fence the worst. The distribution f income however does not reflect this pattern; nor does the istribution of house occupancy rates. Neither of these shows ignificant clusters of income or density but this may well e due to the unreliability of the available information. Africans y custom dislike being counted – the Mayor of W.N.T. hen interviewed confessed that he had never enumerated his hildren.

The diagram showing the intensity of decoration however clearly indicates a zone of intense decoration east of the central area of the township. While the residents here were neither wealthier nor their houses less overcrowded, this was the geographical and spiritual heart of the community. It was the most central and enclosed area of the township and it was the area through which most residents had to pass en route from the main gate in the north-east corner. In this sense it was the most visible to the rest of the community. The elite area in the north-east corner on the other hand was an isolated pocket. The houses were difficult to decorate because they had no dominant street-facing wall and it was, in spite of its being an apparently wealthy area, an area with very little decoration. There was in fact no significant relationship between income (either total household income or income per person per house) and decoration. This is confirmed by the bar-charts which showed that decoration occurred in a pattern unrelated to the particular income of the household or the number of people living in the house.

elow and overleaf: Decorated houses using heliocentric motifs.

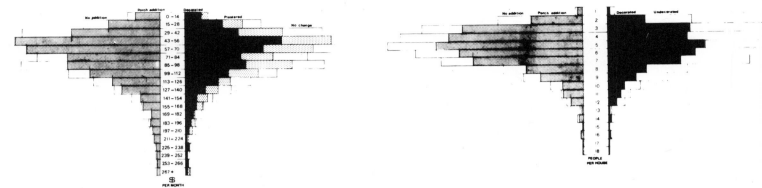

Population distribution, space changes and decoration by household income and house density.

Decoration was an activity which involved a wide range of people in the community. The process of people copying designs from each other spontaneously produced a limit to the whole language of decoration. While none was identical, all the decorations were really variations of about half a dozen basic shapes. By manipulating these and adding colour and texture residents could make surfaces which conveyed either a purely architectonic impression or recognisable images: the razor-blade, for instance, made by inserting three circles into an indented rectangle or the sun made by adding triangular wings on either side of a half-circle. The distinction between abstract decoration and obvious imagery is likely, however, to be stronger in the mind of the un-

initiated than it was in the community. Some residents, for instance, saw certain circular or semi-circular shapes as having to do with the sun, an interpretation unlikely to have come from an outsider to the society.

Certain shapes were explained by their creators as advertising the activities inside the house: a tree shape on the wall because religious meetings were held inside or a horse shape because the house was a gambling saloon; but most were less specific. In fact there seems to be a dichotomy between a set of explanations which suggest a primordial, tribal derivation on the one hand and a more urban, rather banal one on the other. Some, for instance, suggested that 'these are our traditional drawings and white people do

176

Distribution of tribal groups.

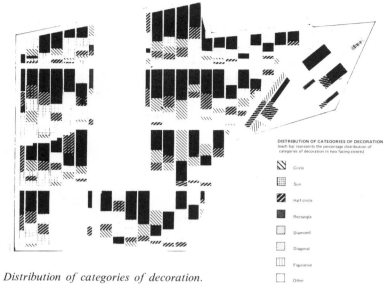

Distribution of categories of decoration.

Geometric wall decorations.

177

not know anything about them' or 'I wanted to show typical Tswana designs.' One Tswana woman even claims to have been sent back to the reserves specifically to learn the designs; but another resident, on the other hand, admits to seeing the design in a geometry book and another in a book on architecture. One resident in fact says that she specifically 'wanted something that would look modern instead of the decorations we do on the farms.' In discussing the circle on his house, a tenant refuted any specifically tribal association: 'The circle is typical European art. Look at the ash-tray you are using.' And while sun shapes suggest inscrutable, heliocentric origins, the sun also appears on Sunbeam Floor Polish tins and suburban wrought-iron gates. Certainly replies like: 'I used green and white because they are my football

colours' or 'I saw the combination on a kiddie's doll house' suggest derivation from an obvious present rather than a removed past.

The pattern of relationships between the decorations and the various tribal groups in the township helps to clarify this ambiguity. Had decorations been linked to tribal affiliations one might have expected that certain tribes who have a strong decorative tradition particularly in respect of mural art, would have played a significant role in the township's decorations. This was not so. Of the major tribal groups in the township, the greater majority were either Nguni (Xhosa, Zulu, Swazi) or Sotho (Tswana, N. Sotho, S. Sotho) and were distributed randomly all over the township. Tswana and Zulu were most numerous throughout but no tribal group decorated much more frequently

Above and facing page: Symmetric and assymmetric motifs.

Distribution of tribal groups by categories of decoration.

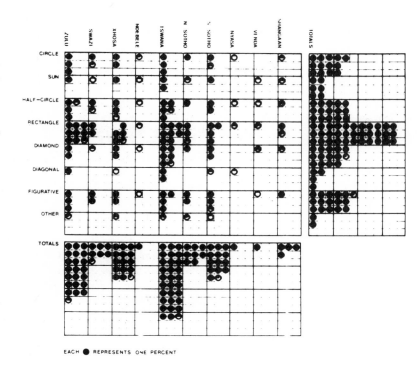

EACH ● REPRESENTS ONE PERCENT

than any other. All decorated more or less in proportion to their numbers in the township, Swazi and Northern Sotho (together only 10 per cent of the township) being the only groups who tended to be more active than others.

If some tribes did not decorate more frequently than others, certain tribes however seem to have preferred certain modes of decoration. One of the ways of categorising the various decorations is according to their predominant shape and a distribution of these throughout the township shows a generally random pattern. While the rectangle and its derivatives were the most popular shape family and the one used by all the tribes in the township, the Nguni group of tribes seemed to have preferred the circle as the basis for their decoration and the Sotho-speaking group to have inclined towards the sun family. The Swazi who were lively decorators had a particularly strong feeling for sun shapes while the Tswana, the most numerous in the township, accounted for most of the diamond and diagonal shapes.

It might be possible to explain these preferences in terms of cultural differences between these tribes; it is certainly not possible to explain them by looking for coincidences between the W.N.T. decorations and those in the rural areas from which these tribes

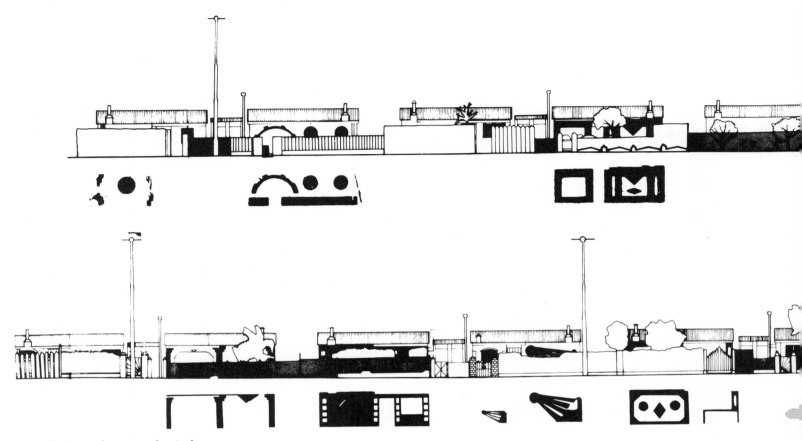

House by house elevations of a single street.

emigrated to the city. In the first place the W.N.T. decorations are generally so different from those of tribal decorations that it is difficult to establish a basis for comparison. Secondly the characteristics that distinguish one mode of tribal decoration from another are not those of shape. Bantu parietal art is essentially architectonic and geometric and the distinctions between tribal expressions generally less qualitative than quantitative. Ndebele decoration, for instance, is really only the more intensive and relentless use of forms which are common in Sotho and other decoration. In addition rural decoration is not static and does not remain unaffected by frequent interchange between city and country, So the Ndebele incorporate a wide range of urban symbols in their later decoration and the Pedi of the Northern Transvaal use symbols from playing cards (as did the people of W.N.T.).[25]

The people of Western Native Township kept in contact with their rural homes and in the early 'forties residents were said to have spent long periods in the country every three years.[26] If this interchange affected the way some thought of decorating their houses (and probably the way their rural relatives felt about theirs) it did not affect the overall quality of the decorations.

For the context of the Western Native Township decorations

Gang slogan on an occupied motor car.

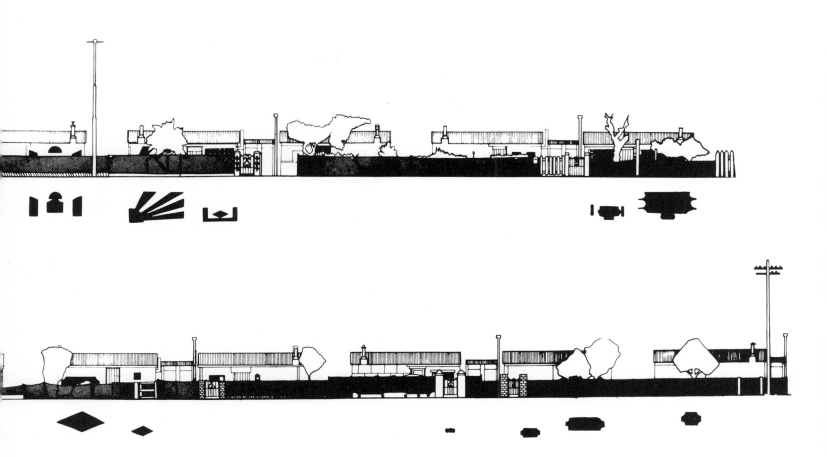

House in the Western Native Township.

cannot be understood by considering people and what they produce as being limited and ultimately tied to their ethnic background. For many this may be a convenient rationale for their own ideologies about race; a way of maintaining their myths about the distinctive potential of one group over another. What in fact happens to people like those who lived in W.N.T. is that they accept, even welcome, the challenge of change from one style of life to another and backed by their sense of security in the place, they endow it with the same spirit and enthusiasm that people do whether they live in huts or villas. (The people of W.N.T. in fact spent the same resources on their houses pro rata to their income as did people of a very much higher socio-economic status.)[27]

For the 'Coloured' people who took over W.N.T. in 1962 there has been little security and less incentive to render the place viable: it has never been their own and it will take a great deal more than just the clearing of the old houses to make it so. For people participate energetically when they have security and hope, poor people as much as rich; and until planning is a process through which these are generated, slum clearance and new house building will succeed only in destroying communities, not in making them.

NOTES

[1] MPHAHLELE, EZEKIEL, *Down Second Avenue*, Faber, London, 1959.

[2] Minutes of the Johannesburg City Council, 1904, 11, 855–890.

[3] LEWIS, PATRICK R. B., *A 'City' within a City – The Creation of Soweto*, University of the Witwatersrand, Johannesburg, 1966, p. 38.

[4] The population graphs are compiled from official census statistics for 1921, 1936, 1946, 1951 and 1960 as well as a wide variety of other sources.

[5] RANDALL, PETER and DESAI, YUNUS, *From 'Coolie Location' to Group Area*, South African Institute of Race Relations, Johannesburg, 1967, p. 1.

[6] Minutes of the Johannesburg City Council, 1904.11, 866–880.

[7] Figures quoted by MAUD, JOHN P. R., *City Government*, Oxford University Press, 1938, p. 135, with the following footnote: 'This figure was given by Dr. Bernstein after making a scientific study of conditions there. In part, but only in part, it can be explained away by the fact that the machinery for registering native births is so defective that the official number of recorded births is considerably smaller than the number of actual births.'

[8] LEWSEN, J., 'The Relationship of the Johannesburg City Council to the Western Areas' in *The Western Areas – Mass Removal?* South African Institute of Race Relations, Johannesburg, 1953, p. 3.

[9] NAKASA, NATHANIEL, 'Writing in South Africa', *The Classic*, Vol. 1, No. 1, p. 58.

[10] MAUD, JOHN P. R., op. cit., p. 101.

[11] FAGAN, H. A., et al., *Report of the Commission of Enquiry into the Disturbances at Moroka*, Johannesburg on the 30th August, 1947, Pretoria, 1948, p. 23.

[12] HELLMAN, ELLEN, 'Urban Areas' in *Race Relations in South Africa*, Oxford University Press, London, 1949, p. 248.

[13] LEWSEN, J., op. cit., p. 4.

[14] LEWIS, PATRICK R. B., op. cit., p. 9.

[15] City of Johannesburg Non-European Affairs Department, *Report on a Sample Survey of the Native Population residing in the Western Areas of Johannesburg*, 1951, p. 224.

[16] From an interview with an ex-W.N.T. resident, Campbell Gwidza.

[17] Descriptions taken from MOTSISI, COSEY, 'Riot', *The Classic*, Vol. 1, No. 2, p. 71.

[18] CALDERWOOD, D. M., *Principles of Mass Housing*, S.A. Council for Scientific and Industrial Research, Pretoria, 1964, p. 63.

[19] EBERHARDT, JACQUELINE, *Survey of Family Conditions with special reference to Housing Needs in Orlando Township, Johannesburg*, quoted in CALDERWOOD, D. M., *Native Housing in South Africa*, p. 24.

[20] From File No. 192/1/4, Non-European Affairs Dept., Johannesburg City Council.

[21] From File No. 71/4/3/3, Non-European Affairs Dept., Johannesburg City Council.

[22] Letter to *The Star*, Johannesburg, 14 October, 1961.

[23] From the Sotho word meaning 'the furrows of a ploughed field'.

[24] GANS, HERBERT, *The Levittowners*, Allen Lane, the Penguin Press, London, 1967, p. 171.

[25] Example cited in WALTON, JAMES, 'Mural Art of the Bantu', *S.A Panorama*, April 1965, p. 35.

Gang slogan on an outhouse lavatory.

[26] HELLMAN, ELLEN, 'The Native in the Towns', in *The Bantu Speaking Tribes of South Africa*, I. Schapera (ed.), Maskew Miller, Cape Town, 1946, p. 429.

[27] BEINART, JULIAN, 'The Process of Urban Participation', in *Proceedings of the Conference: Focus on Cities*, Institute of Social Research, University of Natal, Durban, 1969.

MOBILE SHELTER IN PAKISTAN

Hasan-Uddin Khan

The significance of mobile shelter and the 'truck culture' of Pakistan can only be properly understood in terms of their practical, social and symbolic functions and in the light of attitudes and beliefs which they reflect.

Pakistan has never been a harmonious whole – the people have always been divided. Their roots and allegiances have often differed and all boundaries formed by cultural associations have been in a constant state of change, and have never really had a common basis from which to develop. There is one notable exception, the one unifying factor – the religion of Islam and its cultural parameters. This is the dominant source of historical and aesthetic influence which reflects and recurs in the form, design and colour of all cultural expression in the four regions of Pakistan. This influence from around A.D. 1100 has lent to a 'multi-Muslim' heritage an aesthetic stratum rich in naturalistic emphasis and varied in tradition, due to the various groups that it encountered – from the Hindu, Buddhist, Greek to the later British, nationalistic and technological influences.

Architectural and planning ideas have been very strongly determined by religions in India, as can be traced back to the religious books of the Hindu (Indo–Aryan) culture of the 6th century B.C., although there is no doubt that the principles of the different arts taught were practised long before they were recorded.

Subsequently, in the 2nd century B.C., Greek conquests affected the style of building and planning but this was limited to Northern India. In Southern India the architecture was influenced by the Aryan culture. Here the importance of flowers and gardens in Indian mythology is revealed again and again. Maintenance of gardens was the duty of all citizens. Indeed, in Southern India, different kinds of trees and plants were prescribed in the religious books to be planted in particular places such as temples, around water and beside roads.

Interestingly, flowers are also a pronounced feature of tribal life in Northern India. They are used by men in particular for adornment to signify youth, beauty and the perfection of natural forms.

With the Muslim invasion and culture intrusion into India, there was an attempt to merge the Hindu and Muslim ideologies. However the cultures were far apart.

'Nothing could illustrate more graphically the religious and racial diversity or emphasise more decisively the principle underlying the consciousness of each community than the contrast between their respective places of worship . . . (the mosque and the temple) . . . compared with the clarity of the mosque, the temple breathes mystery in its every particular . . .'[1]

Thus with the conflict of two diametrically opposed cultures there followed a period of confusion and disorder.

On another plane lies the realm of traditional vernacular building which was determined by the social patterns of the people, the climate and locally available materials (the wooden and stone houses in the north, the mud houses in the south).

To speak of an 'all-encompassing Muslim heritage' can be misleading; for although there undoubtedly was such a culture,

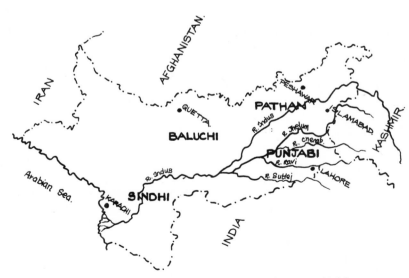

Map of Pakistan showing the four main cultural-tribal groups which have never been historically united. The Pathans of the North-West Frontier province and the Baluchis of Baluchistan have always looked westwards while the Punjabis towards N. India and the Sind have largely been insular.

which was the dominant one, there also existed a variety of divergent rural patterns. In this way two separate physical realities developed – that of the rich and that of the poor – each manifested in the various forms of shelter, art and artefacts.

The dichotomy in expression, derived on one hand from what is regarded as a traditional or rural idology, and on the other from an élitist or 'progressive' ideology, was later to play an important role in the independence struggle against the British.

Up until 1935 the transport of goods was handled by the railways, which were often unreliable in their deliveries. The trucks had one major advantage over the railways – a door-to-door service. At that time, there were no enforced licencing laws or goods carrier taxes for road transport as there were for rail. Hence this method of transporting goods was much cheaper and within the space of three years the road haulage system posed a serious alternative to the railways. The railways led a movement to bring pressure to bear on the trucks so that they were subject to the same conditions, and incidentally improved their own standards to compete.

As the trucking industry took form and goods began to be moved to and from the north to the port of Karachi in the south, and with the coming of independence, the road routes developed very quickly (an indication that in spite of conditions they were recognised as potentially efficient). Roads were bad and breakdowns frequent, the journeys harsh on the drivers and the chance of the trucks being robbed en route began to give rise to *patterns* of truck movement. With this came the embryo of a social network. For instance, the drivers would drive mainly during the hours of daylight and in convoys of four or five. They would stop and rest at meal times in the villages along the routes which in turn created *addas*, or centres at which they would gather. It was the *caravanserai* of the Middle East, which was based on camel travelling distances and oases, transported into the new milieu of the machine age.

> 'Before independence (in 1947), traditionalist ideology could be relatively simple and straightforward, as one of its major functions was to mobilise opinion against colonial government and against foreign imports.'[2]

The difficulties of village enterprises can no longer be blamed on uncontrolled imports as these are subject to import restrictions, and anti-colonial resentment is no longer relevant to policy formulation. The practical problem now concerns the relationship between village enterprises and modern manufacturing methods, between the craft vernacular and the new imported culture of the élita. The whole trucking movement illustrates this dichotomy and presents in microcosm some of the important questions of development in Pakistan; the transition between rural and urban living, the advent of heavy industry, the new mobility, etc.

The development of *two* distinct shelter elements in the process of moving goods around the country may be observed: the adda, or the modern caravanserai, and the truck itself, which becomes a home for the driver and his assistants.

The coming of industrialisation, the transport of raw materials and manufactured goods and the influx of refugees from India after independence caused a massive shift in population to the existing urban centres, especially to Karachi and Lahore. The greatest flow of immigrants came from the north and west parts of the country which were the poorest and slowest 'developing' areas. The city exerts 'pull-forces' – many of which are real and many of which are imaginary. Within Pakistan, the myth of the city became very exaggerated and in the rapidly growing centres (around a 7 per cent per annum population growth rate) some 3–4 per cent is accounted for by the incoming rural dwellers. However, beyond the *idea* of the 'big-city' mythology, the effects of industrialisation on the truckers' thinking and ways of living are as yet unknown, except for the more obvious effects of, for example, the aeroplane on speed as a symbol of power and modernity.

One of the visible effects of industrialisation has been the emergence of a series of specialised settlements – the addas.

With the 'invasion' of the trucks into these settlements came the need to cater for their social and practical requirements. Housing and townships develop around groups of truck stops – especially in the terminals which are inevitably situated in the larger towns. As the addas increase in size, they merge with each other for convenience. They are often situated on or near major communication links. When an area becomes congested – developing in the centre of the city amid further new development, as in Multan and Karachi – the government moves these 'reception' addas to the outskirts of the city near the new regional vehicular arteries. Most cities on the truck routes now have new sectors devoted to this transport traffic.

THE ADDA

The truckers establish their patterns of living with the economic, social and *operational* constraints of the trucking organisation. To the people, whose lives are dictated by the vehicle and their masters who make the policies, it is a way of life rather than a job. They live, breathe and wallow in it, creating a sub-culture which engulfs them.

In the adda, shops are erected and areas for parking are set aside. Workshops and housing units for the shopkeepers' families are built. In some places there is a tendency to construct two-storey buildings with shops at ground level and living quarters on the first floor; in others the housing is situated directly behind the shops with access through small alleyways which are almost always muddy. A very rudimentary drainage is sometimes provided. The plans have provision for greater comfort but in most cases they have not, as yet, been implemented.

The most important single unit is the *chai-khana*, or tea shop. This consists of one or two dark rooms adjacent to an open space. Inside, the kettles for tea are always on the boil – with tea-leaves, sugar and milk, making a strong sweet cup of tea. The ovens and open hearths over coal produce some simple food such as kebabs and *chapati* (a flat unleavened bread). The seating usually consists of wooden benches placed around tables in groups of six or eight. It is in these places that the day's business is discussed, and the

Inside a Chai-Khana, *or tea-shop, in an* adda. *The large urn on the right is heated by a coal fire and contains tea leaves, hot water, milk and sugar. The interior of the* adda *is undecorated.*

drivers tell of their deeds, spin yarns and meet their friends. Here they eat, drink tea and take their drugs. There will usually be a radio to which people listen avidly. The literate will read the daily newspapers to the others and the scribes will write the truckers' letters. The chai-khana is the true hub of both village and adda meeting places, and the main discussion centre.

To service the needs of the vehicles, various companies set up workshop areas in the addas, leasing the land from the government. The companies appoint a manager and staff who often live on the premises, their numbers ranging from three to fifteen. When a new chassis is brought into the adda, the workshop builds a body for it to government specifications.

The bodywork is of wooden pine slats banded and bolted together by metal and wooden cross-pieces. Large iron bolts hold the body to the chassis. After completion, the body is spray painted in the larger workshops but hand brush painted in the smaller ones. Small variations in the bodywork are made according to the owner's wishes, such as the location of semi-secret storage areas, sizes of side windows, etc.

The workshop also carries out all repairs and maintenance for any truck on the spot. (The accident rate of trucks is high in comparison to other vehicles.) Usually, two or three workshops together employ one set of painters. For painting the undercoat the charges are between Rs.500 and Rs.1000, while those who add the design work receive only about Rs.50–Rs.100 (Rs.23 = £1).

In the beginning, trucks were usually painted a khaki or a grey – probably influenced by the army vehicles. The idea of using them as a medium through which to symbolise the creative desire and aspirations of the truckers had not, as yet, caught on. Then, around 1940, the first motifs appeared in the form of lettering. Truck companies had been formed and their names were stencilled or hand painted on the truck sides. (Lettering or calligraphy is the dominant tradition in Islamic culture.) The lettering became more elaborate and was given the name *fancy* by the people in the business.

The front of a Pakistani truck. The bumpers are elaborately worked in metal while the top panel is unusual in not having a religious motif The truck is a standard Bedford of British make.

Front panel above the cabin of a truck. The motifs are patriotic employing national flags, and religious. The 'all-seeing' eyes (left eye on right side and vice versa) are above two roundels depicting the Kaaba of Mecca. The Kaaba is the most common religious motif.

After the preliminaries are completed the truck is ready to receive its 'identity' – the coating of designs. The designers move in and rapidly cover the truck surfaces with the various signs and patterns, directed and watched over by either the truck owner or driver.

The completed truck provides shelter for at least three people, being used rather like a caravan and becoming a second home. For the driver himself, it becomes a first home for he spends more time in and around the truck than he does with his family in his village. He comes to look upon the truck as his prize 'possession', having little else to call his own even though technically it belongs to the company.

Truck painting, like most of Pakistan's folk crafts, is taught by apprenticing young boys to a 'master-painter' or *ustad* (teacher) – a process which is usually kept within the family in each town and handed down in this way from one generation to the next. Thus there is never a surplus of painters in any one place at any time.

Those now working are the third generation of decorators. The first started off as sign-board painters and 'artists' assistants' but then branched off on their own. There are only two or three ustads in each large adda, with the exception of Karachi, Dera Ismail Khan and Peshawar, which have five or six families involved in the business.

The painters are illiterate and untrained in the art school sense.

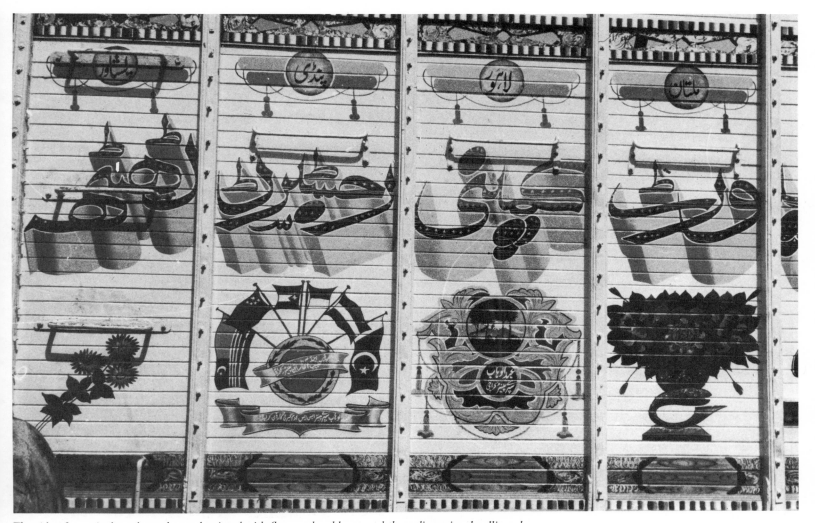

The side of a typical truck, each panel painted with flags and emblems, and three-dimensional calligraphy.

Their ideas, techniques and signs are handed down in the craft tradition and none of them has any knowledge of the 'rules' of painting, perspective, colour theory or composition. Hence their whole attitude, symbols and methods of approach are of a very basic, earthbound nature – a true *ars vulgaris*.

The young boy having decided on his occupation, or. more commonly having it decided for him, becomes involved in the work. At about the age of twelve he is apprenticed to a relative under whom he works for between four and eight years. During this time he is only paid his keep, food and a little pocket money. At the end of this period he moves off to work on his own.

The colours themselves have a life of around one year, although the exterior of most trucks is redecorated at six monthly intervals and the interiors every two years. The ustad is responsible for the overall design of subjects and patterns, leaving his apprentices to fill in and elaborate around his basic painting. At the back of the truck, four or five wooden slats are fitted, on which the artist executes the main large painting, almost always including a landscape.

The calligrapher uses the angular *kufic* and the more popular cursive *naskhi* scripts for all the lettering on the truck. His approach is distinct from that of the painters and although they interact, since the work of each sets off that of the other, they work independently. For the writing, the calligrapher is paid between Rs.25 and Rs.40.

In this process there is yet another specialist – the glass decorator. The groups that paint or etch glass for the windows of the truck come mainly from the northern regions of Pakistan, Multan being the main centre where there is a tradition of decorative work on tiles, pottery and camel skin painting.

As with much vernacular housing in Pakistan, the *interiors* play a more important role than exteriors; for the greater part, exteriors are unornamented.

This brings in the interesting contrast between the 'display on the road' and the plainness of stable or permanent housing. The addas themselves are undecorated on the outside, although in the past five years decoration in the form of bright colours, plastering and wrought-iron work is becoming popular in these settlements.

The amount of money[3] spent on the truck varies from area to area, depending on the origins of the people who are having the work done. In the north, anything up to Rs.6900 (£250) may be spent on a truck's bodywork and cabin interior but in general the cost is usually around Rs.3500, of which Rs.1000–Rs.1800 is spent on decorating the interior of the cab.

The 'artists' receive the smallest cut in the whole process, which if executed by commercial artists would cost ten times as much. Why they are paid so little in relation to the importance of the role they play in the process of getting the truck on the road remains largely unanswered. It is partly due to the fact that paint is a much cheaper material than the plastics etc. used in the other operations in truck building. Also, there is no concept of *value* (in a monetary sense) of art and painting in village or folk life, although there exists a *social* value in the work. But there is the obvious link between the 'fancy-ness' of the trucks and the price.

THOSE WHO SIT IN THE JAWS OF DEATH AND REJOICE, MAY GOD PROTECT YOU – YOU WHO DRIVE THE ROCKET.

FRIEND, IF WE LIVE WE SHALL MEET AGAIN.

I AM NOT WORTHY OF HEAVEN, NOR IS HELL WORTHY OF ME. I COULD BE PLACED IN EITHER AT THY WISH.

COME ALONG FRIEND LETS MOVE THE WORLD'S A SELFISH PLACE.

Examples of calligraphy from various trucks, with their translations.

188

Glass panels on the side of a truck painted by a master glass craftsman from Multan. The doors on the sides are for storage compartments and the paintings depict romantic scenes.

Above and overleaf: Inside cabins of trucks, employing extensive use of plastic materials, silver and gold paper, and mirrors. Truck panel with painted windows and Formica fish.

Although it is clear why more is paid for interiors than exteriors, it is not clear why the exteriors are more personal. For the interiors, elaborate as they are, have a sameness in treatment and materials, and are left to the decorators who work within a given price estimate. It may have something to do with the idea that more people see one's car than one's house – a personal advertisement.

The predominant materials used are plastic and polythene sheets. The 'plastic cloth' is manufactured by sticking coloured pieces of plastic to a clear polythene sheet which is then stretched across the seats, the back and the roof of the cabin. Literally everything is covered by something – the floor by furry nylon mats, the roof is hung with plastic tassels and even the steering wheel is covered by brightly coloured plastic strips. A great deal of tin and

chrome plating is used on both the inside panels of the trucks and on the outside bodywork covering the truck's engine.

THE TRUCKS

There are two parts to the trucker's environment – the immobile shelter of the addas and the mobile shelter – the trucks. The drivers and the truck crew, consisting of an assistant or learner driver and a cleaner/watchman, form the shifting element of the trucking population. Although nominally they live in their own villages, they spend the greater part of their time away from 'home'.

Most of the drivers come from the Pathan and Baluchi provinces – the bleaker hill and desert regions of the west. The men are tough,

189

Most of the while the truck is their home and, being more expensive and more 'modern' than anything else they own or control, 'she' becomes their primary status symbol. There is an interesting split here in referring to the truck in either feminine or masculine terms – the former denoting possession where the woman is an important though secondary 'thing' bound to the man; the latter for the strength and virility of the male in terms of speed and power.

Symbolic expression of an environment is particularly associated with material personal belongings. There is a definite relationship between the two, the possessions being a vehicle and medium for their expression. These relationships are perhaps universal as may be seen from examples as far apart as the heavily decorated weapons and pipes of the Fiji islanders to that of Sindhi furniture today. A clear example of this is found in the mobile home, the elaboration of which may indicate on a large scale the search for permanence. This same phenomenon appears in the gypsy caravans of Europe, the carts of Sicily and East Africa, the wagons of West Africa, the trucks of Mexico and the West Indies, the rickshaws of Thailand and Bengal and, of course, the trucks of Pakistan.

In looking at the art forms in shelter as an expression of a people's desires, a brief look at the home environment of the truck dwellers (the drivers and assistants) gives clues as to why trucks have become the signs of a new sub-culture.

In the tribal areas of Pakhtoonistan and Baluchistan, the people live in a rocky and desert land, which is important for both strategic and communications purposes. In many cases the tribesman is almost a nomad, living in very austere conditions, governed by a strict code which is a mixture of tribal laws and the Islamic faith. The tribesman has had to live in a social and environmental situation which has forced him to present himself as virile, aggressive and strong – expressed in the tribal dances of these areas.

As a result of the economic growth and movement of goods in Pakistan's formative phase of the 1940's, trucks were among the first symbols of progress to be introduced on a large scale. The use of this medium certainly seems to have had an effect on the area. As railways did not exist in this part of the country, the main lines being in the Punjab, the trucks were used on the old trade routes and caravan roads. The tribal leaders, seeing a new way in which to make money, bought some of the vehicles and started their companies to rival those already existent in the Punjab.

The truck was 'handed over' to a driver who was then responsible to his leader for it and we see the growth of a strange triangular relationship between owner, driver and vehicle. Hence the truck, the new symbol of wealth and power, expresses the views of the driver and the owner.

The drivers usually suggest to the artists both the particular signs and the subject matter they want expressed by the signs on 'their' vehicles. For example, a driver might ask the painter to convey a sense of his strength and power, suggesting the tiger as the sign to express this. The painter is then free to choose himself how best to portray a tiger to emphasise this quality.

The larger the truck company, the more the choice of decoration

having grown accustomed to hardship and poverty from birth; they regard driving trucks as a way of bettering their position, both socially and financially. They are paid about Rs.200–Rs.300 a month, which is much higher pay than that of a farm worker who could only hope to earn half as much, or an industrial worker who would get between Rs.100–Rs.250 monthly.

The drivers gain prestige because they are regarded as more 'worldly', having been to the big cities, seen the 'sights' and experienced first-hand the urban mythology. Unlike many poor city dwellers, they have not been humiliated by town life. Their manner and ways seem harsher than those of the villager – they have been exposed to the excitement and pace of the urban areas. They spend a few days in the city between the delivery of goods and collecting their new consignments and on returning to the base adda, they report to their truck owners, settle accounts and then perhaps return to their village for a few days in the month.

Part of the panel on the side of a truck showing the design elements: Calligraphic, *bearing the name of the company, with the letter 'T' possibly derived from* Daily Telegraph *letters.* Naturalistic – *theme of flowers combined with a Karachi fish.* Formalistic – *the bottom of the panel treated as a border, the design brushed on using one stencil in different positions.*

is left to the drivers. A man who owns one or two trucks will take a greater interest in the vehicle and spend a great deal of time supervising the work.

Even though the people involved belong to two different social groups, they are both essentially rural and belong to the traditionally more static sector of society. In urban situations the owners

play a very small part in the sign-making process – to them the truck is merely a wealth-generating possession.

It is for this reason that the tribesman tends to have his trucks painted more extravagantly than the Punjabi or city dweller. The most elaborate trucks come from Dera Ismail Khan in Baluchistan and the only other trucks comparable to them are the new ones of Karachi. This is perhaps largely a function of materials available and the influences from abroad rather than of its inhabitants. For instance, the use of formica originated from Karachi as did the use of fish and aeroplanes as signs.

The difference in areas also causes symbols portrayed on the trucks to become *localised* – or perhaps it would be more accurate to say that the *signs* become localised. For example, the tree as a symbol of life remains the same although the sign may become a palm if from Karachi or a pine if from the north-east.

SYMBOLS AND SIGNS

If a symbol is a sign with the added dimension of value attached to it, then the definition of sign becomes relevant. 'A sign,' says Dr. H. R. Rookmaaker in his book *Synthetist Art Theories*, 'is a direct reference to something and is – while referring to it – immediately connected with the thing itself.' Perhaps the best way to explain them is to give examples. There are natural signs such as seeing smoke out of a chimney as a sign that there is a stove burning in the house, and artificial signs such as traffic signs – they are immediately bound to the situation and give an indication of it. On the other hand a symbol is not directly bound to a thing or situation. A crown is a symbol of sovereignty and power, not a sign that a person is a monarch; the flag is a symbol for a country and so on. The trucks themselves are symbols of modernity and power. Signs and symbols belong to everyday reality and especially in visual imagery, their artistic use may be rich, intelligent and potent with meaning. But the Neo-Platonic line can become far-fetched and can lead to much unverifiable speculation. Aldous Huxley uses Jungian ideas when he says: 'The images of the archetypal world are symbolic; but since we, as individuals, do not fabricate them but find them "out there" in the collective unconscious, they exhibit some, at least, of the characteristics of given reality and are coloured.'[4] However, this view does neglect the ideas of separate development and of a sequential process of storing and so conveying an inheritance or tradition through symbols.

The contradictions in the various theories are at present irreconcilable; hence one must look for and try to understand symbols through the media and environment in which they express themselves. There is a tendency among art theorists to exalt art's functions, which in fact obscures the very reasons for its existence and origins. More often than not, those 'extra-aesthetic' functions can be better understood by a more basic/empirical approach.

So to the trucks. Why is it that they are heavily decorated, and immobile houses are not? This has already been partially answered in the comparison of the various social/geographic origins and life-styles of those involved. In rural surroundings there is no call to express the status and identity through owner-

191

One of the more elaborately decorated trucks, depicting the new symbol of speed, the aeroplane, made of the 'new' material, Formica. The lower panel shows a tank battle of the 1965 war between India and Pakistan.

ship beyond the defined patterns of the group, neighbourhood, village or society. The status, family name and relationships are established and a man can but try and better himself or gain advantages and recognition along *certain well established lines*. He asserts himself within the family group and with the group to other outside groups. Hence his house is often a reflection of his status *within* that group, or class in a village, etc. Any embellishments are seen as attempts either to maintain his status or to break out of his position in society. For example, if he can read he has a certain position and role, or if he becomes rich he does the things expected of him – acquiring symbols of his wealth, e.g. a radio.

When he is displaced from this kind of rural social pattern and gets into an urban situation as a squatter or slum dweller or is flung into a nomadic situation, his normal patterns of relationships with both people and situations change; his position and identity are no longer apparent to his fellow men. He then attempts to re-establish these in many ways. The more static urban dweller begins to build new links based partially on his new urban environment. He begins, little by little, to recreate a new sense of community. This takes time, bearing fruit only after a time span of ten to fifteen years.

The focus of interest in the house is on the interiors, the exteriors being dictated mainly by form, materials and structure. Also the Islamic puritan ethic tends to inhibit a man from 'displaying himself' to the community in such an obvious manner. Hence the concentration on the interior decor and furniture. Again it is interesting to note that even within his house the most highly decorated objects are those which are transportable.

For the trucker, having been dislocated from the norms of his grass-roots, having lost his former visible identity, the exterior of the truck on the road – as a means of expressing his *identity* – assumes an importance which outweighs the failing power of old norms.

While this identity expression or 'coating of arms' may be compared in many ways to the advent of heraldry in the Middle East, it is a phenomenon which has its roots in the loss of the security both of a permanent home and a stable environment. A mobile home poses the need to find a way of creating an atmosphere of stability and a reminder of home.

The driver's motivation to express himself through the decor of his truck is not only a function of his rootlessness. A variety of other sociological reasons play a part, such as the wish to demonstrate a position of power (consisting of personal aggression and sexuality) using the symbolism of a predominantly male-chauvinistic society tempered by religious puritanism.

Whether or not *power* is a 'feeling' based on instinctive aggression is debatable. Using such a model hypothetically it could be argued that: 'Redirection of the attack is evolution's most ingenious expedient for guiding aggression into harmless channels . . .',[5] and one direction is that of self-expression through visual art.

The truck driver is regarded as being very aggressive on the road – he drives fast, almost carelessly, is inconsiderate to the normal automobile and has a higher accident rate than the ordinary motorist.

To attribute this to the aggressive instinct would be simplistic and unhelpful. The very social significance of driving has to be borne in mind. About fifteen years ago, when only the very rich had cars, the man in the street would recognise this as a sign denoting a class difference and showed respect to the man behind the wheel. With the use of trucks by the poorer classes, a system of road etiquette began to develop. To the trucker his vehicle was a way of life, a necessity for his livelihood; whereas to the richer man, his car increased his mobility but he did not have to depend upon it completely.

To the trucker, *his* is the more important vehicle on the road, for he is on a job. Hence he regards the roads as primarily for himself and his kind. So when he hoots at cars and rushes from place to place, he is regarding the road as his domain and all others must get out of his way.

It is true however that he does get a feeling of power that he has not experienced before – that of the throbbing truck and of speed. Again this has a parallel in more affluent societies where the man in the air gets his kicks from taking up aeroplanes or skydiving. The psychological reasons for this show of 'aggression' vary from person to person and from cult to cult.

Apart from making the truck his home, with the driver decorating it to establish himself in the mobile society, the truck is also used as a means of escape. The use of hashish and various stimulants as forms of relaxation and enervation are common amongst the lower exploited classes of the country. Essentially this seems to have the effect of lessening the impact of day-to-day existence and, as such, is a very common form of escapism. New governments see this effect as a socially unacceptable one and try to eradicate it – forgetting or disregarding the reasons for its existence – mistaking effect for cause. It is not surprising that this tradition continues in spite of half-hearted official measures taken against it.

Given the extremely tough working conditions in conjunction with high stress factors of alienation and mobility, it is not surprising that so much use is made of drugs. This may also go some way towards explaining the high accident rate of trucks. A further significant element is a particular brand of male vanity which expresses itself in many small ways, among them the use of flowers for self-decoration, especially in the north. Also in northern Indian culture, perfume (*itar*) for men is very common. Perfume vendors wander around the addas selling their goods to the drivers and other men. It also expresses itself in the trucks themselves through all the decorations and chrome plating that go on to the bodywork.[6]

Symbols[6] may be classified quantitatively by the number or group of people that they affect and a distinction may be made between personal and collective symbolism. Personal symbols, the subject of dream analysis for example, reveal something of the individual dreamer's psychology, depending for their meaning on the personal experience of the dreamer. These symbols are more specific than collective symbols and as such have a more limited use. Collective symbols are easier to identify and depend on a shared popular interpretation. For example, in a tribal dance the symbolism may be clear and certain meanings intricately related to that particular society may be understood by the observer.

In the trucker's context, the act of the driver telling the painter what he wants expresses both a subconscious collective symbolism and his own personal or individual interpretations of those common symbols and his own particular signs. On the other hand, the painter and the interior cab decorator express the symbols in the collective signs of a culture which may be interpreted by a large number of people. This paper is essentially dealing with the collective symbol.

There has always been a conflict between the old ideologies and philosophies of India and Pakistan and the relatively recent introduction of Islamic ideology and the new nationalist and growing socialist ideologies. This process of change has been much gentler than that of the introduction of Christianity to South America, where the religion has been changed and adapted to local customs and traditions. Islam, a seemingly more demanding religion and, in India, a somewhat unifying one (if only by force!) has influenced the functioning of society and has disallowed the expression of many of the old symbols and signs.

The religious element is the most conspicuous in the art of any Islamic culture; besides the concept of *Allah* (God), the *one* power and the transient earthly existence of man, the idea of the dissolution of matter, or ideas of transformation, are important features.

'The ornamentation of surfaces of any kind in any medium . . . result in a world which is not a reflection of the actual object, but that of the super-imposed element that serves to transcend the momentary and limited appearance of a work of art, drawing it into the greater and solely valid realm of infinite and continuous being.'[7]

It is perhaps this element, which has no parallel in the history of art, that makes Islamic art 'religious' – there is very little actual religious iconography in the ordinary sense existing in Islam. This has had a great effect on the pictorial signs and other outward manifestations of the people's lives, irrespective of regional, tribal or cultural differences.

A newer and less integrated movement is that of the political change from nationalism to a form of socialism, which is being reflected in some of the demands of the people. In turn this is reflected in the ever-increasing political themes on the truck façades.

The transition from traditional/rural cultures to the modern/technological cultures produces a *dissociation* or – as Jung puts it – 'a splitting of the psyche' of society at large. It is especially discernible among the older people in the rural areas. More visibly it may be observed in the common forms of alienation resulting from the process of urbanisation. Indeed, the pressures on the driver tend to express and intensify this process, although their situation is to some extent counterbalanced by the possibility of better conditions and escape from a rigid social pattern.

SIGNS

The *positioning* of signs on the truck is also to some extent determined by tradition. On the front of the truck's cabin are the religious signs. They are the first signs seen by all – an utterance of a prayer for protection on the road. These are either formalistic or calligraphic.

On the sides of the truck are the identification signs – the direct name presentation of the company – one side in Urdu, the other in English. The other signs, arranged in panels due to the construction of the bodywork, are the expression of the driver's desires.

The back panel, consisting of wooden slats, forms one large painting which is always a landscape. This is composed of the same elements wherever the truck comes from, although the signs again are localised. The back also has signs for the truck behind in the form of humorous and witty sayings and also the names of main points of call.

The interiors are the formalistic embellishment. They have to a large extent been dealt with already. What remains is to mention that the interiors are a symbol of affluence. When the driver invites anyone to ride in the cabin it is also to show the man his truck and the stuff that he is made of – rather in the spirit that a yachtsman asks someone aboard.

Animals and birds have always played an important role in folklore and in religious tales and have assumed a widespread and easily identifiable symbolism. Among the most frequently painted

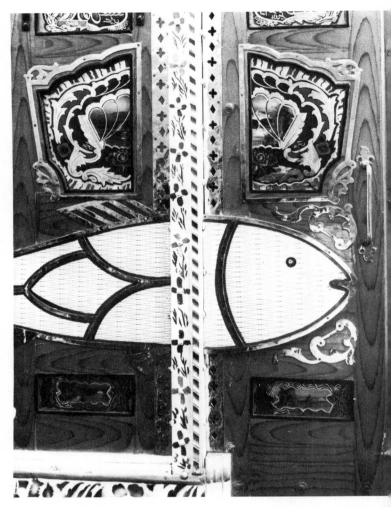

The grain of the timber has been brush-simulated, while a stencilled border divides the fish.

are the lions and tigers which are considered to be the two greatest beasts of the jungle – the monarchs of the animal kingdom. (Interestingly, none of these animals may be found in Pakistan, although tigers are native to the Sunderbunds in Bengal and former East Pakistan). They are symbols of strength, power and dominance. The eagle is by far the most important bird used to represent speed and power, always portrayed with outstretched wings. Animals such as monkeys play an important part in Hindu mythology and consequently have not been incorporated into the Muslim heritage, which has tended to avoid adopting features associated with Hinduism, in an effort to establish a separate identity. The fish, the identification sign for Karachi, Pakistan's only port, is now spreading to all parts of the country.

It is interesting to note the inclusion of a *conscious grouping* of signs in recent years. For example, the deliberate use of a fish/ship

194

eroplane/bird, truck/railway, symbolises the three realms of travel – land, sea and air.

Other animals, such as the elephant, are new signs which have no apparent symbolic value in this context beyond being its direct representation. Again it is interesting to see that the more familiar the sign is to the painter, the more accurately he paints it. So it is not a question of his familiarity with the subject leading him to simplify or abstract it, but rather the opposite.

The only animal that is not included is *man*, for this would be 'un-Islamic'. This is quite unlike Hindu symbolism which encompasses a merging of man, animal and gods (as can be seen from 'Ganesh', the Hindu god of good fortune, who has a human body but the head of an elephant).

'The boundless profusion of animal symbolism in the religion and art of all time does not merely emphasise the importance of the symbol; it shows how vital it is for men to integrate into their lives the symbols' psychic content – instinct.'[7]

The animals are not of course symbolic in themselves. Through their relationships with man and each other, they come to be seen in certain ways, to adopt certain roles and so to acquire symbolic significance through the accumulation and crystallisation of associations in a culture.

The notion that iconography is prohibited in all Islamic pictorial presentation is a false but popular one. There is no prohibition of the representation of living forms in Islam or the Koran. Certain sayings attributed to the Prophet in the *hadith* (collection of the traditional sayings of the prophet) do include a warning to the maker of images that he will be punished on Judgement Day if he tries to imitate God who alone can create living beings. The only places in which figurative representation and painting are suppressed are the mosques and mausoleums. Elsewhere, imagery forms one of the most important elements and a multitude of other pictorial traditions have been assimilated during the long and complex history of Islamic art.

The use of portraiture or figure painting is due to the fusion of the Hindu and Islamic traditions – which is in contrast to other parts of the Muslim world, where the pre-Islamic traditions are usually completely assimilated.

The pictorial signs may be both naturalistic (e.g. landscapes) and formalistic (e.g. patterns). The naturalistic parts of the paintings have many elements in common. The landscapes depict life on the open road – the trees, the sky and the roads themselves. A focal element is the road or a river which winds its way through the centre of a panel, being used as devices for perspective. Seascapes are rare and originate from Karachi.

In general, landscapes are for *identification* purposes, defining the area from which the trucker comes rather than his aspirations.

The general tendency towards rich decoration finds its counterpart in painting in the use of strong decorative colours inherited from the Hindu tradition and the elaborate use of gold in later Mughal painting.

'Mughal painting is one of the most successful applications of Islamic principles to a basically non-Islamic tradition. The development of a realism that goes as to include portraiture is unique even within the great variety of pictorial forms in Islam.'[8]

Other elements in the landscape, such as the trucks themselves, and other 'objects' (for example, houses, aeroplanes) tend to be treated as living beings.

Geometric design springs from the ancient Arab interest in mathematics and astrology and also from flowers; patterns and rhythms existing in nature. All Islamic design includes within it a sense of colour which again plays the same kind of role as tiles or mirrors on a solid wall, giving them a peculiarly ephemeral quality. For example, an arabesque design based on an infinite leaf-scroll pattern that by division of its elements (stem, leaf, blossom) generates new variations of the same original elements, brings about a sense of unity to the bodywork of the truck as both a framing device and as an abstraction of a culture.

Apart from the naturalistic, semi-naturalistic and geometric forms used by the painters in the infinite pattern, *calligraphy* plays an important role in Islamic art and is integrated into every sort of decorative scheme, which serves to reinforce the Islamic and religious traditions of the people. It is used in several ways.

Advertising is the easiest to explain. It is a more direct sign than hitherto existed in Pakistan, belonging to the industrial age and capitalism, being introduced by the companies. Because of this, calligraphy – or to use its local name, *fancy*, although essentially an Islamic art form, is not truly in the folk-art idiom. It is primarily used to show the name and address of the company and is now filtering 'downwards' to be used for advertising others in the trucking operation. For example, each painter puts his name somewhere on the truck and the window painter puts his name on every piece of glass. This is a purely functional aspect of trucking.

The religious sayings are usually taken from the Koran or they are a prayer to God to protect the truck and its inhabitants. This is part of the whole religious scene in the country. Besides the directly religious sayings, the other sayings are all connected with travel.

Two examples of stencils used for the formalistic patterns. They are drawn on cardboard and cut out in long strips. These were adjacent to each other on one truck.

195

There is a rich store of philosophical ideas that exist in folklore and are expressed in words and poetic writings. These are more than just witty or religious – they contain within them the seeds of real and indigenous Pakistani ideology.

A NEW BEGINNING

New materials, economies and technologies, while developing out of changes in the physical environment and society do, in turn, add to or change social dimensions and impose new patterns of living. New symbols appear, are assimilated or born. However they come, it can be seen that they emerge from new perceptions, themselves a response to changed or artificial environmental situations. There have been some significant influences lately – the 1965 and 1970 wars, the trading pacts with Pakistan's neighbours (excluding India), the widespread use of new materials and means of travel from the aeroplane to the moon shots, and the rising socio-political awareness among the poor people.

New signs begin to supersede older ones. The aeroplane fulfils the same function as the bird, the space rocket becomes a powerful new symbol of adventure and progress. These newer symbols can also be seen to be part of a 'class' process, where the lower class has the aspirations of a 'poor' country looking towards the 'rich' nations and, in trying to displace themselves from their own situation, they try to assume the airs, artefacts and mannerisms of that higher class. This occurs in both the social and economic fields of Pakistan's political system.

Around the wars that have been fought against India, a morale boosting mythology has been developed in Pakistan – in the common man's belief in his superiority over his enemy. The signs in the paintings depict the weaponry and some of the better known battles.

Similarly other political gestures such as new monuments, however hideous they may seem, do create a positive response in the poor man, who can see a clear physical expression of an idea or person, developing a symbol from a sign.

'New' materials such as polythene sheets, coloured plastic and the commercial use of formica, have added totally new dimensions to the decorating process. They have meant that the truckers can now move practicably and express themselves effectively.

The truckers are at the crossroads of two cultures – the traditional and the technological – symbolised by their mobile shelter. Both the truckers and the trucks are the bearers of a possible new culture, a culture which has not been inherited from the country's colonial past or an élite culture, but one which will *belong* to Pakistan, having grown from the old roots and new worlds of the common man.

NOTES

[1] BROWN, PERCY, *Indian Architecture,* Vol. II, Muslim Period, Taraporevala Sons & Co., Private Ltd., Bombay, 1964.
[2] MYRDAL, GUNNAR, *Asian Drama,* Vol. II, Ch. 25, Pantheon, New York, 1968.
[3] Prices quoted for 1968.
[4] HUXLEY, ALDOUS, *Heaven and Hell,* Chatto & Windus, London, 1956.
[5] LORENZ, KONRAD, *On Aggression,* Methuen & Co., London, 1961, p. 47.
[6] In this paper, the symbols, ideas on signs and most definitions are based on Jung's books. JUNG, CARL, *Man and His Symbols,* Aldus Books in association with W. H. Allen, London, 1964 with especial reference to: Part I, JUNG, C., 'Approaching the Unconscious', Part III, FRANZ, M. L. VON, 'Process of Individuation', Part IV, JAFFE, A., 'Symbolism in the Visual Arts'.
[7] GRUBE, J., *The World of Islam,* Introduction, Paul Hamlyn, London, 1966.
[8] JAFFE, A., op. cit., p. 238.
[9] GRUBE, J., op. cit., Introduction.

ACKNOWLEDGEMENTS

Susan Wilkinson and Paul Oliver for their help and revision of my work.

THE CONCEPT OF SETTLEMENT IN THE WEST AFRICAN SAVANNAH

David Dalby

In the spring of 1963, a friend and I were walking away from the University of London, across Russell Square. The sky had become overcast, after several days of fine weather, and my friend, a Hausa-speaker from Northern Nigeria, remarked 'The town is cloudy today.' The meaning of his remark was quite clear, but his use of the word 'town' instead of 'sky' reminded me that Hausa, according to the major Hausa–English dictionaries,[1] appears to possess a pair of words with the identical form gàrii, but with the distinct meanings of 'town' and 'sky'. His confusion of 'town' and 'sky' in English was perplexing, however, because if gàrii (= town) were a separate concept in Hausa from gàrii (= sky) he would no more confuse the two concepts in English than an Englishman would confuse the *bark* of a dog with the *bark* of a tree when speaking, say, in French. Was it possible, then, that gàrii did not represent a pair of homophones, with unrelated meanings, but that it designated some broad, environmental concept, covering both 'town' and 'sky'? The strangeness of such an embracing concept, in an Englishman's view, would explain its treatment as two separate items in the relevant dictionaries, all compiled by British lexicographers.

A scientific analysis of the usages of gàrii in Hausa was clearly called for, and the short walk across Russell Square led to the subsequent collection and examination of over two hundred separate phrases containing the word gàrii (many of them with two or more different interpretations depending on the context). These were assembled with the help of Malam A. I. Galadanci and Malam I. A. Kurawa (both of Kano), and from published texts in the Hausa language, and the resulting corpus, with translations and a detailed discussion, were published in a linguistic journal in 1964.[2] The present paper is designed to present the results of this earlier study to a wider readership, drawing on additional, corroborative evidence from a second major language, Manding, also spoken on the West African savannah.

The setting for our study is the open savannah, south of the Sahara, level or undulating grassland broken with areas of scrub and light woodland. The typical settlement type consists of a main village, comprising a complex of mud-built compounds and enclosed by a mud wall or stockade, often with a few outlying hamlets. Land around and within walking distance of the village is farmed on a rotating basis, and is divided into 'fields' where subsistence crops (such as millet) or cash crops (especially groundnuts) are grown. Within or close to the village there are normally several wells. Cattle raising is more the concern of the Fulani people, pastoralists who live in symbiosis with the agriculturalist Hausa in Northern Nigeria and Niger, but Hausa villages have their own complement of livestock, mainly goats and sheep, which are pastured on uncultivated land and sheltered at night within the village itself. Each community has its own village head, responsible to a district head in a larger village or small town, and ultimately to an emir in what used to be the fortified capital of each region.

The first salient fact to come to light about the usage of gàrii was its flexible scale in reference to human settlements. 'Town' is an inadequate translation, since the Hausa term – although referring typically to a village or town – may be used in different contexts to describe any level of human settlement from the entire (inhabited) world to a deserted (but potentially inhabitable) oasis on the fringes of the Sahara. Thus one may say, for example, 'today the gàrii of the world has become one' (i.e. the world has become a smaller place through the ease of travel), or, at the other extreme, 'they reached a gàrii in the Sahara, where there was nothing but wells'. Between these two limits, the term may be applied to any of a whole range of human settlement and territorial units, from an isolated homestead through hamlet, village and town to district or nation. In the context of Hausaland, however, it is clear that the most typical application of the term is to an individual settlement ('village' or 'town') on the savannah. The many other varied applications of the term are best explained as expansions, particularisations or abstractions of this basic meaning of gàrii.

Notwithstanding the flexible scale of application, as just described, the actual boundaries of a settlement described as gàrii may be defined with precision, based on actual usages of the term. In reference to an individual settlement, gàrii may be used either in a comprehensive sense, covering the entire inhabited *and* cultivated area, or in a particularised sense, referring to a part or aspect of the settlement or community: these particularised applications are of assistance in defining the boundaries of gàrii in its total sense of 'human settlement or community'. In the rural setting there is an expressed dichotomy between the 'inner' gàrii, covering the main settlement or centre of habitation, and the 'outer' gàrii,

197

The gàrii – View over a Hausa town.

covering cultivated farmland[3] and any outlying hamlets (which may be up to several miles apart). These two layers of gàrii together stand in contrast to the unoccupied or uncultivated land described as 'behind' or 'beyond' the gàrii: the latter does not imply simply the land outside an actual or theoretical boundary around the settlement, but covers *all* unproductive land, within as well as outside the confines of the settlement, including latrine areas and rubbish dumps as well as uncleared 'bush'. Hence 'throw it behind the gàrii' means simply 'throw it away', and 'he went behind the gàrii' can mean 'he went to the latrine' (i.e. within the settlement) as well as 'he went into the bush' (i.e. beyond the limits of the cultivated land). By contrast, the inclusion of all cultivated land and pasturage within the concept of gàrii is illustrated by the examples 'we reached a gàrii, but (there were) fields only' and 'we reached a gàrii, but (there were) cattle only'. These statements indicate that the travellers were entering the outer part of a gàrii, marked by cultivated land or cattle, but that human habitation was not yet in sight.

Although the boundaries of gàrii may be extended horizontally, to wherever the limits of a community's farmland or pasturage happen to be at a particular time, it is interesting to observe that they do not extend below the surface of the earth, except when referring to wells, the only subterranean component of the traditional rural economy. Hence, when a well has dried up, the Hausa may comment that 'the well *is* the gàrii', i.e. without a well there can be no human settlement. On the other hand, although cemeteries are normally situated within the confines of the 'outer' gàrii, a ghost is described as 'entering' the gàrii when it rises from the grave.

A frequent particularised usage of gàrii is that in which it denotes the actual inhabitants of a settlement, as may happen with comparable terms in many languages: examples such as 'the whole gàrii knows . . .' or 'the gàrii is sleeping' could be paralleled by similar phrases in English, involving 'village' or 'town'. What is more interesting, and different from English usage, is the way in which the gàrii, identified with its inhabitants, is conceived of as contracting at night. When workers leave the fields at dusk, an observer may say that 'the gàrii has arisen' (i.e. to return to their village) or that 'the gàrii has gathered in one place'. When a thief 'breaks the gàrii' at night, the implication is that he has broken through (or climbed over) the closed stockade or wall around the village itself. At dawn, in reverse, one may again say that 'the gàrii has arisen' (i.e. to return to the fields), or 'the gàrii has cleared, or been exposed', a key expression which we shall return to later. When a market is being held, however, the focus of the gàrii is conceived of as shifting to the site of the market, frequently outside the main settlement: hence the phrase 'he (has) entered the gàrii' may be used in the sense 'he has gone to market', even when this involves leaving the village to visit a temporary market outside. On non-market days, the same phrase would imply either that he had entered the village or main settlement itself, from outside, or that he had gone out into the town or village from his own compound within it.

From the particularised usages of gàrii, emphasising aspects of

View over Emir's palace, Kano.

the settlement or community which are of paramount importance at a given moment, it becomes clear that the term applies ideally to an economic and social unit, all the parts of which are interdependent, and any one of which may be identified with the whole. Thus the phrase 'the gàrii has died' may imply, depending on the circumstances, that a village has been abandoned, that the soil is no longer fertile, or that the village head (or other ruler) has died; to say that 'wild animals have killed or devoured the gàrii' means that they have destroyed the crops or carried off the livestock; conversely, the gàrii is said to 'come to life' when an abandoned village is rebuilt on a new site, when the community is enjoying new prosperity, when rains return after a drought or when a new village head (or other ruler) has been appointed. Other phrases with variable reference, relating especially to social or economic decline, include 'the gàrii has spoiled', used when many people have moved away from a village, when its inhabitants have become less religious or when the productivity of its land has declined; and the picturesque phrase 'the gàrii has tightened the drum for us'. In the latter case, the metaphor involves the tightening of the tuning-strings around an 'hour-glass' drum, the implication being that the community is feeling the pinch of poverty or is in some other kind of trouble. The collective nature of a traditional Hausa community is reflected in the fact that an individual Hausa will normally refer to his village or town as 'our' gàrii, only a village head or ruler of a larger community referring to 'my' gàrii. There is a distinction in Hausa also between second person singular and the plural pronouns (corresponding to 'you' and 'your'), and when speaking to a Hausa, other than a chief, about his native community, one should speak of 'your' (plural) gàrii. An exception occurs in phrases where the term gàrii is extended to refer to the economic welfare of an individual, rather than that of a village or town, arising especially in urban situations where an individual's fortunes are more readily separable from those of the community as a whole. Hence someone may say 'this is my gàrii' when he has found prosperity – for example as a trader – after settling in a strange community.

So far in our discussion we have been concerned with the concept of gàrii at 'ground level', and its involvement with the 'sky' has not yet been considered. In the context of a London park, this involvement appeared strange, and to understand it one must picture the quite different relationship between the sky and a rural community on the open savannah. We have already seen how the term relates, in its most typical usage, to an economic and social unit, all the parts of which are independent. These include the inhabitants and their homes, their farmland and their domestic animals. Also included are the wells on which the community is dependent for water, and it is in this context, of a rural economy in an area of low and often uncertain rainfall, that one realises the vital role which local weather plays in the life – and sometimes death – of an individual community. Annual rainfall, over a large part of the Hausa-speaking area, ranges between 20 and 40 inches: the majority of this rainfall is confined to the summer months, when evaporation is at its highest. Water is precious, and rainy weather is not normally described in Hausa as 'bad weather'; the greeting *ruwaa yaa yi gyaaraa* ('the rain has improved things') is used even when the rain has done damage, or has resulted in flooding: to resent the rain would represent ingratitude towards Allah. Parts of the Hausa-speaking areas of Nigeria and Niger are severely affected, at the time of writing this paper, by the 1973 drought. Discussion of the weather is mostly concerned with the weather as it affects the crops and the livestock: such discussion centres especially around the occurrence or absence of rain, and around the forecasting of weather from the presence or absence of cloud. In such discussion it is noteworthy – and understandable – that the boundaries of the term gàrii should be extended vertically upwards, to include the visible sky above the community and the local weather on which it is dependent. Hence such phrases as 'the gàrii has joined its eyebrows', i.e. is frowning, when thick black clouds have covered an almost windless sky; 'the gàrii has been closed, or covered', when there is a veil of light cloud; or 'the gàrii has bared itself', when the clouds have disappeared entirely. Phrases also occur in which only the context enables the listener to know whether they refer to the life of the gàrii on the horizontal plane, or to the weather conditions of the gàrii. Thus 'the gàrii has no certainty' implies either that trade or the local economy is fluctuating, or that the weather is very changeable; while 'the gàrii has stopped still' implies either that trade has come to a standstill and there is no money about, or that it has suddenly stopped raining. Similarly, one may ask someone to wait 'until the gàrii has made a clearance', especially when deferring payment to them: the phrase means either 'until the rains are over' or 'until economic affairs have improved', although in practice the two interpretations often coincide, cash-crops not being ready for sale until after the end of the rains. The same phrase, 'the gàrii has made a clearance', may be applied also in a different context to the clearing of new land for cultivation, or to the pulling down of old houses.

We have already seen how the gàrii, on its horizontal plane, is conceived of as contracting when the inhabitants return to their homes for the night, and as expanding or 'clearing' again at dawn. This expansion involves not only the opening of a village gate or stockade, and the return of its workers to the fields and its livestock to pasture, but also the visual expansion of the gàrii, as dawn 'opens up' the land around the settlement. This is expressed clearly in the phrase 'the gàrii has made a disc', used when the first light has spread around the horizon or, when day has fully dawned, 'the gàrii has cleared or (been) exposed' or 'has (been) cleared or hollowed out'. The term used for 'disc' in the first of these phrases is *faifai*, referring basically to a circular mat used to cover pots or gourds, and the related verb *faifàyee*, used in the sense of 'clear or hollow out' has the additional specialised application of 'hollow out (a gourd)'. We are thus provided with a clear picture of the Hausa imagery behind the concept of the expanding gàrii at dawn, an expansion first on the horizontal plane and then including the sky above the settlement. With the arrival of day the gàrii resumes its full form, of which the sky, like an upturned, hollowed-out gourd, provides the outer limit above ground level.

From this discussion it will have become apparent that the term gàrii represents a key term in the life, culture and language of the Hausa-speaking peoples. This key role is further reflected by the number of abstract usages to which the term is also put, and which one may assume to have developed from the concrete applications already described. The only formal distinction between the concrete and abstract usages is that the definite form of the noun, *gàriǹ*, is never used when the reference is abstract. The most common usage under this category is where gàrii carries the general sense of 'dawn' or 'day', as opposed to phrases describing the arrival of dawn in a particular locality on a particular day. Thus, the phrase 'gàrii cleared' has acquired the general sense in Hausa

Family compound in Kano, Northern Nigeria.

of 'next day' or 'next morning', and is the expression normally used to convey this meaning. Similarly, the set compound *waàsheè gàrii* has the abstract meaning of 'next day', in contrast to the concrete reference of the related phrase *gàrii yaa waashèe* (literally 'gàrii has cleared'), used to describe the arrival of dawn at a particular place. 'Every day of one's life' may be translated into Hausa as 'Every gàrii of the world'; in the latter form, only the context can clarify whether the reference is to every 'day' or to every 'place' in the world.

The extension of gàrii to cover the sense of 'day' is in fact less strange than at first appears to a non-Hausa readership. It needs to be recalled that the link between an agricultural community on the savannah and its open visible environment is much closer than between an urban or forest community and its 'interrupted' visible environment. In the former case, the area farmed by a community is frequently within a clear field of view from the central village,

although of course by *day* only. We have already seen how the gàrii contracts at night, with the closing in of darkness and of nocturnal dangers (i.e. hyenas and other prowling animals, and in former times also human marauders). 'Visibility' and 'familiarity' are of special importance in a community where each individual is acquainted with everyone else and with his personal affairs: the concept of 'night' is thus in opposition to gàrii in its concrete sense of 'individual settlement' (existing in its ideal form only by day) as well as in its abstract sense of 'day'. The contrast between gàrii and the evils of night is reflected in such sayings as 'however deep the night, gàrii will clear'; 'because of a slanderer, gàrii will not refuse to clear'; or 'whoever tells lies at night, gàrii will clear (and expose him)'. The positive implications of gàrii are further exemplified by the use of the adjectival noun *na-gàri*, derived from gàrii and having the sense of 'good person' or 'good thing' (literally 'person or thing of gàrii'): *na-gàri* occurs in regular contrast to the adjectival noun *muugù*, 'bad (person or thing)', as in the aphorism 'a person or thing of gàrii belongs to everyone, a bad person or thing belongs only to himself/itself'.

A further abstract usage of gàrii, stemming from its basic sense of 'settlement' or 'inhabited place', is in phrases where it carries the general sense of 'situation' or 'environment'. Significantly, such usage is frequently in association with the verb *ganii* 'to see', again emphasising the visual connotations of gàrii. Using the noun in an abstract sense, one may say literally, of a person who always knows the right thing to do, 'seeing of gàrii (is) with him', in other words, 'he is aware of his environment or his situation'. In contrast, the phrase 'he has no seeing of gàrii' means that a person is physically blind. To say that people 'have eyes, but not for seeing of gàrii' may imply – depending on the context – that they are unaware of what goes on around them, that they are ignorant of the laws of Islam, that they are illiterate, or that they cannot see the spirit-world. An interesting Hausa proverb, using a similar construction, may be translated literally 'monkey, you are seeing gàrii (but) before you see it, it has already seen you'. The reference is to the fact that a monkey, occupying a concealed vantage-point in an isolated tree, will have already betrayed his whereabouts by disturbing the branches as he climbed the tree: in other words, 'take care, lest you be the one who is harmed first'. Another verb frequently associated with gàrii is *ji*, meaning 'to feel, hear, listen to or obey': in a concrete sense, 'we feel the gàrii' means that our community is feeling the effects of a local shortage. In abstract applications, one may say that a child 'obeys gàrii' if he is obedient, or that he does not 'hear (or obey) gàrii' if he pays no heed to warnings or advice. 'Hearing gàrii' is also a phrase meaning 'echo', or 'unidentified sound', in other words a noise from the surrounding environment.

'Son of the gàrii' is the normal expression used to describe a native inhabitant of a village, town or country, in contrast to 'son of the world', denoting an untrustworthy person who has abandoned his responsibilities to his community. In its abstract application, 'son of gàrii' denotes someone who is at home in a particular situation, or who is master of his circumstances. There is a similar transition from the concrete to the abstract in phrases involving the verb *ci*, meaning 'to eat, consume, conquer or win': thus 'to eat or conquer (the) gàrii' can mean either 'to capture a particular

Houses of a Hausa city. The pointed pinnacles at the corners of the buildings reach up to the enveloping space above.

town or village' or 'to win a game or contest, or otherwise gain the upper hand in a particular situation'. This and the previous usage are combined in the proverb 'With a son of gàrii one always conquers gàrii', i.e. 'With expert help a difficult situation can always be mastered'. Similarly, 'getting gàrii' has the abstract sense of 'getting the (right) opportunity', as in the amusing proverb 'Getting gàrii, a leper (does) a girls' dance among the Indian hemp': the implication here is that given the right opportunity, or circumstances, anything is possible. The multiple applications of gàrii are extended even further at this point, and in its sense of 'situation' or 'opportunity' the genitival form of gàrii is sometimes used where an English preposition or conjunction would be used: thus 'gàrii of running, he dropped the money' means 'while running . . .'; and 'he has come, gàrii of seeing you' means '. . . in order to see you'.

Our final examples from Hausa involve the verb *shaa*, meaning 'to drink, or have one's fill'. Of an old inhabitant of a place, one may say that he has 'had his fill of the gàrii', but in the abstract application of gàrii the phrase would imply that a man was simply very old, that he had had much experience or many troubles, or, if used of a promiscuous woman, that she had known many men. In its general sense of 'human experience', gàrii appears to combine both its spatial and temporal applications.

Before summarising the results of our study of gàrii, it will be useful to compare these results against data from at least one other, unrelated, language spoken in a similar environment. If, as has been argued, there is a direct link between the physical environment of the Hausa and their use of the term gàrii, than one might expect to find terms with a similar range of meaning in languages spoken in other parts of the West African savannah. Hausa is the principal language in the eastern half of that savannah, and a suitable language for comparison is Manding, the principal language in the western half. Manding is unrelated to Hausa, is separated from it by a large number of smaller languages, but – in the form of Manding known as Bambara – is spoken in a similar area of the savannah and on the same latitude as Hausa.

In Manding, the term *dùgu* has applications strikingly similar to those of gàrii.[4] It is the basic term for an individual settlement, i.e. a village or town, and – like gàrii – can be used on a flexible scale to refer to any category of human settlement or territorial unit up to the whole inhabited world itself. Like gàrii also, dùgu comprises the land around a settlement as well as the settlement itself, and dùgu is used as the basic Manding word for 'earth, ground or soil'. There are other particularised usages in which the term, as in Hausa, is identified with a specific part or aspect of the settlement or community, as when one says that 'the whole dùgu has gone to the mosque', or that 'the dùgu is hard or difficult' (in reference to the economic life of a community). In phrases involving the weather, dùgu is used less extensively than gàrii, although it is possible to say 'the dùgu has darkened' when storm clouds have gathered.

The last phrase can also be used to describe nightfall, and in its application to the arrival and departure of daylight the Manding term dùgu provides a striking parallel with the Hausa term gàrii.

The regular way of describing the arrival of dawn is to say that 'dùgu has become white, clean or clear', often as a sequel to the phrase 'the night has washed or laundered' (thus implying that the night has 'washed' the dùgu, leaving it clean at dawn, a formula used in narrative to describe the continuation of events on the following day). The Manding thus have the same concept of the clearing of the field of view, identified with the dùgu, at the dawning of each day, and the association with 'day' is evident in the phrase 'dùgu has come to its end (or its divide)', used at dead of night. The compound 'dùgu-end' (or 'dùgu-divide') has the sense of 'midnight'. As in Hausa, there is an expressed opposition between night and the settlement (viewed in its ideal form only by day); 'may dùgu clear well' is a frequent greeting at night among the Manding, just as 'let gàrii clear' may be used in Hausa as an encouragement during the night. There are also similar sayings in Manding, contrasting the concealment of night with the visibility of day, as for example: 'if you say you are beautiful at night, when dùgu clears, people will see'.

As final points of similarity between the two languages, one may cite the fact that it is normal in Manding to refer to a person's village as 'their' dùgu (and only as 'his' when one is referring to the chief), and that the expression 'son of (the) dùgu' may be used either in the concrete sense of 'native (of a particular community)' or, as in Hausa, in the abstract sense of 'master of a situation'.

CONCLUSION

As far as the Hausa term gàrii is concerned (to which the Manding term dùgu corresponds in most, although not all, respects), one may set up the following table to summarise its applications:

Human Settlement or Inhabited Place
(*basically*: Village or Town with its Surrounding Lands,
Human centred Ecosystem)

(by particularisation): Any part or aspect of a settlement and its community, including:	(by variation of scale): Any inhabited/inhabitable area, from an isolated oasis or homestead to the entire world.
Centre of Habitation	
Chief of the Community	
Human Population	
Livestock	
Local Economy	
Market-area	
Farmland	
Water supplies (Wells)	
Local weather	
Local sky	
(by abstraction): Dawn Day	(by abstraction): Environment Human Experience Surroundings, Situation Objective

204

From the linguistic point of view, the complex applications of gàrii serve to demonstrate how much detailed work is necessary to bridge the conceptual gaps between languages spoken in different cultural and physical environments. Even now, more work remains to be done on the usages of gàrii and on its 'boundaries' with related environmental terms in Hausa, whereas the analysis of the Manding term dùgu has only just begun. The immensity of the task can be grasped when one realises that Africa alone possesses over a thousand languages; and that each language contains a large range of 'key' terms requiring the same kind of detailed analysis as that to which gàrii has been subjected. From the environmental point of view, however, the task is more straight-forward. The study of gàrii has demonstrated the importance of language in providing an understanding of vernacular settlement-types, of their relationship to the environment and of the way they are regarded by their occupants. It becomes clear that no detailed study of vernacular shelter and settlement can be complete without paying adequate attention to the conceptual terminology used by the local population. It would also seem likely that the quite different nature of the concepts involved, in comparison with current Western concepts, may provide new perspectives in the way Westerners view their own relationship with their shelter and environment.

NOTES

[1] ROBINSON, C. H. (1925), BARGERY, G. P. (1934), and ABRAHAM, R. C. (2nd ed., 1962).

[2] DALBY, DAVID, 'The noun gàrii in Hausa: a semantic study', *Journal of African Languages*, III, 3, 1964, pp. 273–305.

[3] Most cultivated land lies in the 'outer' gàrii, but in many settlements there are also fields in the 'inner' gàrii (i.e. among the scattered houses of the main settlement, or or within the town-walls).

[4] Annual rainfall, over a large part of the Hausa-speaking area, ranges between 20 and 40 inches: the majority of this rainfall is confined to the summer months, when evaporation is at its highest. Water is precious, and rainy weather is not normally described in Hausa as 'bad weather'; the greeting *ruwaa yaa yi gyaaraa* ('the rain has improved things') is used even when the rain has done damage, or has resulted in flooding: to resent the rain would represent ingratitude towards Allah. Parts of the Hausa-speaking areas of Nigeria and Niger are severely affected, at the time of writing this paper, by the 1973 drought.

[5] I am indebted to my friends Monsieur Amadou Traoré of Bamako (Mali) and Monsieur Camara Laye of Kouroussa (Guinea), for their kind help in discussing the usage of this term in the Bambara and Mandinka dialects of Manding.

Hausa merchants house.

SEMIOLOGICAL URBANISM: AN ANALYSIS OF THE TRADITIONAL WESTERN SUDANESE SETTLEMENT

Alexander-Phædon Lagopoulos

THE SUDAN AS A CULTURAL UNIT

Ecologically, the Sudan consists of two almost parallel main biomes: arid grassland or semi-desert and tropical savannah and grassland.[1] Within this zone H. Baumann identifies, from west to east, eight cultural areas: the Western Atlantic, that of the Upper Niger, the Voltaic, the Eastern Atlantic, the Semi-Bantu, the Central Sudanese, the bipartite Eastern Sudanese and the pastoral area of north-east Africa. D. Paulme bands together the first four of these and part of the next two into one area, the Western African area, thus defining an area corresponding to the Western Sudanese area of M. J. Herskovits. Both define a cultural area, which M. J. Herskovits calls 'Eastern Sudan', lying east of Lake Chad and, according to D. Paulme, extending to the Red Sea. M. M. Horowitz believes that the Eastern Sudan is culturally heterogeneous, but forms a unity by reason of the observed economic and cultural interdependence, and that the whole of the Sudan – at least its central region – can be regarded as a unity,[2] a view to which we subscribe. In the following study we will deal with the western part of Sudan's cultural area.

BASIC SEMIOLOGICAL CONCEPTS

Semiology is the science of the study of signs; it rests on structural linguistics. The linguistic sign consists of a concept and an optical or acoustical image of a psychological nature. The meaning is the signified and the image is the signifier. Certain basic semiological concepts will be dealt with below.

Social language (langue) and speech (parole). According to F. de Saussure, language (*langage*) presents a social aspect, the social language, which constitutes a system of conventional signs, and an individual aspect, speech, which consists of individual combinations of those signs, obeying the rules of the social language. The two aspects of the language are linked dialectically. Extended speech, the combination that is of the larger linguistic elements termed sentences, is called *discourse* and is no longer bound by linguistic, but by logical restrictions. L. Hjelmslev distinguishes three levels of social language; schema, norme and usage. The opposition 'social language – speech' is closely related to the opposition 'code – message' of the information theory and corresponds to the oppositions 'structure – event' and 'system –

procedure'. According to R. Barthes, the opposition 'social language – speech' is a fairly general one as regards the semiological systems. One difference between linguistic social language and most semiological social languages is that the former is elaborated by the mass of speakers, whereas the signs of the latter are relatively arbitrary and become carriers of a '*logotechnic*'.

Signifier (signifiant-Sa) and signified (signifié-Se). According to L. Hjelmslev, the level of the signifiers and that of the signified of linguistics present two aspects: *form*, which can be described systematically by linguistics, and *substance*, the description of which lies outside the field of linguistics. This verification can be generalised with all semiological systems. The semiological sign frequently possesses a signifier's substance which carries the substantive signifier and is called *pre-signifier* (pre-signifiant). Signs of this sort belong to non-isologue semiological systems. A pre-signifier is presented by semiological systems where the substance of the signifier of the signs is a useful object. R. Barthes calls the signs of these systems *functions-signs* (fonctions-signes).

The effect of the act which connects the signifier and the signified, entailing the creation of a sign as an absolute entity, is called *signification*. The relative position of a sign inside a system of signs establishes its *value*. According to R. Barthes, the relation between signifier and signified is exact and immotivate as concerns sign, while it is inadequate and analogical as concerns symbol. Their analogic relation in the case of a symbol also lends it *expression* beyond signification.

The linguistic sign (morphem) is one of the two unitary elements of linguistics; it is accompanied by meaning (*unité significative*) and belongs to the first articulation of language. A second unitary linguistic element is the phonem, a distinctive unit (*unité distinctive*) 'devoid' of meaning, which belongs to the second articulation of language. Human language is characterised by the existence of those two articulations.

Syntagm (syntagme) and paradigm (paradigme). Syntagm (metonymy) is a linear combination of signs governed by syntactic rules. Paradigm (metaphor), in linguistics, is the set of the signs which are related by sound or meaning or both.

R. Barthes observes that there can exist erratic semiological systems, in which inert pre-signifier material will bear at certain places discontinuous and even disconnected signs; in the interspaces between the signs there are temporarily inexistent syntagms.

In the opinion of F. de Saussure, there are only differences in social language. The differences between linguistic signs become the reason for their classification into three basic dual paradigmatic categories, according to J. Cantineau, in accordance with which the relations between the similar and the dissimilar element of two signs are adopted as criteria. Particular interest is presented by privative oppositions, in which, according to A. Martinet, the signifier of one sign is detected by the existence of a signifier (marque) which is lacking in the signifier of another sign. The one signifier is marked (marqué), while the other is unmarked (non-marqué). The latter is called zero degree of the opposition and does not entail absence of signification, but an absence which possesses signification.

Denotation (dénotation) and connotation (connotation). A system is called denotative when its signs by themselves are regarded, and connotative when its signifiers (connotators) are signs of another system, which is denotative with respect to the first one. It is possible for a number of signs of the denotative system to form only one signifier of the connotative system. The form of the signifiers of the connotative system constitutes *rhetoric* and that of the signified *ideology*. The level of connotation is the symbolic level of a denotative system of signs, and it is there that the aesthetic message must be sought.

Language – object (langage – objet) and meta-language (méta-langage) A system is called meta-language if its signified are signs of another system, called language – object.[3]

INTRODUCTION TO SEMIOLOGICAL URBANISM

The physical space (the artificial environment of ecology) is the result of social action. As with every social phenomenon, it becomes the carrier of a meaning to the group or groups which have created it and, generally, to every individual who is familiar with it directly or indirectly, whether intimately or superficially. In principle, the approach to it on this level falls within the scope of semiology, in order to form ultimately, in our opinion, a branch of urbanism (semiological urbanism), when immediately related to the urbanistic approach. In the present study, a semiological analysis of the settlement of the western part of the cultural area of the Sudan, as defined in the first paragraph, will be attempted.

There are two inverse processes which are explored by semiological urbanism. The first presupposes the existence of a physical space and the activities pursued within it, the perception of which leads to the emergence of a set of signs, related to signifieds of denotation and connotation. The object of its semiological study is *the mental morphology* (according to P. Boudon) of the physical space and the creation of an interpretative structure-model.

The urbanistic sign is a function-sign, because it presents a pre-signifier of a useful character. According to U. Eco, the *signified of denotation of the sign of architecture and urbanism is the function performed by the pre-signifier*: the signified indicates the primary function (*funzione prima*) of the pre-signifier viewed as an element of physical space. This thesis relates to space production, but in so far as the mental image is concerned the signified of denotation does not belong solely to the urbanistic functional level, or to the functional level generally, but may also belong to other levels, such as the social level generally, the economic level, the chronological level, and others. *A pre-signifier may relate, either by itself or with other pre-signifiers, to a series of signified of connotation belonging to the same sign of connotation, having regard to the fact that both the signifier as well as the signified of denotation carried by it form a new signifier, or a part of a new signifier, of a series of signified.* Those last mainly indicate the social role of the pre-signifier (*funzioni seconde*, in regard to space production).

The semiology of the mental morphology of the settlement may comprise two different levels. *The first relates to its theoretical mental image and the second to its actual perceptual image.* This distinction does not lead to the radical separation of the two levels for an individual, because the continuous passage from the one to the other is possible for him.

The second process explored by semiological urbanism relates to the *physical morphology* (according to P. Boudon) of the space, from the scope of its production with the aid of its creators' cultural representations (representations' structure-model). The semiological study of this process can adopt two avenues of approach, one of which explores the mechanisms of the creation of the physical space. This creation sets out from a set of values (ideological level), which, if we isolate the functional level generally, define a set of functions. The latter, which belong to the signifiers of the signified values, are translated into forms. These forms, in turn, become signifiers of the signified functions. One part of urbanistic, and architectural, design falls under semiology.[4]

The following symbols will be used in the semiological analysis of the western Sudanese settlement below: (d) = at the level of denotation; (c) = at the level of connotation.

SEMIOLOGICAL ANALYSIS OF THE WESTERN SUDANESE SETTLEMENT

South Mali

Dogon. The shape of the settlement, according to the Dogon (Dagon, Dagom, Tombo, Habbe-sing, Kado), must be elliptic. The main square, *tay*, according to this model, is located to the north and comprises the council house and the oval altar *anakazu dummo*; the latter is quadrangular in plan and its corners are oriented towards the cardinal points of the compass. The signified (c) of the square, which plays the role of pre-signifier, is the sky (*alagala*) and the primordial field. This field is held to be divided into 60 parts, in the image of the earth and of the world, into 64 parts or into 6,400 (80 by 80 cubits). The signified (c) of the council house is a head, while those of the altar are the egg of the creator Amma, the centre of the world and the point of departure of the (second and third world) creation. North of the square there is the

207

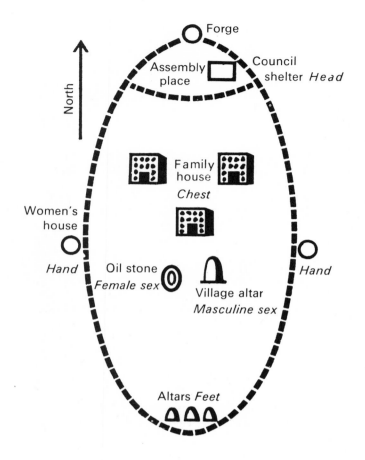

Forge

Assembly place

Council shelter *Head*

North

Family house *Chest*

Women's house

Hand

Oil stone *Female sex*

Village altar *Masculine sex*

Hand

Altars *Feet*

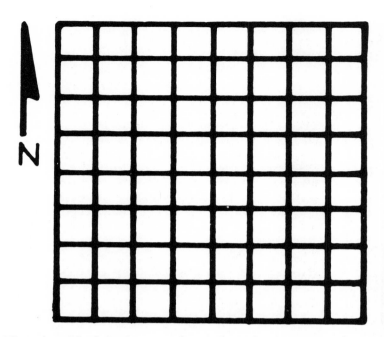

Ellipsoid model of the Dogon settlement (according to M. Griaule, Dieu d'Eau).
Chessboard model of the Dogon settlement.
Plan of the Dogon large house (based on a figure by M. Griaule, L'Image du Monde au Soudan).
The Dogon settlement Ogol (according to M. Griaule et G. Dieterlen, Le Renard Pale).

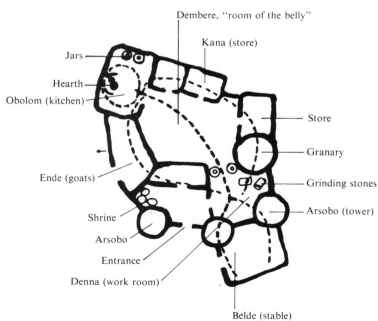

Dembere, "room of the belly"

Kana (store)

Jars

Hearth

Obolom (kitchen)

Store

Granary

Ende (goats)

Grinding stones

Shrine

Arsobo (tower)

Arsobo

Entrance

Denna (work room)

Belde (stable)

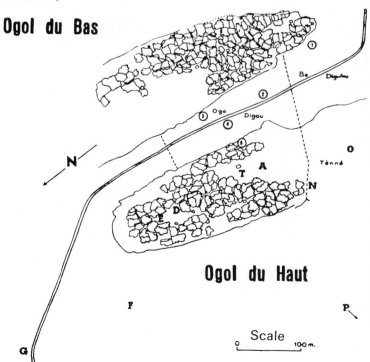

Ogol du Bas

Ogol du Haut

Scale

Dogon house, Mali.

forge, the signified (c) of which is a mythical forge. At the centre of the settlement there is a set of stones, the signified (c) of which is the female genital organ. Respect for women leads to the construction of the foundation altar, having as its signified (c) the male genital organ, outside the settlement, while normally it ought to have stood beside the set of stones already referred to. Three other elements of the settlement have as their signified (c), two of them one hand each and the third the legs. The signified (c) of the entire settlement is a man lying flat on his back.

According to another model, the settlement is square and is oriented towards the cardinal points of the compass; it has a chessboard pattern road system. The signified (c) of this chessboard pattern is the world, the earth and all cultivations. The signified (c) of the terraces of the settlement dwellings are the sky and the white squares of the blanket for the dead, those of the shaded courtyards, the black squares of the blanket and those of the roads, the seams between the strips of the blanket. The signified (c) of the settlement, beyond the blanket for the dead whose signified (c) is the world, is the front of the ancestral habitation having 80 niches.

The settlement, its every neighbourhood and its region have the world as their signified (c). The settlements of the Dogon are frequently bipartite, having as their signified (c) the primordial element from which the world was created. An example of a bipartite settlement is afforded by the Ogol settlement.

209

Granaries, towers and dwellings in Irely, Bandiagara escarpment.

Irely, Dogon village on the Bandiagara escarpment, Mali.

The altars, which stand in and around Ogol, have all the stars as their signified (c). The main altar (*para lebe*), erected by the founder of the settlement and occupying the centre of the main square lebe dala (terrace of the snake-*lebe*) of the Upper Ogol, has as its signified (c) the centre of the world (*adino bogi*).

The signified (c) of the plan of the large house (*ginna*) is the ark, being identified with the world, of Nommo, the organiser of the world, and Nommo himself. It may be inscribed in an ellipse, the signified (c) of which is the cosmic egg. The signs (d) 'kitchen', 'central room', 'work room' and 'antechamber' are converted into signifier (c), referring to the signified (c) of the anthropomorphic level 'head', 'trunk', 'belly' and 'genital organ' respectively. According to the above standpoint, the plan of the house is converted into a sort of summary of its three-dimensional spatial reality. The three-dimensional standpoint of the large house likewise conducts to the level of connotation. The signs (d) 'ground floor floor', 'ground floor ceiling' and 'floor ceiling' of the two-storey house lead to the signified (c) 'earth', 'space between the earth and the sky' and 'sky' respectively.[5]

The Bamako settlement. Formerly, the Bamako settlement comprised a central neighbourhood, Niarela, which was inhabited by the Niare, the founders of the settlement, consisted of three parts and had three gates, one to the north, another to the west and the third to the south. This neighbourhood was surrounded by four peripheral neighbourhoods oriented towards the four cardinal points of the compass. To the north (according to informants, but actually to the west) and to the south (to the east) there lay the neighbourhoods of the merchants and stock-breeders Twati: the northern neighbourhood was occupied by the Ture tribe, and the southern by the Drave. The signified (c) of the Niare, Ture and Drave groups and of the spaces occupied by them is fire. To the east there was the Banãkoro neighbourhood and to the west the Bozola neighbourhood, composed of four social groups of fishermen, occupying different spaces. The signified (c) of these four groups and of the spaces corresponding to them is water, as the complement of fire. The settlement was surrounded by a wall pierced by four gates oriented towards the cardinal points of the compass, at which four roads ended.

210

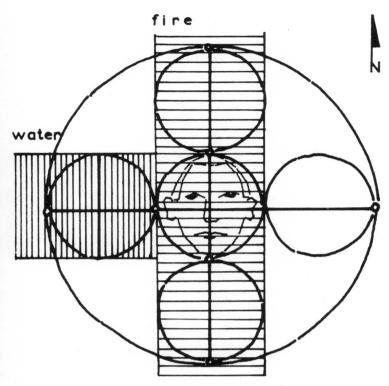

fire

water

Free geometric rendering of the old settlement of Bamako.

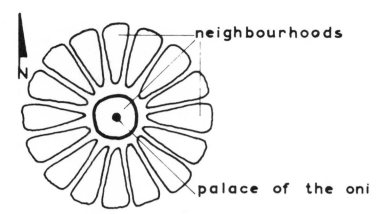

neighbourhoods

palace of the oni

Geometric representation of the Yoruba old settlement of Ife.

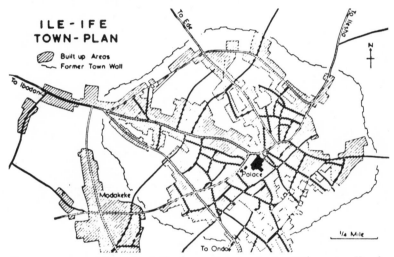

ILE-IFE
TOWN-PLAN

Built up Areas
Former Town Wall

To Ede
To Ilesa
To Ibadan
To Ondo
Modakeke
Palace
¼ Mile

Contemporary settlement of Ife (according to A. L. Mabogunje, Yoruba Towns).

The signs (d) 'central neighbourhood' and 'settlement' lead respectively, on the one hand to signified (c) 'head' and, on the other, to signified (c) 'man with arms outstretched at shoulder height' and 'world'.[6]

Yoruba of Nigeria. The Ketu settlement was elliptic in form; it was surrounded by two concentric walls, having one gate in their northern part, and was notionally divided into two halves. The signified (d) and signified (c) simultaneously of the one half was 'right' and 'west', and those of the other 'left' and 'east'.

According to tradition, the holy city of the Yoruba Ife (Illife, Ile-Ife), a typical Yoruba settlement, once consisted of four peripheral neighbourhoods oriented towards the cardinal points, twelve other peripheral neighbourhoods between them, the above making in all sixteen peripheral neighbourhoods, and a central neighbourhood, in which the palace, *afin*, of the religious chief *Oni* was located. Every set of a peripheral neighbourhood, the clan it contained theoretically and the clan representative had as its signified (c) one of the sixteen Yoruba deities, headed by Olokun (the sea), who, according to tradition, had been born at Ife. At the turn of the century, the city comprised seventeen neighbourhoods, each of which had a representative: these were nine patriarchs and eight chief priests. Similar observations apply to the modern city. The city is a pre-signifier, which becomes the carrier of a signifier (d), and the latter in turn causes the appearance

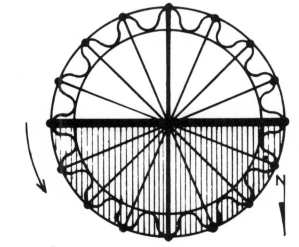

The earth and the world according to Yoruba.

A Yoruba shrine and priest's cult-house. Carved caryatids which support the verandah roof represent gods and spirits of the Yoruba pantheon.

of a sign (c), the signified (c) of which is the beginning of time (i.e. 0 time), the earth, the world and their centres (0 space); the latter are also the signified (c) of the pre-signifier 'palace'. The earth and the world are regarded by the Yoruba as being circular or rectangular and consisting of 16 parts. In outline, they are regarded as being composed of two perpendicular 'road' axes, which are oriented and depart from their intersection point, the centre of the world, where Olorun (sky) resides. The main 'road' is the E–W axis, creating a right and a left region, and the secondary one is the N–S axis. These two axes are considered as carrying the four main regions of the world, which correspond to the four cardinal points of the compass, to the four principal gods and four colours, or the 16 regions of the world.

It seems likely that the signs (d) and the cartographic signifiers (d) of Ife can be classified into three paradigmatic categories: the category of points (to which the sign (d) and cartographic signifier

(d) of the pre-Sa 'palace' appear to belong, as indicated by its relation to the concept of the centre of the world, the intersection of the cosmic axes), the category of lines (pre-signifier: road axes, neighbourhood limits) and the category of surfaces (pre-signifier: neighbourhoods).

The fact of the co-existence of a four-part and a sixteen-part cosmic image, arranged around a central point, probably leads to a dual consideration of the settlement, as composed of four areas or of sixteen neighbourhoods, surrounding the central palace.[7]

Fali of northern Cameroon. The world, according to the Fali of Kangu, the cosmogonic conceptions of which have been adopted by the other Fali, is bipartite. It sprang from two primordial eggs, the egg of a toad, *tokulgi,* the signified (c) of which are a mating pair, the female and the west, and the egg of a turtle, *tabunu,* the signified (c) of which are a mating pair, the male and the east. The shell of the former revolved in the direction of the apparent movement of the sun, while that of the latter revolved in the opposite direction. The interior of each egg revolved in an opposite direction to that of the shell. The two eggs collided at the centre of the world and there sprang from them two square earths, *osi,* which were at first separated by a trench containing the primordial ocean, being subsequently joined together to form the immobile earth, *boktik uribi.* The eastern region of the immobile earth is known – it is the region of the humans – while the western region is unknown and wild; the two regions are considered as quadripartite. According to another version, the land of the humans is bipartite, being composed of the male village, *ri,* and the female cultivated land around it, *hem,* and is surrounded by the wild earth; the contour of the first is circular. If the Fali regard the earth as consisting of two squares, they also conceive it as square, rectangular or circular.

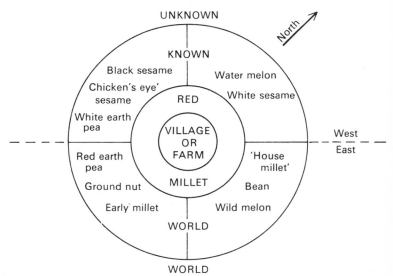

Geometric representation of the cosmic organisation of the Fali settlement Toro and its surrounding fields (according to J. P. Lebeuf, L'Habitation des Fali).

212

The ultimate earth, just as the initial earth and the initial world, is bipartite. It consists of two opposed and complementary regions, the eastern earth of the humans, the signified (c) of which is the male, and the western wild earth, the signified (c) of which is the female. Each region, in turn, consists of two opposed and complementary parts, the signified (c) of the one being the male and that of the other the female. The signified (c) of the earth is a man; he is regarded as consisting of four parts, the head, the trunk, the legs and the arms, arranged around a central element, the genital organ.

The cosmic organisation is reflected by the social organisation. Fali society consists of two main groups, that of the toad and that of the turtle, these have been enlarged to include respectively the varan and crocodile groups.

The Fali settlement consists of the two main social groups already referred to and, theoretically, of four neighbourhoods. The signified (c) of each neighbourhood is one part of the quadripartite earth, and of the quadripartite world, and one part of the human body. The Toro settlement (Gǫbri Bowri), the western mythological village of Tinguelin, one of the four regions of the territory of the Fali of Kangu, consists of four old neighbourhoods, those of Banntoro, Chauǫte, Babãndji and Bantendjum, and a newer one, the Baltokpǫssi. It is surrounded by red millet fields, around which the remaining crops are cultivated, forming four oriented groups. The similarity of the above spatial layout to the concentric spatial organisation of the earth, already referred to, is obvious: the signified (c) of the settlement is the male central part of the earth of the humans, the signified (c) of its cultivations is

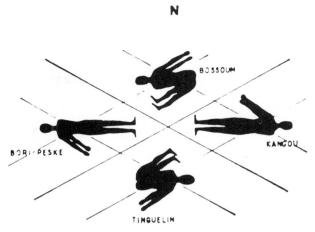

The anthropomorphic Se_c of the four mythical primordial settlements belonging to each part of the Kangu Fali territory (according to J. P. Lebeuf, L'Habitation des Fali).

the female ring, which encloses that part, and that of the space which surrounds them, the unknown earth. At the same time, the signified (c) of each of the old neighbourhoods of the settlement are the earth, the world and the human body, the signified (c) of its four old neighbourhoods are the four parts of the earth and of the world and four members of the human body, while the signified (c) of the complete whole formed by them is the centre of the earth and of the world.

The first born males or males and females of the generations of an extended family are spread over the space in relation to the apparent motion of the sun. Each extended family is composed of one turtle group and one toad group, each of which consists of a male part and a female part. The members of the extended family have as their signified (c) the members of the human body. The dwelling complex of certain social groups has as its signified (c) the clockwise and that of the others the counter-clockwise rotation of the cosmic eggs. Certain pre-signifiers, which are structures or wooden pillars (bal do or ka gu), have as their signified (c) the 'centre of rotation'. The signified (c) of the pillars are the following: 'centre of the world', 'centre of the earth', 'navel', 'phallus' and 'mythical crocodile'.

The Fali dwelling leads to the signified (c) 'shell of the primordial turtle egg', 'shell of the primordial toad egg'; 'earth', 'world', the signified (c) relating to the successive phases of the earth and of the world; 'man' and 'man and woman mating', in which case the sign (d) 'walls of the dwelling' is converted into the signifier (c) of the signified (c) 'woman' (the same sign (d) leads also to the signified (c) 'earth', 'liquid element'), while the sign (d) 'roof' becomes the signifier (c) of the signified (c) 'man' (it leads also to the signified (c) 'sky', 'solid element'). Every structure of the dwelling and every space of the structure, just as the whole of the dwelling, have as their signified (c) the 'earth', 'world', 'mating couple'; every structure has as its signified (c) a member of the

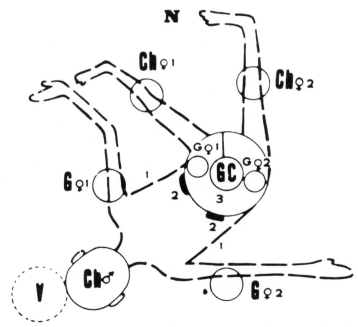

The anthropomorphic Se_c of the Fali dwelling (according to J. P. Lebeuf, L'Habitation des Fali).

213

human body. The Fali dwelling can also lead to a zoomorphic or phytomorphic symbolism.

It has been pointed out that the territory of the Fali of Kangu is quadripartite. Each two parts constitute one region. The one of the two regions thus formed has as its signified (c) the earth of the humans and the other, the wild earth; one part of the region has as its signified (c) the east and the other the west. The four primordial settlements, according to mythology, correspond to the above parts. Each part is deemed to comprise not only one, but also four primordial settlements. The set of the four parts, and the set of the four primordial settlements of each of these parts have a human body as their signified (c). In the first case, it is the body of a man (signified (c): 'sky'), lying on his right side and fertilising the earth, whereas in the second case, the posture of the body differs from one part to another.[8]

Kotoko of southern Chad. The Kotoko are the descendants of the Sao, who created a pre-Islamic culture. The model of their settlements is the Logone-Birni settlement, which, according to tradition, was founded by the Sao. As all Kotoko settlements, it consists of two sections, the eastern *halaka* and the western *alague* (or *alage*). Certain signified (c) of the first of these areas relate to the north, 'up', manliness, strength, activities which have to do with water, white, day and the hot season of the year, and one of its signified (d) relates to the direction of the flow of the river which skirts the settlement to the south, while certain signified (c) of the second relate to the south, 'down', womanliness, passivity, the chase, black, night and the rainy season, and one of its signified (d) relates to the counter direction of the flow of the river. We observe a contradiction at first sight between the signified (c) of the two sections 'north section'–'south section' and their signified (d) 'east section'–'west section'. In other instances, contradictions of this kind are expressions of the contradiction model-reality, but in the present instance the contradiction is resolved by the fact of the correspondence between north-east and south-west.

The dualism of the settlement reflects the dualism of the earth and the world. Both are regarded as consisting of a northern and a southern region parted by a river, having as its signified (c) a man

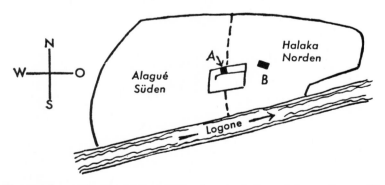

The Kotoko settlement Logone-Birni: A. tukuri, B. guti (according to W. Muller, Die Heilige Stadt).

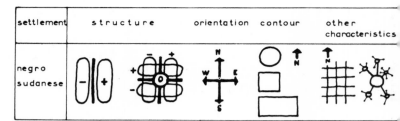

Main characteristics of the Sudanese settlement (according to A.-Ph Lagopoulos, L'Influence des Conceptions Cosmiques . . .).

lying on his back, on one bank of which there stands the tree *mahilage*, having as its signified (c) the axis of the world and the phallus of the recumbent man. Earth and world are regarded also as quadripartite. The signified (c) of the settlement are 'earth', 'world', 'man'.

The two sections of the settlement are considered as being separated by a central zone related to the palace, the signified (c) of which is the world and its centre. The palace grounds contain the *tukuri* building, the construction of which is ascribed to the Sao. The building consists of two volumes, a north volume with 'man' as its signified (c) and a south volume with 'woman' as its signified (c). The passage between them, which runs east–west, is a pre-signifier leading to the signified (c) 'axis of equilibrium of the palace', 'axis of equilibrium of opposites', 'axis of the settlement', 'axis of the earth', 'axis of the world'. That explains why it corresponds to the zone running north–south, which separates the two sections of the settlement and is considered as an axis. The signified (c) of the *tukuri* relate to 'earth', 'world', '0 time (commencement of time)'.

East of the palace there was the *guti*, a structure of spiral ascent, which resembled the Mesopotamian ziggurat. The ascent, which ran counter to the apparent motion of the sun, has as its signified (c) 'cosmic disorder', while the descent, in the reverse direction, has as its signified (c) 'cosmic order', 'creation'. Other signified (c) of the *guti* are '0 time', 'centre of the world', *'mahilage'*, 'cosmic axis', 'man standing upright', 'phallus'.[9]

CONCLUSIONS

The following symbols will be used for the mathematical formulae in this chapter:
a. As regards the level of reality: the symbol 'pre-Sa' instead of the term 'pre-signifier'.
b. As regards the level of denotation: the symbol 'Si_d' instead of the term 'sign', 'Sa_d' instead of 'signifier' and 'Se_d' instead of 'signified'.
c. As regards the level of connotation: symbol (Si_c' instead of the term 'sign', 'Sa_c' instead of 'signifier' and 'Se_c' instead of 'signified'.

The image of the western Sudanese settlement, as formed by its inhabitants, that is to say its mental morphology, is identified in principle with the cultural representations, the model, of its founders. This conclusion means that the signs (d) and signs (c) to which the physical space of the settlement relate are, in principle, the same as those which governed its creation. An analogous phenomenon is observed with respect to the dwelling and the region. The above conclusion applies to all non-Western settlements, but not to the Western settlement. *The model referred to is governed by the level of connotation, more particularly by the mythological sphere, and is socially acknowledged.* Concerning non-Western cultures, it is of general application, if 'f' is a mathematical mapping:

Procedure of the creation of the settlement:
$$\left\{ z \mid z = Si_c \right\} \xrightarrow{f_1} \left\{ y \mid y = Si_d \right\} \xrightarrow{f_2} \left\{ x \mid x = \text{pre-Sa.} \right\}$$

Procedure of the creation of its image:
$$\left\{ x \mid x = \text{pre-Sa} \right\} \xrightarrow{f_2^{-1}} \left\{ y \mid y = Si_d \right\} \xrightarrow{f_1^{-1}} \left\{ z \mid z = Si_c. \right\}$$

The image of a Western culture settlement is always governed by the signified (d) and, simultaneously, by the signified (c) of different lexica. The set of signs (d) and the set of signs (c) of the settlement are not socially established, but they do not cease to have a social origin. Furthermore, the creation of the Western settlement is spontaneous or, in certain instances, the product of design on the part of a minority of specialists, who impose a logo-technic.

The settlement model from which the western Sudanese settlement originates and to which it relates is composed of a set of signs (d), the cartographic signifiers (d) of which jointly form a simple geometric pattern. This set corresponds mainly to an essentially horizontal standpoint and sometimes to an essentially vertical standpoint of the settlement.

Both the signs (d) of the western Sudanese settlement, and of the non-Western culture settlement generally, as well as their signifiers (d), which are manifested in their cartographic rendering, may be classified into three paradigmatic categories: that of points (e.g. the sign (d) of the palace of Ife, one of the signs (d) of the *guti* of Logone-Birni), *that of lines* (e.g. the signs (d) of the roads of the settlement in the case of the Dogon and the Yoruba, the sign (d) of the axial zone of the Kotoko settlement, the sign (d) of the bounds of the neighbourhood in the settlements which have been studied) *and that of surfaces* (the sign (d) of the neighbourhoods); furthermore, the first two of these categories subdivide into two sub-categories, as we shall see immediately below (types of signs (d) by K. Lynch). There may exist uncertainty over the classification of a given sign (d) or signifier (d), or its classification under two categories simultaneously may be possible: an example of this is afforded by the *guti* of Logone-Birni, the signified (c) of which are the cosmic axis (sign (d): line) and the centre of the world (sign (d): point, derived from the intersection of the cosmic axis with the plane of the settlement). These categories are the same as those deduced from the researches of K. Lynch, who studied certain images of contemporary inhabitants of Boston, Jersey City and Los Angeles. K. Lynch identified five types of signs (d): the landmark, the node, the path, the edge and the district. The unitary elements of all the spatial scales of the semiological

standpoint of the settlement fall into the categories and sub-categories referred to.

The set of the signs (d) of the western Sudanese settlement ($\{y \mid y = Si_d\}$) forms one or more syntagms. *These are governed by syntactic laws, two of a general nature expressions of which appear to be the dualistic pair of the form $+/0$ or $+/-$, in the latter case consisting of bi-polar semantic elements, and the triadic form $+/0/-$, consisting of two pairs of the form 'marked – unmarked'.* Forms of this type are: centre – circumference, north – centre – south, east – centre – west, right – middle – left, up – middle – down, male – female.

To non-Western cultures, the syntactic laws of the signs (d) derive from the level of connotation. To Western culture, the laws governing the signs (d) of the city derive from the levels of denotation and connotation, and appear to identify with those referred to above. Thus, for example, K. Lynch observes that the district is chosen because of its homogeneity, that is to say its heterogeneity with respect to the surrounding districts, while the landmarks are usually chosen because they contrast with their surroundings, from the standpoint of spatial scale, orientation, age or cleanliness.

The model of the western Sudanese settlement obeys certain rules. These rules characterise all non-Western settlements, and also apply equally to the architectural and to the regional scale: *To each pre-signified and, by extension, to each sign (d) usually corresponds one sign (c) and conversely:*
$$\{x \mid x = \text{pre-Sa}\} \Leftrightarrow \{y \mid y = Si_d\} \Leftrightarrow \{z \mid z = Si_c\}.$$
This rule has proved valid generally in all the examples we have analysed, with the exception of the Toro settlement of the Fali: its four old neighbourhoods lead up basically to the level of connotation and, to a secondary degree only, the newer Baltok-possi neighbourhood. Pre-signifiers related to social groups may also lead to signs (c) (e.g. the toad, turtle, varan and crocodile groups of the Fali). Frequently, the location of the social pre-signifiers having certain signified (c) coincides with urbanistic pre-signifiers possessing the same signified (c) (see e.g. the Bamako settlement).

The above conclusions prompt us to accept that the signs of the settlement of non-Western cultures are predetermined socially, hence that *they present a rigidity.* Conversely, the settlement of Western culture presents a continuous development which, so far as regards the formation of its image, *allows flexibility in the selection of the signs;* this image is a function of movement within the settlement. The flexibility is frequently so great as to lead F. Choay to believe, quite rightly, that the modern city has become disorganised from a semiological standpoint.

We find the counterpart of the relationship between the formation of the images of the non-Western and the Western settlement in the relationship between the technique of the leading representatives of the pre-war and the modern cinema. During the period 1925–30 the technique of montage was at its zenith Eisenstein, a typical exponent of this technique, tries to predetermine the signs of the cinematographic discourse, using shots. The modern approach to the cinema, on the contrary, is more delicate and composite, and has as its unitary element a cinematographic sequence, which allows the viewer greater freedom in the choice of signs.

The signified (c) may be of different scales; there is no relation necessarily between their scale and that of the pre-signifiers. Thus, for example, taking also into account other pre-signifiers beyond the urbanistic ones, the pre-signifier of the Fali 'structure pillar', 'structure space', 'dwelling structure', 'dwelling', 'settlement neighbourhood', 'settlement', 'part (one-fourth) of the territory' and 'territory' refer to the same signified (c) 'man', 'earth' and 'world'; more particularly, the pre-signifier 'neighbourhood' refers to the signified (c) 'man', 'part (one-fourth) of the earth', 'earth', 'part (one-fourth) of the world' and 'world', while the pre-signifier 'settlement' refers to the signified (c) 'man', 'centre of the earth', 'centre of the world', 'central part of the earth of the humans', 'earth' and 'world'. The preceding examples also lead to the conclusion that *different pre-signifiers have the same signified (c)* (this conclusion is in apparent contradiction with the preceding mathematical formulae.

It is possible for the signified (c) of a pre-signifier of the settlement to be the signified (d) of a pre-signifier of another kind. An example of this is to be found among the Dogon, for whom the signified (c) of the terrace, of the courtyard and of the road of their settlement are respectively the white and the black square, and the seam of the blanket for the dead.

There may exist contradictions between one or more signified (d) of the same pre-Sa and one or more signified (c) of the same pre-signifier of the settlement. We encountered such contradictions in the Logone-Birni settlement of the Kotoko: they related to the signified of its sections halaka and alague. The modern settlement may also present such contradictions.

It is possible for the set of elements, to which the signified (c) of a lexicon of the settlement refer, to make up one entity perfectly (e.g. the two sections and the central zone of Logone-Birni refer to three signified (c), the whole of which corresponds perfectly to the earth or the world) *or imperfectly* (e.g. the settlement of the Dogon, where we have the signifieds (c) 'genital organ', 'right hand', 'left hand' and 'legs', the whole of which, though not corresponding to the entity 'man', nevertheless refers to the latter).

The set of Si_d of the image of the western Sudanese settlement presupposes the placing of a subject in a specific spatial scale. Placing in a different spatial scale leads to a different set of signs (d). The pre-signifier and the cartographic signifier (d) of one scale frequently consists of a sub-set of the pre-signifiers and the signifiers (d) respectively of the immediately more analytical scale. Thus, the set of cartographic signifiers (d) of the image of the more general spatial scale of Ife comprises only one signifiers (d), relating to the whole of the settlement, the set of signifier (d) of the next scale comprises four signifiers (d), relating to the four regions of the settlement, and one relating to the palace, and the set of signifiers (d) of the scale next after comprises sixteen signifiers (d), relating to the sixteen neighbourhoods of the settlement, and one relating to the palace.

The foregoing conclusion also applies to the image of the Western settlement. Furthermore, according to K. Lynch, the set of

signs (d) appear to be constant in the case of a given individual placing himself in a specific spatial scale. The set of signs (d) may also be affected by other parameters other than the spatial scale, such as the hour of the day and the season of the year.

To come again back to the western Sudanese settlement, placing in a given spatial scale may lead to different sets of signs (d). An example of this is afforded by the settlement of the Dogon, which presents one set of signs (d) when it is viewed as elliptic and another set when it is viewed as a chessboard pattern. Certain elements of the settlement, limited in number and/or of a specialised kind, scattered over the whole of the settlement, may be converted into carriers of signs (d) and signs (c). Thus, the set of the altars of Ogol of the Dogon relate to a set of signs (d), having the whole of the stars as its general signified (c). According to J. Castex and Ph. Panerai, the same phenomenon is observed in the case of the set of the monuments of the Western settlement.

The western Sudanese settlement presents a series of sets of signified (c), which corresponds to the set of signs (d) of a spatial scale. If we symbolise with $Se_c O$ a signified (c) which belongs to an urbanistic lexicon O (suc-code), that is to a set of signs and their laws corresponding to a specific attitude towards reality, and with A (= cosmic), B (= anthropomorphic), C (= temporal, ... N a series of such lexica, we have:

$$a\,|a = Se_c\,A\,\underset{\rightarrow}{f_1}\ b\,|b = Se_c\,B\,\underset{\rightarrow}{f_2}\ c\,|c = Se_c\,C\,\underset{\rightarrow}{f_3} \ldots \underset{\rightarrow}{f_{n-1}}\,n\,|n = Se_c\,N$$

and mSre specifically:

$$a\,|a = Se_c\,A \Leftrightarrow b\,|b = Se_c\,B \Leftrightarrow c\,|c = Se_c\,C \Leftrightarrow \ldots \Leftrightarrow n\,|n = Se_c\,N.$$

The lexica A, B and C predominate over the others. The above mathematical expression reflects the principal characteristic of the systems of classification of non-Western cultures. Each set of signs (d) of a spatial scale leads to a series of sets of signified (c) corresponding to this scale. At the same time, the elements of the sets of signified (c) may be independent of the spatial scale to which the signs (d) relate. The first conclusion also applies to the Western settlement.

The set of signs (d) and of signs (c) of the western Sudanese settlement satisfy the three main characteristics, according to J. Piaget, of a structure: *the totality, governed by structural laws, the transformation and the autoregulation*, which entails the conservation of the structure and its maintenance within certain limits with the assistance of feed-back mechanisms. The same conclusion also applies to the sets of signs (d) of the Western settlement.

From the standpoint of semiology, the western Sudanese settlement, just as every settlement generally, is a non-isologue system and consists of function-signs. While the set of signs (d) of the Western settlements forms usually an erratic system, that of the western Sudanese and generally of non-Western settlements is generally a non-erratic system.

The image of the non-Western, just as that of the Western, settlement is governed by a code, resembling a linguistic social language, which appears to be characterised by the existence of a series of articulations. This code governs the set of the signs (d) of the settlement, which takes the place of speech. One 'sentence' of the peech seems to be a number of signs (d), which constitute one ntity for a given subject. It appears to be a fact that, if a subject s placed in the more analytical spatial scale, one or more 'sentences' vhich it will form with the signs (d) corresponding thereto, may orm a sign (d) of the next scale. The set of signs (d) of the settle- nent form a discourse. Discourse entails rhetoric. In contrast to he non-Western settlement, its signifiers for the Western settle- nent derive only from certain of the signs (d) of the settlement. *Through its rhetoric, the set of signs (d) of the settlement refers to deology of the social group or one of the social groups of the settle- nent. A fundamental and general ideology, to which all the sets of igns (d) of the western Sudanese settlement refer, is its cosmic and ts human essence.*

Orientation in a settlement is a function of the elements which an be transformed into urbanistic pre-signifiers, having regard to he fact that *the existence of distinct signs (d) is a necessary pre- equisite of orientation.* K. Lynch is in agreement on this point:

he believes that in the modern Western settlement spatial orienta- tion is due to its legibility (imageability, visibility). *Orientation is not due solely to the existence of pre-signifiers and their signs (d), but mainly to their interrelations.* In the case of the western Sudanese settlement, and the non-Western settlement generally, the signs (d) are related, not only among themselves, but also with fixed points or directions; this relation may be actual (level of denotation) and/or theoretical (level of connotation). Such points are the four cardinal points of the compass and their centre. The interrelation of the signs (d) of the settlements referred to is not solely spatial, but also temporal, the latter being due basically to the signifieds (c) of the temporal and the cosmic lexica; the signified (c) of the latter are interconnected through narrative elements. To non- Western cultures, space and time are indissolubly connected. The fact that two sets of signified (c) of the western Sudanese settlement correspond to one temporal and one cosmic lexicon determines orientation within the settlement.[10]

REFERENCES

ODUM, E. P., *Fundamentals of Ecology*, W. B. Saunders Co., 1971³, p. 381 (fig. 14–9) and LEUZINGER, E., *Afrique. L'Art des Peuples Noirs*, Ed. Albin Michel, Paris, 1962², map 1.

BAUMANN, H., *Les Peuples et les Civilisations de l'Afrique*, Payot, Paris, 1962, pp. 89, 91–92; PAULME, D., *Les Civilisations Africaines*, 'Que Sais-je?', PUF, Paris, 1965, pp. 98–99, 112–113 and HOROWITZ, M. M., 'A Reconsideration of the "Eastern Sudan" ', *Cahiers d'Etudes Africaines*, Vol. VII, 3e Cahier, MCMLXVII.

SAUSSURE, F., DE, *Cours de Linguistique Générale*, Payot, Paris, 1971, pp. 23–39, 97–102, 106–107, 123–124, 155–166, 170–175, 180–184; BARTHES, R., Rhétorique de l'Image and Eléments de Sémiologie, *Communications*, pp. 4, 1964, 41, 42, 48, 50–51 and 92–97, 101, 103–132 respectively; WELLS, R. S., 'De Saussure's System of Linguistics', in *Structuralism. A Reader*, M. Lane (ed.), Jonathan Cape, London, 1970, pp. 87, 93–96, 102–103, 117; FAGES, J. B., *Comprendre le Structuralisme*, E. Privat (ed.), Toulouse, 1968, pp. 19–33, 53; GREIMAS, A. J., *Sémantique Structurale, Recherche de Méthode*, Libr. Larousse, Paris, 1966; ECO, U., *La Structure Absente. Introduction à la Recherche Sémiotique*, Mercure de France, 1972; 1968), 272, 297 and BENSE, M., Συνοπτική Θεμελίωση τῆς Σύγχρονης Αἰσθητικῆς, Δευκαλίων, Χρόνος, 1, 2, Μάρτιος—Μάϊος 1970, e.g. 143, 147, 148–149, 157–158.

BOUDON, P., *Recherches Sémiologiques: Le Phénomène Urbain*, Paris, 1968, pp. 5; 13–14, 32, ECO, U., op. cit., pp. 269, 270–271, 272, 273, 274–276, 304–305, 311; ALEXANDER, Ch., *Notes on the Synthesis of Form*, Harvard Univ. Press, Mass., 1966 (1964), pp. 46–59, 76–77 and CASTEX, J. et PANERAL, Ph., 'Notes sur la Structure de l'Espace Urbain', *L'Architecture d'aujourd'hui*, No. 153, dec. 1970-jan. 1971, pp. 32, 33. See also LEFEBVRE, H., *Le Droit à la Ville*, Ed. Anthropos, Paris, 1968, pp. 62–63.

GRIAULE, M., *Dieu d'Eau*, Fayard, Paris, 1966, 'L'Image du Monde au Soudan', *Journal de la Société des Africanistes*, Tome XIX, Fasc. II, 1949, 'Myth de l'Organisation du Monde chez les Dogons du Soudan', *Psyché*, Symbolisme d'un Temple Totémique Soudanais', in *Le Symbolisme Cosmique des Monuments Religieux*, Série Orientale Roma, XIV, Roma, 1957, 'African Art', in *Larousse Encyclopedia of Prehistoric and Ancient Art*, Paul Hamlyn, London, 1966 and 'Systèmes Graphiques des Dogons', in 'Signes Graphiques Soudanais', *L'Homme*, 3, 1951, pp. (41, 68–69, 72, 74, 83, 89, 90, 92–94, 107–108, 112–113, 150), 86–87, 445, (30–32, 33), 82 and 25 respectively; GRIAULE, M. et DIETERLEN, G., *Le Renard Pâle*, Univ. de Paris, Travaux et Mémoires de l'Inst. d'Ethnol., LXXII, Paris, 1965 and 'Afrique Noire', in *Symbolisme Cosmique et Monuments Religieux*, Musée Guimet, Paris, 1955, pp. 32–33, 61, 79, 83, 97, 101–102, 106, 128, 129, 162–163, 169, 178, 254, 266–268, 276, 293–301, 307, 320, 323–342, 345–348, 349–350, 352, 390, 393, 417–418, 470, 479, 490 and 102, 103, 104, 106 respectively; LAGOPOULOS, A.-Ph., *L'Influence des Conceptions Cosmiques sur l'Urbanisme Africain Traditionnel*, Athènes, 1970 and 'Semeiological Analysis of the Traditional African Settlement', *Ekistics*, Vol. 33, No. 195, Febr. 1972, pp. 132, 136, 137–140 and 144 respectively; SERVIER, J., *L'Homme et l'Invisible*, R. Laffont, Paris, 1964, pp. 85, 86, 254, 263, 264 and ZAHAN, D., *La Viande et la Graine*, Présence Africaine, Paris, 1969, pp. 129–130.

⁶ PÂQUES, V., *L'Arbre Cosmique dans la Pensée populaire et dans la Vie Quotidienne du Nord-Ouest Africain*, Inst. d'Ethn., Musée de l'Homme, Paris, 1964, pp. 173–175.

⁷ FROBENIUS, L., *Mythologie de l'Atlantide*, Payot, Paris, 1949, pp. 19, 26–28, 34, 40, 41, 42, 144–145, 147, 159–160, 161–163, 164–166, 230, 238, 248, 254–255, 258; Λαγόπουλος, Α.-Φ., Δομική Πολεοδομία: Ὁ Οἰκισμός ὡς Τ.Ε.Ε., 1973, pp. 94–95; LAGOPOULOS, A.-Ph., 'Semeiological Analysis . . .', p. 144; BAUMANN, H., op. cit., pp. 348, 364, 365; MABOGUNJE, A. L., *Yoruba Towns*, Ibadan Univ. Press, 1982, pp. 4–6; FRASER, D., *Village Planning in the Primitive World*. Studio Vista, London, pp. 43–44, 45–46; Πάπυρος-Λαρούς, Παγκόσμιος Μυθολογία, Τόμ. Β', 'Αθῆναι, 1964, pp. 244, 249–250; CASSIRER, E., *The Philosophy of Symbolic Forms*, Vol. 2, *Mythical Thought*, Yale Univ. Press, U.S.A., 1955, p. 87 and MAQUET, J., *Les Civilisations Noires*, Marabout Univ. Belgique, 1967, p. 190.

⁸ LEBEUF, J. P., *L'Habitation des Fali, Montagnards du Cameroun Septentrional*, Libr. Hachette, Paris, 1961, 'Dessin et Ecriture chez les Fali', *Abbia*, mars 1967 and 'Système du Monde et Ecriture en Afrique Noire', *Présence Africaine*, ler trim. 1965, pp. ;49–50, 367–560, 584–586), 27 and 130, 133–134 respectively; LAGOPOULOS, A.-Ph., *L'Influence de Conceptions Cosmiques . . .* and 'Semeiological Analysis . . .', pp. 155–160 and 146 respectively; Λαγόπουλος, Α.-Φ., op. cit., p. 104; LEBEUF, A., 'Le Système Classificatione des Fali (Nord-Cameroun)', in *African Systems of Thought*, International African Institute (ed.), Oxford Univ. Press, London, 1965, pp. 329–330 and Πάπυρος-Λαρούς, op. cit., p. 249.

⁹ LEBEUF, A. M. D., *Les Principautés Kotoko. Essai sur le Caractère Sacré de l'Autorité*, Ed. du Centre National de la Recherche Scientifique, Paris, 1969, pp. 55, 58, 59, 85–87, 91–96, 153–154, 155–156, 311–312, 313, 314, 315; LEBEUF, A. et J.-P., 'Monuments Symboliques du Palais Royal de Logone-Birni (Nord Cameroun)', *Journal de la Société des Africanistes*, Tome XXV. Fasc. I et II, 1955, pp. 25–26, 29–30, 31–34; LEBEUF, J.-P. et DETOURBET, A. MASSON, *La Civilisation du Tchad*, Payot, Paris, 1950, pp. 11, 13, 38, 50; MÜLLER, W., *Die Heilige Stadt*, W. Kohlhammer, Stuttgart, 1961, pp. 163, 165, 166–169 and LAGOPOULOS, A.-Ph., *L'Influence des Conceptions Cosmiques . . .* and 'Semeiological Analysis . . .', pp. 160, 163–165 and 144–145 respectively.

¹⁰ See also Πάπυρος-Λαρούς, op. cit., pp. 96–97, 99, 102–114, 117–121, 122, 126, 127, 129, 130–136, 137, 159, 160; LAGOPOULOS, A.-Ph., 'Semeiological Analysis . . . and *L'Influence des Conceptions Cosmiques .i. '*, pp. 146–148 and 166–167, 279,

280, 282 respectively; LYNCH, K., *The Image of the City*, The MIT Press, Cambridge (Mass.), 1965 (1960); BARTHES, R., 'Sémiologie et Urbanisme', *L'Architecture d'aujourd'hui*, No. 153, déc. 1970–jan. 1971, same author, 'Rhétorique de l'Image' and 'Eléments de Sémiologie', *Communications*, 4, 1964, pp. 48–49 and 124–125, 126 respectively; CHOAY, F., 'Remarques à propos de Sémiologie Urbaine', *L'Architecture d'aujourd'hui*, No. 153, déc. 1970–jan. 1971; ECO, U., op. cit., p. 293; CASTEX, J. et PANERAI, Ph., op. cit., p. 33; LEFEBVRE, H., op. cit., pp. 54–55, 71, 73; PIAGET, J., *Le Structuralisme*, 'Que Sais-je?', PUF, Paris, 1968, pp. 5–16; GREIMAS, J., op. cit., pp. 23–25; LÉVI-STRAUSS, C., *Anthropologie Structurale*, Plon, Paris, 1958 and *La Pensée Sauvage*, Plon, Paris, 1962, pp. 166–170 and 83, 84–86, 179 respectively; ELIADE, M., *Le Sacré et le Profane*, Gallimard, Paris, 1965, 'Structure et Fonction du Mythe Cosmogonique', in *La Naissance du Monde*, Ed. du Seuil, Paris, 1959 and *Cosmos and History. The Myth of the Eternal Return*, Harper Torchbooks – The Bollingen Library, New York and Evanston, 1959[2], pp. (31, 41–42, 43, 52, 57), (475, 478, 490) and 9–10 18–20 respectively; DURKHEIM, E. and MAUSS, M., *Primitive Classification*, Cohen and West, London, 1970[2] (1901–2); CASSIRER, E., op. cit., pp. 89, 106–107 JACCARD, P., *Le Sens de la Direction et l'Orientation Lointaine chez l'Homme*, Payot, Paris, 1932, e.g. pp. 8–10, 17, 19–20, 108–109, 114–118, 124, 170, 176–187 242, 256–257, 344–346 and KEPES, G., 'Notes on Expression and Communication in the Cityscape', in *The Future Metropolis*, L. Rodwin (ed.), Constable and Co Ltd., London, 1962, pp. 205, 208.

NIIKE: THE SITING OF A JAPANESE RURAL HOUSE

Keith Critchlow

To establish a basis of comparison for this study I am going to suggest that we consider those aspects of Japanese architectural activity involving siting, orientation and construction, as a protective medicine. In doing this I am going to compare it with Chinese acupuncture, which has known a history of three and a half thousand years and which continues today to expand in its scope, and to astound with its effectiveness. Under chairman Mao's directive that 'Chinese medicine and pharmacology are a great treasure house; efforts should be made to explore them and raise them to a higher level',[1] new energy has been poured into the study and practice of this ancient art.

Acupuncture is based on an ancient discovery that there is a relationship between the surface of the body and the interior organs. It was found that there are certain points of the body, which, if punctured or burned, resulted in a beneficial effect on disorders within, and in many cases remedied serious ailments. The practice was recorded in the Shang Dynasty in 1558 B.C. but it was not until the end of the Chin Dynasty in A.D. 420 that the Emperor Wei Teh had ordered a bronze statue to be made which demonstrated the 'points' and the 'channels' connecting them. Later in the Sung Period, somewhere between A.D. 1102 and A.D. 1106, dissection was practised, but from then until today, in spite of the vast increase in the skills of medical science, no anatomical basis has been discovered to reveal how the system of acupuncture works.

Today the Chinese are forging ahead with techniques which have stretched Western observers to the limits of their credulity. Currently hospitals throughout China are performing major operations where the patient is anaesthetised locally by the insertion of a single needle.

The implications of such recovered and developed ancient knowledge are vast when related to the many millions spent each year in the United States and the British Health Service on tranquillisers, drugs and operation expenditure. Yet they are far deeper in terms of the philosophical tolerance that is demanded by a system that is totally effective, but whose physiological basis has yet to be demonstrated in medical terms. I have myself, for the past five years, been in the care of a British acupuncture expert since I watched my father being cured by him of *pectoris angina*. My father agreed to the experiment as he was faced with habitual drug-taking for the rest of his life, 'western' medicine having no known cure for this heart condition. I amused myself with the thought that logical positivism would have to dismiss as impossible more than two thousand years of the relief of human suffering. We have good reason to review the bases of many of our western axioms.

The Japanese too have begun to publish texts in English on the art of acupuncture and the authors describe it as a therapy '... whose application successfully alleviates many ills before which Western medicine remains disarmed'. They then go on to state a position which enables me to draw a parallel with Japanese architectural siting practices. 'It is not necessary to believe the ancient Chinese philosophy underlying acupuncture in order to practise it successfully but only to accept it as a working hypothesis until such time as it can be replaced by a more satisfactory theoretical framework.'[2]

There are certain ritualistic methods for setting out the correct place, orientation and features for a house, courts and out-houses which are used both in China and in Japan. The better known is the Chinese art of *Feng Shui* (pronounced 'fung shway'), which also includes the burial of ancestors as an essential part of the total siting of a Chinese family. Feng Shui no doubt has had its proportion of obscurantist, if not dishonest, practitioners but it has suffered, as did acupuncture for so many years, from almost total dismissal by western observers. The roots of this neglect seem deeply embedded in the difference of standpoints between the Chinese and western philosophical systems. M. Freedman, in his study of Chinese lineage and society, inevitably was confronted with Feng Shui, as it was inseparable from the Chinese concept of family lineage. He made no attempt to make a fully definitive statement on the art, but he did put forward a most perceptive and sensitive explanation of his own perplexity in trying to understand the traditional belief in Feng Shui. 'It is difficult for somebody brought up in a tradition which distinguishes sharply between man and nature to grasp at once the basic premise of Feng Shui; one may stand by the side of a Chinese friend and admire the view; . . . coastal south eastern China . . . produces splendid vistas. One's own pleasure is aesthetic and in a sense objective – the landscape is out there and one enjoys it. One's friend is reacting differently. His approach is cosmological. For him the viewer and viewed are interacting, both being part of some greater system. The cosmos is Heaven, Earth and Man. Man is in it and of it. So . . . my characteristic reaction may be to say . . . I find it beautiful. My friend's may well be to remark that he feels content. . . . Man is in Nature. The landscape affects him directly in the ideal case making him feel relaxed and confident. They (the Chinese) are asserting a human response to forces working in the cosmos: and just as the landscape may affect man, man may affect it.' Freedman goes on to make a valuable if literal translation of Feng Shui as 'winds and waters'. 'The *Chi*, the cosmic breaths which constitute the virtue of the site, are blown about by the wind and held by the waters. An ideal site is one which nestles in the embrace of hills standing to its rear and on its flanks.'[3]

Two factors emerge from the above. First, the roots of our so called western attitudes, and second the meaning of *Chi*, or material force to the Chinese.[4] On the first count I think that it is by no means obvious that we have always had a different view of nature from the Chinese one, in spite of our biblical directive that man was to have 'dominion' over birds and beasts and the plants of the field. This could have as positive a meaning in terms of responsibility through consciousness as the latterly oft-cited negative one, i.e., to rule over (dominate) – and hence finally to the sadly contemporary 'exploitative' attitude. For the second factor there is a long tradition, aptly summarised by the great Sung synthesist Chu Hsi in the twelfth century, of the inseparable 'essences' (or 'breaths') of the elements and their material coagulations. They are always in varying proportions of grossness or subtlety. The Chinese would not understand our mental dichotomy of 'mind, matter' or 'man, nature' or 'spirit, body' as they have a minimum three-term system which is known as Heaven, Earth and Man. 'Heaven expands, Earth changes and Man educates and nourishes.'[5] The Chinese considered man primarily as a moral creature uniting Heaven and Earth. 'Therefore the way of the ruler is rooted in his own personal life and has its evidence (in the following) of the common people. These words of Mencius would not be amiss in a Little Red Book! Lu Hsiang-Shan (a contemporary of Chu Hsi in the Sung period) also typifies and condenses fundamental Chinese attitudes in the following: 'The affairs of the universe are my own affairs. My own affairs are affairs of the universe.' 'Moral principles inherent in the human mind are endowed by Heaven and cannot be wiped out.' 'Moral principles are nothing but those principles right before our eyes.' When asked where he put his effort Lu said 'I devote my effort to the area of human feelings and human affairs, practical situations and principles of things . . .'. 'Men living in the world all share the same material force.'[6] It is interesting to speculate that the roots of our own western dichotomous attitudes could be attributed to Descartes' reduction of a three-term psychological system (Body, Soul, Spirit) to a two-term dualism of Mind and Matter. While there is a three-term system – as for example, experience or empiricism at one point, ideas or principles at another – values or human morality become the integrating function. In other words, whatever physical world you experience and whatever ultimate psychological realities you contribute to, ultimately your 'way of

life' or moral behaviour links, realises and integrates these poles in daily life.

That Mao should find such relevance in Marx's dialectical materialism and augment it in his own way in the light of China's rich philosophical heritage is almost typified in Marx's often quoted eleventh thesis on Feuerbach 'The philosophers have only interpreted the world in various ways; the point however, is to change it'.

We have seen the dramatic results of Mao's encouragement of acupuncture and we can only speculate as to whether Feng Shui will also have its renaissance. The main difference between these analogous sciences is that architectural principles do not contain such immediate and dramatic results because the results of planning or siting are on a far longer time scale. The contemporary Chinese policy of balance between industrial, urban and rural needs appears to be a high priority in a little-polluted present-day China.

This preamble on the relation between ancient and modern oriental practices is an attempt to give some background to the accompanying diagrams which are a synthesis of certain ancient and contemporary Japanese practices and philosophies. Japan's traditional and ancient *Shin Taoism* (Shinto) has many parallels with the ancient nature philosophy of China Taoism and the most important fruits of the Chinese flowering of culture during the Sung period was directly imported into Japan in the twelfth and thirteenth centuries, including the skills of acupuncture, now highly regarded in modern Japan.

One more quotation from Lu Hsiang-Shan (from a poem written on the way to a meeting with Chu Hsi) lays the ground for another disarmingly simple practice of the ancient eastern sages – that of profound simplicity. 'Work that is simple and easy will in the end be lasting and great. Understanding which is devoted to isolated details will end up in aimless drifting. . . .'[7] It is the apparent over-simplicity of the oriental *Yin-Yang* active and passive universal modes, together with the five elements of Fire, Earth, Metal, Water and Wood and the twelve zodiacal creatures that has baffled those western scholars who delight in layers of causality.

It is questionable whether we can attribute the study and categorisation of the astronomical bodies to farming communities whose daily and yearly routine leaves no time for such detailed observation. But they nevertheless have inherited, because of its simplicity, a zodiacal tradition from some distant sages, which has become vernacular practice. This would seem to verify the fact that the ancients knew the profundity of instituting a system the terms of which would be plain to all, and which would be perpetuated by its continued appropriateness. It is with this in mind – that there is possibly a great wisdom underlying the apparent simplicity of these traditional practices, as has emerged with the value of acupuncture – that the following diagrams have been devised.

The diagrams are based on, and augment, the exhaustive fieldwork of Richard Beadsley, John Hall and Robert Ward in the Japanese village of Niike in the Okayama prefecture on the island of Houshu.[8] After seven years of consecutive study they speak of

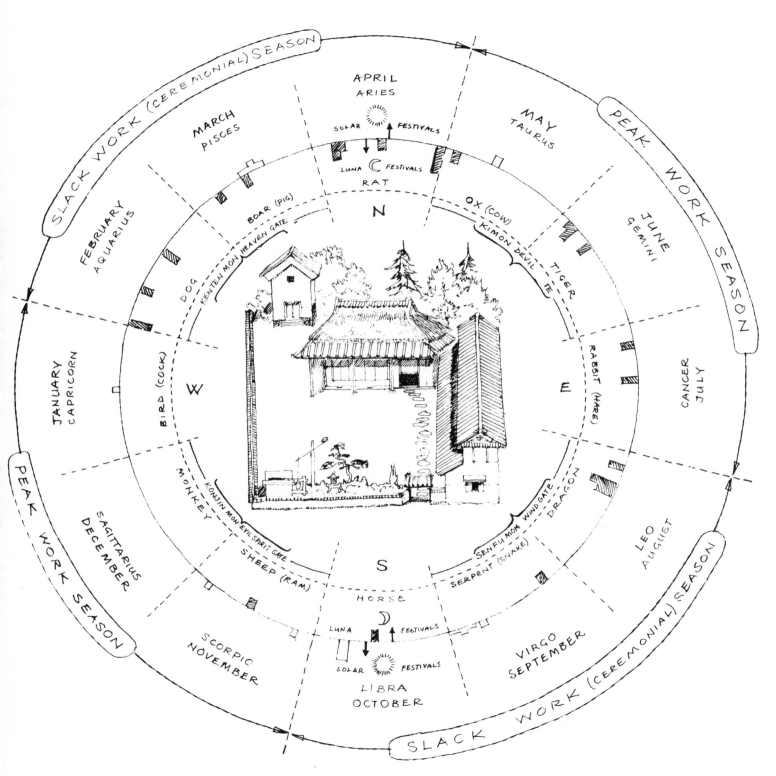

SLACK WORK (CEREMONIAL) SEASON

PEAK WORK SEASON

PEAK WORK SEASON

SLACK WORK (CEREMONIAL) SEASON

APRIL
ARIES

SOLAR ☼ FESTIVALS

LUNA ☾ FESTIVALS

RAT

MARCH
PISCES

FEBRUARY
AQUARIUS

JANUARY
CAPRICORN

MAY
TAURUS

JUNE
GEMINI

CANCER
JULY

BOAR (PIG)

KENTEN MON HEAVEN GATE

DOG

BIRD (COCK)

MONKEY

KONJIN MON EVIL SPIRIT GATE

SHEEP (RAM)

N

W

E

S

HORSE

SENFU MON WIND GATE

SERPENT (SNAKE)

DRAGON

RABBIT (HARE)

TIGER

OX (COW)

KIMON DEVIL TE

SAGITTARIUS
DECEMBER

SCORPIO
NOVEMBER

LUNA ☽ FESTIVALS

SOLAR ☼ FESTIVALS

LIBRA
OCTOBER

VIRGO
SEPTEMBER

LEO
AUGUST

Diagram One: Generalized image of a typical homestead in Niike.

221

the tentativeness of their conclusions and the limitations of any holistic generalisation. In presenting the following diagrams I would doubly reinforce this sentiment but hope that they will stimulate in others the same urge to get to the root of those ways which men in the past devised to establish better harmonic relations between the parts of the cosmos than presently prevail in our current 'western' exploitative and divisive behaviours.

DIAGRAM ONE

The picture in the centre of this diagram represents a generalised image of the typical homestead arrangement of one household of the Niike community, the whole village comprising about twenty such homesteads. The houses, outbuildings, utility yards and assorted farmyard structures are in a closely-knit site, approximately square or rectangular, and of roughly 60 ft. per side.

Sometimes the whole area is surrounded by a mud wall capped with tiles and with an arched entrance. The enclosure is often formed by the juxtaposition of households as well as by the meeting of stone walls assembled from the levelling activities of the sloping sites. As in the Chinese system the hill is 'behind' the village. The house tends to be at the back (north) of the plot leaving a large multi-purpose area for animal tethering, crop drying, chickens, pigs, etc. The striking uniformity of these households can be attributed to the rules of Hogaku. These directional rules govern the whole planning of the homestead, from the entrance to the relationships between buildings, and even to the planning of the rooms within the house. It differs from the Chinese Feng Shui inasmuch as the topographical features and the human/landscape relationships are hardly in evidence, apart from the previously mentioned hill behind and the view over the economically vital paddyfields to the south. The public buildings and cemetery seem not have significant relationships with the dwellings.

The hogaku system is basically zodiacal in character. The centre of the house is the midpoint of a horizontal zodiacal circle which, as it is divided up, apportions zones for appropriate functions, animal, human and architectural. It is not, however, a static system; rather it is like the face of a clock, the planets moving around it like so many hands which determine auspicious and inauspicious dates for particular functions, and into which the birthdays of the inhabitants are also closely interwoven. There are however, some stable relationships within this circle which relate to constant values. These are two axes: south-east through to north-west which is consistently auspicious, and north-east through to south-west which is consistently inauspicious. The former, starting in the south-east, known as Senfu-mon, or 'Wind gate', represents the flow of household income; and the north-west exit is known as the Kenten-mon or 'Heaven gate'. At this corner of the site is the tall, one-roomed storehouse for the family fortune or valuables – a physical symbol of the 'fortunate' flow from the entrance diagonally across the site to the Heaven gate. The polarised bad fortune which potentially flows in the diametrically opposite way, from the Kimon (Devil gate) to the Konjin-mon

(Evil Spirit gate) in the south-west, is blocked off by the L-shape plan of house and outhouse which are backed against this undesirable influence. However, a space of some sort must be left in both these corners to allow an evil influence to depart, should it happen to have entered the site. In some villages around Niike a baleful force known as 'circling Konjin' moves regularly around the zodiac possibly one of the planets, but apparently little is made of this in Niike itself.

When one observes the placing of the zodiacal animals and remembers that when it was devised, and for whom, it must have had some basis (unless one takes the easy way out and condemns the accomplishments of the whole oriental tradition as so much primitive superstition) some interesting points arise as to the placing of the often found chicken house in the 'bird' direction and the ox or cowshed in the general 'ox' section. The 'dog' may probably relates to the guarding of the treasure house in its section. The relation of the monkey to the well, or a dragon to the long storehouse, needs a somewhat more subtle explanation. To suggest a connection between dragons and fertility as a landscape phenomenon in the Chinese system and the storage of 'fertiliser' in this outhouse may be too 'western' a speculation. But whatever the relation between the physical needs of a fundamentally rice-producing community and the original wisdom of the animal attributions of the zodiacal system, it is significant that both the astronomer-sages and the most humble peasant were using familiar terms. Theirs was a wisdom which goes far beyond the exact correspondence of symbols as it ensures a cohesiveness of symbolic usage throughout a civilisation.

Discussion of the site fortunes has so far been restricted to the first two circles of information around the household: compass points being ascribed zodiacal positions and animal symbols, and auspicious and inauspicious flows of influence through the site. The next circle has a series of larger and smaller diagonally shaped rectangles projecting in toward the site. These are ceremonial and ritual days, determined by the lunar calendar – the lunar festivals. From the same circle are unshaded rectangles projecting away from the site; these are solar-determined festivals. These festivals are a study in themselves and exhaustive information on them is to be found in Village Japan;[8] the significance here is their importance in the Niike year and their close relationship to the nature of the villagers' livelihood – rice farming. It shows how the more ancient lunar calendar dominates (this is also because of the practical use of moonlight for night work). But more significantly it demonstrates those times when people have time to consider both cultural and cosmic matters – when nature relieves them from the toil in the rice fields. The corresponding occidental zodiacal names and months have been put in to assist comparison with our parallel system.

DIAGRAM TWO

Although in Niike the populace will turn to moxibustion and acupuncture (Hari-Kyu) only when modern 'western' medicinal drugs available have failed, the system is still in use rurally. The

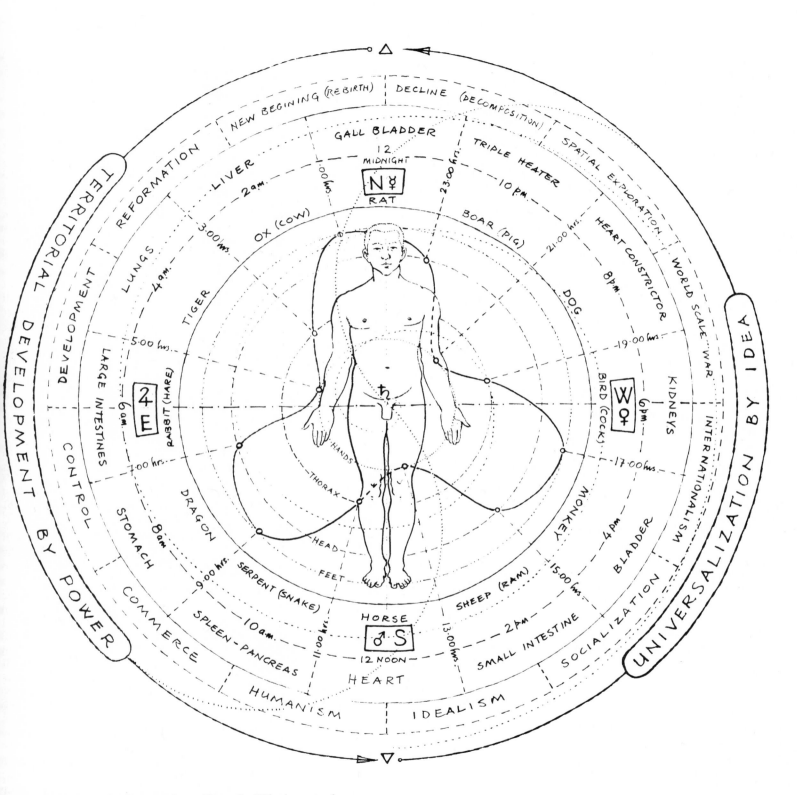

Diagram Two: Generalized image of a resident of a Niike homestead.

223

point of this article is to attempt to bring together some differing aspects of traditional symbols and practices to aid the reader to find further connections for himself. Here we have the connection between the zodiacal allocations for the twenty-four hour day and the flow of *chi* or vital 'breath' of the body. Modern commentators in Japan translate chi's (*Ki* in Japan) as biorhythm and energy fluctuation[9] and it corresponds to the recently discovered full-day biological 'clock' inherent in all human cells which can be upset so drastically when jet travel puts the 'clock' out by traversing normal time barriers. Let us take the generalised image in the centre of this diagram as a hypothetical resident in one such household described in Diagram One. It is not feasible to indicate on the figure all of the 'meridians' or series of points (in some way connected to the major internal organs) which are the precise positions for the application of needles when needed. What is shown however is the connection between the zodiacal animals representing two-hourly intervals of the whole twenty-four hour day, and each of the twelve 'regular' meridians. The 'energy' – giving life to the body, activating each separate organ is said to 'flow' along these well-defined channels translated as 'meridians'. Of these twelve meridians, ten are directly relatable to recognised organs in our western system; the remaining two are related to integrative functions rather than organs and have been translated as 'heart constrictor' and the 'triple heater' (a type of metabolic complex).

Four concentric circles can be seen circumscribing the body. These represent, from smallest to largest, the hands, thorax, head and feet. The darker three-lobed pattern which relates to these positions in the body demonstrates that the major energy flow (or ki) has traversed the whole system three times during the twenty-four hours. This not only relates the basic health of the individual to the hours of the day and their zodiacal characteristics, but also determines the correct time for the doctor to apply the appropriate needles. The cardinal directions have been 'boxed in' with their allocated planet, Saturn taking up the centre. The dashed line outside these have in them the central 'hour' of the two-hour periods for zodiacal sign and outside these the name of the relevant 'meridian'. The exact two-hour periods are given in hourly periods from 01.00 hours to 23.00 hours.

If we find the household siting principles difficult to rationalise it is not surprising for the very reasons that Freedman so aptly described: we tend to 'start' our thinking from a standpoint 'outside' the situation, not as a part of it. It is also probably due to this that the western scientific community has been so reluctant to concede any basis for acupuncture – even in the face of dramatic results produced in the presence of western doctors in China. We cannot expect dramatic demonstrations of the validity of this Japanese rural siting tradition any more than Feng Shui from China. But evidence has emerged from quite an unexpected area which may give us some basis (in our terms) for justifying these siting techniques. This is the remarkable research of A. V. Krylov[10] into the effect he has named 'magnetotropism' in plants; that is the discovery that there was a direct relation between the fertility and resistance to microorganisms in wheat germ, and the planet's geomagnetic field.

The orientation of the Niike household and farm building places them relative to the earth's magnetic field; the Chinese Feng-Shui professors actually use a magnetic compass for the art. Some of the conclusions of A. V. Krylov in his own words speak for themselves:

1. 'It was established that the geomagnetic field definitely affects growth processes in plants.'
2. 'It was shown that the effects of magnetic fields, both of the Earth and of permanent magnets on the life activities of sprouts was more pronounced when the seeds – in dry state – were orientated with the radicles toward the magnetic poles.'
3. 'It was shown that magnetotropism (growth of root toward magnetic poles) is accompanied by changes in the rhythm of growth of both root and stalk. The growth of both was enhanced in sprouts from seeds whose radicles were oriented toward the south magnetic pole and weakened when oriented in the opposite direction.'[11]

We have to be cautious in extending conclusions to more complex forms of life but even with grain storage there is a basis for the orientations.

The final set of categories around our figure are the allocations of a modern Japanese philosopher, George Oshawa, who claims a traditional basis for his teachings. His thesis is that human affairs are affected collectively over very long periods of time and can be recognised in the patterns of world history. They are also founded on a zodiacal division of time; which is a twelvefold division of one complete turn of our galaxy, calculated as approximately two hundred million years. Oshawa applies a logarithmic spiral to the time scales, so that while one complete turn of the spiral travels through all twelve 'houses' or divisions, the actual number of years gets shorter; hence he draws history as a spiral closing in toward the centre. This spiral can be seen in the diagram as a dotted line starting in the south, which represents about 138 century B.C. and proceeds to close into the centre. As it again passes the south point the time is now the fourth century A.D. and the next time the nineteenth century A.D. The logarithmic proportions to the ages work in the following way – a zodiacal section during the Mediaeval age was approximately two hundred years the Modern age seventy years and the Present twenty-five years. Oshawa's model based on an ancient Shinto concept of time accounts for the 'speeding up' of human affairs until it reaches a critical point, reverses and begins to expand again. The whole of this system is embraced by a major duality of character which has been indicated by a lightly dotted Yin-Yang Serpentine Line, one half as Yang-dominated representing territorialisation by Power, the other, Yin-dominated, representing universalisation by Ideas. These two aspects Oshawa uses to represent the major cosmo-sociological forces operating, as he believes, in the human consciousness as our planet passes around the galaxy. A seasonal effect is produced by our alternately coming closer to the centre in the galactic 'summer' and moving farthest from the centre during the galactic 'winter'. It is not put forward that the ancients knew of the galaxy in our terms, but it is suggested that their acute observation of the effects of the position of the parts of the solar

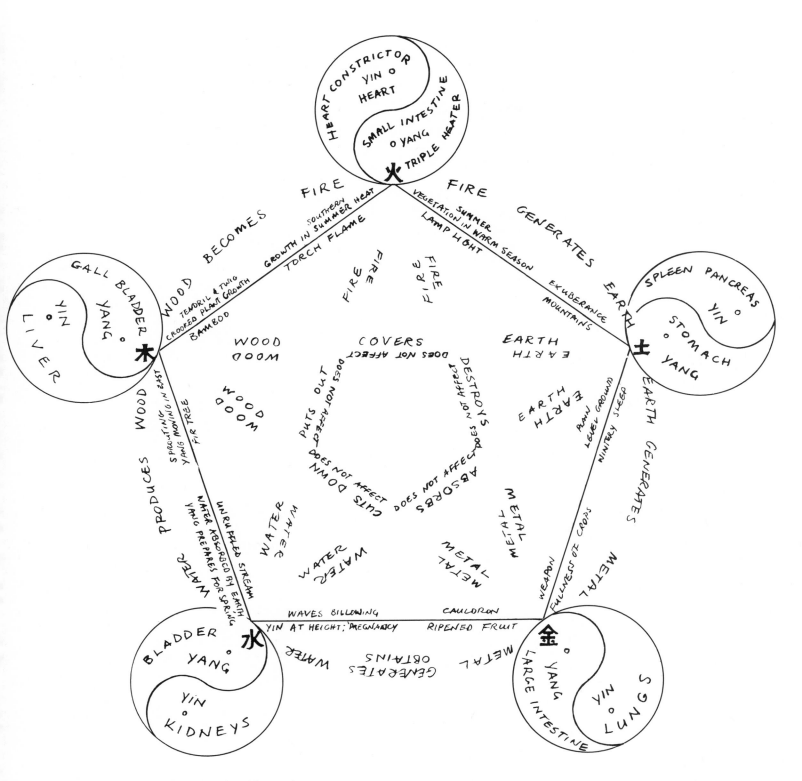

Diagram Three: The pattern of the 'essences' or 'elements'.

system, and the calculated times it took for a cycle to repeat (known as a 'platonic year' in occidental terms), could have been the basis for their approach.

DIAGRAM THREE

This five-fold pattern of the essences, is a schema devised to arrange certain properties and characteristics of the Chinese and Japanese system of elements. These, however, are not to be considered quite as literally as we tend to translate them. Each element in its most subtle form is an essence or Chi which coagulates, from its material force, into physical form as its grossest expression. The five nodes of the pentagon are represented by the essence of Fire (top) and going around clockwise followed by Earth, Metal, Water and Wood. The Oriental has always understood that human experience corresponded to the elements on the basis of like knowing like. The outer circle and the sequence just named is known as the 'generative cycle'. Along the straight arms of the pentagon are seasonal aspects in relation to the elements, as well as the prime representatives of each element. They are passive toward their clockwise neighbour and active toward their anticlockwise neighbour. Inside the pentagon is a double line of relationships between opposite elements in the form of a five-pointed star. These are the destructive and passive relationships between the essences, i.e., Fire destroys Metal, through melting it, but Metal does not affect Fire.

The Yin-Yang circles projecting from each node of the pentagon represent the three left- and three right-hand wrist pulses of the Chinese–Japanese acupuncture diagnostic system. The top position (Fire) contains two pulse positions, one from the right wrist and one from the left wrist as they both relate to Fire. In acupuncture diagnosis great importance is placed on the 'reading' of the twelve pulses: that is, the two readings, deep and surface, for each of the six wrist positions. In the diagram the Yang meridian represents the surface pulse and the Yin meridian the deep pulse. This connection between the essences and the meridians is an integral part of the trained acupuncturist's knowledge. The interrelations between the elements also holds good on another level between the organs, their meridians and the life energy that flows through them.

There are further layers of symbolism between the fire elements and tastes, sounds, viscera, human frame, colour, social relationships, weather, musical instruments, grains, sacrifices, sense organs, affective states, states of government. Unfortunately the more the oriental system makes analogous connections the more critical and sceptical becomes the western mind. It is better to take the system in digestible quantities remembering the motivation behind the philosophy. A human being was seen as the best endowed creature of the material forces of the cosmos, and humanity was seen as a link between the subtle expansiveness of Heaven and the gross receptiveness of Earth, through the proportioning of the elements. Man had a particular responsibility not only to understand (heavenly attribute) but to assist in the changes of the world (earthly attribute) through nourishment and education (human moral attribute). Here we can return to our opening observations on acupuncture and consider, if we are so disposed, the philosophical connections between the respective roles of points on the surface of the human body and the sites or 'points' on the surface of the land. In the first case the points are only of use if the organism is in disorder or disease. In the second the dwelling position is considered beneficial to the health of the environment if it is placed well and enables the inhabitants to perform their role of nourishing, tending and harmonising the vicinity. Both reflect a tradition based on a more subtle understanding of the relations of parts to the whole than we can boast of in the west. Our problem lies in dismissing those things which do not conform to our particular external instruments. To the Japanese and Chinese tradition it was always understood that the ultimate instrument is man's own body. The tuning of this instrument is the responsibility of each owner.

Who better than Lu Hsiang-Shan to close this all too brief introduction to oriental siting techniques, with his poignant observation that 'the universe has never separated itself from Man. Man separates himself from the universe.'[14]

[1] Chairman Mao Tse-Tung, quoted in WEN, HUI; WEI-KANG, FU and others, *Acupuncture in Anaesthesia*, Foreign Language Press, Peking, 1972, p. 1.

[2] MANAKA, YOSHIO and URQUHART, IAN A., *Acupuncture, A Layman's Guide*, Weatherhill, London and Tokyo.

[3] FREEDMAN, M., *Chinese Lineage and Society*, London.

[4] *Sources of Chinese Tradition*, Volume 1, p. 465.

[5] ERKES, EDUARD (trans.), *Ho Shang Kung's Commentary of Lao-Tse*, Artibus Asiae, Switzerland, 1958.

[6] *Sources*, op. cit.

[7] It also highlights the difficulties our contemporary industrial culture has created by proliferating its languages and specialisations until nobody can cope with the 'whole' because we no longer have a science of the whole.

[8] BEADSLEY, R. K., HALL, J. W. and WARD, R. E., *Village Japan*, University of Chicago Press, p. 186 – Work cycles and ceremonials.

[9] If an acupuncture practitioner came to treat a villager in his homestead he would bring with him a similar, invisible, zodiacal symbolic tradition which would guide him as to the correct time to apply his diagnosed treatment. See MANAKA and URQUART, op. cit.

[10] KRYLOV, A. V., 'Magnetotropism in Plants' in FEDYNSKII, V. V. (ed.), *The Earth in the Universe*, Moscow, 1964 (Trans., Israel, 1968).

[11] Op. cit.

[12] *Source Book in Chinese Philosophy* (Trans., Wing-Tsit Chan.), Oxford University Press, 1963, p. 582.

Notes on the Contributors

BEINART, Julian

Professor of Architecture and Urban Design at Massachusetts Institute of Technology, Julian Beinart was formerly professor of Urban and Regional Planning, University of Cape Town. He has written widely on African urbanisation and popular arts and has made a prolonged study at the native townships of Johannesburg.

CRITCHLOW, Keith

A world authority on geodesics and spatial geometry, Keith Critchlow has made a life-long study of esoteric and 'Lost' knowledge. He is the author of *Order in Space* and a book on Oceans, and many articles on geodesics. He lectures at the Architectural Association, London.

DALBY, David

Formerly reader in West African Languages at the School of Oriental and African Studies of London University, Dr. David Dalby is Director of the International African Institute. He was the organiser at the International Manding Conference held in London in 1972, edited with R. J. Harrison Church the symposium, *Drought in Africa*, and has published many works on African linguistics.

HAKANSSON, Tore

An anthropologist with a special interest in the arts in tribal societies, Tore Hakansson is based in his native Sweden. His writings have been widely published in anthropological journals. He is currently working on a collection of folk-tales from Africa and Afro-merica.

KHAN, Hasan-Uddin

An architect and planner who was educated at the Architectural Association, Hasan-Uddin Khan is currently consultant on the master plan for four cities in the Kashmir. He became interested in mobile shelter while studying communications and planning in Karachi.

KHOSLA, Romi

Now an architect in Delhi, Romi Khosla has made several expeditions to the Tibetan borderland and Sikkim, documenting the Buddhist monasteries, their architecture and decoration. He has published several studies of this declining culture.

LAGOPOULOS, Alexander-Phaedon

Alexander-Phaedon Lagopoulos is an Architect-Engineer and professor of Town Planning at Thessaloniki University, who holds a Doctorate in Engineering (Athens) a Doctorate in Ethnology (Sorbonne) and was Elève Titulaire in Urban Geography at the Ecole Pratique des Hautes Etudes. He has published other papers on Semiology and tribal shelter.

LEWCOCK, Ronald and BRANS Gerald

Fellow of Clare Hall, Cambirdge, Ronald Lewcock was formerly Howard Fellow at Columbia, and lecturer at the University of Natal. An Australian, he has published widely on his research in shelter in many parts of the world, including his chapter 'Zanj, the East African Coast' in *Shelter in Africa*. In this study he is joined by the anthropologist Gerald Brans.

MORGANTHALER, Fritz

A medical doctor and psychiatrist in Zurich, Switzerland, Dr. Fritz Morganthaler has joined the anthropologists P. Parin and G. Parin-Matthey in a number of expeditions during which he has made psychoanalytical studies of tribal people. He is the joint author of *Les Blancs Pensent Trop* and other works.

OLIVER, Paul

Editor of the series, which includes *Shelter and Society* and *Shelter in Africa*. Paul Oliver was formerly Head of the Graduate School of the Architectural Association and is now Director of Art and Design at Darlington College of Arts. He is also the author of several books on Afro-American music, including *The Story of the Blues*.

OZKAN, Suha and ONUR, Selahattin

Both faculty member of the Middle East Technical University at Ankara, Turkey Suha Ozkan and Selahattin Onur have made joint studies of housing in Central Anatolia and squatter housing in Turkey. As post-graduate students Ozkan was formerly at the Architectural Association and Onur at the University of Essex.

PIEPER, Jan

Graduate of the University of Aachen, Germany, Jan Pieper has made several trips to India and Nepal where he has lived for a couple of years. He was a post-graduate student at the University of London Development Planning, a lecturer at the University of Aachen and is now an architect in Germany.

POLITIS, Eugenie
A native of Chios, Eugenie Politis has studied the art and architecture of the island for several years. She is a graduate of the Royal College of Art where she studied stained glass and has since executed a number of major commissions in this technique.

RAPOPORT, Amos
After lecturing at the University of California, Berkeley and the School of Environmental Studies, London University, Amos Rapoport returned to Australia to become Professor at the University of Sydney. He is now Professor of Architecture at the University of Wisconsin, Milwaukee. Amos Rapoport is the author of *House Form and Culture* and contributed "*The Pueblo and the Hogan*" to *Shelter & Society*.

WALTON, James
Resident in South Africa James Walton has devoted much of his life's work to the study of vernacular shelter in which he is a world authority. He is the author of *African Village, Windmills, Water-mills and Horse-Mills of South Africa* and many monographs, and was the founder of the Vernacular Architecture Group in Great Britain.